Order and rebellion

Manchester University Press

Order and rebellion

Labour's managerial politics from Miliband to Starmer

Emmanuelle Avril and Eric Shaw

Manchester University Press

Published by Manchester University Press
Oxford Road, Manchester, M13 9PL

www.manchesteruniversitypress.co.uk

British Library Cataloguing-in-Publication Data
A catalogue record for this book is available from the British Library

ISBN 978 1 5261 9227 1 hardback
ISBN 978 1 5261 9228 8 paperback

First published 2026

EU authorised representative for GPSR:
Easy Access System Europe, Mustamäe tee 50, 10621 Tallinn, Estonia
gpsr.requests@easproject.com

Typeset
by New Best-set Typesetters Ltd

Contents

Tables

Preface

> How to encourage freedom without which political parties will become moribund, whilst not destroying the cohesion without which they will cease to be effective instruments of government?
>
> Michael Foot[1]

The words of former Labour leader Michael Foot vividly sum up the dilemma of political management within the party. In the years under Ed Miliband, Jeremy Corbyn and Keir Starmer from 2010 to 2024, the Labour Party wrestled with this dilemma with particular intensity, with profound and far-reaching repercussions for the party's fortunes. This book covers the years in opposition in which the party had to deal with loss of power, the New Labour legacy and the challenge resulting from the election of a radical left-wing leader; it concludes with the early months of the Starmer government until the end of 2024. It provides an in-depth account of what took place within the party during this period, including how leaders coped with deep divisions over policies, core values, strategy, power structure and indeed the very purposes of the party. The book analyses the different managerial strategies pursued by the three leaders, the factors which determined their choice and their outcomes and consequences.

The book draws upon a wide range of primary and secondary sources. The former include party texts, reports and internal party documents, and are heavily based on an ambitious programme of interviews with key players, conducted between October 2022 and October 2024, with a view to both understanding decisions from the point of view of those who were 'in the room' and testing the validity of some our hypotheses. The research for this book also involved direct observation of key party events (such as local party meetings, annual conferences and election campaigns) which can give a sense of the 'real feel' of the party while allowing for illuminating informal, spontaneous exchanges with various party players, from the grass roots up. This approach focused on capturing meaning helped to ensure that attention could be paid to what lies below the surface and to more low-key, gradual yet crucial changes not picked up by media coverage or the many one-off studies of specific, prominent events.

Along the way, we encountered problems in securing interviews with party officials in place during the Corbyn leadership and, even more so, the Starmer leadership, which contrasted with the relative ease for both authors of arranging interviews during the New Labour years. In contrast with this earlier period, there appears to be a loss of interest in engaging with the academic community. We can only speculate about the reasons for this apparent culture shift, with three possible reasons suggesting themselves: the tight managerial regime instituted under Starmer, a shift in the outlook of party officials and a changed environment marked by the advent of social media.

Why study party management? Party management is one of the most vital functions performed by leaders of political parties. It is about promoting cohesion and regulating disagreement in such a way as to prevent it sliding into fractious discord. It is also about control, ensuring the effective governance of a party while preserving a measure of internal democracy. Parties are voluntary associations composed of people brought together to promote some common ends, and in parties of the left these will necessarily include ideals as well as electoral victory. Aside from the inevitable clashes of personal ambition, mass parties with a governing vocation, such as the Labour Party, will necessarily include within their ranks members who differ considerably over how they construe these ideals, how best they can be advanced and how they can be reconciled with gaining public office. As a result, conflict has been endemic as competing institutions, groups and individuals have wrestled for control over resources, positions, power and policy.

Conflict causes problems, since effective electioneering requires teamwork, cooperation and a willingness to subsume differences for the good of the party as a whole. There is always a danger that the collision of ideas, ambitions and interests may degenerate into toxic and fractious strife, blighting a party's prospects at the polls. The problem is a particularly acute one for social democratic parties committed to membership engagement, the free expression of opinion and democratic decision-making. But energetic debate and the airing of differences can have beneficial effects: they allow for the ventilation of new ideas, encourage greater participation and promote the mobilisation of consent.[2] A party that suppresses debate will become dull, inert and bereft of vigour and vitality, unable to rejuvenate itself: monolithic and tightly regimented parties will succumb to elite control and soon atrophy. In short, 'too little conflict may encourage stagnancy, mediocracy, and groupthink, but too much conflict may lead to organizational disintegration'.[3] The tension between the two has been a powerful and recurrent theme in Labour's history.

Striking the right balance is the function of party management. This term is very frequently used in political discourse but, equally, very rarely defined. One exception is Minkin's characterisation of party management as 'The attempt to control problem-causing activities, issues and developments in order to ensure that outcomes were produced which the managers considered to be in the party's best interests. How the best interests were understood was usually closely related to advancing the aims and objectives established by the party leadership.'[4] In his study of party management under Blair, Minkin brilliantly used this definition to explore the many intricacies of Labour's internal politics,[5] but our purpose in this book is a more modest one and we have opted for a more restrictive definition: party management as a leadership function oriented to sustaining the party's cohesion and enhancing leadership control. By party *cohesion*, we refer to 'the extent to which group members can be observed to work together for the group's goals'.[6] 'Promoting cohesion entails regulating and containing disagreements so they do not disrupt the minimal degree of order and harmony [...] essential if a party is to act as an effective team.'[7] It is about mobilising, directing and maximising collaborative efforts in the pursuit of common goals. *Control* can be understood as the establishment of an effective system of governance, or 'decisional efficacy', that is, the leadership's ability to take prompt decisions which members feel obligated or are induced to accept.[8] Measures of effective party management, then, are the leadership's ability to retain members' allegiance, formulate binding policies and manage internal conflicts.[9]

What factors determine the effectiveness of party management in the Labour Party? Here we distinguish between three broad variables: managerial control capability, the scale of managerial challenges and strategies of party management. A Labour leadership's managerial control capability is contingent upon two factors: prescribed managerial powers as laid down in the party's Rulebook and, no less important, its access to them.

Managerial challenges refer to four key variables which operate either to intensify or mitigate the impact of conflict. These are:

- legitimacy, that is, the degree to which the leadership's rule is legitimated and underpinned by procedural consensus;
- ideological coherence, that is, the degree of agreement over the party's core aims and values;
- strategic convergence, that is, the degree of agreement over both the fundamental purposes of the party and the means of advancing them;
- normative order, that is, the degree to which the internal life of the party is regulated by shared norms of behaviour.

Strategies of party management refer to the preferred methods and mechanisms used by party managers to advance the two key managerial objectives of cohesion and control. Here we differentiate between two major managerial traditions and strategies which have been deployed over the years: the centralist and the pluralist.

The book investigates how these strategies played out under three leaders: Ed Miliband, Jeremy Corbyn and Keir Starmer, who all shared the experience of managing the Labour Party in opposition, with limited incursions into earlier periods (the New Labour years, the Wilson years) to provide a wider historical context and points of comparison. Most of the eleven chapters are arranged to follow the chronology of events, starting with the Miliband leadership, then Corbyn and finally Starmer, but the book also includes five thematic chapters: Chapter 1 provides context by looking at external factors bearing on party management; Chapter 2 outlines the theoretical framework; Chapters 6 and 7 provide case studies of Brexit and antisemitism, while Chapter 10 focuses on candidate selection. While a key dimension of the book is the specific nature of party management in opposition, it also covers the first six months of the Starmer government, which helps to understand the impact of party management choices while in opposition on the conduct of the party in power.

Thanks to our long-standing familiarity with and intimate knowledge of the Labour Party, and by placing ourselves in the Lewis Minkin tradition as 'internal critics' of the party, we have sought to provide a nuanced and systematic study of Labour's internal politics in the years in opposition after 2010. We thus hope to offer a balanced and illuminating exploration of the politics of party management in one of the most strife-ridden and turbulent periods of the party's history, the Corbyn leadership, and to furnish an analysis of the character, purposes and underpinnings of the Starmer managerial regime. In so doing, we also shine new light on often ill-understood or over-simplified controversies (e.g., over antisemitism and the Israel–Palestine issue, and divisions over Brexit and future relations with the European Union) which will continue to trouble the party. This diachronic as well as thematic examination of Labour Party management is in turn framed by the larger issues which we deem to lie at the heart of any assessment of the role of political parties and of politics more generally, those of pluralism and trust.

Notes

1 Michael Foot, *Parliament in Danger!* (London: Pall Mall Press, 1959), p. 21.

2 Françoise Boucek, 'Rethinking factionalism. Typologies, intra-party dynamics and three faces of factionalism', *Party Politics*, 15:4 (2009), 473.

3 M. Afzalur Rahim, *Managing Conflict in Organizations* (Westport, CT: Quorum Books, 2001), p. 12.

4 Lewis Minkin, *The Blair Supremacy: A Study in the Politics of Labour Party Management* (Manchester: Manchester University Press, 2014), p. 1.

5 Minkin, *The Blair Supremacy.*

6 Ergun Özbudun, *Party Cohesion in Western Democracies: A Causal Analysis* (Beverly Hills, CA: Sage Publications, 1970), p. 305.

7 Joop J. M. Van Holsteyn, Josje M. Den Ridder and Ruud A. Koole, 'From May's laws to May's legacy on the opinion structure within political parties', *Party Politics*, 23:5 (2015), 10.

8 Harry Eckstein and Ted R. Gurr, *Patterns of Authority: A Structural Basis for Political Inquiry* (London: John Wiley, 1975), p. 453.

9 *Ibid.*, p. 445.

Acknowledgements

First and foremost, our gratitude goes to Lewis Minkin, sorely missed colleague and friend, who inspired us to research Labour Party management in the first place and whose eye for detail, combined with an impressive ability to see larger patterns, set the bar very high. We could never claim to match his superlative command of everything Labour, but this book, which we dedicate to him, represents our modest attempt to walk in his footsteps.

We are of course hugely indebted to all those who agreed to in-depth interviews or other forms of communication, in some cases on repeated occasions: Luke Akehurst, Simon Alcock, Terry Ashton, Ann Black, Katy Clark, Jon Cruddas, Louise Ellman, Andrew Fisher, Simon Fletcher, Peter Hain, Diane Hayter, John Lansman, Neal Lawson, Ruth Lister, Tim Livesey, Chris McLaughlin, Iain McNicol, John McDonnell, Karie Murphy, Marc Stears, Larry Whitty, Rosie Winterton, Stewart Wood, Anna Yearley. Some interviewees wished to remain anonymous; only they will know who they are. We are also immensely grateful to those who provided us with documentation. We also owe an enormous debt of gratitude to the many current or past Labour Party members who, through informal discussions and exchanges and providing invaluable information, gave us precious insight into their experience of life in the Labour Party: in particular Maggie Paun, John Stolliday, Phil Yeoman, as well as the vast number of random conference delegates, visitors and party staff who took the time to have conversations with us. We are also indebted to the editors of

LabourList for their knowledgeable and insightful articles, to Michael Crick for his equally invaluable work on candidate selection, to Simon Wren-Lewis's blog *Mainly Macro* and to Laurence and Sam Freedman's blog *Comment is Freed* for essential background information and penetrating comment.

We are particularly grateful to Luke Akehurst, Ann Black, Jon Lansman, Tim Livesey, Simon Fletcher and Stewart Wood, who read and provided many extremely helpful comments on sections of the book in manuscript. Academics Ivor Gaber, Nick Randall and Mark Wickham-Jones also provided invaluable feedback. We take full responsibility for any remaining shortcomings or errors.

We extend our thanks to the team at Manchester University Press, particularly to the brilliant Rob Byron, whose enthusiastic support for this project, professionalism and flexibility were a wonderful help in allowing the book to take the shape we wanted; and to Judith Oppenheimer for her meticulous and highly professional copy-editing.

Finally, and not for the first time, this book could not have come into existence without the patience and ceaseless support of our families. Our most heartfelt thanks must go to them.

Emmanuelle Avril and Eric Shaw, April 2025

A note on political labelling

We have sought to classify groups or tendencies in the Labour Party by the use of various labels. They are not entirely satisfactory, but we have generally relied upon common usage, especially within the party.

The party right. This refers to those who support traditional Labour values of equality and poverty alleviation, but only to the extent that they do not seriously challenge key economic and social institutions. They also tend to place a heavy emphasis on adapting party policy to existing public opinion. We roughly equate the right with 'New Labour', but also use the term 'Blairite' to refer to those furthest to the right and who often identify themselves in this way. It has become common recently to refer to the party right as 'the centrists', but in general we have avoided this term.

The hard left. This refers to those with a strong hostility to capitalism, who seek to replace it with a socialist system, rooted in the values of equality and social justice, and favour major extensions of public ownership and a much more regulated economy. We equate the hard left with the Bennite left of the 1980s and the Corbynite left during the Corbyn years.

The soft left. This is an imprecise term, but in our terminology it refers to those with a stronger commitment to key Labour values such as equality and poverty alleviation and a more critical approach to capitalism than those on the right of the party. Equally, it rejects both the right's willingness to shed principles if they conflict with public opinion and the hard left's belief that socialist policies were either really popular or could easily be made so if asserted sufficiently strongly, favouring instead a mix of receptivity and persuasion.[1]

The radical left. This refers to left-wingers outside and further to the left of the Labour Party, though significant numbers joined the party under Corbyn.

We are disinclined to use the term 'centrist', in part because, as noted above, the term is often used as a synonym for the right, and in part because there is no centrist current occupying an ideological position distinct from either the soft left or the right.

However, it is very important to stress that these labels represent points along a left–right spectrum, that each shades into the other, that none are particularly homogeneous and that there is much fluidity over time among them.

Note

1 John Denham, 'Pragmatism and the left: Whither the soft left?', *Renewal*, 32:1 (2024), 24.

Abbreviations

ASLEF	Associated Society of Locomotive Engineers and Firemen
BAME	Black, Asian and Minority Ethnic
CAC	Conference Arrangements Committee
CGT	Capital Gains Tax
CLP	Constituency Labour Party
CLPD	Campaign for Labour Party Democracy
CWU	Communication Workers Union
EHRC	Equality and Human Rights Commission
FBU	Fire Brigades Union
FPTP	First-Past-the-Post
GLU	Government and Legal Unit
GMB	General and Municipal Workers' Union
HQ	Headquarters
IFS	Institute for Fiscal Studies
IHRA	International Holocaust Remembrance Alliance
ISIS	Islamic State of Iraq and Syria
JLM	Jewish Labour Movement
JVL	Jewish Voice for Labour
LOTO	Leader of the Opposition's Office
NCC	National Constitutional Committee
NEC	National Executive Committee
NHS	National Health Service
NPF	National Policy Forum

Abbreviations

PLP	Parliamentary Labour Party
PR	Proportional Representation
OMOV	One Member, One Vote
RMT	Rail, Maritime and Transport Workers Union
SCG	Socialist Campaign Group
SDP	Social Democratic Party
SNP	Scottish National Party
StWC	Stop the War Coalition
TUC	Trades Union Congress
TSSA	Transport Salaried Staffs' Association
USDAW	Union of Shop, Distributive and Allied Workers

1
Party management and the party's external environment

> That's the sole key to politics in the modern world: how to manage change. Resist it: futile; let it happen: dangerous. So – the third way – manage it. But it can't be managed unless there are rules of management, value judgements as to how and why we are managing it in a particular way.
>
> Tony Blair[1]

External factors have a bearing on party management, since party cohesion is also subjected to the centrifugal forces which originate from the outside, in the changing, complex and uncertain environment within which the party operates. The aphorism which states that the only constant in life is change applies with acuteness to organisations and their external surroundings. This calls for an examination of the interface between party management and the party's external environment or, perhaps more accurately, how the latter feeds into the former, that is, how the party interprets the constraints of its changing environment and chooses to adapt to those changes.

A party's external environment can be broadly defined as composed of all the outside factors or influences that impact on the operation of party management: changes may affect the constitutional arrangements, legislation and any types of rules regulating the political process; change may affect the electorate and the expectations of the electorate as a whole (or of specific groups within it), as with Brexit; new domestic and international policy challenges may confront the party with new issues; competing parties may rise or decline. Given that these different factors will push and pull in different directions, a party needs to arbitrate between the conflicting demands of a changing environment and adopt organisational responses to move in the (perceived) correct direction.

External factors encompass the whole environment in which the party operates: social, cultural, legal, political, regulatory, statutory, economic, etc., at all levels, including local, regional, national and even international. Globalisation, Europeanisation and now Brexit have had a major impact on the way the Labour Party positions itself ideologically and on the organisational choices it has made to align with or push back against these trends. Successive Labour leaders have striven to conceptualise the relationship of the party's values and objectives in relation to capitalism and to the hegemonic position of economic liberalism in the Western world. Ben Jackson identified the three main constraints which have weighed upon Labour governments: geopolitics, the economic context and a hostile media environment, 'causing divisions in Labour's electoral coalition, and they will almost certainly do the same to Starmer as they did to MacDonald, Attlee, Wilson, Callaghan, Blair and Brown'.[2] These are covered later in the book in relation to the case studies provided in the chapters.

In this particular chapter, however, we deal with the more specific British environment defined by the rules of the political game, which determine the state of party competition in Britain, the economic and social context which have a bearing on UK voters' attitudes and expectations and the various tools available for parties to communicate with their audiences. Party management is the activity whereby leaders choose to react to this environment based on their interpretation of how best to navigate constraints. As with the larger global trends, they may seek to adapt or to transform their environment.

Here we focus on changing conceptions of how the party relates to its environment. We examine this by exploring how organisational responses illustrate the clash between rival conceptions of the party, of its role and of its representative functions. We identify three main types of external factors which we think are most relevant to party management: political and institutional factors (the rules of the game, the party system);

socio-economic factors (the prevalence of certain issues, the expectations of the electorate); and the communication and technological environment (the tools and methods used to reach out and mobilise support).

Theories of party change

In this first section, we briefly draw from the main theories of party change. In the public debate, these tend to revolve around the adapting or transforming question. Yet the adaptation/transformation dichotomy is too crude, and a more nuanced understanding will prove more useful in thinking about the processes at work. For example, Kenneth Janda borrows from organisational change theory to put forward a refined version of the Nadler–Tushman typology of party change which classifies change along the two dimensions of scope (whether the change is incremental, involving only parts of the organisation, or strategic, involving most of the organisation) and timing (whether the change is anticipatory – and occurs in advance of environmental events – or reactive, and follows those events) in relation to external events, leading to four main types of adjustments: tuning, adaptation, reorientation, recreation.[3] The literature on climate change, for example, has shown that a process of adaptation which comes with transformation (transformational adaptation) is conceptually different from 'incremental' adaptation, in which existing practices are simply adjusted to make them better suited to changing conditions without disrupting the system.[4] Yet the distinction is not always straightforward, since adaptation may be transformational at one level and not another, and a series of incremental adaptations may cumulatively have a transformational effect.

There is a tendency to focus on critical junctures and periods of sudden change as the most significant ones, whereas periods of consensus and continuity may be equally important. Significant changes which take place incrementally and gradually may be overshadowed by more spectacular surface changes. During a period of continuity, a range of ideas may set and congeal over time to the point when changing them or attempting to go back to the old ways will be perceived as heresy.[5] In this sense, the politics of consensus can be defined as providing a reduced space within which politics is deployed rather than a mere convergence of views around objectively best policy and best practice. Colin Hay speaks of a 'settlement' and the internalisation of a set of values which makes ideas that challenge orthodox thinking very difficult to make look credible.[6] Even relatively timid questioning of the orthodoxy will trigger violent reactions in those who sustain the consensus, even though the context has changed. We will see how this played out during the Miliband and Corbyn years.

Leaders are limited not just by objective external constraints but also, and we argue as importantly, by their own perceptions and interpretations of these constraints. Proponents of 'ideational institutionalism'[7] have demonstrated that underlying normative ideas can have as strong a constraining effect as formal institutions. A set of dominant and commonly accepted ideas will act as a powerful mental straitjacket to determine the range of responses that political leaders will find acceptable when external institutional or material conditions change. It follows, from a party management perspective, that ideational power is 'the capacity of actors (whether individual or collective) to influence other actors' normative and cognitive beliefs through the use of ideational elements. This may occur directly, through persuasion or imposition, or indirectly, by influencing the ideational context that defines the range of possibilities of others'.[8] This is exemplified by the success of Tony Blair, Gordon Brown and other 'modernisers' in defining the process of change in terms of the counterposition between 'New' and 'Old' Labour.

The axiomatic view is that all organisations need to evolve because, like living organisms, they are subjected to the process of entropy and have to renew and reinvent themselves in order to survive. This was reflected in the move from a conception of organisations as 'machines', which had prevailed in the age of scientific management, to 'organisms', a biological metaphor which encapsulates the idea that an organisation which fails to evolve will be doomed to extinction.[9] The evolutionary metaphor emphasises 'survival' as a key aim, and logically places greater emphasis on the relation between the organisation and its environment. This shift in narrative comes with an ethos of change, as change is justified in the name of modernisation and democratisation. This was an all-powerful rhetoric during the New Labour years, when adaptation to change came to be erected as the key imperative. On the face of it, this focus has remained: the 2019 election manifesto promised to deliver 'Real Change'; Starmer's 2024 manifesto was encapsulated in the even vaguer notion of 'Change'. But, of course, change means very different things to different leaders: is change sought to shape the party to fit the environment, or is the aim to bring change to the environment?

Change, as the ability to adapt rather than transform, underpins the political marketing approach. A leader who is seen to be proactive is seen as a strong leader only to the extent that he/she conforms to the existing orthodoxy. The way he kept a tight hand on the party is what people most admired in Blair. But the Miliband leadership illustrates another approach, seeking to (partially at least) reshape the environment. The exact reasons why Labour's policy-making process came to a halt two years before the 2015 election are examined in Chapter 3, but what can be said here is that Miliband's trajectory illustrates how a leader straying too far from the orthodoxy will be whipped back into conformity: a set of bad polls forced Miliband to retreat to more consensual positions, so much so that in the end he was accused of having nothing distinctive to offer the voters, thus paving the way for a more daring leader. But Corbyn's challenge to the status quo was deemed too dangerous, so that an array of conservative forces aligned to ensure his project would never materialise. Keir Starmer's return to orthodoxy is so complete that his leadership looks directionless.

We also need to pay attention to whether the party is in power or opposition. What is the role and power of the Leader of the Opposition in a country where the opposition is institutionalised as Her Majesty's Opposition and as a government in waiting?[10] How can opposition leaders shape their party's organisation and outlook? Do opposition parties tend to be more radical or more risk averse, or both, taking radical action internally but taking a very conservative stance outwardly? Most of the time, British Oppositions are in the difficult position of responding to the government and to events. Keir Starmer has been flexing his muscles internally ('a changed party'), in a way which recalls New Labour's transformation of the party into a vehicle for government, but in fact offered a lot of continuity with the conservative agenda. On the other hand, in his first two or three years as leader, Ed Miliband managed to set an agenda which his opponents could not ignore, taking on Rupert Murdoch (over the phone-hacking scandal) and the *Daily Mail* (for defaming his father's name), and denouncing capitalism as 'predatory'. Corbyn, of course, went even further in challenging the rules. However, as detailed in subsequent chapters, in both of these latter cases an ambition to rethink the economic orthodoxy was thwarted as much by internal resistance as it was by opposition outside the party. In opposition, there is nothing a party can do to change external factors. Once in government, it can. This is why it is so important that, while in opposition, the party is clear about how to alter the environment to its advantage.

A turbulent environment, a constantly changing party system and increased voter volatility make adaptation particularly challenging, especially when a party is competing with one or several other parties for the same 'hunting grounds'.[11] But a culture of adapting to change and being too reactive may not always be the best course, as a destabilised environment may return to a previous position or evolve positively. Being able to change and renew is seen as a value in itself, but short-termism and reinvention may be dangerous for a political party, since party reform takes time, inducing a time lag between the diagnosis (often too superficial) of a particular set of changes and the implementation of these changes. The party may then end up playing catch-up, or else too rapid a change might create confusion internally, eroding feelings of solidarity. It is therefore vital for a party to have a clear shared vision of what the party is, where it wants to go and how it plans to get there, not least because it offers a project around which members can unite.

The institutional environment

Since the UK remains the only democracy in Europe to use first-past-the-post (FPTP) to elect its parliamentary representatives,[12] a study of the effect of this voting system on party management is essential. Indeed, FPTP, a simple majority mode of election, is typically described as having historically favoured the two leading parties, Conservative and Labour, and being associated with the emergence of a two-party system – even if the theory of cleavages describes a chicken-and-egg situation, where the two-party system both emerged out of and reinforced the British class structure.[13]

The terms of the debate can be summed up as, on the one hand, the notion that the system is hugely disproportional and thus fails to reflect the variety of opinions, and, on the other, the idea that FPTP delivers large majorities which allow a party to govern and fulfil its promises to the voters (hence the importance of party manifestos – a tool through which winning parties can be held to account). FPTP just about makes it impossible for new parties to emerge – or even for midsize parties to make an impact (although there have been a few exceptions). Yet this needs to be nuanced, as new or changing parties may seek to 'break the mould' (the Social Democratic Party [SDP] came close in the early 1980s, then Change UK never did), or gain sufficient traction in terms of the national vote to be seen as serious competitors. The direction of the mainstream parties may be influenced by the emergence of protest parties, as was the case for UKIP, and now Reform UK. And even if FPTP provides some protection against insurgent parties, this comes with a price in party management terms, since, in Labour's case, it may invite elements – especially on the left – who in other systems would form their own party, to involve themselves in the party, as the disruption resulting from the Corbynite influx illustrated.

As a result of these contradictions, the relationship of the Labour Party with the voting system is complex, with conflicting opinions coexisting in the party. For some, a commitment to electoral reform is an indispensable step to widening support, transforming the party and unlocking British politics. For others, the present system still offers the best hope of majority Labour governments, of avoiding deals with the party's rivals and the watering down of Labour's social democratic agenda. The Labour Party has come to embrace a constitutionally conservative approach, favouring a system that offers the prospect of the party winning office on its own and – notionally – being able to enact a radical policy of social reform.[14] Yet this perception that Labour is favoured by FPTP needs to be set against the facts. Even if the electoral bias inherent in FPTP has shifted back and forth between the two majority parties over time,[15] and clearly favoured Labour in the 2024 general election due to the party's remarkable efficiency in winning seats, overall it is in fact a system which, because of the geography of its vote and weaker party alignment on the left,[16] has benefited Labour less than the Tories. Labour's historic landslide in 1997 was won on the back of less than a third (28 per cent) of the electorate (i.e. of those entitled to vote). The Electoral Reform Society's analysis indicated that the 2019 general election 'saw an increase in vote share for smaller parties – from 18 percent in 2017 to around 25 percent in 2019', which, it stated, 'reflects the long-term trend towards multi-party politics'.[17] The picture is even more concerning if one adds the dimension of turnout: at the 2019 general election, turnout was 67.3 per cent across the UK, bearing in mind that turnout is the percentage of those registered to vote, not of those eligible to vote. According to the Office for National Statistics, only 68 per cent of those aged 20–24 years who were eligible to vote and 75 per cent of Black, Asian and Minority Ethnic (BAME) voters were registered in 2018. Labour's landslide on 4 July 2024 hides worrying signs: despite capturing 211 more seats than in 2019, Labour's majority was won with even fewer votes. In other words, by securing 63.4 per cent of the seats on just 33.7 per cent of the votes, Labour's victory amounts to 'the largest over-representation for any party in post-war history'.[18] The collapse in turnout (which fell to 59.7 per cent), especially in Labour-held seats, reflects the steady decline in public trust. Overall, just 20.1 per cent of eligible electors cast a ballot in Labour's favour. In this context, there is concern that FPTP might unravel Labour's success. Labour's triumph masks a demobilisation of its vote, especially within lower-income groups.

Undeniably, FPTP has, in some periods, such as between 1997 and 2010, when the party greatly increased the efficiency of its campaigning, helped Labour garner the seats necessary to form (sometimes substantial) majorities, thus allowing it to implement its programme. But, given the current trends in voting behaviour outlined below, it might not deliver next time, especially as other competing parties are also becoming adept at playing the system. In addition, should Farage's Reform UK party significantly manage to increase their vote share without this being reflected in terms of representation in the House of Commons, the current voting system would look even more unsustainable. Yet the Starmer leadership is still reluctant to consider a move to some form of Proportional Representation (PR).

The Labour Campaign for Electoral Reform (LCER), which originated in the 1970s as the Labour Study Group for Electoral Reform, has been particularly active during the long periods of opposition. In 1997, after eighteen years in opposition, the incoming New Labour government was committed to changing the voting system, setting up the Jenkins Commission, but a promised referendum on the issue never materialised. Labour did not campaign for reform to the Alternative Vote, a stepping stone to full PR, in the referendum on electoral reform of 5 May 2011, organised under Cameron as a trade-off for Liberal Democrat (Lib Dem) participation in the government. The campaign within Labour gathered pace again from 2015, leading to the LCER joining with a number of other groups and Labour MPs in September 2020 to launch Labour for a New Democracy.

PR has been growing as a popular cause among Labour members and MPs. In 2022, a big push took the form of a virulent campaign spearheaded by ex-Momentum organiser Laura Parker and Labour to Win Luke Akehurst (and other MPs such as John McDonnell and Stephen Kinnock), thus drawing people from across factional divides. At the 2022 annual Conference, a PR motion was backed by a majority of Conference delegates on a show of hands – but was not included in the Manifesto (as only two-thirds majorities on card votes are binding and Starmer was unwilling to commit to it). Addressing an annual Conference fringe meeting in Liverpool in September 2024, the academic Rob Ford called Labour's recent victory an 'electoral jenga pile' to describe a majority that was as remarkable as it was insecure:[19] the fact that four out of ten voters wanted something else than what they got is a recipe for unpredictable outcomes. PR is also a way to bring Labour closer to other, smaller progressive (i.e. anti-Tory and anti-Reform[20]) parties such as the Greens and the Lib Dems, who will undoubtedly make this their ask in any future deal. PR is now one of the most demanded issues within Constituency Labour parties, and many of the new intake of MPs are pro-PR.[21] The pluralist-minded Andy Burnham, addressing the meeting, was very critical of the political culture fostered by FPTP, which, he said, coupled with the whip system, infantilises elected representatives and produces a narrow, shallow party culture which does not allow people to think long term.

For now, the risk-averse Starmer leadership is walking a fine line over electoral reform, acknowledging its adverse effect on public trust but refusing to endorse an alternative, especially as this would involve formalising electoral alliances. This is understandable, as Labour was in 2024 able to play the 'efficiency bias' of FPTP to the full. Yet, opening discussions on electoral reform could allow the Labour government to take ownership of the issue rather than be forced into it, while bringing about the culture of compromise seen in multi-party systems, something which might have prevented hard Brexit, as will be seen in Chapter 6.[22] But this would require a culture change that current party management methods do not allow for.

Class structure and voting behaviour

The voting system in place has a bearing on electoral strategies, since under the FPTP system parties need to build coalitions of voters out of diverse social groups so as to devise a 'broad church' appeal, a difficult balancing act which has the potential to affect the coherence of the party's programme. The Labour Party has to stretch itself thin across a range of socio-economic groups with conflicting expectations and needs. In addition, the understanding of the best electoral strategy for the party varies over time; conflicting electoral strategies over which constituency of voters to prioritise may divide the party. For example, under Corbyn, the polarisation of the electorate over Brexit was such that the party found itself pulled in opposite directions, not being able to prioritise one group over the other (for a detailed account, see Chapter 6). Labour rebuilt the 'Red Wall' in the 2024 election, but tensions remain between the social conservatism associated with the Red Wall and the social liberalism of most Labour voters.[23]

It is a truism to say that changes in the electorate's composition and the changing role of class structures have had a huge impact on Labour's fortunes. The values of the voters and their perception of what a Labour government can bring are influenced by socio-economic change. The long-term decline in party alignment and partisan identification as a result of the post-war shrinking of the working class has been charted by analyses of voting behaviour.[24] This literature identified the growing fragmentation of the electorate with the gradual but steady decline in the percentage of the vote garnered by the two historic majority parties, reflecting, *inter alia*, dwindling working-class identification with Labour. Historically therefore, the Labour vote has tended to be 'softer'. To a large extent, the Red Wall narrative is the latest iteration of these trends. The need to stretch itself across a coalition of voters, added to the increased volatility and fragmentation of the electorate, can account for the struggle of Starmer and his team to articulate a clear message and to come up with a convincing overarching narrative. Large groups of voters can shift decisively, so that the ground recaptured in the Red Wall and in Scotland could be lost again just as quickly if Labour is seen not to deliver.

Meanwhile, the axiomatic view that elections are won in the centre is hardly ever questioned. While Miliband and Corbyn did have an ambition to reconnect the party with the working class, the electoral strategy for 2024 again stressed the need to triangulate so as to obtain a Labour victory by moving back to what was purported to be the 'centre ground'. This was a strategy devised to win the maximum number of seats: the fact that it meant that Labour was going to lose vote share in its safest seats was seen as of no consequence, since this has little impact on the number of Labour seats relative to the Conservatives: 'The decisive group were Conservative to Labour switchers – 14 per cent of Labour's vote share. In a Conservative–Labour contest, every one of their votes counts double.

They subtract one vote from the Conservative pile and add one to Labour. This is what makes them decisive. They are the most important group to win.'[25] As these voters were thought of as 'squarely in the middle of England and Wales: ideologically, demographically and attitudinally', this was where Labour needed to move.

We take this spatial view of electoral politics to be fundamentally misguided, not only because there are at least two cleavages but also because many voters even on the left–right spectrum hold to a combination of views which are both left wing (e.g., on the National Health Service [NHS]), and right wing (e.g., on social security benefits), so that even talking about the 'middle ground' or of a 'centre' conceptually makes no sense. This means that even if the scale of Labour's 2024 victory seems to have vindicated this strategy, it is not a sign of massive popular endorsement. In practice, the Starmer programme was not centrist so much as aligning policy (at least in public) closely with majority voter preferences (hostility to immigration, a 'tough' law-and-order approach, pledges not to raise taxes, but pro-NHS and workers' rights), which did not coalesce into a clear narrative.

Another key dimension highlighted in the literature on parties has been the member/voter dichotomy. Since the 1980s, there has been an ongoing concern that Labour Party members and activists are not representative of the voters and are therefore hampering the party's electoral appeal, not least because delegates may force the party to adopt (in the eyes of the leadership) unpopular policies. Certainly, it was an axiom of New Labour strategic thinking that activists held views that were substantially out of line with both members and targeted voters, and this was used to justify rule changes designed to minimise activist influence. However, membership surveys have looked into these disparities, seeking to show that the ideological gap was in fact not that wide and more a matter of degree than disagreement.[26]

Yet the demographics of the Labour Party membership are undeniably a far cry from its traditional working-class base. In 2021, Tim Bale drew a portrait of Labour's post-Corbyn membership finding them to be 'overwhelmingly white, well-educated and largely middle class and middle-aged, with many of them living in southern England'.[27] Measuring class by using the National Readership Survey marketing categorisation, he found that '74 per cent of Labour members fall into the ABC1 category, leaving 26 per cent in the C2DE category'. Other findings were that 'the party's members are a little more left-wing than the party's 2019 voters and significantly more so than voters as a whole', but also 'far more socially liberal'. In the same vein, Owen Jones, although a Corbyn ally, commented that 'the idea of left-wing middle-class professionals descending en masse on working-class communities to campaign at election time is fraught with issues, mostly arising from contrasting experiences and different priorities and outlooks'.[28] The fact that a quarter of Labour members live in London at the time of this writing is significant in discussions of how to close the North/South divide: the areas where the Labour vote was historically most solid (the 'heartlands') are also those where very little groundwork has taken place. This difference in outlook and priorities between the membership and the electorate has, as we shall see, been a major source of tension between the proponents of the ethic of power, for whom tailoring policy to the preference of targeted voters is a priority, and those who believe that the party's principles should not be so lightly discounted.

Technological innovations

Since the 1990s, there has been a growing body of literature on technology-led changing expectations among voters, with the idea that citizens now expect more responsiveness and transparency, as well as more participation and direct input in decision-making processes. As mass parties, whose organisation has traditionally been a tool of social integration, are struggling to retain the link with the voters, they are under pressure to devise new ways to connect with civil society. In the context of the 'postmodern' – as defined by Pippa Norris – or 'permanent' campaign characterised by a more proactive and better coordinated media and voter management,[29] and the transfer online of a large volume of societal interactions, web-based technologies have provided parties with the opportunity to improve their 'nodality',[30] their ability to sit at the centre of information and social networks. In Labour's case, the erosion of the party's informal system of community involvement through networks of local councillors, trade union officials, Labour clubs and tenant associations, has forced the party to find new tools to interact with the voters.[31] From the early 1990s, political marketing techniques were seen as the answer to improve the party's outreach, since they would make the party more responsive to the needs of the voters.[32]

The development of new technologies has changed the way political parties function. New technologies have affected the environment in which parties operate, the way the parties interact with their environment and the internal functioning of parties. A common feature of technology-based models is the belief that there is a natural congruence between certain democratic forms and the new internet tools used to communicate and mobilise. Yet the impact of internet-led organisational change is contested.[33] The myth of 'digital democracy' has been questioned, as the expansion of channels of expression and communication arising from the new technical possibilities has not led to the democratisation of processes. Contrary to the 'extravagant expectations about information technology on governance and democracy',[34] the new devices and tools can in fact follow 'old organizational patterns', with a small group of informed users/insiders controlling the flow of information.[35] Indeed, these new ways of engaging with the electorate, facilitated by an in-built architecture of participation, were also conducive to more centralised approaches.

Indeed these new technological means in conjunction with a political marketing approach coincided with a questioning of the role of members and activists in relation to voters. During the 1990s, in the New Labour years, the party's conception evolved from a crude members/voters dichotomy to one which saw activists, members and voters as placed on a continuum – the further out you went, the more moderate the ideological positioning, a seemingly common-sense view which, as the Corbyn experience showed, does not always stand the test (see Chapter 5). This reflected the notion that members' views are unrepresentative of the voters, an axiom encapsulated by May's law that the grass-roots members of a political party will be more ideological than both the party leadership and the party's supporters. This meant that voters' perspectives should be collected directly, as activists (specifically Conference delegates) could not be trusted to reflect concerns in the wider population. It followed that, in terms of input, the weight of activists needed to be diluted, with looser forms of affiliation allowing more moderate supporters to have a greater influence.

Colin Smith identified the emergence of a new 'leadership party' model in which leaders were able to rely on direct democracy tools to engage directly with voters and do away with internal processes and members.[36] Other scholars have interpreted this shift to direct democracy as part of a process of the 'hollowing out' of parties. Enfranchising the more passive – and it was assumed more 'moderate' – members would, firstly, dilute the influence of the more radical activists; and, secondly, by side-stepping intermediate party organisations, leave the membership individualised and atomised, impotent before an organised and cohesive leadership.[37] Appeals to the more passive members and reliance on individualised postal balloting, Peter Mair maintained, would lead to a more deferential party.[38] The resulting tighter party management in the Labour Party, designed to smother dissent, was particularly noticeable in the way the centre asserted greater control over Constituency Labour Party functions such as candidate selection (detailed in Chapter 10). This went hand in hand with the professionalisation of outreach functions such as campaigning and electioneering.

The reliance on focus groups, a pillar of Labour's conversion to marketing techniques, also marked a shift towards a mechanistic view of human behaviour. Even if the reliability of the data collected through focus groups has been called into question,[39] and if New Labour's loss of popularity and eventual collapse shows how the best information and communication management techniques are unable to control public opinion in the long term, this belief is still ingrained in Labour's approach. Indeed, the Corbyn leadership continued to rely on focus groups, and the appointment of Deborah Mattinson as Director of Strategy to Starmer pointed to a continued reliance on these methods, as detailed in Chapter 11. Mattinson's study of voter opinion in Red Wall seats afforded an insight into the role played by focus groups. In exploring the attitudes and perceptions of former Labour voters who switched to the Tories in 2019, she uncovered a huge resentment towards those on social benefits for 'milking the system' and preferring to live on benefits rather than to secure gainful employment.[40] There was also palpable anger towards immigrants, who were deemed to be undercutting the wages of British workers, while at the same time refusing to work, claiming benefits which they then sent home.[41]

These perceptions usually had a tenuous relationship to reality, although a strong one to right-wing tabloid reporting. Mattinson herself had earlier acknowledged that 'many voters do not understand how politics works [...] voters find it hard to understand the issues, hard to relate to the politicians, and hard to trust the process'.[42] However, focus group findings were used as guides to how Labour should position itself on key policy issues, such as immigration, the criminal justice system and the alleged aversion to paying more taxes. One interesting example of tailoring Labour's policy to focus group findings was to use 'the flag, veterans, dressing smartly at the war memorial, etc. [to] give voters a sense of authentic values alignment'.[43] This was also reflected, for example, in the 2023 and 2024 backdrop of the annual Conference, which played down traditional Labour symbols and displayed very prominently a Union Jack colour scheme to emphasise the party's patriotic credentials, so that the identity of the party as one walked into the hall was not immediately obvious (some delegates even commented that it had the look of a far-right rally[44]). The problem was that not only did this entail ignoring traditional Labour values, but policy shaped by poorly informed public opinion is unlikely to offer rational responses to major problems.

Technology has the potential to challenge and sustain party management. In the Labour Party, it has tended to allow for increased centralisation and efficiency of processes, while delegating functions to the local, or even individual, level. It is worth noting that all these tools (polls, focus groups, geomarketing, etc.) were construed by their advocates as a means to 'democratise' election campaigning, since they made the party more responsive to the wishes of the voters.[45] Put together, all these methods betray an economicist conception of human behaviour which does not differentiate between political behaviour and that of consumers of a product.[46] Crucially, for the purpose of this book, they rest on the notion that the party's environment can be controlled.

Rival conceptions of the party: electoral machine or social movement

The history of the Labour Party, by nature both a party and a movement, is intimately bound with social movements. Once an established political party at the turn of the twentieth century, Labour's ties with trade unions acted as the link between the parliamentary party and its working-class support base. But extra-parliamentary mobilisation has not been limited to the unions: the party has also been particularly porous to a range of social movements and high-profile campaigns, starting with the Suffragettes. The period from the 1960s to the 1980s, marked by the increased salience of non-material issues and a growing concern with participation, saw the rise of a variety of New Social Movements such as the Campaign for Nuclear Disarmament, with strong ties with the left of the Labour Party, women's liberation and gay liberation, as well as campaigns on issues of race and the environment, among others. Many socialist societies affiliated to Labour, such as BAME Labour, LGBT+ Labour or SERA (Labour's Environment Campaign), are themselves single-issue campaigning organisations,[47] so that many of these movements and campaigns are embedded in the Labour movement and not sitting outside of it. This caused an influx of new members carrying transformatory values, who had been socialised elsewhere and brought outside norms and behaviours into the Labour Party,[48] the consequences of which were to cause tensions which, at times, as in the late 1970s and early 1980s, seriously disrupted the party (see Chapter 2). These political and cultural fractures recurred more recently with Momentum as the change in leadership election rules and Corbyn's candidature provided the opportunity for this self-defined 'social movement' to try and change the party from within, with an 'insider-outsider strategy, linking movements and the party to create a movement party'.[49]

The clash between two rival party conceptions, as electoral vehicle and as movement, was not only prefigured in the late 1970s and early 1980s but, more recently, in two major campaigns which transcended parties and took the form of mass mobilisations. The first was the campaign in 2014 for Scottish independence, powered by a mass movement which attracted many whose involvement in politics had previously been peripheral or non-existent. The second was the 2016 European Union (EU) referendum, when, once again, campaigns cut across party boundaries and sought to reach out to voters previously not engaged in partisan politics. In many ways, a similar pattern of campaigning and communication occurred with Jeremy Corbyn's two leadership campaigns, which drew a variety of new people, some of whom had never been politically engaged, with new mobilisation strategies and online tools allowing Labour to aggregate interests across ethnic and social divisions.

The tools of digital organising which Momentum brought into the party arena fostered a 'party-as-movement mentality',[50] bringing new approaches and techniques to the process, yet without radically challenging the underlying strategy to win elections. James Dennis found that, at the national level, Momentum's use of online and social media tools was very similar to that exercised by the party itself, to ensure that Momentum-backed candidates were elected to key positions.[51] Indeed, although Momentum was conceptualised by its organisers as a member-led democratic social movement embedded in the Labour Party, focused both on promoting popular power and furthering the party's electoral prospects,[52] Momentum's critics, on the other hand, saw it simply as a vehicle to mobilise factionally so as to win internal elections and selections and generally take the party over.

The combination of adopting a mass-movement orientation and opening up the party to new forces comes with a risk of bringing in the wrong kind of people who might not be easily assimilated into the existing party culture, and might come with their own agenda and want to change it.

This, as we see in the following chapter, occurred in the Labour Party from the early 1970s onwards, which not only witnessed the influx of more middle-class, better-educated and younger people with different aspirations and values but also organised attempts at infiltration by the Trotskyist Militant Tendency. The arrival of new members under Corbyn led to a clash of behaviours and norms resulting from the encounter between conflicting ways of thinking about collective action. The new members, socialised in social and protest movements to a different set of practices and behaviour, often came into open conflict with traditionalists. In the end, Momentum's main efforts concentrated on internal elections, either by winning seats on the National Executive Committee or by taking control of Constituency Labour parties to ensure the selection of left-wing candidates,[53] with little engagement with the party's culture.

The 'cartel party' model[54] had posited the inability of contemporary political parties to articulate the demands of the social groups they were supposed to represent – a disconnection from their social base, which needed to be repaired. A growing membership was seen as a response to this problem. But how the membership was going to engage with the party's structure, as we shall see, was another matter. In Corbyn's Labour, the social movement and the party sat alongside one another and never merged, until they separated. Although he claimed that Labour was now more than a conventional party, the party remained more or less unchanged, and the most significant 'democratisation' of party structures – the leadership election rule changes – were engineered by the right of the party to align the membership with the wider electorate.

But merging social movement thinking with the functioning of a mainstream traditional party was always going to be a challenge. Muldoon and Rye's analysis of the 'party-driven movement' (which they take Momentum to be an exemplar of) stresses the fundamental ambivalence of this hybrid model on three levels: strategy (working inside and outside the party), political aims (aiming to transform the party and society) and, crucially for our argument, organisation, i.e. 'the desire to maintain autonomy while participating within party structures'.[55] Yet their conclusion that the effect of this 'has brought about changes to culture and organisation [...] that may yet prove to be relatively stable' is not verified. The foreign body has been flushed out, at least 100,000 of the newcomers have gone,[56] and all that is left are the usual number of left-wingers, intent on keeping the fight within the party.

Momentum's trajectory confirms the view that a 'potential barrier to this strategy is the organisational traditions and strength of the party concerned'.[57] In the case of Momentum, it was the movement which in the end was forced to change and adapt to the party's ways, not the other way around. This is also because of the party's history and earlier experiences of entryism, which meant that Labour had built organisational resistance to attempts to infiltrate it. The feeling of diffidence towards outside movements coming into the party to change it was coincidentally heightened by the fact that, even if Militant and Momentum had little in common, as detailed in Chapter 5, the M used by Momentum to brand its paraphernalia (for example, at the 2019 New Members' reception) seemed to stress the parallel, something which younger delegates may not have realised.[58] As a result, it was Momentum itself which was 'acculturated': while large sections of the 2015 intake had by 2024 left the party, many of the members who had been drawn into the party by Corbyn decided to stay on after his departure, thus adopting the culture of consensus and solidarity described in Chapter 2.[59]

Before the Corbyn experiment put paid to it, the premise was that a more democratic party would be more attractive to new kinds of members drawn from social movements and campaign groups, which would in turn help reconnect the party with its electorate.[60] But the unexpected results of experiments with party structures have put an end to any talk of a further opening of the party. What will be the cost of reverting to more traditional top-down forms?

Conclusion

Concerning external factors, party management is the process whereby groups within the party, especially at the leadership/strategic level, interpret these changes and devise the best – in their view – ways to respond. A difficulty lies in the problem of knowing whether phenomena are long-term structural trends or epiphenomena. Another is that party change is often out of step. Reactivity, which is regarded as a key organisational strength, may be dangerous if the situation the party adapts to reverses. Or the opposite may occur when a party takes too long to grasp the significance of changes and sticks to old responses. Also, the effects of changes are rarely immediate; they develop over time, which means that a recipe for success might not work in a different context.

Classical theories of party change, which have had the most bearing on party management thinking, posit the ability of actors to adopt strategies which are best for adapting to, or even transforming, constraining structures while taking advantage of facilitating structures. Yet they also tend to underestimate the importance of uncertainty and the risk of relying on inadequate information, and thus exaggerate the degree to which 'non-ideological' leaders make rational choices. The fact that the Starmer leadership so signally failed to increase the Labour vote in the 2024 general election (covered up by the talk about 'voter efficiency') is a case in point.

In analysing Labour's responses to external challenges, it appears that choices have not always been optimal. One major factor for this is linked to the dominant mindset prevailing at the top of the party at a given period. Parties seeking to adapt do not always make what would appear to be, in retrospect, the best choices, or else are faced with intractable dilemmas to which they fail to find satisfactory solutions (as seen with the case studies of Brexit and antisemitism in this book). Since it is impossible to state with any certainty that one or several key factors led to success or failure, a more interesting approach consists in unpicking the reasons why and how certain decisions were made, since it is the quality of the decision-making process and of strategic thinking that is the most valuable lesson to be drawn. There is a lack of focus on long-term factors which will help to maintain or enhance the party's institutional strength. Engaging in strategic planning would help to increase internal debate and idea formation and unite members around common objectives. Yet the electoral cycle precludes any long-term vision.

A Labour government has a chance to change the rules of the game, yet it shows little inclination to do so. Instead, it would seem at this point, the leadership is falling into old habits, closing the hatch to reduce outside influence and thus weakening its links with wider society, regarding party activists essentially as a problem to manage rather than a valuable source of input into the policy process, while a very selective targeting strategy has left whole swathes of the country completely untouched. A major hindrance which has blighted the Labour Party for decades is the inability to read the signs correctly.

Notes

1 Tony Blair, 'The challenge of change', Speech to the Global Ethics Foundation (Tübingen University, 2000).
2 Ben Jackson, 'A hundred years of Labour governments', *The Political Quarterly*, 95:2 (2023), 215–18.
3 Kenneth Janda, 'Toward a performance theory of change in political parties' (12th World Congress of the International Sociological Association, Research Committee 18, Session 4, Modelling party change, Madrid, Spain, 1990), pp. 3–4.
4 Richard J. T. Klein et al., 'Adaptation, opportunities, constraints, and limits', in Christopher Field et al. (eds), *Climate Change 2014: Impacts, Adaptation and Vulnerability. Part A: Global and Sectoral Aspects*. Contribution of Working Group II to the Fifth Assessment Report of the Intergovernmental Panel on Climate Change (Cambridge: Cambridge University Press, 2014), pp. 899–943.
5 Richard Heffernan, 'The possible as the art of politics: Understanding consensus politics', *Political Studies*, 50:4 (2002), 742–60.
6 Colin Hay, 'Anticipating accommodations, accommodating anticipations: The appeasement of capital in the "modernization" of the British Labour Party, 1987–1992', *Politics and Society*, 25:2 (1999), 234–56.
7 Martin B. Carstensen and Vivien A. Schmidt, 'Power through, over and in ideas: Conceptualizing ideational power in discursive institutionalism', *Journal of European Public Policy*, 23:3 (2015), 318–37, DOI: 10.1080/13501763.2015.1115534
8 *Ibid.*
9 Gareth Morgan, *Images of Organizations* (Newbury Park, CA: Sage, 2008).
10 Nevil Johnson, 'Opposition in the British political system', *Government and Opposition*, 32:4 (1997), 487–510.
11 Angelo Panebianco, *Political Parties: Organisation and Power* (Cambridge: Cambridge University Press, 1988).

12 The other nation being Belarus. France also uses a 'one-person-takes-all' system, but with a two-round system which means that the winner will need to gather over 50 per cent of the vote.
13 Stein Rokkan and Seymour M. Lipset, *Party Systems and Voter Alignments: Cross-National Perspectives* (New York: Free Press, 1967).
14 Jasper Miles, *Labour Party and Electoral Reform* (London: Bloomsbury, 2023).
15 For a long-term analysis of the effects of FPTP see Charles Pattie and David Cutts, 'Playing the system: Electoral bias in the 2024 UK general election', *The Political Quarterly*, 96:1 (2024), 65–73, DOI: 10.1111/1467-923X.13471
16 James Moules, 'Nearly half of Labour voters weak supporters or tactical voters', *LabourList*, 9 December 2024, labourlist.org
17 Jessica Garland, 'Voters left voiceless: The 2019 general election', The Electoral Reform Society, 2020.
18 Alan Renwick, 'Election 2024: The performance of the electoral system', The Constitution Unit, 10 July 2024, https://www.ucl.ac.uk/constitution-unit/ [consulted 23 March 2025].
19 Personal notes from Conference taken at the 'Labour 4 PR' fringe meeting, Sunday 22 September 2024.
20 The idea of a 'progressive' alliance has so far translated into anti-Tory tactical voting. In 2024, even though there was no official Labour–Lib Dem 'anti-Tory coalition', YouGov data found that voters were 'arranging themselves in this way anyway', something made easier by 'the interchangeability of the views of both parties' voters'. In fact, it appeared that 'the opinions and positions of Labour and Lib Dem voters are near identical across a whole range of issues'. See Matthew Smith, 'What do Liberal Democrat voters believe?', YouGov, 2 July 2024, https://yougov.co.uk/politics/articles/49891-what-do-liberal-democrat-voters-believe [consulted 23 May 2025].
21 Mike Wright, 'Over 100 MPs join new parliamentary group supporting electoral reform for Westminster', Electoral Reform Society, 25 November 2024, electoral-reform.org.uk
22 Thomas Quinn, Nicholas Allen and John Bartle demonstrate that 'the incentives for intra- and inter-party competition associated with two-partism helped to foreclose a softer Brexit', since the broad church party model associated with FPTP forces the leadership to focus on issues of internal cohesion at the expense of cross-party alliances: 'Why was there a hard Brexit? The British legislative party system, divided majorities and the incentives for factionalism', *Political Studies*, 72:1 (2022), 227–48, DOI: 10.1177/00323217221076353
23 Both the 'Red Wall' vote and the 'middle England' vote are something of a myth since neither constitutes a homogeneous group.
24 David Denver, *Elections and Voting Behaviour in Britain* (Basingstoke: Palgrave Macmillan, 1994).
25 Labour Together, 'How Labour won. 2024 Report', Labour Together, 2024, https://www.labourtogether

26 Patrick Seyd and Paul Whiteley, *Labour's Grass Roots: The Politics of Party Membership* (Oxford: Clarendon Press, 1992); Patrick Seyd and Paul Whiteley, *New Labour's Grassroots: The Transformation of the Labour Party Membership* (Basingstoke: Palgrave Macmillan, 2002).

27 Tim Bale, 'Ploughed under? Labour's grassroots post-Corbyn', *Political Quarterly*, 92:2 (2021), 220–8.

28 Owen Jones, 'Mass membership alone doesn't make a social movement', *Guardian*, 27 July 2016.

29 Pippa Norris, The rise of the postmodern campaign? In Pippa Norris, *A Virtuous Circle, Political Communications in Postindustrial Societies* (Cambridge: Cambridge University Press, 2000), pp. 162–80.

30 Christopher Hood and Helen Margetts, 'Looking ahead: The tools of government in the digital age', in Christopher Hood and Helen Margetts (eds), *The Tools of Government in the Digital Age* (Basingstoke: Palgrave Macmillan, 2007), pp. 184–203.

31 Gerry Hassan and Eric Shaw, *The Strange Death of Labour in Scotland?* (Edinburgh: Edinburgh University Press, 2012).

32 Jennifer Lees-Marshment, *Political Marketing and British Political Parties* (Manchester: Manchester University Press, 2001).

33 Emmanuelle Avril and Christine Zumello, 'Towards organizational democracy? Convergence and divergence in models of economic and political governance', in Emmanuelle Avril and Christine Zumello (eds), *New Technology, Organizational Change and Governance* (Basingstoke: Palgrave Macmillan, 2012), pp. 1–20.

34 Peter Shane, *Democracy Online: The Prospects for Renewal through the Internet* (New York: Routledge, 2004), p. 155.

35 Matthew Hindman, *The Myth of Digital Democracy* (Princeton, NJ: Princeton University Press, 2009).

36 Colin Smith, 'Political parties in the information age: From "mass party" to leadership organizations', in Ig Snellen and Wim Van De Donk (eds), *Public Administration in an Information Age. A Handbook* (Amsterdam: IOS Press, 1998), p. 184.

37 See, for example, Richard S. Katz and Peter Mair, 'The ascendancy of the party in public office: Party organizational change in twentieth-century democracies', in Richard Gunther, José Ramón Montero and Juan Linz, *Political Parties: Old Concepts and New Challenges* (Oxford: Oxford University Press, 2002); Piero Ignazi, 'The four knights of intraparty democracy: A rescue for party delegitimation', *Party Politics*, 26:1 (2018), 160–9.

38 Peter Mair, 'Partyless democracy: Solving the paradox of New Labour', *New Left Review*, 42 (2000), 21–35.

39 The group setting in which the sessions are conducted as well as the role of moderators induce emotional pressure on participants, potentially rendering the results useless. The focus group methodology is mostly about sounding

a very small group of participants about policies, and by definition is not representative.

40 Deborah Mattinson, *Beyond the Red Wall: Why Labour Lost, How the Conservatives Won and What Will Happen Next?* (London: Biteback, 2020), p. 23.

41 *Ibid.*, p. 67.

42 Deborah Mattinson and Zoe Tyndall, 'Meet the swing voters', *Progress*, December 2013.

43 Aditya Chakrabortty and Jessica Elgot, 'Leak reveals Labour plan to focus on flag and patriotism to win back voters', *Guardian*, 2 February 2021.

44 Personal notes of the 2023 and 2024 annual Conferences, Liverpool. Similar feelings were expressed by Labour MPs in March 2024, unhappy about the dominant use of the union flag in election campaign material, which they felt might alienate ethnic minority voters.

45 See, for example, Lees-Marshment, *Political Marketing*.

46 Emmanuelle Avril, 'Paradoxes of the cyber party: The changing organizational design of the British Labour Party', in Jeremy Hunsinger, Lisbeth Klastrup and Matthew Allen (eds) *Second International Handbook of Internet Research* (Dordrecht: Springer, 2018), DOI: 10.1007/978-94-024-1202-4_12-1

47 Full list of Socialist Societies currently affiliated to the Labour Party, available at https://labour.org.uk/about-us/socialist-societies [consulted 23 March 2025].

48 Adam Lent, 'The Labour left, local authorities and new social movements in Britain in the eighties', *Contemporary Politics*, 7:1 (2001), 7–25, DOI: 10.1080/13569770123873

49 Adam Klug and Emma Rees, 'The 3 lessons Jeremy Corbyn's movement can teach US progressives', *Guardian*, 23 March 2018.

50 Andrew Chadwick and Jennifer Stromer-Galley, 'Digital media, power, and democracy in parties and election campaigns: Party decline or party renewal?', *The International Journal of Press/Politics*, 21:3 (2016), 283–93, DOI: 10.1177/1940161216646731

51 James Dennis, 'A party within a party posing as a movement? Momentum as a movement faction', *Journal of Information Technology & Politics*, 17:2 (2020), 97–113.

52 Adam Klug, Emma Rees, and James Schneider, 'Momentum: A new kind of politics', *Renewal*, 24:2 (2016).

53 Steven Fielding, 'Labour: Why Jeremy Corbyn still struggles to turn his dream of a social movement into reality', *The Conversation*, 23 September 2018, theconversation.com

54 Richard Katz and Peter Mair, 'Changing models of party organization and party democracy: The emergence of the cartel party', *Party Politics*, 1:1 (1995), 5–28.

55 James Muldoon and Danny Rye, 'Conceptualising party-driven movements', *The British Journal of Politics and International Relations*, 22:3 (2020), 485–504.

56 As discussed in Chapter 10, inside sources say that this estimate may be severely underestimated and that in gross terms the number of Corbyn-era members who quit would be at least twice this number.

57 Muldoon and Rye, 'Conceptualising party-driven movements'.

58 Personal Conference notes 2019.

59 Personal Conference notes 2021 and 2022.

60 Luke Savage, 'The case for party democracy', *Jacobin*, 22 September 2016.

2

Labour's managerial structures, challenges and strategies

> Sons and brothers at a strife!
> What is your quarrel? how began it first?
> – No quarrel, but a slight contention.
>
> *Henry VI*, Part 3, referring to the Wars of the Roses

In this chapter, we address three major issues in the management of the Labour Party: the sources and degree of the leadership's managerial control capability, the character and scale of managerial challenges the party has faced since the mid-1970s and the differing strategies of party management that have been deployed to meet these challenges. *Managerial control capability*, we suggest, varies according both to the scale of managerial powers as stipulated in the party's Rulebook and, crucially, to the leadership's ability to utilise them. The nature and intensity of *managerial challenges*, we argue, is a function of four variables: the extent to which (1) the power structure is legitimated; (2) the party is ideologically cohesive; (3) agreement exists over the role and strategy of the party; and (4) the internal life of the party is regulated by shared norms, or standards of behaviour. By *strategies of party management*, we mean the preferred methods and mechanisms employed by leaders in their role as party managers to advance the two key managerial objectives of cohesion and control. Here we distinguish between two historical approaches to party management, the centralist and the pluralist.

Managerial control capability

How members of a political party behave is shaped and regulated by its rules, protocols and institutional arrangements. A party is a micropolitical system governed by its constitution, which establishes its institutional format, the rights and responsibilities of its various component parts and their mutual relationships. It has mechanisms for making decisions, resolving disputes, facilitating accountability, recruiting candidates for public office and administering discipline. The Labour Party is a heavily rule-bound organisation in which the Rulebook specifies in considerable detail the roles and remits of its various constituent units. Briefly, these were (as of 2010): the annual Conference, the Parliamentary Labour Party (PLP), the National Executive Committee (NEC), the National Constitutional Committee (NCC), the Shadow Cabinet (or Cabinet), the National Policy Forum (NPF), Constituency Labour parties (CLPs) and the various affiliated organisations (mainly trade unions but also the so-called socialist societies).

Almost immediately, we confront a paradox: Labour has at various times been compared to a Michelsian-style elite-driven organisation; but formally and to a substantial degree, in practice, 'internal pluralism has always been a defining feature of the Party, amplified by its network of affiliated organisations, democratic internal arrangements, and divided central authority'.[1] This reflects the two constitutional principles that underpin Labour's institutional design: federalism and the separation of powers. Reflecting its origins as a partnership between trade unions and socialist bodies, Labour has a hybrid constitutional shape, in part unitary and in part federal. The unitary aspect is articulated in the National Executive's responsibility for the internal governance of the party; its federal aspect in the fact that the party also contains affiliated organisations, the trade unions, which are sovereign bodies in their own right with their own leadership, decision-making systems, staffing and resources: although the party regulates its relationship with the unions, it has no direct control over them. This federal dimension is institutionalised in the major role the unions play at all levels of the party's structure, including 50 per cent of the vote at Conference, and major representation on the NEC and other key party committees.

The second principle, the separation of powers, regulates the unitary dimension of the party. Rather than being concentrated in a single body, powers and jurisdictions are distributed between various institutions, most notably the Leader's Office, the Shadow Cabinet (or Cabinet), the PLP, the Annual Conference, the NEC, the NPF and the NCC. The combination of these two principles, federalism and the separation of powers, has meant that natural tendencies – springing from the UK system of parliamentary government – towards the centralisation of power in the hands of the parliamentary leadership are constrained by a system of checks and balances.

Of particular importance is the fact that *constitutionally*, the prerogatives directly conferred upon the party leader are meagre, while those assigned to the NEC are numerous and detailed; *this is particularly the case in the managerial sphere*. The NEC is designated as 'the governing body of the party initiator, administrator and policy executor'.[2] It consists of ex officio members (leader, deputy leader, treasurer) plus elected representatives of the PLP, CLPs and affiliated unions and socialist societies, though the precise balance between these elements has varied over time. Crucially, the NEC and not the parliamentary leadership is primarily responsible for discharging most managerial tasks. Its enumerated powers and responsibilities include:

- the duty to uphold, enforce and determine the final meaning of the constitution, rules and standing orders of the party and to take any action it deems necessary for such purpose, including disaffiliation, disbanding, suspending or otherwise disciplining any party unit;[3]
- the power to propose to party Conference amendments to the constitution, rules and standing orders;[4]
- the power to provide guidance for all aspects of the party organisation, including the rules governing the selections of candidates to public office and the administration of discipline;[5]

- the right to adjudicate in disputes that may arise at any level of the party;[6]
- the right, in pursuance of its duties, to suspend, expel or take other administrative action against individual members of the party;[7]
- overall responsibility for the management and governance of the party.

In 2010, three other bodies were entrusted with significant managerial rights and responsibilities: the Organisation Committee of the NEC, the Disputes Panel of the Organisation Committee and the NCC. The Organisation Committee is a sub-committee of the NEC. Its responsibilities include conducting investigations, overseeing internal elections and ensuring that the selection of candidates for both local and national elections is in accord with the party's procedures.[8] The NEC Disputes Panel is a subsection of the Organisation Committee. It is responsible for 'hearing membership appeals, re-admission applications, party disputes and conciliation [...] minor investigations and local government appeals were referred to the NEC'.[9]

In 1986, as a result of legal difficulties caused by the attempts to ban the Trotskyist Militant Tendency and expel its members (see below), the NEC's judicial functions were passed to a new body, the NCC. Consisting of eleven members separately elected from the NEC, it was charged with determining disciplinary matters presented to it by CLPs or by the officers of the party; and it acted as a final court of appeal. It is empowered 'to impose such disciplinary measures as it thinks fit' and its decisions are final. At the same time, a new disciplinary offence was created: conduct that was prejudicial or, in the opinion of the NCC, grossly detrimental to the party.[10]

Both the NEC and the General Secretary have the right to delegate their powers to elected officers, committees and national and regional officials.[11] In practical terms, this meant – and the point here is crucial to understanding later events during the Corbyn era – that the performance of many of the duties and responsibilities of the NEC was delegated to the party apparatus at headquarters (HQ) and in the various regional offices.

In only one sentence does the Constitution allude to the leader's managerial role: 'the Leader shall, *as a member of the NEC*, uphold and enforce the constitution, rules and standing orders of the party and ensure the maintenance and development of an effective political Labour Party in parliament and in the country'.[12] Yet, paradoxically, for most of the party's history, party management has unambiguously been a leadership function with the NEC operating as its managerial arm. How can we account for this?

The key to this lies in the complex relationship between the leadership, the National Executive, the Shadow Cabinet, the PLP and the larger affiliated unions. The leadership's managerial control capability varies according to the existence of three conditions. First, a system of institutional integration in which the NEC, the Shadow Cabinet and other influential party bodies (such as the Conference Arrangements Committee [CAC]) voluntarily accept the primacy of the leader in managerial (and other) matters. This in turn depends upon the existence of a pattern of concurrent majorities in which the faction or wing of the party that controls the leadership also controls the NEC and other key bodies. The third factor is the acceptance of the convention by all key players that party management is properly a leadership prerogative.[13] Where these three conditions are in place, and only when they are in place, a high measure of managerial control capability is in operation. They are of course not always in place, or, rather, only to varying degrees, and, as a result, the effectiveness of managerial control can vary significantly. Much, of course, depends upon the magnitude of the managerial challenges the leadership encounters.

Managerial challenges

Legitimacy and procedural consensus

In the preceding section we have examined the rules governing the conduct of party members; if they violate them, they will be disciplined or even expelled. But in voluntary organisations like political parties, where the mass of members can neither be paid, incentivised nor easily compelled into submission, systems of rule must ultimately rest on mass consent. This, in turn, presupposes a high degree of legitimacy. Legitimacy can be defined as the condition where power holders are deemed to have the right (within the rules) to make decisions binding upon all members, who in turn are obligated to respect or accept them.[14] However, in political parties like the Labour Party, resilient patterns of legitimacy will depend upon a broad measure of procedural consensus which embraces not only the rules themselves but also the principles which underpin them, or what David Easton calls a 'legitimating ideology'. This he defines as a set of norms and values 'that justify the way power is organized, used, and limited and that define the broad responsibilities expected of the participants in the particular political relationships'.[15] A procedural consensus greatly eases the task of party management, since instead of having to rely on sanctions, inducements and exhortations, leaders can anticipate compliance with their decisions because members willingly accept them.

As an avowedly democratic party, Labour's legitimating ideology necessarily took the form of a theory of party democracy. This came to embrace two fundamental principles: firstly, that those who occupied positions of authority should be elected by and accountable to the party membership; and secondly, that the party's programme should be approved by the membership, a principle articulated in the notion of Conference sovereignty. However, there was always considerable ambiguity about how these principles, and the rules designed to give effect to them, should apply in practice. Much of this revolved around the precise relationship between the parliamentary and extra-parliamentary wings of the party. Thus, shortly after his unhappy years spent as leader, Michael Foot pin-pointed what he called an 'extraordinary feature of the [Labour] party constitution, the existence of two sovereign authorities. The National Executive, answerable to the party Conference, has not the power to dictate to the Parliamentary Labour Party, but nor has the Shadow Cabinet, answerable to the Parliamentary Party, the power to dictate to the National Executive, less still the party Conference.'[16] Where a system of institutional integration and concurrent majorities exists, then the problems that arise from them are almost by definition manageable. But, in his interlude as leader, Foot faced a situation where the left controlled the NEC and the majority of CLPs, the right controlled the Shadow Cabinet and the PLP, and Conference was finely balanced between the two.

What was a difficult situation became virtually unmanageable because intensifying division between left and right over the performance of the 1974–79 Labour government had led to a fracture not only over the policies themselves but also over the way they had been made, more specifically over the degree to which the actions and choices of Labour in office should be bound by the election manifesto. The left, invoking the doctrine of Conference sovereignty, insisted that the responsibility of Labour in government should be to implement the party manifesto, whereas the right maintained that the parliamentary leadership and the PLP should be the final arbiter of policy. In effect, in this period, Labour's procedural consensus disintegrated, with left and right no longer agreeing over the principles that should govern the organisation and exercise of power in the party.

The party right, the leadership and most MPs increasingly challenged the traditional doctrine of party democracy on three grounds. Firstly, Conference was undemocratic as it was dominated by block votes wielded by a few union leaders, which meant that the principle of Conference sovereignty was no longer acceptable. Secondly, the constituency parties were often run by a small number of left-wing activists unrepresentative of the wider party membership and, a fortiori, of Labour voters. Thirdly, the notion that Labour MPs should be individually accountable to (and replaceable by) these activists and collectively accountable to Conference contravened the conventions of the British system of parliamentary government which held that no outside body had the right to direct the behaviour of MPs. In contrast, for the left, most party activists and the more left-wing unions, the problem was that, once in office, there were no mechanisms to prevent a Labour government flouting manifesto commitments – which, they claimed, happened with the 1974–79 governments. Hence what was required were rule changes that would enforce greater accountability of

Labour MPs individually and collectively to the institutions of the wider party. After Labour's defeat in 1979, they campaigned for three major constitutional changes:

- replacing the existing system in which only MPs could vote to select the leader by an electoral college which represented all sections of the party;
- instituting a system of mandatory reselection for the selection of parliamentary candidates in which all MPs would be required to fight a competitive election before being readopted as the party candidate;
- giving the NEC sole control over the drafting of the manifesto, in place of the existing system where it was jointly agreed by the NEC and the (Shadow) Cabinet.

The PLP fiercely resisted the three constitutional reforms, and conflicts within the party degenerated into a veritable civil war. As the editor of the left-wing weekly *Tribune*, Richard Clements, wrote in December 1980, 'Left, right and centre, the Labour party seems to be gripped by a collective hysteria. [It] is fast beginning to look like the worst example of a sectarian organisation tearing itself to pieces in doctrinal and unfraternal argument.'[17] The outcome was a full-blown crisis of legitimacy as the authority of the leader, Michael Foot, was openly defied and efforts to block the constitutional reforms proved fruitless, with two of them, mandatory reselection and an electoral college for the selection of the leader, passed by Conference. Equally, desperate appeals by Foot could not prevent a section of the right, including some prominent figures, from defecting to form a new party, the Social Democratic Party, a schism that had a devastating impact on Labour's performance in the 1983 general election.

The crisis deepened further the following year, when, almost contemptuously brushing aside the pleas of his leader, Tony Benn activated the new electoral college by challenging Denis Healey for the deputy leadership.[18] The rancorously fought contest, very narrowly won by Healey, further embittered divisions in the party. By this time (September 1981), the pendulum of the party was already swinging back to the right, aided by adept organising by right-wing union leaders. But with the party in complete turmoil and Mrs Thatcher basking in the glory of the successful expedition to recapture the Falkland Islands from the Argentinians, an election was called in 1983. The result was catastrophic for Labour, and Foot swiftly resigned. In the leadership contest, the first to be conducted using the electoral college, Foot's protégé Neil Kinnock defeated Roy Hattersley by a handsome margin.

The new leader set about patiently building a broad coalition which eventually encompassed the right and elements of the left. This process was helped by the so-called 'realignment of the left', which was to have profound and enduring consequences. A section of the left, which included Kinnock, had already broken away by refusing to vote for Benn in his bid for the deputy leadership. A wider split now occurred, triggered by the crisis over the Militant Tendency. Militant was a Trotskyist organisation, a front for the shadowy Revolutionary Socialist League, which had for a decade engaged in a policy of infiltrating the Labour Party. An investigation launched by the NEC into its stronghold, the Liverpool Labour Party, revealed details of its use of unscrupulous methods, including the bullying and intimidation of opponents, and the decision was taken to proscribe it and expel its cadres. One section of the left (the 'soft left') swung behind the leadership and firmly backed the proscription of Militant, while the other (the 'hard left') adamantly opposed it.[19] The former, which included such figures as Robin Cook, John Prescott, Michael Meacher, Bryan Gould and David Blunkett, was better disposed to the Kinnock leadership than the hard left, and these and other of its representatives came to occupy senior positions on the front bench. This left isolated the more oppositionalist 'hard left', led for many years by Tony Benn, whose influence steadily shrank over the years, reaching a nadir by 2015.

The 'realignment of the left' reversed the process of polarisation. Two other developments encouraged the repair of the procedural consensus and the restoration of leadership legitimacy. The first was the institution of the electoral college. Under this method, the leader was for the first time elected by the whole party rather than by a small number of MPs, which gave Kinnock and his successors a much stronger claim to represent the will of the majority and hence a democratic mandate. The second development was the growing acceptance of One Member, One Vote (OMOV) as the most democratic method for conducting party elections and selections. This was progressively extended to elections to the NEC, the selection of Conference delegates, voting in the electoral college and, finally, in 1993, under Labour's new leader John Smith, who had replaced Kinnock after Labour's unexpected 1992 election defeat, to the selection of parliamentary candidates. It appeared that at long last a new consensus had emerged in the party over the appropriate way in which power should be structured, apportioned and exercised.

Ideological coherence

Ideology can operate as a unifying or a disruptive force in political parties. By ideology, we mean the 'fundamental goals, ideals and principles about the nature of the good society which define a party's vision and form the basis of a governing platform'.[20] Where a shared ideology exists, it acts as a potent force uniting members in the collective pursuit of shared ends. It can also act as a shock absorber, mitigating the effects of disagreements over policy, strategy and organisation. But where members disagree about fundamental aims and ideals, the impact of these disagreements will be compounded and magnified.

But what, precisely, were Labour's 'fundamental goals, ideals and principles'? Here, a certain amount of inference and even conjecture is required, for, unlike most other social democratic parties, the party never promulgated an official and definitive declaration of its aims and values[21] – a function that the much-discussed Clause IV of the constitution was far too thin to fulfil. Yet it is possible to identify certain common values and ethical motifs which have persisted throughout its history, which have supplied a general framework for policy and strategy. An inspection of manifestos, speeches and other documents over the years makes it possible to distil three core principles which, to varying degrees, have acted as points of ideological convergence within the Labour Party: the pursuit of equality, the relief of poverty and collectivism.

The belief in social equality, declared Tony Crosland, one of Labour's foremost theorists as well as a prominent politician, was 'the most characteristic feature of socialist thought'.[22] Precisely what equality meant was a matter of lively dispute but – at least until the arrival of New Labour – there would have been broad assent to Crosland's 1974 definition: 'By equality we meant [...] a wider social equality embracing also the distribution of property, the educational system, social-class relationships, power and privilege in industry – indeed all that was enshrined in the age-old socialist dream of a more "classless society"'.[23] Equality of outcome, understood in this sense, was 'central to Labour's thinking'.[24] It was accepted that a measure of inequality was inevitable to provide incentives, to reward skills in short supply, to foster investment and so forth – but the accent should be on *justifying* these inequalities. There was also broad agreement that these inequalities were structural in character, embedded in a pattern of social and economic arrangements characterised by profound class inequalities stemming from the operations of an unfettered market economy. Inequality in Britain could be defined as class based, Crosland contended, in that the stratification patterns took the form of 'a few broad and deep incisions into the social body, as opposed to innumerable shallow cuts', and that 'these deep incisions coincide[d] to form a single set of national divisions'. It followed that inequalities could be reduced only by addressing their systemic causes.[25]

The second value was defined by Crosland as giving to poverty relief 'an exceptional priority over other claims on resources'.[26] This included guarantees of a level of income sufficient for all people to participate in the life of the community, access to decent housing, education and healthcare, and a large measure of employment security. It was, further, the duty of the state to afford adequate protection to all its citizens against the vagaries and uncertainties of life. Public provision on such a scale required a highly interventionist state and generous public spending, which, in turn, entailed a progressive tax regime in which material resources could be recycled to help those most in need.

The third value, collectivism, embodied the notion of *citizenship rights to collective goods* such as healthcare, education and social benefits delivered to all on the basis of socially recognised need. Collectivism was institutionalised in terms of a large public realm insulated against the compulsions of the market and governed by a distinct set of principles: public service, solidarity and the pursuit of the common good.[27] From this, it followed that the delivery of such collective goods and services by public (i.e. non-profitmaking) organisations animated by a public service ethos was not simply a means, but *an end in itself*, with the public domain supplying 'a space for forms of human flourishing which cannot be bought in the marketplace'.[28]

These three values formed the basis of Labour's consensus. There were major disagreements over what they meant in practice, how they should be applied and, indeed, whether they offered too modest a set of aspirations; they were capable of varying interpretation and therefore allowing for both diversity and change.[29] Thus there were always disagreements, often serious ones, 'about the precise nature of the objectives to be sought, the means of their achievements, or the priority of their pursuit'.[30] But for much of Labour's history, there was broad agreement that the party should be creating a much more equal society from which poverty should be eradicated and with collectively provided services delivered according to need by non-profitmaking public organisations.

This consensus was first challenged in the late 1970s and early 1980s, in the wake of the perceived shortcomings of Labour governments of the 1960s and 1970s. Radical insurgents claimed that the Croslandite social democratic consensus had failed and must be replaced by a more full-blooded socialist programme committed to a major expansion of public ownership, the institution of an elaborate system of economic planning and much tighter regulation of the economy. This programme was adopted by Labour as the basis of the 1983 manifesto – and was thoroughly discredited by Labour's calamitous defeat in the election that year. Neil Kinnock, the new leader, then navigated a retreat from the radical prospectus of the early 1980s and a return to more mainstream social democratic politics.

The next challenge to the party's ideological core was more potent and much more far reaching in its effects. It came from the right of the party, as a generation of highly capable and energetic young, self-labelled 'modernisers', notably Tony Blair, Gordon Brown, Peter Mandelson and Philip Gould, sought in effect a rupture from the past, symbolised by their popularisation of the terms 'Old Labour' and 'New Labour'. Labour's traditional stances on taxation, public ownership and the provision of public services were denounced as backward looking, dogmatic and alienating. 'Old Labour', Gould averred, had lost touch with 'the values, instincts and ethics' of the bulk of voters.[31] 'New Labour' in its stead offered a new paradigm, in essence a hybrid of traditional social democracy and neo-liberalism. In the words of two leading economists, it accepted 'many of the premises of market fundamentalism but [believed] in the capacity of the tax and benefit system to deal with undesirable consequences'.[32] Here we briefly consider its revisions of Labour's traditional consensus.[33]

New Labour accepted key postulates of neo-liberal thinking: egalitarianism demanded heavy and steeply progressive taxation which eroded incentives, stifled enterprise and innovation and retarded economic growth. It alienated both the business community, whose cooperation was essential to any government, and angered voters deeply resistant to any additions to the 'burden of taxation'. Lower taxation, in contrast, would boost investment, productivity and growth; and generous rewards for 'wealth creators' would reignite the spirit of enterprise and risk taking vital to enhancing the UK's competitiveness.[34] Greater equality, neither feasible nor desirable, was replaced as an ideal by meritocracy, which involved making it much easier for the able, energetic and ambitious of all social backgrounds to secure the positions and the rewards their talents merited. To this end, New Labour implemented a whole raft of policies, including much improved childcare provision, various community initiatives and, above all, improved access to higher-quality education.

In contrast, New Labour remained fully committed to the traditional goal of poverty alleviation and what came to be called 'social exclusion'. Major strides were made in reducing poverty through raising child benefits and pensions, a huge programme of targeted tax credits and the introduction of a Minimum Wage. Under Blair and Brown, the overall level of poverty, measured relatively as the percentage of households with incomes less than 60 per cent of the national median, fell.[35] Perhaps the most impressive achievement was the Sure Start programme, which provided a network of thousands of centres providing support and facilities to children of pre-school age.

New Labour's reappraisal of established party principles was most emphatic in its retreat from collectivism. Under the rubric of 'modernisation', it challenged monopoly public service provision, claiming that it was prone to inertia, waste and inefficiency, and producer domination. 'Modernisation' took many forms, but the most important were the introduction of internal markets, consumer choice, a more commercial ethos and outsourcing of the delivery of services to the private sector. The boundary between the public and private sectors became more porous, and profit seeking was allowed to penetrate areas of social life from which it had previously been excluded.[36] David Marquand concluded that New Labour 'pushed marketization and privatization forward, at least as zealously as the Conservatives did'.[37]

There was considerable pride within the party in New Labour's record of major improvements in the public services, particularly the NHS, but also education, and substantial inroads into poverty among older people and the young. But meritocracy failed to resonate as an alternative to greater material equality for a range of reasons, not least that given by Crosland that 'the greatest rewards would go to those with the most fortunate genetic endowment and family background',[38] and also, as argued by Michael Young, that it would be utterly corrosive of social cohesion and harmony.[39] Most contentious of all was the New Labour enthusiasm for marketisation, commercialisation and outsourcing in the public services. 'The history of social democracy,' Robin Cook, the soft left former Foreign Secretary, wrote shortly before his death, 'can be expressed as the struggle to set limits to the market and to define those areas where priorities should be set by social policy rather than commercial forces. Yet this government is dismantling the barriers that its predecessors had erected to keep those commercial forces off the public-service turf.'[40]

The New Labour neo-liberal/social democratic synthesis did not furnish an alternative source of ideological cohesion because it had so few disciples.

But the effects of the loss of ideological cohesion were not immediate. Among the reasons for this was the fact that many of those most disillusioned quit the party – the membership slumped between 1997 and 2010 – or retreated into inactivity. Others were mollified by New Labour's achievements and by its prowess and the polls. Yet the decay in the party's ideological consensus meant that, when circumstances became less propitious, internal fractures would open and the task of sustaining party unity would become much more onerous. This first became evident after the party's dismissal from office in 2010, when the backlash against New Labour began, leading to the election of Ed rather than David Miliband, though its real and dramatic impact was deferred until 2015.

Party role and strategy

Labour throughout its history has been divided, and sometimes seriously so, not only over policy and the distribution of power, but also over strategy. More specifically, a perennial source of tension has been the precise balance between electability and the pursuit of ideals. Many students of political parties have distinguished between two orientations to politics: the office-seeking, whose priority is winning votes and obtaining office; and the policy-seeking, for which the integrity of policy is more important.[41] For example, Kitschelt distinguishes between two ideal-types of motivational patterns within social democratic parties, lending themselves to two different strategic road maps. On the one hand, the 'pragmatists', who favour aligning party policies as closely as possible to voter preferences, assumed to congregate in the centre of the political spectrum. On the other hand, the 'ideologues', who believe that 'a purist appeal to party objectives will eventually convince voters of the party's correctness'.[42] The former is particularly common among leaders, whose overriding priority is to win elections and thereby gain entry into government; the latter, in contrast, is mainly to be found among members, and especially activists, largely drawn into politics by ideals.

There is plainly more than a grain of truth in this reasoning, but we suggest this is too narrowly conceived and overly dichotomous. We start with a broad question: what is politics as a practical activity actually for? In responding to this question, we draw very loosely though heavily upon Weber's classic and much dissected essay, 'Politics as a Vocation'. Weber is concerned with the meaning of 'the vocation of politics' and distinguishes, either explicitly or by inference, between three distinct orientations to politics or, in his terminology, ethics: the ethic of power, the ethic of responsibility and the ethic of conviction.[43] We understand by 'ethic' in this context a particular way of assigning meaning to politics, and the standards of conduct appropriate to it.[44] An ethic, then, constitutes a predisposition to act in a particular way and for a specific set of purposes. The three ethics are presented by Weber as ideal types,[45] but, in what follows, we deploy them as empirical categories operating with the Labour Party, presenting them as composites since 'human motivation is almost always an impure and heterogeneous blend of different, often conflicting, impulses and affects'.[46] For these reasons, it is important to emphasise that the distinctions between the three ethics are matters of *weighting* and *priority*. Thus, in utilising the three categories, we define them according not to their *exclusive* but their *principal* motive force.

What distinguishes those animated by the ethic of power is the insistence that, since without power nothing can be accomplished, obtaining it must be *the overriding priority*; nothing can be done to help the poor, the socially marginalised and the distressed, if the party, through its unwillingness to compromise, consigns itself to opposition. It follows from this that politicians should act as political entrepreneurs, formulating policy products that match the preferences of voters as these are registered (through opinion polls and focus groups), even if this means jettisoning some cherished principles.

For much of Labour's history, those animated by the ethic of power represented only a minority current: Herbert Morrison was perhaps one example, Harold Wilson another. Only with the arrival of New Labour did its influence become paramount. 'Modernisers', led by Blair, Brown, Mandelson (Morrison's grandson) and Phillip Gould, believed that 'Old Labour', distracted by dogma and tradition, had been too slow to adapt its policies to prevailing public sentiment. As outlined in Chapter 1, what characterised the New Labour approach, according to Jon Cruddas, a Downing Street aide under Blair before becoming an MP, was 'the method by which policy is scientifically constructed out of the preferences and prejudices of the swing voter in the swing seat in order to reproduce itself through dominating Middle England – New Labour's marketplace. Policy is the product of positioning.'[47] Ideas, he wrote, 'became the raw material to achieve political position and engineer the retention of power. [...] Votes are the form of exchange, policies the commodities and elected office the derived profit.'[48] From this approach, we can infer – although these were never spelt out – two key precepts, which we call opinion alignment and power accommodation. The former stipulated that, on matters of high public salience, policy should correspond as closely as possible to what voters wanted. The latter prescribed avoiding any measure likely to alienate powerful institutions – most notably the press, major global corporations and the City – whose power, prestige and access to resources gives them the capacity to influence voters and whose cooperation was required to facilitate the delivery of policies.

The ethic of conviction is the mirror image of the ethic of power. The ethic of conviction, as we use the term, was composed of two key components: the notion of politics as a calling and a 'monist' approach to truth and reality. Politics as a calling held that political activity was meaningful only to the degree that it was motivated by dedication to a cause, and that cause, for Labour politicians, should be a socialist transformation of society. If politics was to amount to more than (in Weber's phrase) a 'frivolous intellectual play' or the base pursuit of self-advancement, it must be driven by commitment to larger purposes and ideals.[49] The ethic's exponents did not (as critics claimed) ignore electoral considerations; rather, they assumed that what they offered was what the voters really wanted or could be persuaded to want. Adherents of the ethic of conviction often viewed politics through the prism of Marxist notions of class conflict, distinguishing between those (themselves) who as socialists represented the real interests of the working-class, which lay in the application of socialist principles, and those on the right of the party who stood for class compromise, hence the dilution of those interests. They had a strong sense that they would be justified by history.

The ethic of conviction also exhibited a pronounced tendency towards 'monism', the belief that 'to all true questions there must be one true answer and one only, all the other answers being false'.[50] Hence the importance of always taking a principled stance, even if this was (temporarily) unpopular, such as over gay rights, negotiations with the Irish Republican Army or nationalisation. Because they defined themselves as principled, there was a propensity to consider those who disagreed with them as opportunists and careerists primarily interested in the gratifications afforded by public office. This helped to engender the 'betrayal thesis', which over the years figured so prominently in the lexicon of the left.

For nearly all of Labour history and until Corbyn's astonishing triumph in 2015, disciples of the ethics of conviction were confined to the sidelines. Many left-wing Labour leaders have appeared to espouse this ethic, but this tended to be largely rhetorical. When given ministerial responsibilities, their behaviour conformed much more closely to the ethic of responsibility: examples included Stafford Cripps, Aneurin Bevan, Michael Foot and Barbara Castle; the one notable exception was Tony Benn, in the latter half of his career. Under Corbyn, the complete irreconcilability between the ethics of conviction and of power was a major cause of the civil war that enveloped the party.

The ethic of responsibility requires 'acting pragmatically in pursuit of ends that are both realistic and collectively desirable'.[51] In the words of the leading soft left politician Bryan Gould, 'the demands of practical politics will inevitably require compromise and trade-offs' – but that policy should, notwithstanding, be guided by the 'touchstone of principles'.[52] Parties should be programmatic in orientation, in the sense that policies should 'have a special meaning in terms of the programme to which members are presumably devoted and for which they joined the party'.[53] To a greater extent than the ethic of conviction, the ethic of responsibility emphasises the constraints which limit the discretion of political parties; the feasible should never be neglected in the pursuit of the desirable. Again, unlike the ethic of conviction, compromise is regarded not only as unavoidable but also, at times, as beneficial. As the soft left MP Lisa Nandy maintained, 'the airing of different points of view, the clash of ideas, leadership that can challenge and compromise, gives us better decisions'.[54]

While exponents of the ethic of responsibility understood that account must always be taken of public opinion, they rejected the proposition that the choice was either to follow it blindly or simply ignore it; they favoured engagement with the voters. Sometimes the accent should be on principle rather than popularity, for example always helping those most in need in the midst of the clamour about 'scroungers' on the welfare state. Sometimes it should be the reverse, for example being willing to drop policies they believed to be both sensible and principled but appeared to be unsellable, such as the non-nuclear defence policy of the 1980s. There were no iron rules: it all depended on judgement and circumstance. In Weber's words, the ethic of responsibility sought to steer between the 'mere opportunism born of avidity for power' and the 'intoxication of ideologists'.[55] Prior to New Labour, this was the most widely diffused ethic in the party. It was practised both by left-wingers (when they came to assume the practical responsibilities of office) such as Richard Crossman, Michael Foot and Barbara Castle, but also by those to be found on the centre and right of the party, for example Roy Jenkins and Tony Crosland, both of whom were prepared to take unpopular decisions (respectively over civil rights and egalitarian educational policies). However, with the rise of New Labour as the dominant force on Labour's right, the ethic of responsibility was increasingly identified with the soft left of the party.

Disagreement between adherents of these three ethics has always been a feature of Labour politics, though its intensity has varied over time. Thus, we shall see that the Miliband era witnessed a conflict between the ethic of responsibility and the ethic of power, the Corbyn era between the ethic of conviction and the ethic of power, and the Starmer leadership once more between the ethics of power and responsibility. As we shall see, this lies at the root of the choice of managerial strategies. This clash of ethics, because it is inherent in the politics of the left, is a seam that runs throughout Labour history and will continue to do so.

Normative order

Parties, especially social democratic ones, are not simply associations in which members pool their efforts to achieve some common goal but also communities knit together by a common culture. Labour, as Cronin observed, 'was never just a political party. It was a movement, a way of thinking and feeling, and an intense set of loyalties and antipathies.'[56] The politics of the Labour Party cannot be understood without appreciating its culture or, in Drucker's terminology, its ethos.[57] This we define as the 'basic assumptions and beliefs that are shared by members of an organization, that operate unconsciously, and that define in a basic "taken-for-granted" fashion an organization's view of itself and its environment'. They are learned responses to the problems of how a party can cohere, adapt and sustain itself in a competitive environment.[58]

The basic constituent of a culture are norms of behaviour. Elster has defined norms as 'injunctions to behaviour that (i) are non-outcome-oriented, (ii) apply to others as well as to oneself, (iii) are sustained by the sanctions of others, and (iv) reinforced by internalised emotions'.[59] As March and Olsen pointed out, 'although self-interest undoubtedly permeates politics, action is often based more on discovering the normatively appropriate behaviour than on calculating the return expected from alternative choices. As a result, political behaviour, like other behaviour, can be described in terms of duties, obligations, roles, and rules.'[60] Members who remain in a political organisation for any length of time, especially those who play an active part, become habituated to its tacit understandings, conventions and ways of doing things; these supply standards of behavioural propriety and set the tone and temper of a party.

However, in Labour's case, identifying these norms is inordinately difficult precisely because they are taken for granted and rarely articulated; and because of the difficulty of gathering data other than by immersion in the party's inner world. As Marquand pointed out, they are 'nebulous, impalpable, the subtleties of which are extraordinarily hard to catch on paper'.[61] As a result, our efforts to pin down the key norms necessarily have to be tentative and even, to a degree, conjectural: but they are no less important because they cannot be scientifically established. With these caveats in mind, on the basis of observations (including participant observation) over many years, of interviews and by utilising a range of primary and secondary sources, we identify three major norms in Labour's culture: loyalty, solidarity and civility.

Loyalty takes the form of attachment to the party *as an institution* and is most commonly to be found among longer-term members. It is, however, a complex phenomenon which can take different forms. At its most basic, the object of loyalty may be the party itself, its traditions, its rituals and practices: rather like loyalty to a favoured football team. It may, alternatively, have an element of contingency: loyalty to the party as long as it stays true to its principles. And it may take the more specific form of loyalty to the leader, who is seen in some way to embody the party and its public face, a sentiment which tends to intensify as an election draws nearer.

We define solidarity as 'unity or accordance of feeling, action, etc., especially among individuals with common interests, sympathies or aspirations'.[62] As a norm, it was woven within Labour's fabric, a transposition to the party of the class solidarity that underpinned trade unionism: 'the canon of solidarity', Crossman observed, was fundamental to 'the spirit of trade unionism'.[63] Class solidarity was the belief that working-class life could be improved only through collective effort, anchored in strong and enduring ties of comradeship and mutual obligation. As such, it seeped into the party's own collective consciousness in its formative years, morphing gradually into a specifically *party* solidarity, shared by long-standing members quite irrespective of class background. Indeed middle-class – by socio-economic standards – Labour Party members have tended to subjectively identify as working class. As a result, Labour, like other social democratic parties, became not only an association for the advancement of shared aims and interests, but a 'community of solidarity' bound together by ties of fellow feeling and mutuality.

The main significance of civility, Labour's third norm, was that it operates as a force regulating the expression of disagreement. While it does not preclude sharp clashes of opinion and heated – even vehement – debate, it enjoins members to respect the convictions of others, to accept that those with differing views hold them in good faith, that personal attacks are unacceptable and that mutual tolerance is an essential part of civilised debate. It holds that disagreements should not prevent those from different wings of the party from working together or indeed from socialising (the drink in the pub after a meeting). Of course, party members did not always live up to this norm, but it nevertheless stipulated how they ought to behave, and this had an important restraining effect. The fact that many media commentators depict Labour as a party which relishes nothing more than fighting with itself reflects a lack of familiarity with how debate, *in most normal times*, is conducted within CLPs.[64]

To the extent that these interlinked and mutually reinforcing norms were internalised and embedded in party life, they imparted a powerful impulse towards unity and stability: 'an emotional reflex to preserve the party', and an instinct 'to keep the "Labour family" together – to conciliate, negotiate and broker a deal between the conflicting parties'.[65] They did not always forestall acute strife, but they did prevent it from exploding into schismatic behaviour (save for the SDP in 1981) of the type that fractured socialist parties on the Continent. As long as these three norms permeated the collective psychology of the party, a high degree of normative order or integration could be said to exist. This in turn operated as a conflict/shock absorber, acting as a powerful force assuaging conflict, facilitating party cohesion and therefore easing the task of party management.

However, a party's normative order is not fixed but is constantly being renegotiated and reinterpreted as the environment which the party inhabits alters, the composition of the membership changes and new challenges emerge. Periods of normative breakdown are most likely to occur with the conjuncture of two processes: a rapid influx of a significant number of new recruits, and severe collisions within the party over issues of strategy, ideology and power. Normative breakdown has so far occurred twice in Labour's post-war history, the first in the period from the late 1970s to mid-1980s, the second under Corbyn. Here we confine ourselves to a discussion of the former, as the second will be addressed in subsequent chapters.

From about the mid-1970s, the composition of the party underwent a substantial alteration as older, solidaristic-minded working-class members were replaced by a new cohort of younger, usually more highly educated and middle-class members, idealists influenced by the upsurge in student protest and the resurgence of socialist thinking in higher education in the period.[66] Many of them possessed, Eric Deakins MP averred, 'the normal middle-class characteristics: articulate, self-assured, confident in manner and view', and 'tending to dogmatism'.[67] They were less instinctively loyal, less respectful towards authority and more truculent in manner and style. They were often rebellious in temper: 'remove the diadem, and take off the crown!' Austin Mitchell MP noted the emergence of 'a whole new culture' manifested in 'an end to submissiveness and deference', and 'a greater willingness to question, argue and dispute'.[68] A relatively small but hyperactive and therefore disproportionately influential number of these activists were members of Trotskyist organisations, especially the Militant Tendency, who imported into some local parties (mainly in Merseyside and London) the style of splenetic sectarian intolerance typical of such bodies.[69] Overall, there was an inclination among many to respond to policies of which they disapproved with accusations of leadership 'betrayal'.

To a number of observers, these political, cultural and sociological changes, by no means limited to the UK, spelt the end of social democratic parties as 'communities of solidarity', as the 'spirit of discipline in a culturally and sociologically relatively homogeneous organization' was gradually extinguished.[70] But this is to take too narrow and rigid a view of party culture. Culture consists of sets of learned responses and, as such, evolves with new experiences and new challenges, particularly the shock of electoral debacles. 'In situations of disorientation, crisis and search for meaning, actors are in particular likely to rethink who and what they and others are, and may become.'[71] Party members have agency, and their norms evolve as they encounter, reflect upon and adapt to new situations, modifying their thinking and behaviour accordingly. Many of the left-wing insurgents of the 1970s and early 1980s came over time to be socialised into a greater appreciation of the importance of solidarity, loyalty and civility. Increasing numbers came to concur with soft left frontbencher Bryan Gould's insight that 'the betrayal theory' had inflicted serious damage on the party by engendering 'a constant climate of suspicion and grievance which makes it difficult for the Labour Party to maintain the unity and discipline rightly expected of a party seeking office'.[72] There developed, in response to the demoralising sequence of electoral defeats, a much greater sensitivity within the grass roots to the effects of their behaviour on Labour's image, a greater appreciation of the need for party cohesion and a greater disposition to acknowledge the functional importance of leadership. Seyd and Whiteley, who researched party membership in this period, observed that while most members adopted a principled approach to politics, they also wanted to win elections and they understood this meant compromises: the learned experience in the long years in opposition under Kinnock and Smith.[73] All this helped restore allegiance to the leadership, a greater willingness to give it the benefit of the doubt and to work collaboratively for common ends.

But in the early 1990s a new challenge to party culture was posed from a very different quarter as Blair, Brown, Mandelson and others deliberately embarked on a strategy of '*Kulturkampf* aimed at displacing the party's inherited political culture'.[74] Blair, a hugely capable and astute party manager, sought to engineer a transformation not only of the party's ideology, programme and power structure but also in 'its modus operandi, its thinking, its programme and above all its attitudes'.[75] Thus loyalty to the party was reconfigured as loyalty to Blair and the 'New Labour project'; and solidarity was redefined in terms of the modernisers' *esprit de corps* and more broadly of pride in belonging to a winning team.

But this *Kulturkampf* was by no means wholly successful. While some members socialised into the new way of thinking, many more departed or sank into sullen passivity. They were, to a degree, replaced by a new type of activist – sharp-suited rather than casually dressed, heavily focused on the mechanics of electioneering, Blairite true believers, some of whom displayed a rigidity and intolerance comparable to the left-wing insurgents of the early 1980s.[76] But there were not many of these. As Blair himself acknowledged: 'There was a cadre of people who believed in New Labour and understood it, instinctively and emotionally as well as intellectually, but they were small in number, uncertain in influence and still feeling their way, as in a sense I was.'[77] Most constituency parties were unreceptive to the New Labour ethos, which failed to sink deep and secure roots, and Blair's ambition of transforming party culture was never fulfilled, as was to become evident after 2010.

Approaches to party management

So far we have analysed the resources available to party managers and the problems and challenges they faced; we now turn to their responses. Throughout Labour's history, patterns of party management tended to oscillate between two major traditions: centralism and pluralism. These differed according to two variables: the degree of reliance on discipline and the degree of centralisation. By discipline, we mean a relationship in which the leadership 'wins submission by the ability to impose an alternative to [the target's] preferences [...] that is sufficiently unpleasant or painful so that these preferences are abandoned'.[78] By centralisation, we mean the extent to which the activities of members and lower-level units are subject to directives issued by the centre rather than being left to their own discretion.[79]

After an initial period of party building, in the 1920s, in response to external challenges, especially the threat of Communist infiltration, as well as internal pressures, Labour evolved a centralistic pattern of party management. Discipline, both in the PLP and the wider party, was seen as vital to maintain both party unity and an efficient system of internal party governance. MPs who flouted majority decisions ran the risk of suspension or expulsion from the PLP or even the party. Thus Stafford Cripps (a few years later to become Chancellor of the Exchequer) and Aneurin Bevan (soon to be Minister of Health) were both expelled in 1939 for campaigning for the formation of a Popular Front, in defiance of a Conference decision. Bevan only narrowly escaped expulsion again in 1955 for persistently challenging majority decisions, and Michael Foot, a future party leader, lost the whip in 1961. Equally, during the heyday of managerial centralism from the mid-1930s to the early 1960s, the NEC devised and operated a range of central controls to regulate and limit the rights of subordinate party units, MPs and members to form factions (for example, the Bevanite Group was forced to dissolve in 1955), to remove sitting MPs and to associate with outside groups, through the institution of the so-called 'proscribed list' of banned organisations.[80]

Managerial centralism was regularly attacked, especially from the left of the party. One of its most perceptive critics was Richard Crossman, a friend and ally of Harold Wilson, party leader from 1962 to 1976. In 1955, he argued that 'old-fashioned, rigid regimentation' was unsuitable to a modern party both because it was counter-productive, stoking rather than allaying antagonisms, and because it facilitated the growth of oligarchy in the party.[81] In the mid-1960s, as a senior PLP manager, Crossman, with Wilson's full support, established a much more pluralistic managerial regime;[82] and a little later, under General Secretary Ron Hayward (elected in 1972), the same regime was extended to the wider party as the NEC relaxed controls, for example no longer blocking efforts of CLPs dissatisfied with their MPs from deselecting them, and abolishing the proscribed list.[83]

Managerial pluralism's core proposition was that 'experience proves that disciplinary action is no remedy for serious discontent, still less for disunity'.[84] Wilson, in his years as leader both in government and opposition, was plagued by constant rebellions but regarded attempts to quell them by rigorous enforcement of leadership decisions as counter-productive and opted for more conciliatory methods.[85] As he told Barbara Castle, a friend and political ally, in an 'impassioned outburst': 'all along I have believed my duty was to be the custodian of party unity'.[86] At one point he exclaimed that while his critics preferred to parade their consciences, he had 'waded through shit' to prevent the party splitting.[87] And as Bernard Donoughue, a senior Wilson aide, wrote, 'he fudged and ducked and weaved' in his attempts to hold the party together, especially over the highly divisive issue of membership of the EU.[88] Later events would demonstrate that this was an impressive achievement.

James Callaghan, Wilson's successor, was a politician (in this respect) in very much the same mould. With his long experience, he had an intimate knowledge and instinctive feel for Labour's traditions, customs and habits; though tough and ruthless, he saw himself as a conciliator – although at the end he was overwhelmed by the sheer force of party schisms which by the 1980s tested the liberal, pluralist regime to its limits.[89] Under Callaghan's successor Michael Foot (leader from 1980–83) – both a former rebel and long a pluralist standard-bearer – that regime came close to disintegration. Presiding over a party wracked by multiple and dangerous cleavages, faced with Tony Benn's highly disruptive bid to be elected deputy leader, the SDP schism and a huge row over Trotskyist infiltration of the party, Foot found there was little he could do to preserve either cohesion or an effective system of internal governance.

For reasons discussed earlier, circumstances eased under the resolute leadership of Neil Kinnock from 1983 to 1992. He was prepared to take tough disciplinary action against the highly disruptive Militant Tendency and often tried to project himself as a firm and forceful leader. But many of his instincts were pluralist. As his biographer noted in 1987, he well understood 'the importance of keeping the Party behind him in everything he has done, both to safeguard his own position and to avoid more internal contention'.[90] With considerable skill, acumen and determination, Kinnock constructed a broad alliance which backed the expulsion of Militant's leading cadres and which eventually eliminated the entryist threat. Kinnock's successor in 1992, John Smith, was an accomplished party manager, more emollient by nature than his predecessor, and he adopted a 'relaxed and accommodating method of leading the party'.[91] In marked contrast to his successor, he did not believe that confrontations with the left were either a wise or necessary way of asserting his own authority. Instead he favoured collegiality and an inclusive approach which sought to reach decisions as far as possible through a process of coalition building, inclusivity and mutual adjustment.[92]

But this approach, and the ascendancy of managerial pluralism, did not survive his untimely death and Tony Blair's election as leader in 1994. The new leader was impatient with what he saw as pluralism's recipe of fixing and deal making, prevarication and short-term tactical manoeuvring.[93] Party management was for a purpose, and his purpose – the 'New Labour project' – was bold, ambitious and bracing. The party had to learn to conduct itself 'in a fundamentally different manner both in office and in opposition' if it was to be transformed into an effective election-fighting machine.[94] This could be accomplished only by a leadership with total mastery over the party. In the words of Blair's senior strategist Philip Gould – an eager disciple of the ethic of power – 'only a unitary system of command could give Labour the clarity and flexibility it needed to adapt and change at the pace required by modern politics'.[95]

An astringent managerial regime was installed, overseen by 'a comprehensive interlocking managerial machine operating under the guidance of the Leader's Office'.[96] The various institutions of decision-making, the Shadow Cabinet, PLP and the NEC were interlocked, and the primacy of the leader was firmly established. The NEC, with its arsenal of managerial powers, became a bastion of loyal responsibility to the leader. Along with this was a major change in the culture of party officialdom. The conception of the role of party officials evolved from being the 'civil servants of the party' into culture-carriers of party modernisation, a new political technocracy committed to 'the New Labour project'.[97] One example of this was the extended and more partisan role they played in candidate selection.[98]

In apparent contradiction to this centralising drive was the expanded use of OMOV and various forms of direct consultation and the democratisation of the policy-making process. But OMOV was designed to attenuate the role and influence of constituency party organisations seen as dominated by left-wing activists by transferring functions to the more passive, presumed to be more 'moderate' and more amenable, through direct balloting. As Seyd and Whiteley commented, Blair wanted 'pliant, supportive and inactive members, still willing to give money but not demanding influence over party policies in return'.[99] The democratisation of policy-making, however, took the form of the implementation of a wide-ranging package of reforms entitled 'Partnership in Power', adopted by Conference in 1997. Formally, the objective was to offer multiple opportunities for ordinary party members to participate in policy-making through a newly established National Policy Forum. In reality, this functioned as a 'dignified part' of Labour's constitution, furnishing 'a veneer of democracy disguising centralisation and control'.[100]

In all this the leadership was following the remorseless logic of the ethic of power. Since members were more oriented to the realisation of ideals and less exclusively focused on optimising the vote, their contribution to policy formation needed to be minimised, and the same applied to all the institutions of the extra-parliamentary party. Thus, the role of Conference, still formally the party's sovereign body, dwindled as the leadership stage-managed its proceedings, converting it into a platform for photo opportunities and soundbites aimed at television audiences. Party managers were equipped with a whole range of agenda-managing and procedural mechanisms enabling them to divert serious misgivings over government policy into relatively innocuous channels. The outcome was a 'heavily managerialised party'.[101] Already by 2000, Peter Mair concluded that 'the leadership seems intent on installing a degree of control over the Labour party without precedent'. In its striving for 'iron control', it had engaged in 'manipulation of internal procedures to ensure that only those on message would reach key positions inside the party or on lists of candidates for public office' and had taken multiple steps to suppress internal party dissent.[102]

But intense managerialisation was accompanied by a loss of party vitality. During the mid-1990s, Labour's membership leapt from a very low base to reach a peak, at 405,000, in 1997.[103] Thereafter it slumped continuously, falling to a mere 166,000 by 2008, the lowest ever recorded.[104] As a leading expert on party membership concluded, New Labour's leadership, policies and management of the party had both alienated many existing members and failed to attract many new ones.[105] Equally, there was evidence of declining levels of activism and decomposing and atrophying party organisation on the ground, especially in Labour heartlands. Constituency representation at party Conference fell progressively from 501 in 2007, to 465 in 2008, 444 in 2009 and 412 in 2010.[106] Dismal numbers of members were taking part in the selection of parliamentary candidates or bothering to vote in internal party elections.[107] It was thus a deflated, demoralised and diminished party that Gordon Brown's successor was to inherit when Labour was ejected from power in 2010.

Notes

1 Martin Forde (chair), *The Forde Report* (London: Labour Party, 2022), p. 29, https://labour.org.uk/wp-content/uploads/2023/01/The-Forde-Report.pdf [consulted 23 March 2025].

2 Lewis Minkin, *The Labour Party Conference: A Study in the Politics of Intra-party Democracy* (Manchester: Manchester University Press, 1978), p. 4.

3 Labour Party Rulebook, 2013. Chapter 1, Clause VIII. 3. A; Clause X 5.

4 *Ibid.* 3. H.

5 *Ibid.* 3. N.

6 *Ibid.* 4.

7 *Ibid.* 3. A.

8 Labour Party NEC, Terms of Reference, March 2016.

9 *Ibid.*

10 Labour Party Rulebook, 2013. Chapter 1, Clause IX, 2C; Lewis Minkin, *The Blair Supremacy: A Study in the Politics of Labour's Party Management* (Manchester: Manchester University Press, 2014), p. 67.

11 Labour Party Rulebook, 2013. Chapter 1, Clause VIII. 5.

12 Labour Party Rulebook, 2013. Chapter 1, Clause VII, 1 v. Emphasis added.

13 As Minkin has demonstrated, the relationship between the party and the unions is regulated by a set of norms and conventions – what Minkin calls 'the rules' – whose fundamental principle was the acceptance by both of different spheres 'each with its own roles, responsibilities and autonomy. The more left-wing unions, it should be noted, did, at times, query and challenge this convention.' Minkin, *The Blair Supremacy*, p. 13.

14 Dennis Wrong, *Power: Its Forms, Bases and Uses* (Oxford: Blackwell, 1979), p. 49.

15 David Easton, *A Systems Analysis of Political Life* (New York: John Wiley and Sons, 1965), p. 292.

16 Michael Foot, *Another Heart and Other Pulses* (London: Collins, 1984), p. 160.

17 Eric Shaw, *Discipline and Discord: The Politics of Managerial Control in the Labour Party, 1951–87)* (Manchester: Manchester University Press, 1988), pp. 245, 251.

18 The college initially comprised three sections, the PLP, the CLPs and the affiliated unions, and initially gave the CLPs and the PLP 30 per cent each and the unions 40 per cent. This was later replaced by an equal division between the three.
19 The hard left (led by Tony Benn but also including one of his junior lieutenants, Jeremy Corbyn) opposed expulsions on the grounds that the sectarian Militant represented a legitimate strand of opinion within the party. The soft left held that the Tendency was a dangerous and disruptive body whose aims were incompatible with those of the party.
20 Diane Sainsbury, 'Theoretical perspectives in analysing ideological change and persistence', *Scandinavian Political Studies*, 4:4 (1981), 273–94.
21 With one exception, the publication of an official statement of aims and values, largely compiled by then deputy leader Roy Hattersley in 1988, but which aroused little interest in the party. See Karl Pike, 'Mere theology? Neil Kinnock and the Labour Party's aims and values, 1986–1988', *Contemporary British History*, 34:1 (2020), 95–117.
22 Tony Crosland, *The Future of Socialism* (London: Jonathan Cape, 1964), p. 77.
23 Tony Crosland, *Socialism Now* (London: Jonathan Cape, 1974), p. 16.
24 David Lipsey, 'The meretriciousness of meritocracy', *Political Quarterly*, 85:1 (2014), 37.
25 Crosland, *The Future of Socialism*, p. 118.
26 *Ibid.*, pp. 76–7.
27 David Marquand, *Decline of the Public: The Hollowing Out of Citizenship* (Cambridge: Polity, 2004), p. 27.
28 *Ibid.*
29 W. H. Greenleaf, *The British Political Tradition. The Ideological Heritage* (London: Routledge, 1983), pp. 14–15.
30 *Ibid.*, p. 8.
31 Philip Gould, *The Unfinished Revolution* (London: Little, Brown & Co, 1998), p. 19.
32 Paul Collier and John Kay, *Greed Is Dead: Politics after Individualism* (London: Allen Lane, 2020), p. 82.
33 For a much more detailed exposition see Eric Shaw, *Losing Labour's Soul?* (Abingdon: Routledge, 2007), especially chapters 5 and 8.
34 Peter Mandelson and Roger Liddle, *The Blair Revolution: Can New Labour Deliver?* (London: Faber and Faber, 1996), p. 64.
35 Paul Gregg, 'New Labour and inequality', *Political Quarterly*, 81:1 (2011), 16–30; Ruth Lupton et al., *Labour's Social Policy Record: Policy, Spending and Outcomes 1997–2010* (London: LSE Centre for Social Exclusion, 2013).
36 Jon Cruddas and John Rutherford, 'Ethical socialism', *Soundings*, 44 (Spring 2010), 11.
37 Marquand, *Decline of the Public*, p. 118.

38 Crosland, *Socialism Now*, p. 16.
39 Michael Young, *The Rise of the Meritocracy* (London: Penguin, 1958); Michael Young, 'Down with meritocracy', *Guardian*, 29 June 2001.
40 Robin Cook, 'How Labour can win back the 4 million voters we lost', *Guardian*, 17 June 2005.
41 Gijs Schumacher, Catherine E. de Vries and Barbara Vis, 'Why do parties change position? Party organization and environmental incentives', *The Journal of Politics*, 75:2 (2013), 210.
42 Herbert Kitschelt, *The Transformation of European Social Democracy* (Cambridge: Cambridge University Press, 1994), pp. 209–10.
43 Max Weber, 'Politics as a vocation', Reprinted from Hand Gerth and C. Wright Mills (eds), *Max Weber: Essays in Sociology* (New York: Oxford University Press, 1946).
44 Joshua Cherniss, *Liberalism in Dark Times* (Princeton, NJ: Princeton University Press, 2021), pp. 8–9.
45 That is, analytical devices for elucidating behaviour.
46 Wrong, *Power*, p. 83.
47 Jon Cruddas, 'New Labour and the withering away of the working class?', *Political Quarterly*, 77:1 (2006), 206.
48 Jon Cruddas, *The Dignity of Labour* (Cambridge: Polity, 2021), p. 68.
49 Weber, 'Politics as a vocation', pp. 36–7.
50 Isaiah Berlin, *The Power of Ideas* (Princeton, NJ: Princeton University Press, 2000), p. 30.
51 Nick O'Donovan, 'Responsibility in the political thought of Max Weber', *Polity*, 43 (2011), 86.
52 Bryan Gould, 'Constructing a left politics', *Soundings*, 42 (2009), 136.
53 Leon Epstein, *Political Parties in Western Democracies* (London: Routledge, 1980 [1967]), p. 262.
54 Lisa Nandy, *All In: How We Build a Country that Works* (London: HarperCollins, 2023), p. 200.
55 Joshua L. Cherniss, 'An ethos of politics between realism and idealism: Max Weber's enigmatic political ethics', *Journal of Politics*, 78:3 (2016), 711.
56 James Cronin, *New Labour's Pasts* (London: Pearson Longman, 2004), p. 19.
57 Henry Drucker, *Doctrine and Ethos in the Labour Party* (London: Routledge, 1979).
58 Edgar Schein, *Organizational Culture and Leadership* (San Francisco, CA: Jossey-Bass, 1985), p. 6.
59 Jon Elster, 'Rationality and the emotions', *The Economic Journal*, 106:438 (1996), 1389.
60 James G. March and Johan P. Olsen, 'The new institutionalism: Organizational factors in political life', *American Political Science Review*, 78 (1984), 744.
61 David Marquand, *The Progressive Dilemma* (London: Weidenfeld & Nicolson, 1990), p. 197.

62 *Shorter Oxford Dictionary.*
63 Richard Crossman, *Introduction to Bagehot, The English Constitution* (London: Fontana, 1963), pp. 41–2.
64 The evidence base for these observations has relied upon participant observation over many years and in different settings. The distinctiveness of civility as a Labour Party norm is also demonstrated by contrasting the ways in which debates are conducted in the party compared with in far-left organisations.
65 Michael Calderbank, 'How likely is a Labour Party split?', *Red Pepper*, 4 August 2016.
66 Patrick Seyd and Paul Whiteley, *Labour's Grass Roots: The Politics of Party Membership* (Oxford: Clarendon Press, 1992), pp. 33–4, 37.
67 Eric Deakins, *What Future for Labour?* (London: Hilary Shipman, 1988), p. 26.
68 Austin Mitchell, *Four Years in the Death of the Labour Party* (London: Methuen, 1983), p. 21.
69 Shaw, *Discipline and Discord*, pp. 265–6.
70 Gerassimos Moschonas, *In the Name of Social Democracy* (London: Verso, 2002), p. 143.
71 James G. March and Johan P. Olsen, 'The logic of appropriateness', ARENA Working Papers (2016), p. 16.
72 Quoted in Eric Shaw, *The Labour Party Since 1979: Crisis and Transformation* (London: Routledge, 1994), p.165.
73 Seyd and Whiteley, *Labour's Grass Roots*, p. 45.
74 Cronin, *New Labour's Pasts*, pp. 4, 2.
75 Tony Blair, *A Journey* (London: Hutchinson, 2010), p. 48.
76 Observations at Conference and at CLP level.
77 Blair, *A Journey*, p. 200.
78 John Galbraith, *The Anatomy of Power* (Boston, MA: Houghton Mifflin, 1983), p. 22.
79 Harry Eckstein and Ted R. Gurr, *Patterns of Authority: A Structural Basis for Political Inquiry* (London: John Wiley, 1975), p. 53.
80 All these matters are discussed in Shaw, *Discipline and Discord.*
81 Richard Crossman, 'Reflections on party loyalty', *New Statesman*, 2 April 1955.
82 Richard Crossman, *The Diaries of a Cabinet Minister. Vol. 2, 1966–68* (London: Hamish Hamilton and Jonathan Cape, 1976).
83 Shaw, *Discipline and Discord*, p. 184.
84 Douglas Houghton, 'The Labour backbencher', *Political Quarterly*, 40:4 (1969), 455. Douglas Houghton MP was at the time chair of the PLP.
85 Eric Shaw, 'The problem of party management', in Peter Dorey (ed.), *The Labour Governments 1964–1970* (London: Routledge, 2006), pp. 34–52.
86 Anne Perkins, *Red Queen: The Authorized Biography of Barbara Castle* (London: Macmillan, 2003), p. 359.

87 Steve Richards, 'What would Harold Wilson do?', *The New European*, 14 July 2018.
88 Bernard Donoughue, *The Heat of the Kitchen: An Autobiography* (London: Politicos, 2003), p. 157.
89 Eric Shaw, 'The Labour Party', in Anthony Seldon and Kevin Hickson (eds), *New Labour, Old Labour: The Wilson and Callaghan Governments 1974–79* (London: Routledge, 2004).
90 Michael Leapman, *Kinnock* (London: HarperCollins 1987), p. 189.
91 Michael Foley, *John Major, Tony Blair and a Conflict of Leadership* (Manchester: Manchester University Press, 2002), p. 115.
92 Minkin, *The Blair Supremacy*, p. 84.
93 Foley, *A Conflict of Leadership*, pp. 155–6.
94 Cronin, *New Labour's Pasts*, p. 2.
95 Gould, *The Unfinished Revolution*, p. 240.
96 Minkin, *The Blair Supremacy*, p. 136.
97 *Ibid.*, p. 134.
98 *Ibid.*, p. 169.
99 Patrick Seyd and Paul Whiteley, 'Why Blair needs his grass roots', *New Statesman*, 6 December 1999.
100 Patrick Seyd and Paul Whiteley, *New Labour's Grass Roots: The Transformation of the Labour Party Membership* (Basingstoke: Palgrave Macmillan, 2002), p. 176.
101 Minkin, *The Blair Supremacy*, pp. 303–30.
102 Peter Mair, 'Ruling the void', *New Left Review*, 42 (2006), 175, 184.
103 John Marshall, *Membership of UK Political Parties* (London: House of Commons Library, 2009), p. 9.
104 Paul Whiteley, 'Where have all the members gone? The dynamics of party membership in Britain', *Parliamentary Affairs*, 62:2 (2009), 250.
105 Patrick Seyd, 'Corbyn's Labour Party: Managing the membership surge', *British Politics*, 15:1 (2000), 4.
106 Minkin, *The Blair Supremacy*, p. 754.
107 Richard Heffernan, 'Labour's New Labour legacy: Politics after Blair and Brown', *Political Studies Review*, 9:2 (2011), 171–2.

3

'No matter how hard he tried, he could not break free': Miliband, New Labour and the party's programme

> If we departed a millimetre from New Labour, we were in trouble.
>
> Tony Blair[1]

The party setting

Four former cabinet ministers entered the race for the party leadership in 2010, after Labour's eviction from power and Gordon Brown's resignation: Ed Balls, Andy Burnham, as well as David and Ed Miliband. They were joined by a fifth candidate, Diane Abbott, a no-hoper representing the hard left Socialist Campaign Group (SCG). The two Miliband brothers soon emerged as the front-runners, David representing the New Labour wing of the party, Ed the soft left. It was widely assumed, not least by David himself, that he would coast to victory: he was senior in political stature as former Foreign Secretary (Ed had been Environment Secretary), was better known and seemed to be more popular among voters. However, he was just beaten by his younger brother on the fifth ballot, though he had won majorities in two of the three sections of the electoral college, parliamentarians and members. Ed Miliband's victory stunned and dismayed the Blairites,[2] many of whom were never quite reconciled, and they convinced themselves he had won only because of a 'stitch-up' masterminded by UNISON, the General and Municipal Workers' Union (GMB) and, especially, Unite. The extreme narrowness of his victory also meant that Miliband's legitimacy was constantly questioned.

Blair and Brown had constructed a formidable apparatus of centralised power in the party, but this, we have suggested, depended on the capacity of the leadership to wield control over and integrate all the major levers of power. Miliband was a soft left leader presiding over a party where the right was strongly embedded in the Shadow Cabinet and the PLP and, to a degree, in the party machine too. As Mandelson later commented, from the outset Miliband 'could count his real supporters on the fingers of one hand and […] even they were prone to doubts', adding that as for the 'Blairites' (presumably including himself), 'it was only a matter of time before they came for him in the night'.[3] Hence the new leadership had an insecure grip over the party. Miliband sought, as we shall see, a change of programmatic direction and a new ideological identity for the party, but whether he had the means to secure this was always a moot point, given the unpromising party setting and also the media environment in which he operated.

Traditionally, the Shadow Cabinet was elected by the PLP, though portfolios were allocated by the leader. In 2011 the PLP agreed that, in future, the Shadow Cabinet would be picked by the leader, which in theory could have buttressed Miliband's position. Yet he felt he had no option but to fill the key posts in the Shadow Cabinet with those who had occupied major ministerial positions in the outgoing government, such as Yvette Cooper, Andy Burnham, Douglas Alexander and Ed Balls, none of whom sympathised with his political goals. In theory, he could, at some point, have appointed more loyalists, but did not do so for a variety of reasons. Firstly, he felt that the claims of the ex-ministerial heavyweights to senior front bench posts could not realistically be denied – and anyway, they would be more dangerous sulking on the back benches. Secondly, he was a pluralist who believed that the Shadow Cabinet should reflect the spread of opinion in a PLP in which the left as a whole was decidedly a minority. Thirdly, he thought appointments should be made on merit, which was why he promoted talented MPs such as Rachel Reeves, Jim Murphy, Chuka Umunna and Tristram Hunt, even though they were not from his wing of the party.[4] In consequence, as one senior advisor recalled, 'we never really had a Shadow Cabinet that bore the imprimatur of Ed's politics'.[5]

Miliband's problem was personal as well as political. The ex-ministerial heavyweights considered themselves, in terms of experience, ability and seniority in the party, as equal in status to Miliband, except for Balls, who saw himself as his superior; and they struggled to reconcile with the fact that he, rather than they, had secured the leadership. Constantly preying on their mind was the thought – as one Miliband aide put it – that 'this guy's my peer, I'm better than him, what the fuck is he doing as leader?'[6] There was a further complication. The most senior front bench position was Shadow Chancellor of the Exchequer, a job Ed offered his brother. Since David turned it down, he selected Alan Johnson who, however, resigned for personal reasons in early 2011. After David rejected a second offer, Ed felt he had no option but to appoint Balls. The two Eds had worked closely together as advisers to Brown for several years, but their relationship had deteriorated. Miliband recognised Balls's mastery of economics, his penetrating intelligence and his stature in the party, but equally he knew him to be brashly self-confident, assertive and at times abrasive. With his 'huge ego', he was regarded as 'not a natural team player', and so it proved; in the words of one senior Miliband aide, working with him could be 'a total nightmare'.[7] The consequences would be serious: effective leadership had to be based on agreement between the leader and his Shadow Chancellor in the crucial area of economic policy, but it was always evident that Balls had little sympathy with Miliband's desire to move beyond the New Labour paradigm.

The allegiance to Miliband of most of those in the Shadow Cabinet with New Labour affinities was shaky. They saw him as too left wing, too intellectual and too other-worldly and, as time passed, as inadequate as a parliamentary performer and as a communicator. Frontbenchers are formally bound by collective responsibility and therefore obligated to show loyalty to the leader – a convention that Starmer later very strongly enforced. But those critical of Miliband interpreted the discipline of collective responsibility very flexibly.[8] They felt under no obligation to keep their reservations to themselves, and indeed were quite willing to impart them in off-the-record briefings to journalists, including those from right-wing newspapers. When describing Miliband as arrogant, aloof and indecisive, the press was always able to attribute these epithets to 'informed party sources'.[9] As Roy Greenslade, former editor of the *Mirror*, noted, 'right-wing editors have been aided and abetted in their attempt to terminate Miliband's political career by citing criticisms from a range of Labour MPs'.[10] Some Shadow Cabinet members were sufficiently emboldened to challenge Miliband's authority either openly or 'by disdainful body language'.[11] The fact that Miliband was saddled with a Shadow Cabinet he did not control 'created an inherent instability from the outset'[12] – and he never felt strong enough to replace these sceptics by those upon whom he could rely.

Equally, Miliband also faced substantial difficulties in managing the PLP.[13] Unlike Corbyn, Miliband had a significant minority of MPs who had voted for him, but, despite the prodding of some allies such as Jon Trickett, he was unwilling to forge them into an organised soft left current which could buttress his leadership, fearing this would only promote factionalism.[14] Most MPs were in fact more or less loyal, but there was a cohort of truculent Blairites very resentful of what they saw as Ed 'trashing our record' in government and thus they constantly sniped at him.[15] Matters were not improved by Miliband's reluctance to spend time with the troops in the bars and tearooms of Westminster Palace. As one close aide observed, 'We used to have terrible trouble getting him to go and talk to MPs. He just hated doing that. [...] MPs always complained that they couldn't get time with him, that he wouldn't see them. That was a real problem.'[16]

Most MPs judge leaders on their ability to win elections; much can be forgiven if the leader is an electoral asset, but Miliband's poor public image appeared to drag the party down – a ComRes poll in May 2014 suggested that 40 per cent of voters were less likely to vote Labour because of Miliband [17] – thereby sapping his authority both in the Shadow Cabinet and in the PLP.[18] Miliband lacked the extraordinary communication skills of a Tony Blair, and never developed the same ease of manner and effortless fluency. But his difficulties in projecting himself to the British public were greatly aggravated by the deep and abiding hostility of Britain's overwhelmingly right-wing press.

The media setting

Most voters pay little attention to, nor do they display much interest in, politics and are rarely able to judge the qualities or performance of politicians; they necessarily rely on images purveyed to them by the media. The media thus have a considerable capacity both to set the agenda of policy and to influence perceptions of leaders and events. The lesson that Blair and his allies drew was that the press, especially the *Mail* and the Murdoch papers, had to be placated. 'It's almost impossible,' he wrote, 'to understand how, for the Labour party in the 1980s, we just kind of felt submerged by the weight of media opposition.' Defending the 'inordinate attention' of New Labour to courting the media, he added, 'In our own defence, after eighteen years of opposition and the, at times, ferocious hostility of parts of the media, it was hard to see any alternative.'[19] Furthermore, the influence of the right-wing press was not confined to their readers. As the BBC's former business editor, Robert Peston, pointed out, the *Mail* and the *Telegraph* played a major role in setting the Corporation's news agenda.[20] 'Never underestimate,' Greenslade commented, 'the agenda-setting capabilities of a dominant right-wing press.'[21]

Labour leaders, in short (with the significant exception of Blair), have always had to wrestle with deeply negative press coverage, but, as one expert pointed out, the speed and virulence of the attacks on Ed Miliband when he assumed the Labour leadership late in 2010 were extraordinary and relentless.[22] From the outset he was 'Red Ed', a doctrinaire socialist, an enemy of freedom wholly in thrall to his Marxist extremist father (Ralph), a man – the *Mail* claimed – who 'hated Britain'. Relations were further soured by the fact that, unlike his two predecessors, Miliband was unwilling to spend time wooing, flattering and pandering to powerful media figures.

Press antagonism to Miliband deepened further because he had the temerity – against the advice of his more timorous and spineless colleagues

– to denounce the tabloids over the phone-hacking scandal, with its revelations about their industrial-scale hacking, phone-tapping, bugging and other illegal practices, especially by the Murdoch papers the *News of the World* and the *Sun*, but also the *Mail* and others. He told the Leveson Inquiry, set up to investigate phone-hacking, that 'organisations like News International had huge power and I think politicians were reticent to speak about some of these practices that were exposed. I include myself in that. There came a moment when I found it impossible not to speak out. I knew at that moment I was crossing a Rubicon.'[23]

This was treated as an outrageous act of lèse majesté and attacks by the *Express*, *Telegraph*, *Times*, and especially the *Mail* and the *Sun*, intensified and were unceasing (and continue to this day). In one example chosen entirely at random, the *Mail* referred to Miliband as 'cringe-making', a 'huge liability' and someone who 'looks weird, sounds weird, is weird'.[24] The assaults reached a peak of utter absurdity with the 'bacon sandwich' episode. In May 2014, the (right-wing) *Evening Standard* published a photograph of Miliband munching a bacon sandwich, which went viral, endlessly reproduced on television, quiz and comedy programmes,[25] with hundreds of thousands of views on YouTube. The 'bacon sandwich' entered popular folklore as the one thing voters knew about Miliband. It seemed to encapsulate in one still all that people were incessantly told – and that opinion surveys and focus groups revealed – were the characteristics most commonly associated with Miliband: he was 'odd', 'pathetic', 'geeky', 'weak', 'indecisive' and, in particular, 'weird'.[26]

Miliband's unpopularity was such that the fear began to mount that Labour would be unable to win an election under his leadership, and the mutterings grew louder. Indeed, at one point in November 2014 a coup was planned to remove him. But both Labour's rules and its culture inhibited efforts to eject a leader, and the moment of danger passed.[27] But, if his survival as leader was rarely imperilled, his lack of support within the PLP, combined with his poor standing in the polls, greatly hampered Miliband's efforts at renewing and redefining the party's policies and ideology.

'No matter how hard he tried, he could not break free'

Miliband, neo-liberalism and New Labour

Miliband's ambition, at least initially, was the bold one of replacing the New Labour neo-liberal/social democratic synthesis which had defined its approach to policy-making by a more radical programme, which his ally John Denham called a 'distillation of soft-left politics'.[28] In Miliband's view, Blair and Brown had too easily succumbed to the axioms of neo-liberal thinking, the pillars of which, he believed, had been demolished by the financial crisis. 'We were stuck in a mindset of the 1990s,' he had told the Fabian Society in May 2010, 'which feared the idea of government taking on the power of markets' and which perceived globalisation as 'an untameable force of nature to which we must adapt or die'.[29] While he acknowledged the major improvements in the public services and poverty alleviation under the Blair and Brown governments, he saw as their greatest flaw the failure to make any significant inroads in massive levels of inequality, especially of wealth.[30]

Marc Stears, the new leader's close friend and senior aide, summed up Labour's essential choice as both he and Miliband saw it: 'whether a Labour government should be aiming to accept the prevailing order pretty much as it currently exists, trying to operate largely within it, or whether it should be aiming for a more fundamental shift'.[31] For the new leader, the aim should be the latter, with greater equality as Labour's driving purpose. According to Stears, he had 'always been obsessed with inequality'[32] and he believed strongly that 'large inequalities of income and wealth scar our society', were grossly unfair, inhibited the life prospects of many and undermined the sense of community.[33] He was heavily influenced by Richard Wilkinson and Kate Pickett's acclaimed 2010 study, *The Spirit Level*,[34] that chronicled the corrosive effects of vast disparities in income and wealth upon the quality of people's lives, with dire effects upon physical and mental health, crime, social cohesion and many other chronic social problems.[35]

Inequality could be lessened, Miliband concluded, only by changing the way the economy operated. Significantly for someone who identified himself with the left, he did not advocate a socialist economic system based on extensive public ownership, workers' control and planning, but accepted the inevitability of capitalism: the question, in his view, was what type of capitalism? Here he and his chief economic advisor, Stewart Wood, were influenced by the 'varieties of capitalism' literature developed by scholars in the preceding decade. Capitalism, they argued, could take very different forms. In particular – and greatly simplifying a nuanced and sophisticated analysis – they differentiated between two variants: the lightly regulated Anglo-American model and the more coordinated and socially regulated model found particularly in Northern Europe.[36]

This was the theoretical framework from which Miliband, in his address to the 2011 party Conference, borrowed when he drew his distinction between 'predatory' and 'responsible' capitalism. The former was characterised by financial speculation, short-termism, asset-stripping, 'cosy cartels' and vested interests; its inevitable outcomes were unacceptable disparities in income, wealth and power, poor working conditions, precarious employment, stagnant pay and a low-skill, low-productivity economy. Further, economic activity was skewed by an inflated and inadequately regulated financial sector prone to wild speculative gyrations – which was why the UK had suffered so severely from the financial crash.[37] The latter variant, as practised in Germany and the Nordic countries, was characterised by the promotion of long-term investment and innovation, retraining and reskilling schemes, steady growth, and governance structures which engaged employees in decision-making; its outcome included less inequality, superior welfare systems and more secure employment.[38]

With his critique of 'predatory capitalism', Miliband was reviving themes – such as corporate greed, disregard for the public good and the excessive power of capital – virtually ignored by the previous leadership. He was also exploring ideas similar to those which had been formulated over many years by the influential centre-left economics commentator Will Hutton. In 2010, Hutton had published a book criticising New Labour's acceptance of the Thatcherite economic model with its obsession with financial engineering, short-term profit-seeking and maximisation of share values. Because they had accepted neo-liberal rostrums, Hutton concluded, neither of New Labour's key economic policy-makers, Brown and Balls, 'had a clue of what was about to hit the British economy, courtesy of the over-leveraged and effectively non-regulated financial sector'.[39] He advocated a more activist state, a more closely regulated financial sector, more inclusive patterns of corporate governance and a stakeholders' model of capitalism, in effect what Miliband termed 'responsible capitalism'.

For many, especially on the New Labour wing of the party, such theorising seemed detached from the real world they and their constituents inhabited, and few MPs would have been aware of, or at least interested in, the 'varieties of capitalism' literature. What struck them, and forcefully, was the castigation of 'predatory capitalism', which they read simply (and wrongly) as an attack on big business, per se. They were dismayed by what seemed to them as Miliband's shredding of a fundamental New Labour axiom, the crucial importance of a rapprochement with the City and the corporate sector.[40] The reference to 'predatory' capitalism was, according to Shadow Home Secretary Yvette Cooper, 'anti-business, anti-growth and ultimately anti-worker for the many people employed by large companies in the UK'. Miliband had 'allowed the impression to arise', Shadow Business Secretary Chuka Umunna complained, 'that we were not on the side of those who are doing well' and 'creating wealth'.[41] And predictably, the attack on 'predatory capitalism' precipitated a torrent of abuse from the press.

In truth, Miliband and his advisors had not really thought through their analysis of capitalism, nor had they prepared the ground for its reception. They took fright at the storm it had provoked, and all references to 'predatory capitalism' were hastily excised from Labour's lexicon. But the commitment to egalitarian policies persisted, and Miliband's next initiative, the idea of 'predistribution', was more thoroughly grounded. The concept, its originator the American political scientist Jacob Hacker wrote, was designed to promote 'market reforms that encourage a more equal distribution of economic power and rewards even before government collects taxes or pays out benefits'; and it offered a response to the problem of how to promote greater equality in fiscally straitened circumstances.[42] It meant tackling 'not just the symptoms of huge inequalities in market power' but the primary causes, the rules that shape the way markets work.[43] This analysis appealed greatly to Miliband in that it seemed to resolve political problems – the limits to redistribution – as well as advancing his crucial goal of equality.

Traditionally, Labour's strategy was redistributive – to recycle the proceeds of economic growth through taxation to finance expanded public programmes and increased cash transfers, and by these means to tackle inequality and poverty. As a direct consequence of the crash, Britain faced a huge fiscal shortfall which, Miliband and his advisors felt, limited the amount of money available. 'The redistribution of the last Labour government relied on revenue which the next Labour government will not enjoy,' Miliband explained: hence the importance of a new economic model that did not rely so heavily on fiscal policy, that *predistributed* as well as *redistributed*.[44] The objective was ambitious: to find ways of reconfiguring the rules, incentives and institutional structures of the economy in such a way as to generate both more egalitarian outcomes and a more productive economy. It was, Wood argued, an attempt to 'reclaim that productivity story for the left and say there's a left agenda here about making a country more equal, not through tax and spend, but through re-engineering the economy'.[45]

The leadership floated a whole raft of proposals in the following months to give tangible expression to 'predistribution', including reforms to enhance the bargaining power of wage-earners, tighter regulation of the banking system to curb speculative activity, a British Investment Bank to foster long-term investment, an interventionist industrial policy to support key industrial sectors, new rules on corporate takeover bids, better vocational training, workforce participation in decision-making and steps to curb excessive corporate pay. However, the sheer range of policies placed under the umbrella of predistribution highlighted a lack of specificity about what it entailed. Serious encroachment into inequality would require pressing ahead with such radical measures as widening the ownership of capital assets, worker representation on corporate boards and enhancing collective bargaining rights.[46] But the cautious strand in the leader's mental make-up made him hesitate about anything that might further alienate powerful financial and business interests already irked by talk of 'predatory capitalism'.

Predictably, the idea did not elicit much serious discussion within most of the media, whose attention span rarely extended much beyond dissecting soundbites and regaling their readers and listeners with Westminster gossip. Instead, they concentrated on scoffing at the ungainly word 'predistribution', or simply dismissing it as another instance of 'Red Ed's' 'lurch to the left'. But more worrying was the scepticism, if not outright resistance in the party. Most Labour MPs reacted with annoyance and even bewilderment at what they saw as the leader's inconsequential theorising about the dynamics and motive-forces of the economic system; surely these were idle distractions from the real nitty-gritty of politics? Debates about reshaping the rules and institutions underpinning British capitalism seemed, to many MPs, as the ivory-tower cogitations of a North London intellectual with absolutely no relevance to ordinary people.[47] Many Labour MPs believed – insofar as they thought of these matters at all – that the New Labour synthesis of free market economics and redistributive politics was an essentially sound one. In their view, and in that of the party's strategists and polling analysts too, the leadership should be focusing on tangibles: on formulating 'retail' policies targeted at voters rather than talking about inequality.[48] And for Ed Balls, who was detached from the discussion about 'predistribution', all this was essentially a distraction from what should be the principal aim of Labour's economic policy: regaining its economic credibility. In what was becoming something of a pattern, having aired an idea and encountered stiff resistance, Miliband then abandoned it.

Miliband did launch one further initiative in his quest for ideological redefinition: 'One Nation Labour'. This, Miliband told the 2012 party Conference, expressed the party's aspirations for 'a country where everyone has a stake', 'where prosperity is fairly shared' and 'where we have a shared destiny, a sense of shared endeavour and a common life that we lead together'. It meant acknowledging that New Labour, 'despite its great achievements, was too silent about the responsibilities of those at the top'.[49] The speech was warmly praised by two veteran commentators, Polly

Toynbee and Steve Richards, the latter describing it as 'one of the cleverest and most significant party Conference speeches'.[50] It had its roots in Blue Labour, an idea originating in the thinking of Maurice Glasman (ennobled by Ed Miliband) and developed, among others, by Jon Cruddas, Jonathan Rutherford and Marc Stears. Blue Labour was, in part at least, a revival of ethical socialism. It was an attempt to explore and respond to a widespread sense of loss and disorientation, especially among the working-class, as familiar rhythms of traditional life, communal ties and customs were disrupted by globalisation. It sought to resuscitate the language and ethos of place, dignity of work and patriotism. Like a comet, it briefly blazed before sinking into the sunset, leaving a trail across the political skies: One Nation Labour.

But what did 'One Nation Labour' actually *mean*? For Stears, who drafted much of the speech, it 'was a moderated version of what Blue Labour had been about [...] it was a speech about ethos and the common good'.[51] For Jon Cruddas, it was 'trying to reimagine a left patriotism' linked to bold schemes of social reconstruction.[52] And for Stewart Wood, it was another attempt to break with the prevailing neo-liberal consensus, but in a way that would not reopen old wounds.[53] But the concept lacked policy substance, coherence and precision, and many senior frontbenchers were never really committed to it. Most saw it as a piece of tactical repositioning and a rebranding exercise, a deft move to outmanoeuvre the Tories by appropriating their 'One Nation' slogan.[54] And it rapidly became 'little more than an all-purpose prefix on the party's press releases'.[55] Not surprisingly, it failed to gain any traction with the electorate and Miliband himself soon lost interest.[56] It had the same short shelf life as 'predatory capitalism' and 'predistribution'.

By the middle years of his leadership, Miliband was increasingly troubled by much more immediate and pressing concerns, in particular managing mounting tensions within the party over how to respond to the Coalition's huge and immensely damaging programme of spending cuts. As so often in the case of the Labour Party, short-term tactical and presentational concerns began to squeeze out longer-term thinking and policy planning, and the priority, overwhelmingly as the next election crept closer, was to consolidate and extend Labour's narrow lead in the polls which emerged in 2012. Above all, how could it convince the British public that it could be trusted to manage the economy competently?

Austerity and economic credibility

The dramatic loss of public confidence in Labour's capacity to manage the economy was a prime cause of its drubbing at the polls in 2010. The Tories, assisted by most of the media, were remarkably successful in convincing the bulk of the electorate that responsibility for the global financial crash precipitated by the collapse of the US sub-prime market and rooted in massive speculative activity in opaque financial products actually lay with Gordon Brown spending too much money in the UK. This narrative, delivered in a series of easily digested soundbites, proved to be a powerful one: the financial crash had occurred on Labour's watch. Labour had brought the economy to its knees, had 'maxed out' on the nation's credit card and failed to 'mend the roof when the sun was shining'. It had disregarded the injunction that 'you can't spend what you don't have'. It was 'all Labour's mess'; with the UK as a result teetering at the edge of bankruptcy, the Conservative–Liberal Democrat coalition had no option but to rescue the country's tattered finances by administering a stiff dose of austerity.

The idea that Brown was the principal cause of a global financial crash was, one might generously say, quixotic in the extreme. The UK's deficit and debt levels had risen dramatically, but this was as a direct consequence of the massive costs of the Brown government's bailing out the banks. Prior to the financial crash, in 2007/8, deficit and debt levels were lower than when Labour had assumed office in 1997.[57] The cause of the crash, according to the Treasury's top official, Sir Nicholas Macpherson, was 'a banking crisis pure and simple'.[58] 'The last government', the leading Oxford economist Simon Wren-Lewis insisted, 'did not borrow excessively [...] The recession was a consequence of overleveraged banks and the collapse of the US housing markets.'[59] In short, the deterioration in public finances was attributable not to government policies – though the policy of 'light-touch regulation' of the City had certainly contributed – but to the crash itself and the steps taken to prevent a 1930s-style depression. As the Institute for Fiscal Studies concluded, while the UK's public finances 'were not particularly strong compared with those of other advanced economies', equally they 'were not in a bad state on the eve of the crisis'.[60]

How was Labour to respond? Should it try to explain to the British public that the causes of the global financial crisis were a mite more complicated than the pattern of UK public spending? No, the leadership judged this would be too difficult. It accepted the advice of party strategists and pollsters as well as most of those on the New Labour wing of the party who argued that Labour's culpability for the crash was so deeply embedded in the popular psyche and so endlessly repeated by the media that any attempt to dislodge it would take a huge amount of time and energy and probably would not succeed.[61] As the rising Blairite frontbencher Chuka Umunna put it: to complain 'in ever more strident and louder terms' that the crash was in fact caused not by Brown's extravagance but by bankers was futile. 'The harsh political reality is that the electorate rejected this. Screaming "you're wrong" at the electorate is not a good strategy for a party seeking to win back its trust.'[62] It was a miscalculation of huge proportions. As Stewart Wood later ruefully reflected: 'We thought that avoiding the question was somehow going to make the question go away.'[63] The failure to challenge the myth that Brown caused the crisis was, in the words of the *Guardian*'s economics editor Larry Elliott, a 'catastrophic political blunder',[64] and it was to have long-term disabling consequences for Labour.

Almost immediately, Labour was confronted with the problem of how to respond to the Coalition's drastic programme of expenditure cuts. The unions and the party left clamoured for steadfast and determined resistance to austerity. In March 2011, the Trades Union Congress (TUC) organised a mass protest attended by more than 250,000 people. Two years later, left-wingers in the party and the unions, including Jeremy Corbyn, John McDonnell and Len McCluskey, launched the 'People's Assembly Against Austerity'. [65]

Miliband's initial response to austerity was Keynesian. He shared the assessment of his soft left ally Peter Hain that the best way to reduce deficit and debt levels was through an expansionary strategy, with additional public spending and investment taking up the slack of depressed private demand.[66] As Stewart Wood reasoned, 'with interest rates basically at zero now was the time to be borrowing more, to be spending more, to be investing more, to counter austerity'. Deflation, in contrast, would only strangle the recovery.[67] Miliband's problem was that many of his critics on the New Labour wing of the party did not share this view. The Keynesian alternative of spending your way out of a recession, they believed, could not be sold to the voters and, indeed, would merely reinforce their conviction that a future Labour government would be fiscally reckless. Furthermore, information about the economy was filtered through the media, and most British media organisations, including the broadcasters, largely recycled received neo-liberal wisdom about the unavoidability of harsh spending cuts. As Paul Krugman commented, at a time when the austerity paradigm had been discredited among most macroeconomists 'to the point where hardly anyone still believes it', it was still uncritically accepted and regurgitated by the bulk of the UK media.[68] The BBC, in particular, was guilty of this.[69]

Almost immediately, Miliband came under pressure from the right of the party. Labour must exert, Roger Liddle, a former Blair advisor, insisted, 'ruthless financial discipline'. To Patrick Diamond, another former senior Blair advisor, Labour's priority must be to regain fiscal credibility, and this meant not only accepting the inevitability of fiscal retrenchment but being 'much clearer on the specifics of the spending cuts it will support'.[70] To re-establish its reputation for economic competence meant reassuring the voters it would exercise the utmost restraint on spending. Indeed, a group of Blairite commentators called for 'zero-budgeting across the whole of Whitehall, questioning every line of public spending, with nothing off the table'.[71]

There was another problem that the party's left largely ducked, but the right was aware of: many voters, far from objecting to them, actually *approved* many of the cuts in welfare benefits. The Blairite Work and

Pensions Shadow Secretary, Liam Byrne, spelt this out plainly to delegates at Labour's 2011 Conference: 'many people on the doorstep at the last election felt that too often we were for shirkers, not workers. We've got to deal with that if we want to get re-elected.' He added: 'Decent Labour voters see their neighbours lie about all day and get benefits while they are working their socks off, and say, "Why should I vote Labour when they let this happen?"' The following year, he rammed the message home: 'Labour is the party of hard workers, not free riders. The clue is in the name. We are the Labour party. The party that said that idleness is an evil.'[72]

These pronouncements angered many on the left of the party and in the unions, but academic research covering this period substantiated the facts upon which they were based. For example, most voters were convinced that benefit cheating and 'sponging off the state' was rife and that huge amounts of money were being lavished on those too lazy to work. A majority of voters believed that poverty was a lifestyle choice and that most unemployed people could find a job if they really wanted one.[73] And these perceptions infected how voters viewed Labour. When focus groups were asked who they thought it represented, one of the stock images was of 'a slob lounging at home on his sofa'.[74] Voters believed that Labour was 'the party of people on benefits', Byrnes's successor as Works and Pensions Shadow, Rachel Reeves, declared, 'and by word and actions it had to convince them that we are not the voice of those who are out of work. Labour is a party of working people, formed for and by working people.'[75]

The economist Simon Wren-Lewis posed the question: because a large slice of the electorate believed those on welfare were scroungers, 'should Labour therefore pretend this is true?'[76] The response of the Blairites, 'transfixed by dire polls showing voters see [Labour] as soft on welfare',[77] was an emphatic 'yes'. Whether voters' views derived from ignorance, prejudice or the dominant media narration and were way out of line with empirically verifiable fact was irrelevant: the only reality that Labour needed to ponder was what people believed. Further, if the price of getting back into office, and therefore of being able to help the needy, was to align its stances to public opinion, even when misguided, surely this was a price worth paying?

But Miliband was troubled about such arguments. Being 'tough on welfare' might please the voters, but benefit sanctions were already punitive. Why should those who were already often poor, deprived and struggling to make ends meet suffer more? Furthermore, was it rational and sensible to allow policy to be shaped by a distorted version of reality? But right-wingers in the party could adduce the clear findings of focus groups and opinion surveys, and grudgingly and without conviction, Miliband began to inch towards their point of view.

But what of the economic case against austerity? In a speech in August 2010, Balls had contended that 'the coalition's plans for rapid deficit reduction now are not just unfair but also unnecessary and economically unsafe'.[78] But by 2012, reasoning that the deficit was becoming structural as well as cyclical, he had changed his mind – and he also induced Miliband to do so. The two agreed on a statement that, in future, Labour would neither oppose all cuts nor would they commit to reversing them.[79] This provoked an angry response from the left and the unions. Unite's leader, Len McCluskey, complained of a 'policy coup' by the Blairites and warned that Miliband was being 'dragged back into the swamp of bond market orthodoxy'.[80] His criticisms were echoed by the leaders of the party's other largest union affiliates, UNISON and GMB. But Miliband was not to be deflected from his new path, and indeed in the following year he approved a major speech by the Shadow Chancellor pledging a future Labour government to a 'tough deficit reduction plan' governed by 'strict fiscal rules' and 'iron discipline' over spending – even to the extent of adhering to the Coalition's public spending targets for 2015/16.[81] By 2014, Miliband indicated that in office he would accept many of the Coalition's cuts, impose a cap on most welfare spending and undertake not only to 'balance the books' but to seek to achieve a budgetary surplus by the end of a parliamentary term.[82] 'Austerity's victory over Keynesianism,' Robert Skidelsky later commented, 'was complete.'[83]

Framing the manifesto

These pronouncements set the parameters for the next manifesto. Initially, this was the responsibility of the party's policy review, first headed by Liam Byrne, then by Cruddas. Cruddas favoured a radical policy agenda but, as the election date drew closer, his policy review was increasingly shunted aside and control over the manifesto process was transferred to what Cruddas called 'the professional political apparatus', the party's strategists, focus group advisors and election experts. From 2013 onwards, the key figures were Spencer Livermore, Head of Campaigns, Torsten Bell, Head of Policy, Greg Beales, Executive Director, responsible for strategy and party polling, Greg Cook, Head of Political Strategy, and Shadow Foreign Secretary Douglas Alexander, who became chair of general election strategy. As their influence expanded, that of Miliband's more left-wing advisors, such as Stewart Wood, Tim Livesey and Cruddas himself, dwindled.[84] As Wood recalled, if 'you said anything other than what the Blairite orthodoxy is, you were considered to be caring more about ideas than winning'.[85]

Caution now became the watchword. After Osborne's so-called 'omnishambles' budget in 2012, the polls had moved in Labour's favour.[86] To solidify its lead, the professional political apparatus advised, the party should play safe and concentrate on offering policies which provided obvious gains for the voters. This shaped the tone and content of the manifesto, *Britain Can Be Better*. The language of 'early Miliband', of 'predatory capitalism', financial speculation and City short-termism made no appearance. There was a heavy accent on fiscal discipline. The manifesto pledged that additional spending would be financed only by revenue (although Labour would borrow to fund capital investment); cuts would continue until the deficit was eliminated; borrowing and the national debt would be progressively reduced and a surplus delivered on the current budget 'as soon as possible in the next parliament'.[87]

But if Miliband tempered his ambitions, he did not abandon them. The manifesto contained a whole series of redistributive measures, including a 50p tax rate on higher incomes, the so-called 'mansion tax' on houses worth more than £2 million, the tax on bankers' bonuses, the abolition of non-dom tax exemptions[88] and the freezing of electricity prices. It was Labour's most egalitarian manifesto since 1992.[89] But in the party's launch of its manifesto, Miliband tended to downplay the egalitarian message. He emphasised that outside the NHS, education and international development, spending would fall 'until the books are balanced'.[90] In fact the party's very orthodox stance on spending was further tightened by a last-minute, unscheduled and unauthorised shift. After the manifesto was agreed at the so-called Clause 5 meeting of the NEC and the Shadow Cabinet and just prior to printing, a mysterious preface surfaced. On the initiative of Torsten Bell, Spencer Livermore, Ed Balls and Douglas Alexander, but with the consent of Miliband, it contained a material change in the manifesto: a commitment to a 'triple budget responsibility lock' guaranteeing that a Labour government would cut the deficit every year, irrespective of circumstances, would not commit to any new policies that would require additional borrowing and would deliver falling debt levels by 2020 – which put a question mark around some of the redistributive pledges in the manifesto. It was hardly the clearest of messages, nor the most convincing.

The polls predicted a minority Labour government but, in the event, the party suffered yet another devastating defeat. The Tories gained an absolute majority, the first time since 1992. Labour won 30.4 per cent of the vote, a minuscule gain of 1.5 per cent over the dire 2010 result, but with a net loss of twenty-six seats, mainly because of the party's almost complete wipe-out in Scotland, with forty out of forty-one seats seized by the Scottish National Party (SNP). Miliband immediately announced his resignation.

The ethic of responsibility vs the ethic of power

Blairites wasted little time in setting the terms of the debate in the inevitable post mortem. The central organising theme was Ed Miliband's 'lurch to the left', with former Blairite stalwart Alan Milburn deploring Miliband's strategy as a 'hideous and ghastly experiment' which had ignored 'the fundamentals of winning elections'.[91] The Blairite drumbeat was that his conversion to fiscal discipline was too slow, too hesitant and too lacking in conviction; he had stubbornly ignored persistent New Labourite demands for a more astringent stance on the deficit and the debt. His talk about 'predatory capitalism' and his insistence on fiscal redistribution had gratuitously alienated the business community.[92] As Matthew Taylor, Blair's former head of strategy, admonished: 'The enthusiasm with which some Labour politicians bash the unacceptable face of capitalism in contrast to their relative silence about the virtues of enterprise gives credence to the argument that Labour is anti-business.'[93] In consequence, the Tories had maintained a consistent lead as the party best able to manage the economy.[94] Miliband had carelessly flouted the New Labour maxim that elections are won on the centre ground; as a result, Tristram Hunt opined, Labour moved more 'out of step with the prevailing mood of the nation' than at any time since 1983.[95] Miliband had, Burnham lamented, failed 'to counter the perception that Labour gave an easy ride to some people in society who did not want to help themselves'.[96]

These critics were right in claiming that Miliband remained far less impressed than they were about the strengths and virtues of British capitalism, was unconvinced by austerity and felt that Labour's priority should be to combat inequality. In his heart, he was a disciple of what we have called (following Weber) the ethic of responsibility and not the ethic of power favoured by his New Labour critics. But the divide between the two ethics did not only lie between Miliband and these critics but also within his mind. On the one hand, he was convinced that there was 'little point in being in politics unless you believe in something and want to really change things'.[97] But, on the other hand, as his chief of staff Tim Livesey recalled, inside his head there was 'a little pragmatic worm eating away'.[98] He tended to be bold in conception but cautious and risk-averse in execution. He was always torn between radical ambitions and tactical wariness and found it difficult to resolve the tension.[99] Much of Miliband's hedging, evasions and indecisions, for which he was often berated by critics on both left and right, were due to this inner tension between the two ethics: between opting for the policies he felt were the right ones (in terms of both those which worked best and were consistent with party principles) and those which seemed more expedient.

The latter eventually tended to prevail because Miliband's instinctive circumspection was reinforced by institutional pressures. Strategists, public opinion analysts and other members of the 'professional political apparatus', largely recruited in the New Labour years, urged a play-safe, retail and transactional approach to electioneering which avoided anything controversial. Added to all this was the relentless pounding meted out to him by the press, which sapped his confidence and made him fearful of taking risks. As he told an aide, 'I'm going to get another battering. And I can't afford that. I'm not going to do it.'[100]

As a result, he disappointed both the right and the left of the party. For the right, he had been too tardy and too half-hearted about cutting the deficit and debt levels: not robust enough on 'fiscal discipline'. But ultimately more damaging was the critique from the left, from his fellow Keynesians. The Nobel prize-winning economist Paul Krugman expressed himself 'astonished' by the limpness of Labour's response to 'the austerity push' and by its willingness 'to accept claims that budget deficits are the biggest economic issue facing the nation'.[101] It had, Wren-Lewis noted, allowed 'the lie that Labour governments are always fiscally profligate [to be] cemented in stone'. By 'constantly triangulating between sensible macroeconomics and what the focus groups were telling them', he added, Labour under Miliband was left with 'a policy that failed to convince'.[102]

In March 2024, Rachel Reeves, a New Labour luminary, implicitly conceded that the Keynesian critique of austerity was right, and the Blairites were wrong. 'The austerity programme', she maintained in her Mais Lecture, 'to cut public spending harder and faster than most other European countries, squandering the gains of the previous thirteen years [...] did not just hollow out the public realm and widen inequality, it also undermined our economic resilience. Sucking demand from the economy and cutting investment corroded British infrastructure and sent private investment tumbling.'[103] But this was not a view articulated at the time by her New Labour allies and was eventually, if very reluctantly, swallowed by Miliband. By being too lame and feeble in its critique of austerity, Wren-Lewis wrote, Labour left the Coalition off the hook – despite the fact that it 'presided over the worst recovery from a recession for hundreds of years, and an unprecedented fall in real wages'.[104] Why, the election expert Ivor Crewe wondered, was it 'left to Martin Wolf in the *Financial Times* and Paul Krugman in the *New York Times*' to make the Keynesian case for public investment in infrastructure as the engine for growth? Labour lost not because of Miliband's 'lurch to the left' but because all that Labour offered was 'a gentler, kinder austerity policy, and of course that simply appeared to concede the Conservatives' central thesis against the Labour Party'.[105]

Conclusion

Labour, as we have emphasised, is constitutionally a pluralist party but, where the circumstances are conducive, can operate in a highly centralised manner, as under New Labour. Two of these conditions, institutional integration under the aegis of the leader and a pattern of concurrent majorities, did not exist under Miliband. His New Labour critics were solidly ensconced in the Shadow Cabinet and the parliamentary party, and hence he never had full mastery of the party. Added to this, his preferred mode of managing conflict was through consensus and inclusivity. Confidence in him on both the front bench and back bench was always brittle, and the circumstances of his election meant that his legitimacy was always being queried. His ambition was to induce the party to adopt a soft left programme, but he lacked the muscle to achieve this, as perhaps he eventually realised; the 'pragmatic worm', the ethic of power, grew larger and larger. He struggled to free himself from the entanglements of New Labour but could not do so; he was never in a position, nor perhaps did he have the inclination, to brandish a Brown-style 'great, clunking fist'. As Cruddas later reflected, 'I was quite angry about it at the time, but with hindsight, I can see more and more the pressures that worked on him … it's tragic.'[106]

Notes

1 Quoted in Lewis Minkin, *The Blair Supremacy: A Study in the Politics of Labour's Party Management* (Manchester: Manchester University Press, 2014), p. 765. The quotation in the chapter title comes from Pink Floyd's song 'Hey You'.
2 We use the term 'Blairite' as a synonym for New Labour in this chapter. It includes those 'Brownites' (which effectively disappear as an organised group) who on issues of substance agreed with the Blairites, including Ed Balls, Yvette Cooper and Douglas Alexander. A minority of former 'Brownites', including Ed Miliband himself and Stewart Wood, were effectively part of the soft left.
3 Peter Mandelson, 'Labour will never be credible without convincing people of its economic credentials', *Observer*, 10 May 2015.
4 Interview, senior aide.
5 Interview, Stewart Wood.
6 Interview, senior aide.
7 *Ibid.*
8 Interviews, Stewart Wood; Peter Hain.
9 Rafael Behr, 'The making of Ed Miliband', *Guardian*, 15 April 2015; Mehdi Hasan and James Macintyre, *Ed: The Milibands and the Making of a Labour Leader* (London: Biteback Publishing, 2011), pp. 240–1, 326–8; Eunice Goes, *The Labour Party under Ed Miliband* (Manchester: Manchester University Press, 2016), p. 62.
10 Roy Greenslade, 'Ed Miliband: Genuine crisis or monstering campaign?', *Guardian*, 10 November 2014.
11 Behr, 'The making of Ed Miliband'.
12 Interview, Jon Cruddas.
13 Interview, senior aide.
14 Len McCluskey, *Always Red* (New York: OR Books, 2021), p. 162; Interview, senior aide.
15 Interview, Peter Hain.
16 Interview, Stewart Wood.
17 Stephen Fielding, '"Hell, No!" Labour's campaign: The correct diagnosis but the wrong doctor?', in Anthony Geddes and Jonathan Tonge (eds), *Britain Votes* (Oxford: Oxford University Press, 2015), p. 63.
18 Interviews, Peter Hain; Stewart Wood.
19 Tony Blair, 'The Prime Minister's Reuters Speech on Public Life', *Political Quarterly*, 78:4 (2007) 280, 276.
20 Ivor Gaber, *The "othering" of "Red Ed", or how the Daily Mail "framed" the British Labour leader*', *Political Quarterly*, 85:4 (2014) 473.
21 Greenslade, 'Ed Miliband: Genuine crisis'.
22 Gaber, '*The "othering" of "Red Ed"*', 277.

23 'Leveson Inquiry: Murdoch too powerful – Ed Miliband', *BBC News*, 12 June 2012.
24 Daniel Johnson, 'Blunders that made Mr Weirdo unelectable', *The Mail*, 3 December 2014.
25 Fielding, '"Hell, No!" Labour's campaign', p. 63. The photo was also republished by the *Sun* during the election campaign.
26 Tim Bale, *Five Year Mission: The Labour Party under Ed Miliband* (Oxford: Oxford University Press, 2015), p. 71.
27 *Ibid.*, p. 258.
28 John Denham, 'Pragmatism and the left: Whither the soft left?', *Renewal*, 32:1 (2024), 27.
29 Goes, *The Labour Party under Ed Miliband*, p. 47.
30 Ed Miliband, 'Inequality and left politics', *Renewal*, 25:2 (2017), 6–7.
31 Marc Stears, 'Fundamental questions', *Renewal*, 23:3 (2015), 34–9.
32 Dimitri Batrouni, *The Battle of Ideas in the Labour Party* (Bristol: Bristol University Press, 2020), p. 99.
33 Ed Miliband, Hugo Young lecture, 10 February 2014.
34 Batrouni, *The Battle of Ideas*, p. 99.
35 Richard Wilkinson and Kate Pickett, *The Spirit Level* (London: Penguin, 2010).
36 See, for example, Peter Hall and David Soskice (eds), *Varieties of Capitalism. The Institutional Foundations of Comparative Advantage* (Oxford: Oxford University Press, 2001).
37 See, for example, Stewart Wood, 'We need to talk about the "Middle"', *Open Democracy*, 15 February 2013, opendemocracy.net
38 Ed Miliband, Speech to the Labour Party Conference, 27 September 2011.
39 Will Hutton, *Them and Us: Changing Britain – Why We Need a Fair Society* (London: Little, Brown, 2010), pp. 147–8.
40 Interview, Marc Stears.
41 Matt Dathan, 'Yvette Cooper's epiphany: Ed Miliband was too anti-business', *Independent*, 19 May 2015; Chuka Umunna, 'Where Labour went wrong – and what we must do to put it right', *Observer*, 10 May 2015.
42 Martin O'Neill, 'Predistribution: An unsnappy name for an inspiring idea', *Guardian*, 12 September 2012.
43 Stewart Wood, 'Responsible capitalism is Labour's agenda', *Guardian*, 9 January 2012.
44 Ed Miliband, Predistribution speech to Policy Network, 6 September, 2012.
45 Interview, Stewart Wood.
46 Martin O'Neill and Thad Williamson, 'Philosophical foundations for "good capitalism"', *Renewal*, 20:1 (2012) 1, 4.
47 Interviews, Jon Cruddas; Stewart Wood.
48 Interview, Jon Cruddas.
49 Bale, *Five Year Mission*, p. 131.
50 Batrouni, *The Battle of Ideas*, p. 79.

51 Quoted in *Ibid.*, p. 84.
52 Quoted in *Ibid.*, p. 85.
53 Wood, 'We need to talk about the "Middle"'.
54 Dimitri Batrouni, 'One Nation, disconnected party', *British Politics*, 12 (2017), p. 437.
55 Bale, *Five Year Mission*, p. 155.
56 Batrouni, 'One Nation', p. 443.
57 Ruth Lupton et al., *Labour's Social Policy Record: Policy, Spending and Outcomes 1997–2010* (London: LSE, Centre for Analysis of Social Exclusion, 2010).
58 Patrick Wintour, 'Labour overspending did not trigger financial crash, says senior civil servant', *Observer*, 3 May 2015.
59 Charlie Cooper, 'The myth: Excessive government borrowing got us into this mess', *Independent*, 3 May 2013.
60 Carl Emmerson, Paul Johnson and Robert Joyce, 'The Green Budget' (London: Institute for Fiscal Studies, 2015), p. 16.
61 Sean McDaniel, 'Social Democracy in the Age of Austerity: The Cases of the UK Labour Party and France's Parti Socialiste, 2010–17' (PhD thesis, University of Warwick, 2019), 169; Phil Cowley and Dennis Kavanagh, *The British General Election of 2015* (Basingstoke: Palgrave Macmillan, 2015), p. 72. As Stewart Wood later conceded: 'We didn't really confront the elephant in the room' (Interview, Stewart Wood).
62 Chuka Umunna, 'It's not "Tory lite" to recognise that Labour's problem is economic credibility', *Guardian*, 29 June 2015.
63 Quoted in McDaniel, 'Social Democracy in the Age of Austerity', p. 169.
64 Larry Elliott, 'Jeremy Corbyn is right to blame the banks, not Labour, for the financial crisis', *Guardian*, 10 August 2015.
65 Bjorn Bremer, *Austerity from the Left: Social Democratic Parties in the Shadow of the Great Recession* (Oxford: Oxford University Press, 2023), p. 164.
66 Peter Hain, *Back to the Future of Socialism* (Bristol: Policy Press, 2015), pp. 258–9. He spelt out the Keynesian case in detail, arguing that economic recovery could be most effectively engineered by an interventionist 'entrepreneurial' state embarking on large-scale infrastructure projects. *Ibid.*, pp. 75–110.
67 Interview, Stewart Wood.
68 Paul Krugman, 'Economics and elections', *New York Times*, 6 April 2015.
69 Simon Wren-Lewis later wrote that political commentators on the BBC 'allowed coalition ministers to repeat their "clearing up the mess" metaphor without serious challenge. Indeed it became part of the deception'; Simon Wren-Lewis, 'Recognising the success of macroeconomic myths', *Mainly Macro*, 29 May 2015, https://mainlymacro.blogspot.com/
70 Both quoted in Hain, *Back to the Future of Socialism*, p. 68.
71 Greg Cooke et al., *In the Black Labour: Why Fiscal Conservatism and Social Justice Go Hand-in-hand* (London: Policy Network, 2011), p. 5.

72 Kiran Stacey, 'Labour's hypocrisy on "shirkers vs workers"', *Financial Times*, 8 January 2013.
73 Peter Taylor-Gooby, 'Why do people stigmatise the poor at a time of rapidly increasing inequality, and what can be done about it?', *Political Quarterly*, 84:1 (2013), 31–42; Emma Briant, Nicholas Watson and Gregory Philo, 'Reporting disability in the age of austerity: The changing face of media representation of disability and disabled people in the United Kingdom and the creation of new "folk devils"', *Disability and Society*, 28:6 (2013), 874–89.
74 Bale, *Five Year Mission*, p. 150.
75 Amelia Gentleman, 'Labour vows to reduce reliance on food banks if it comes to power', *Guardian*, 17 March 2015.
76 Simon Wren-Lewis, 'Austerity's apologists on the left', *Mainly Macro*, 15 February 2016. For example, the public believed that 41 per cent of the welfare budget was spent on the unemployed; the real figure was 3 per cent. Again, people thought 27 per cent of the welfare budget was claimed fraudulently; the real figure was 0.7 per cent. TUC, 'TUC support for benefit cuts dependent on ignorance, TUC-commissioned poll finds', 4 January 2013. Research demonstrated that public perceptions of the benefit system corresponded far more closely to right-wing press depictions than with the facts. See, for example, Karen Rowlingson, Michael Orton and Eleanor Taylor, 'Do we still care about inequality?', in *British Social Attitudes: The 27th Report* (London: Sage, 2012); Tracy Shildrick and Jessica Rucell, *Sociological Perspectives on Poverty* (York: Rowntree Foundation, 2015); Neil Gavin, 'Below the radar: A U.K. benefit fraud media coverage tsunami – impact, ideology, and society', *British Journal of Sociology*, 72 (2021), 707–24.
77 Polly Toynbee, 'Labour – roll up your sleeves and demolish these disastrous howlers', *Guardian*, 6 January 2012.
78 Ed Balls, Speech to Bloomberg, 27 August 2010.
79 Patrick Wintour, 'Ed Miliband backs Ed Balls's stance on spending cuts', *Guardian*, 16 January 2012.
80 Len McCluskey, 'Ed Miliband's leadership is threatened by this Blairite policy coup', *Guardian*, 17 January 2012.
81 Ed Balls, 'Striking the right balance for the British economy', Labour Party website, 3 June 2013.
82 Rowena Mason, 'Labour cannot afford to undo coalition spending cuts in next government', *Guardian*, 30 May 2014.
83 Interview, in Bremer, *Austerity from the Left*, p. 156.
84 Interviews, Jon Cruddas; Tim Livesey.
85 Interview, Stewart Wood.
86 In fact, appearances were misleading; as Stears later wrote, 'our polling data was wrong. Our relationship with the public was far more fragile than we imagined'. See Stears, 'Fundamental questions', p. 36.
87 Labour Party, *Labour Party Manifesto, Britain Can Be Better* (2015).

88 Non-dom (short for non-domiciled) rules give tax concessions to people living in the UK but who are not deemed domiciled for tax reasons.
89 Labour Party, *Labour Party Manifesto, Britain Can Be Better* (2015).
90 Nicholas Watt, '"I am ready" says Ed Miliband as he launches Labour election manifesto', *Guardian*, 13 April 2015.
91 Fielding, '"Hell, No!" Labour's campaign', p. 55.
92 Bale, *Five Year Mission*, p. 219. During the election campaign, a letter signed by 103 senior business leaders (including a number who had backed New Labour) warned that a 'change in course' would 'put the recovery at risk' and would 'threaten jobs and deter investment'. Benn Quinn and Angela Monaghan, 'More than 100 business leaders sign letter backing Tories', *Guardian*, 1 April 2015.
93 Patrick Wintour, 'Ed Miliband: Wealth creation means tackling inequality', *Guardian*, 7 February 2015.
94 Patrick Diamond, Giles Radice and Penny Bochum, *Can Labour Win? The Hard Road to Power*, Policy Network (London: Rowman and Littlefield, 2015), pp. 18–19.
95 Tristam Hunt, 'The forward march of Labour', Speech to Demos, 20 May 2015.
96 Rowena Mason, 'Liz Kendall will back white working-class young', *Guardian*, 30 May 2015.
97 Interview, senior aide.
98 Interview, Tim Livesey.
99 Interviews, Stewart Wood; senior aide.
100 Interview, senior aide.
101 Paul Krugman, 'The austerity delusion', *Guardian*, 29 April 2015.
102 Wren-Lewis, 'Recognising the success of macroeconomic myths'; Simon Wren-Lewis, 'The economic consequences of George Osborne: Covering up the austerity mistake', *New Statesman*, 17 April 2015.
103 Rachel Reeves, Mais Lecture, 19 March 2024.
104 Wren-Lewis, 'Recognising the success of macroeconomic myths'.
105 Ivor Crewe, 'Not a social democratic moment', *Renewal*, 23:3 (2015), 25.
106 Interview, Jon Cruddas.

4

Miliband and organisational tensions

The punch in Strangers' bar that probably gave Corbyn the leadership.

Stewart Wood[1]

Managing the party on the ground

The New Labour model of the party was of a hierarchically ordered, tightly managed, professionally organised machine primarily geared to contesting elections. During its years in control, the role of activists had been curbed and power shifted from the party on the ground, including the annual Conference, to the party in public office. Miliband's aspiration, in contrast, was to transform Labour into an outward-looking, mass campaigning party engaged in the life of local communities, a party which valued members for the contributions they could make, not merely a resource to be exploited.[2] But, as with policy, so too with organisation, there was a gap between the grandiosity of the vision and the practicalities of implementation, and nothing of great substance was achieved – with one great exception. Ironically, that exception, the disbanding of the electoral college and its replacement by OMOV as the mechanism for selecting the leader, was the outcome less of his initiative than of his reaction to circumstances largely out of his control. In what follows, we firstly examine Miliband's largely abortive plans to reform the party and then turn to the circumstances that culminated in the new system for selecting the leader.

Refounding Labour

To give effect to his project of reinvigorating the party, Miliband commissioned the *Refounding Labour* inquiry headed by Peter Hain, long a champion of the mass campaigning party model. The report, published in 2011, uncovered a party which had decayed under Blair and Brown, with a hollowed-out membership which had dwindled from 400,000 in 1997 to around 150,000 in 2010, and with a seriously depleted activist base, apathetic in some areas, complacent in others.[3] Constituency meetings were often poorly attended and 'bogged down in procedural detail', frustrating and alienating members and deterring potential recruits.[4] As a result, many CLPs had become very insular in outlook, bureaucratic and detached from local communities.[5] Because New Labour regarded activists as potential troublemakers, the activist base of the party had been neglected. It had in many areas atrophied and become inert.[6] Large numbers of members, Hain later wrote, had become 'deeply disillusioned by what they felt had been turned by New Labour into an ideology-free zone, a party dominated by careerist professional politicians'.[7]

Hain told delegates at the party Conference in 2011 that debated the report that 'we have to build a people's movement for Labour in our neighbourhoods, our workplaces, that is what we mean by Refounding Labour'.[8] This notion of a 'movement party' envisaged involving people broadly sympathetic but reluctant to join the party and led to one of *Refounding Labour*'s few substantive proposals: the creation of a new category of 'registered supporters'. The idea had its origins in an experiment pioneered by Tony Blair in his Sedgefield constituency.[9] In 2004 (while Blair was still leader), the Labour Supporters' Network was established, described on the Labour Party website as 'a way for people to register their support for Labour without having to join the party'.[10] Now *Refounding Labour* envisaged registered supporters being able to 'take part in our party, improve our organisation on the ground, build our links into communities and, most importantly, help deliver successful election results'.[11] In its original conception, registered supporters would link up with a party-inspired effort of working 'closely with civic activists and social entrepreneurs, building local alliances with community groups which share a common sense of purpose' such as fighting hospital closures and cutbacks in public transport: active campaigning which would demonstrate the relevance of party politics to people's lives. Rather than being animated by a heavily procedurally bound culture, the party could act as an instrument of wider political mobilisation.[12] The *Refounding Labour* report was overwhelmingly carried by Conference, but its concrete proposals (perhaps filleted) were modest and fell short of any significant reorganisation of the party, for which, anyway, the party machine lacked any enthusiasm.

But the idea of transforming Labour persisted in a related form: that of community organising. This concept had its origins in community-organising schemes in the US popularised by Barack Obama's much-publicised background as a community organiser and his application of the techniques during his successful presidential campaign in 2008, though it also reconnected with the party's own traditions as one segment of a wider Labour movement. David Miliband exhibited considerable interest in the idea and sought to apply it in efforts to mobilise support for his leadership bid.[13] The idea was then taken up by Ed, with Stears's enthusiastic advocacy. He had been impressed by reports of the work of Arnie Graf, a Chicago-based veteran of community organising who was invited to conduct a root-and-branch review of the party. His report confirmed Hain's bleak findings: a hierarchical structure with procedure-riddled and uninspiring meetings, underpinned by a deadening bureaucratic culture. Calling for greater openness and more appreciation of the value of members, he urged changing the party's internal culture to conform more closely to a community-oriented movement-style model.[14] Two of Graf's recommendations are worth noting. The first was the introduction of open primaries for candidate selection, with candidates selected by all Labour voters: this represented too radical a rupture with tradition and was rejected. The second was the recruitment of community organisers whose remit would include neighbourhood campaigning in alliance with local pressure groups to weave local parties much more closely into the fabric of local communities.[15]

Graf's ideas neatly synthesised with Hain's. Miliband was enthusiastic, and so too was Iain McNicol, the party's General Secretary. Under his aegis, steps were taken to shift party resources away from HQ and into the party on the ground, and a community organising manual was compiled. But the impetus for reform soon began to fade. Most senior party officials charged with implementing Graf's report were sceptical. They were socialised into a New Labour culture for whom the party should operate as a well-oiled, professional machine, run by specialists in winning elections and heavily directed from the centre. Officials feared that Graf's (and Hain's) plans would divert resources from the – expensive – essentials of effective electioneering, such as the commissioning of focus groups and the recruitment of professional marketing and advertising expertise. As one Miliband aide recalled, 'they were very cynical about ideas of wanting to involve members and the public' and dismissed anything that could be construed as idealistic 'as nonsense or as naïve'.[16]

Graf's report was never published nor widely circulated, and, because of foot-dragging by party officials, little progress was made in implementing his proposals. Under multiple pressures, Miliband's interest in party revitalisation waned. 'Ed in his heart wanted to do it,' his chief of staff mused, 'but in his head, he didn't think it was worthwhile. It was a luxury we couldn't afford, and we didn't have the time.'[17] The project was effectively abandoned after the appointment of Douglas Alexander as Campaigns Co-ordinator in 2013, a strong proponent of New Labour-style, tightly managed campaigning; he effectively induced Graf to resign.[18] As with policy, so too with organisation. Miliband's initial ambitions for transformative change were not realised. But the idea of community organising did not vanish.

Managing the party machine

The fate of Graf's grand scheme pinpointed one of the problems Miliband faced throughout his leadership: the lack of a dedicated, enthusiastic and loyal party machine of the type that helped drive the New Labour project. This became evident in the 2010 leadership election when most officials displayed an unabashed partisanship for the older Miliband. As one (Ed) Miliband aide recollected, 'the whole machinery built, constructed and refined by Blair was co-opted by David Miliband's campaign',[19] including, it was rumoured, the supply of supposedly confidential data; and party officials responded with dismay and were 'absolutely dumbfounded' when the younger brother's victory was announced.[20]

Not surprisingly, the relationship of the new leader's staff with senior party officials was initially quite strained and never became entirely harmonious. And there was one upset early in Miliband's leadership. Ray Collins had been persuaded to resign as General Secretary in 2011, and there were two contenders, Chris Lennie, the Deputy General Secretary, and Iain McNicol, a GMB official, to replace him. Miliband backed Lennie, but McNicol was elected: the episode illustrated the limits to Miliband's influence over the NEC.

Miliband's chief of staff, Tim Livesey, described the party organisation he inherited as 'a very powerful performance machine that really just rode roughshod over anybody that disagreed with it'.[21] Miliband disapproved of New Labour-style command and control; he wanted the restoration of a system which involved less policing of the activities of party members and an end to interventions to promote favoured candidates in parliamentary selections and party elections: in a word, abandoning the 'covert-management system run from headquarters'.[22] The aim was, Livesey declared, 'to democratise, to enfranchise, to stop this incredible controlling instinct that basically shuts everybody out of politics, including your membership, let alone the electorate'.[23] These moves towards decentralisation and 'light-touch regulation' were manifested in the key area of candidate selection. All party leaders will seek to help those whom they regard as capable, talented and politically well-disposed to secure winnable seats, and Miliband was no exception: he played a significant role in Keir Starmer's adoption as a Labour candidate in 2015. But he was less keen than his two predecessors – and much less so than his two successors – on intervening in a systematic and forceful manner. Indeed he upset two senior staffers in his office for not finding them safe seats.[24] All this reflected his general desire to ease central controls and encourage a more open, liberal and pluralist culture in the party.

Given that senior party officials had been appointed and promoted under New Labour, some friction between the party apparatus and the Leader's Office was inevitable. But the potential for conflict between these two bodies was also inherent in Labour's pluralist constitutional format because of their different compositions, functions and lines of accountability. In August 2011, Miliband was sufficiently concerned to persuade senior businessman and long-standing Labour supporter Sir Charles Allen, the former chief executive of ITV and chairman of EMI, to report on how the relationship between the Leader's Office and party HQ could be improved. The report, completed in March 2012, proposed a new Executive Board consisting of six Executive Directors plus General Secretary Iain McNicol, Tim Livesey, the chief of staff, and his deputy Lucy Powell.[25] It was not, for various reasons, at all well received by party staff, but matters eventually calmed down. Though relationships between party HQ and the Leader's Office were at times difficult, they were nothing like as tumultuous as under Miliband's successor, Jeremy Corbyn.[26] One particular reform is worth noting, since it was to prove counter-productive. To help improve coordination between party HQ and the Leader's Office, in 2013 it was decided that two senior members of the Leader's Office should be designated as Directors of the Party. As the *Forde Report* (discussed in detail below) found, this actually 'added to the confusion of lines of responsibility and jurisdiction and eventually, in the Corbyn era, led to tension and conflict'.[27]

Managing the party–union relationship

Though there were tensions between the leadership and the affiliated trade unions over how best to respond to Tory austerity and over the Coalition's public sector pay freeze, for the most part, the relationship operated more smoothly than under Blair and Brown – not unexpectedly, since Miliband had been the unions' preferred candidate. This inevitably led to relentless, predictable and inaccurate media allegations that he was 'under the thumb' of the 'trade union barons'. As we shall see below, many on the Blairite wing of the party favoured a looser connection with the affiliated unions, which Miliband did not. But he did have his reservations about the form that relationship should take. He felt that the unions' 50 per cent share of the Conference vote weakened its democratic credentials and, as part of the Refounding Labour project, he proposed a reduction. But not only did he fail to prepare the ground by consulting with the unions; he chose to frame the matter provocatively as a challenge to union power. 'We cannot go on with a system,' a party source declared, 'in which unions have 50% of the vote at Conference, and just three general secretaries of three unions control four-fifths of that union vote. Currently, the union leaders are playing hardball, but they need to wake up.' Another party source added that 'If we are going to have a Conference which has more power, then it has to come to decisions in a way that the leader feels he can defend.'[28] This was, to put it mildly, an undiplomatic and clumsy way of presenting the issue, a very poor piece of political management calculated to alienate the unions from whom he would require some support to gain Conference approval. Facing defeat at Conference, Miliband had no option but the rather humiliating one of backing down. But this incident was to set the scene for later events.

The New Labour wing, though ousted from the leadership, remained a potent force in internal party politics. In particular, the Blairite ginger group Progress, funded very generously by wealthy business donors, was – or was alleged to be – playing a major role in the promotion of Blairite candidates in winnable seats. In December 2011, Unite produced an internal report which expressed concern that 'Labour party policies are often determined by a small group of advisers – far too often dominated by old thinking, neo-liberalism and the organisation Progress'. The report, accepted by the union's executive, urged a much more energetic role for the unions in the internal affairs of the party, especially in candidate selections. It drew attention to the 'crisis of working-class representation', with only 4 per cent of MPs from manual professions as compared to 55 per cent from public relations, politics and the media, and it recommended a campaign to encourage Unite members to join constituency parties and to persuade Unite activists to seek selection as Labour candidates and work closely with other affiliated unions 'to secure the adoption of trade union (or union-friendly) candidates in winnable constituencies in particular'.[29] As McCluskey elaborated in his memoirs, with many constituency parties having few members, even a modest influx of Unite recruits could have a sizeable impact on selection outcomes.[30] In June 2012, the document was leaked to the *Guardian*, which melodramatically described it as heralding 'renewed civil war between the Blairite wing of [the] party and its union backers'.[31]

As it happened, the event that was to precipitate the 'civil war' had already taken place. In February 2012, the former army major and Labour MP for Falkirk, the somewhat bibulous Eric Joyce, headbutted and punched a Conservative MP and then laid into Labour MPs who sought to restrain him. Criminal charges followed and Joyce was excluded from the Labour Party, creating a vacancy for the candidacy for his – it was then imagined – safe Labour seat of Falkirk. From this inebriated punch thrown in anger flowed a series of events which eventually culminated in the election of Jeremy Corbyn as leader of the party.

The process of selecting a new Labour candidate for Falkirk began in the spring of 2013. The major employer in the constituency was the Grangemouth oil refinery, whose workforce was organised by Unite. Unite, in line with its strategy described above, was keen that one of its members should be selected, and the leadership had one in mind: Karie Murphy, at the time the office manager of Tom Watson, then Labour's campaign coordinator and (at the time) a close friend of Unite's head, Len McCluskey. To ease Murphy's selection, Unite recruited new members to the party from within its own ranks, and the constituency's membership quickly doubled from a rather pathetic figure of less than a hundred to over two hundred.

Rumours began to circulate that Unite had resorted to improper practices to fix Murphy's selection. The Shadow Defence Secretary, Jim Murphy (no relation), and Blairite grandee Peter Mandelson accused the union of signing up Unite members en bloc without their knowledge or approval, forging signatures and coercing Unite union members into signing direct debit forms to join the party in a determined drive to stitch up the contest.[32] The abuses of trade union power in the Labour Party were a regular media meme and the pugnacious left-winger Len McCluskey was a particular bête noire: as a result, what was essentially a story of purely parochial interest was very extensively publicised and soon morphed into a national scandal – indeed a crisis for Miliband's leadership.

Miliband was placed in an extraordinarily difficult position. As we have seen, he felt vulnerable to the charge of being at the beck and call of the unions and was always being prodded, as a senior aide recalled, 'to show he was going to stand up to the trade unions and not let them walk all over him. It was a really dangerous moment for Ed.'[33] The Blairites, however, sensed an opening which could be exploited to curtail trade union influence: as the *Observer* journalist Andrew Rawnsley put it, Falkirk presented a 'fantastic opportunity' to tackle 'the disproportionate power wielded in party leadership votes, candidate selection and decision-making by a small number of union officials'.[34]

Miliband took this advice: he would show that he was not weak and indecisive, as he was so often depicted, by a forthright dressing down of Unite.[35] In a forceful speech, he denounced the union's behaviour in Falkirk as 'a politics of the machine. A politics that is rightly hated. What we saw in Falkirk is part of the death-throes of the old politics.' It was, he concluded, no longer acceptable that trade union members were often affiliated automatically: they 'should choose to join Labour' and 'not be automatically affiliated'.[36] It was throwing down the gauntlet to the union in the most goading manner. Under Miliband's prompting, the NEC placed the Falkirk party under 'special measures', thereby transferring control over the selection to the NEC. It then launched an investigation. The confidential report, which was soon leaked, pulled no punches: major irregularities such as forgery, bullying and the enlistment of Unite members into the party without their consent had been unearthed. As a result, the NEC suspended Unite's candidate, Karie Murphy, as well as Steve Deans, a Unite official and her campaign manager, and then, dramatically, referred the matter to the police for possible criminal investigation.

McCluskey was furious, particularly with Miliband, and their relationship was never fully repaired. The allegations against Unite, he angrily rebutted, were without foundation and were orchestrated by Progress. In the past, 'every manoeuvre has been deployed, often with the assistance of Labour headquarters, to parachute favoured candidates into safe seats'. Unite had simply been trying to redress the balance, and the offensive over Falkirk was the Blairites' retaliation.[37]

Behind the scenes, some of Miliband's allies had questioned his judgement in jumping to conclusions before the evidence about the allegations had been fully examined.[38] As so often happens, as events unfolded, it became clear that the preferred media narrative of 'union bully boys' was, at best, an oversimplification. It transpired that the spin placed upon the report by those who leaked it to the *Guardian* was misleading; it had in fact presented a more nuanced and ambiguous picture. It did confirm that people had been recruited en bloc by Unite, some without their knowledge, but the more extreme claims about malpractices, forgery and criminal irregularities could not be adequately corroborated. Unite had indeed, as was alleged, paid the membership fees of new members, but added that this was allowed under party rules. Under Blair, the NEC had launched a scheme called Union Join which allowed trade unions to subsidise the first year's fees of new recruits at a discounted rate as a way to incentivise recruitment; and General Secretary Iain McNicol knew that Unite was using the scheme in Falkirk. Murphy and Deans were eventually cleared of any wrongdoing and reinstated, though by then the former had withdrawn from the selection contest. Shortly after, the police decided there was insufficient evidence to proceed with a criminal investigation.

But, though Unite had not, for the most part, directly breached party rules, it had used tactics which were scarcely democratic. It was not, as one senior aide observed, quite the stitch-up that was portrayed, but it was 'murky' and 'definitely not in the spirit of the rules'. By paying the fees of about a hundred new recruits and as a result doubling the very low membership of the party, it was difficult to avoid the conclusion that Unite was packing the constituency to select its candidate. Encouraging potential supporters to join a CLP to influence a selection contest was not exactly an unknown practice, but the scale of the membership increase and the fact that the candidate was close to a major union leader hardly shed a glowing light on either the union or the party.[39]

The leadership was in crisis: Miliband had taken a very aggressive stance towards Unite and then had been forced to retreat, and the whole episode had attracted a lot of unflattering publicity. The leadership decided that the best way to defuse the crisis was the time-honoured one of commissioning an inquiry, furthermore one given a broad remit of investigating the party–union connection. Ray Collins, the former General Secretary of the party and previously a senior union official, a shrewd and experienced political operator and consensus builder, was given responsibility for conducting the review. As we have seen, in 2011 Miliband had contemplated changes to the party–union relationship but had had to abandon them. Now, he judged, might be the time to reconsider the matter, but by taking a different approach.

After considerable discussion in the Leader's Office, officials hit on the idea of proposing the end to the traditional system of collective affiliation to the party. Under this system, members of affiliated trade unions automatically paid the political levy unless they chose to 'opt out'. The income raised was then assigned to the unions' political funds – funds specially set up to allow unions to contribute money for political purposes. It was then up to the unions to decide how many of these levy-payers should be affiliated en bloc to the Labour Party. This would affect the percentage of votes a union could wield as a proportion of the 50 per cent of Conference votes.

The Collins report made two major recommendations, both arrived at after close consultation with the Leader's Office. The first was that collective affiliation should be replaced by a system which required that trade union members make personal choices. Union members who wished to join the party, as affiliated members, would have to make a conscious decision to do so. The second recommendation took the process of 'individualisation' of the party a step further and was even more far reaching: to replace the electoral college by OMOV as the mechanism for selecting the leader. This was odd, since, though the matter was obviously a crucial one, it had not been discussed and did not even figure on Labour's agenda until the commissioning of the report. We look at the wider context below, but at this stage it is worth noting how it emerged: the result of a deliberate (and successful) decision to divert attention from the controversy over disputed candidate selection procedures.[40]

The suggested new system for electing the leader was as follows:

- The Electoral College for leadership elections would be abolished and replaced by a new system based on the principle of OMOV.
- The eligible electorate should be composed of three classes: members, affiliated supporters and registered supporters. The 'affiliated supporters' consisted of those people who belonged to organisations (overwhelmingly trade unions) affiliated to the Labour Party, who paid the political levy and opted to be part of the party; 'registered supporters' were those people willing to affirm their loyalty to the party and principles and who paid a modest amount for the right to take part in leadership elections but were not full members.
- In future, union members would only become 'affiliated supporters' with full membership rights if they chose to do so. Because they already contributed (indirectly) to the party through the political levy, there was no requirement for any additional payment, but they would need to affirm in writing that they supported Labour values. An important corollary of this was that in place of the one third reserved to the unions under the electoral college, the voting weight of these affiliated supporters was determined strictly by the number of those who voted, which, it was anticipated (correctly), would mean a significant slide in their percentage of the total vote.[41]
- Responsibility for nominating and shortlisting leadership candidates would remain with MPs. The existing system required that candidates be nominated by 12.5 per cent of PLP members. To ensure that all candidates commanded a substantial body of support from among MPs, this threshold was raised to 15 per cent.[42]

Collins, with the help of Miliband and his aides, worked hard to persuade, to cajole and to reassure the unions, especially the 'big four' (Unite, UNISON, GMB and the Union of Shop, Distributive and Allied Workers [USDAW]), who hesitated about the proposals.[43] Initially, the general secretaries of three of the four, UNISON, GMB and USDAW, were very doubtful about the package. The GMB's Paul Kenny declared that he doubted many of his 650,000 members would be willing to join the party, while McCluskey apparently told his executive that he would expect only 75,000 Unite members to join Labour, as opposed to the one million currently affiliated.[44] As a result, they might come under pressure to reduce their affiliation fees to the party. They were also, of course, aware that the package was designed to weaken the capacity of trade union leaderships to manage their members' voting choices. The problem for the leadership was that the package would only pass Conference if there was a significant degree of union support.

The champion of the Collins package, unexpectedly, was the most left wing of the big four unions' leaders, Len McCluskey. In a reversal of Unite's traditional stance, he called the package 'really good' and 'morally defensible'. He stated boldly that 'I can no longer defend putting 1 million of my members as affiliates to the Labour party when our own internal polling demonstrates that a large chunk of that 1 million vote for other parties.'[45] When he exhorted his trade union colleagues to accept the package, McCluskey records in his memoirs, he received a bewildered response: 'Paul Kenny (GMB), Dave Prentis (UNISON), and Billy Hayes (Communications Workers Union, CWU) got me in a room and demanded, "What the fuck are you playing at? You know this is ridiculous."'[46] McCluskey countered that 'what's being offered to us is, in my eyes, extraordinary. We had the most right-wing PLP of my lifetime forfeiting their position of privilege.' The unions were being offered a unique 'opportunity to cut out the PLP, who are a drag anchor on everything we're doing'.[47] At the same time, the unions' existing strong representation at Conference, on the NEC and the NPF would remain intact. They were convinced.

Perhaps more surprisingly, there were few objections from MPs to the abolition of the electoral college. The PLP was abandoning its one third share of the selectorate that elected the leader, itself a reduction from the 100 per cent share it had enjoyed prior to 1981, but there was scarcely any opposition. There were several reasons for this apparently surprising fact. Firstly, OMOV had already been applied to candidate selection, to the election of CLP delegates to Conference and in elections to the NEC and other key party bodies, and using it for leadership election was no more than a logical extension of the principle.[48] After all, it was used by most social democratic parties abroad and, indeed, by all the major parties in the UK.

Secondly (and crucially), the quid pro quo was the reduction of union power in the party, a long-standing Blairite goal. Behind the scenes, senior Blairites, including Blair and Mandelson, had been agitating for OMOV for some time for precisely this reason.[49] As Matthew Taylor explained, OMOV 'would replace what masqueraded for democracy', that is, 'the capture of the party by key interests (principally trade union hierarchies) and an unrepresentative cadre of hard left activists'.[50] Tony Blair himself unambiguously and enthusiastically applauded the introduction of OMOV as 'a long overdue reform, something I should have done myself. It puts individual people in touch with the party and is a great way of showing how Labour can reconnect with the people of Britain.'[51]

Thirdly, while the PLP would no longer have the right directly to choose the leader, they would have the right to determine the shortlist from whom the electorate would make the final selection. As McCluskey commented, 'instead of having a disproportionate influence on the vote itself, MPs would be the gatekeepers, limiting the choice put before members'.[52] And this gatekeeping role was, as we have noted, enhanced by increasing the proportion of nominations required from 12.5 per cent to 15 per cent of parliamentarians.[53] Fourthly, MPs were confident in entrusting the final say in electing the leader to the party membership. Since the 1980s, the right of the party had promoted a series of party reforms designed to dilute activists' influence by enfranchising the more passive members, a process from which they had seemed to benefit in party elections and candidate selections. If OMOV had been in operation in 2010, David, the more Blairite Miliband brother, would have triumphed. As Jon Cruddas noted, the Blairites totally bought into the notion that widening the franchise would benefit the right of the party: it was, indeed, 'a hallmark of Blairism'.[54]

Such thinking also reflected the view of scholars of political parties. By circumventing activists entrenched in local party organisations, the reasoning ran, OMOV severely eroded the institutional power of those most likely to resist a more moderate leadership.[55] The individualisation of participation, replacing collective deliberations, would further bolster the power of the leadership by isolating and even atomising the rank and file, left more or less powerless in the face of the tightly organised party elite.[56] Evidence to substantiate this line of reasoning was furnished by research published in 2017, based on a cross-national data set combined with an expert survey. It confirmed the hypothesis that shifting power from better-informed, more motivated and more radical activists to the less engaged ordinary members had the effect both of strengthening the leadership and fostering more centrist politics.[57] Much of the hard left reached the same and – for them – sombre conclusions about the consequences of introducing OMOV and for that reason objected to it, as indeed they had continuously since the idea was first floated in the early 1980s.

With very few objections, the reform package sailed through the PLP and the Shadow Cabinet. The NEC agreed the Collins report by a crushing majority of twenty-eight votes to two (the dissenters were hard left CLP representatives), and it was ratified by a special conference in March 2014 by a substantial majority, with dissent confined to left-wing CLP delegates and a number of smaller leftish unions.[58]

Creating the new category of 'registered supporters' was later to be condemned by right-wingers in the party for opening the sluice gates to 'far-left entryists' who played a key role in delivering victory to Corbyn. The *Times* columnist and formerly Tony Blair's chief speech writer (a role he has also played for Starmer) Phil Collins wrote: 'It was Mr Miliband who drafted the rules under which new members have flooded the Labour party at £3 a time, with no qualification period, to vote for an unelectable.' Similarly, Luke Akehurst, a key organiser for the party right and subsequently an MP, referred disparagingly to these affiliated supporters as the 'flotsam and jetsam washed in from the mailing lists of single-issue pressure groups or far left micro-parties', recruited to 'outvote hard-working Labour activists'.[59]

One can, if one wishes to be kind, ascribe such views to memory lapses. As we have seen, the idea of registered supporters originated in an experiment pioneered in Blair's Sedgefield constituency party and was then taken up by the *Refounding Labour* report. As Miliband's chief whip, Rosie Winterton, recalled, this was 'what Tony had always wanted to do. He had always toyed with it but didn't think it would be possible to achieve.'[60] The supposition that the registered supporters' scheme would lead to the recruitment of centrist-minded people was one shared by Tom Baldwin, Miliband's Director of Communications, and why many found the idea attractive.[61] And finally, David Miliband (and others) supported the scheme because it appeared the closest to achieving what he ideally favoured, US-style primaries. Indeed, it was for this reason that the fee of £3 was set – by the NEC and *not* by Miliband – at so low a level.[62]

In truth, the decision to alter the mechanism for electing the leader was not a carefully planned initiative. It was, as one senior advisor put it, a highly reactive and improvised response to multiple pressures in highly stressful circumstances.[63] Ray Collins's package, Cruddas averred, 'was quite an elegant way of squaring the circle of the institutional stakeholders in the party and the membership, navigating the tricky Falkirk problems and eliciting the support of both McCluskey and Blair: what's there not to like?'[64] What possibly could go wrong?

Notes

1 Interview, Stewart Wood.
2 Interview, Tim Livesey.
3 Peter Hain, *Back to the Future of Socialism* (Bristol: Policy Press, 2015), p. 236.
4 Labour Party, *Refounding Labour* (London: Labour Party, 2011), pp. 15, 18.
5 *Ibid.*, p. 6.
6 Interview, Peter Hain. In Blair's words, 'political activism always had that tinge of the oddball about it'. Tony Blair, *A Journey* (London: Hutchinson, 2010), p. 118.

7 Hain, *Back to the Future*, p. 225.
8 Victoria King, 'Labour delegates vote to scrap shadow cabinet elections', *BBC News*, 26 September 2011.
9 Lewis Minkin, *The Blair Supremacy: A Study in the Politics of Labour's Party Management* (Manchester: Manchester University Press, 2014), p. 129.
10 Emmanuelle Avril, 'The evolution of decision-making in the British Labour Party: From grassroots to netroots?', in Emmanuelle Avril and Christine Zumello, *New Technologies, Organizational Change and Governance* (Basingstoke: Palgrave Macmillan, 2013), pp. 102–16.
11 Labour Party, *Refounding Labour*, p. 15.
12 *Ibid.*, pp. 241, 243.
13 James Scott and Jane Wills, 'The geography of the political party: Lessons from the British Labour Party's experiment with community organising, 2010 to 2015', *Political Geography*, 60 (2017), 124–5.
14 Marc Stears, 'Post-democracy, democratic renewal and the recent history of British politics', *Juncture*, 22:3 (2015), 216–19.
15 Scott and Wills, 'The geography of the political party', p. 126.
16 Interview, senior aide.
17 Interview, Tim Livesey.
18 Toby Helm, 'Revealed: Labour Party power grab puts old guard back at heart of election strategy', *Observer*, 8 December 2013.
19 Interview, Tim Livesey.
20 Interviews, Tim Livesey; former senior party official.
21 Interview, Tim Livesey.
22 Minkin, *The Blair Supremacy*, p. 772.
23 Interview, Tim Livesey.
24 Interviews, Tim Livesey; senior aide.
25 Tim Bale, *Five Year Mission: The Labour Party under Ed Miliband* (Oxford: Oxford University Press, 2015), pp. 96–7.
26 Patrick Wintour, 'Labour Party in turmoil after disastrous HQ meeting', *Guardian*, 14 March 2012. It is worth noting that senior staffers later to be accused by Corbyn aides as seeking to undermine his leadership (such as Emilie Oldknow, John Stolliday and Patrick Hannigan) worked co-operatively with his predecessor. Interviews, Tim Livesey; senior aides.
27 Martin Forde (chair), *The Forde Report* (London: Labour Party, 2022), p. 29.
28 Patrick Wintour, 'Ed Miliband plans to curb union hold over Labour', *Guardian*, 2 August 2011.
29 Unite, *Political Strategy*, December 2011.
30 Len McCluskey, Always Red (New York: OR Books, 2021), p. 173. In addition, McCluskey was also responding to growing pressure within his union to disaffiliate from the party or divert funds from political to industrial activities, as urged by, among others, Sharon Graham, a senior official who eventually succeeded McCluskey as General Secretary. Interview, senior aide.

31 Patrick Wintour, 'Unions fight Labour's Blairite faction "in struggle for party's soul"', *Guardian*, 15 June 2012.
32 Patrick Wintour, 'Unite union accused of manipulating Labour selection procedures', *Observer*, 12 May 2013; Nicholas Watt, 'Jim Murphy: Union has overstepped mark in selection of Labour candidate', *Guardian*, 3 July 2013.
33 Interview, senior aide.
34 Andrew Rawnsley, 'The Unite row is a grave crisis that Ed Miliband could turn into a great opportunity', *Observer*, 7 July 2013.
35 Interview, senior aide.
36 Ed Miliband, Speech on the unions and party funding, BBC Politics Live, 9 July 2013.
37 Len McCluskey, 'Yes, Labour's selection process has been abused, but not by the unions', *Guardian*, 9 July 2013.
38 Rajeev Syal, 'Karie Murphy withdraws as Labour candidate for Falkirk after union row', *Guardian*, 7 September 2013.
39 Rajeev Syal, 'Labour Party's Falkirk membership inquiry report – analysis', *Guardian*, 4 February 2014; Interview, senior aide. McCluskey later acknowledged that using the scheme which was discontinued had been unwise. McCluskey, *Always Red*.
40 Interview, Tim Livesey.
41 Ray Collins, *Building a One Nation Labour Party: The Collins Review into Labour Party Reform* (London: Labour Party, 2014); Peter Dorey and Andrew Denham, '"The longest suicide vote in history": The Labour Party leadership election of 2015', *British Politics*, 11:3 (2016), 259–82.
42 Collins, *Building a One Nation Labour Party*, p. 27.
43 Interview, Tim Livesey.
44 Bale, *Five Year Mission*, pp. 179–80.
45 Patrick Wintour, 'Labour must shift policies or risk ruin, says Len McCluskey', *Guardian*, 17 July 2013.
46 McCluskey, *Always Red*, p. 193.
47 *Ibid.*, pp. 198, 196.
48 Indeed the proposal for electing the leader on the basis of OMOV was first championed in 1981 by David Owen and others shortly before they quit the party to form the Social Democratic Party.
49 Interview, Tim Livesey.
50 Quoted in Minkin, *The Blair Supremacy*, p. 129.
51 Andrew Grice 'Tony Blair backs Ed Miliband's internal Labour reforms', *Independent*, 28 February 2014.
52 McCluskey, *Always Red*, p. 198.
53 Initially, Collins proposed doubling the threshold to 25 per cent. But the unions objected and the 15 per cent suggested by UNISON leader Dave Prentis was agreed: McCluskey, *Always Red*, p. 198.
54 Interview, Jon Cruddas. See also Minkin, *The Blair Supremacy*, pp. 54–5.

55 See, for example, Richard Katz and Peter Mair, 'The ascendancy of the party in public office: Party organizational change in twentieth-century democracies', in Richard Gunther, José Ramón Montero and Juan Linz, *Political Parties: Old Concepts and New Challenges* (Oxford: Oxford University Press, 2002); see also Anika Gauja, *Party Reform: The Causes, Challenges and Consequences of Organizational Change* (Oxford: Oxford University Press, 2016), p. 83; Piero Ignazi, 'The four knights of intra-party democracy: A rescue for party delegitimation', *Party Politics*, 26:1 (2018), 160–9.

56 Kenneth Carty, 'Are political parties meant to be internally democratic?', in William Cross and Richard Katz (eds), *The Challenges of Intra-party Democracy* (Oxford: Oxford University Press, 2013), p. 21; Ignazi, 'The four knights', p. 7.

57 Gijs Schumacher and Nathalie Giger, 'Who leads the party? On membership size, selectorates and party oligarchy', *Political Studies*, 65:1 (2017), 162–81.

58 Minkin, *The Blair Supremacy*, p. 105; Bale, *Five Year Mission*, p. 218.

59 Phil Collins, 'Ed Miliband's sulk led to Labour's downfall', *Prospect*, 14 September 2015; Luke Akehurst, 'Opinion. Labour Party Conference 2021: Significant progress has been made on tackling antisemitism, but there is still a mountain to climb', *Fathom*, October 2021.

60 Interview, Rosie Winterton.

61 David Aaronovitch, 'Eight years hard Labour', *Tortoise Media*, November 2023, tortoisemedia.com

62 Interviews, Simon Fletcher; senior aide.

63 Interview, Stewart Wood.

64 Interview, Jon Cruddas.

5
High hopes: the forward march of Corbynism

> The party is walking eyes shut, arms outstretched, over the cliff's edge to the jagged rocks below.
>
> Tony Blair[1]

> Blairism is dead and unmourned.
>
> Len McCluskey[2]

Corbyn's election

After Ed Miliband's hasty resignation, four candidates secured sufficient nominations to enter the race to replace him: Andy Burnham, Yvette Cooper and Liz Kendall, all frontbenchers from the party mainstream, and Jeremy Corbyn, a leading member of the hard left SCG of MPs. Corbyn had been first elected in 1983 and had played a minor role in the Bennite insurgency of the early 1980s; he had agreed to stand because no one else of any seniority was available. When John McDonnell was invited by Corbyn to manage his campaign, his initial response was, 'It'll be a mistake. We'll be annihilated and out for a generation.'[3] By 2015, the hard left was at its weakest for years, wilting on the margins of Labour's politics. With no expectation of victory, the Corbyn campaigners' hopes were to use a rare opportunity to reach a wider audience, their goal to avoid humiliation.[4]

To qualify under the new rules, candidates required nomination by 15 per cent of the PLP, about double the strength of the SCG. A somewhat motley group of MPs, including right-wingers such as Margaret Beckett and Frank Field, who had no intention of voting for him, agreed to nominate the Islington MP, confident that he had no prospect of winning. Even then, Corbyn was able to squeeze in the requisite number of nominations only at the very last moment.

It was then with mounting bewilderment and apprehension that MPs observed the thousands who were flocking to Corbyn's meetings, and the enthusiasm, adulation even, with which he was greeted. This turned to horror, shock and disbelief when a poll midway through the contest indicated that Corbyn was far and away the front-runner.[5] Tony Blair encapsulated the feelings of many MPs – including a chorus of New Labour grandees and political commentators – when he castigated 'a politics of parallel reality in which reason is an irritation, evidence a distraction, emotional impact is king and the only thing that counts is feeling good about it all'.[6] But the more Corbyn's supporters were belittled 'as immature, deluded, self-indulgent and unrealistic', the more their resentment at the Westminster elite's arrogance and condescension mounted, and the greater the groundswell for Corbyn.[7]

The Corbyn wave proved unstoppable. With almost 60 per cent of the total vote, Corbyn won emphatic majorities of all three categories of electors devised by the 2014 reform: full members, registered supporters and affiliated supporters (Table 5.1). Corbyn had been awarded a resounding mandate. The hard left had mutated at a stroke from little more than an

Table 5.1 Leadership election 2015 results

Candidate	Party members		Registered supporters		Affiliated supporters		Total	
	Votes	%	Votes	%	Votes	%	Votes	%
Jeremy Corbyn	**121,751**	**49.6**	**88,449**	**83.8**	**41,217**	**57.6**	**251,417**	**59.5**
Andy Burnham	55,698	22.7	6,160	5.8	18,604	26.0	80,462	19.0
Yvette Cooper	54,470	22.2	8,415	8.0	9,043	12.6	71,928	17.0
Liz Kendall	13,601	5.5	2,574	2.4	2,682	3.8	18,857	4.5

Source: Labour Party

isolated, dwindling and largely irrelevant band into the party's ruling bloc. How could a 66-year-old serial rebel, who had spent more than three decades on the back benches with minimal support from his parliamentary party, win such an astonishing victory?

For many in the PLP and the media, the explanation was straightforward: an influx into the party of a mix of wild-eyed utopians, fanatics and the deluded.[8] Matters were rather more complex, and a range of factors were at work. Firstly, Corbyn's three rivals seriously misjudged the mood of the party. They assumed that members would share their analysis of Labour's defeat: that Miliband failed to commit sufficiently firmly to 'fiscal discipline', was too obsessed with inequality and was too anti-business – in short, had pushed the party too far to the left. In fact, most members felt the opposite: Miliband had been too tepid in condemning the Coalition's economically and socially disastrous austerity programme and had not been sturdy enough in defending its many casualties. His fault was not, as the Blairites claimed, that he had reneged on New Labour but that he had failed to do so. Many in fact shared the scornful judgement of the stance taken by Corbyn's three mainstream rivals, pronounced by two Nobel economic laureates, Paul Krugman and Joseph Stiglitz. In the words of the former, every candidate aside from Corbyn 'bought fully into that conventional nonsense' that the Brown government's over-spending caused the crash, and that austerity was essential to restore a fiscal balance. In the words of the latter, by advocating 'a kinder version of austerity, a milder version of austerity', Labour moderates had 'wimped out'.[9]

The errors of the three mainstream contenders were compounded by an ill-fated miscalculation by the acting party leader, Harriet Harman. The government had introduced yet another tranche of welfare cuts, including limiting child tax credits to two children, imposing a cap on household welfare benefits and enforcing an extended freeze on working-age benefits: all measures that would further impoverish those who had already suffered most from austerity. Harman persuaded the Shadow Cabinet not to oppose these measures on the grounds that Labour was already widely seen by the voters as 'too soft on welfare'.[10] When Burnham demurred, Harman replied: 'But Andy, we lost that argument. You may have noticed that we lost the election.' Indeed the point of abstaining, a senior Labour aide added, was 'to teach Labour a lesson' in electoral realities.[11] Most party members were appalled and outraged.[12] Corbyn, in contrast, openly defied the whip on this issue, proclaiming, 'I am not willing to vote for policies that will push more children into poverty.'[13] As one influential Corbynite involved in the election campaign recalled, this vote was 'the turning point of the 2015 election.'[14]

So far, we have considered how the judgements and calculations of the various players influenced the final result. Now we turn to four underlying conditions that facilitated Corbyn's victory. The first was the collision between different orientations to the role and purposes of the party, the clash between the ethic of power, on the one hand, and the ethics of responsibility and conviction, on the other. At its simplest, the issue was this: to what extent should one relinquish principles in the quest for votes? For the three mainstream candidates, it was common sense that, having been decisively rebutted by the voters, the party should adapt its policy stances to public preferences – for example, on welfare benefits. Bryan Gould, a one-time stalwart of the party's soft left and, as we have seen, a protagonist of the ethic of responsibility, had been observing the leadership contest from his New Zealand eyrie. He described how he had 'watched in disbelief as Labour leaders have sought to explain their unwillingness to stand firm and fight for what they supposedly believe in [...] "We can't fight the electorate" is the siren call. How are the voters likely to view a party that so manifestly lacks the courage of its convictions? Will they not conclude that Labour is fatally short of both courage and convictions?'[15] It all smacked of Groucho Marx's declamation, 'Those are my principles, and if you don't like them ... well, I have others.' Corbyn, in contrast, was seen as a politician whose hallmarks were honesty, consistency and unflinching integrity.[16] He was, in Gamble's crisp phrase, 'the outsider speaking truth to power.'[17] In short, what was from one perspective electoral realism was from another what Krugman called the 'strange, sad moral and intellectual collapse of Labour moderates.'[18]

The second condition that eased Corbyn's path to victory was the introduction of OMOV for selecting the leader, or, rather, its unanticipated consequences. As we have seen in Chapter 4, it was widely assumed that OMOV would benefit the right, both because the more passive members would be more 'moderate' and because the by-passing of constituency organisations had rendered activists isolated and atomised. In Labour's case, both these suppositions proved to be entirely wrong, and for three major reasons. Firstly, the presumption that the more passive party members were *substantially* more 'moderate' than activists proved to be incorrect; indeed there was never much empirical evidence to support it. Secondly, the atomisation thesis took no account of Labour's pluralist and federal political arrangements. The affiliated unions could always act and often have acted as support bases for dissident groups, ready to supply an array of resources. Thus a group of left-wing unions, including the party's largest affiliate, Unite, made available to the Corbyn camp office space, technical equipment, staffing assistance and other assets.[19] Added to this was Labour's informal pluralism, the long-standing role played by hard left ginger groups, especially the Campaign for Labour Party Democracy (CLPD), founded in 1973, whose members (most notably Jon Lansman) had acquired very considerable organisational acumen and experience over the years and who provided a ready pool of volunteers for the Corbyn campaign.

Thirdly, the atomisation thesis ignored the politics of extra-parliamentary organisation and mobilisation. The SCG, as it became progressively more isolated in the PLP, attached itself to and became a significant part of a flourishing ecosystem of radical protest.[20] Operating as a hub around which many campaigns revolved was the Stop the War Coalition (StWC), a radical leftist body most of whose leading cadres were drawn from the Socialist Workers Party and Communist factions. Founded in September 2001 to mobilise popular resistance to Western intervention in the Global South, it had organised a massive demonstration in London against UK involvement in the Iraq war, one of the largest in British history. Corbyn had had strong connections with the StWC since its inception, indeed served as its chair for several years and had developed close relations with Stop the War radical leftists such as Seumas Milne and Andrew Murray, who became two of his closest advisers.[21] With its resources, membership lists, networks and campaigning experience accumulated over twenty years, StWC was described by Murray as 'perhaps the major tributary in the flood that lifted Corbyn to the leadership'.[22] In addition, the Corbyn campaign could call upon the backing of other extra-parliamentary protest organisations (such as the Occupy movement) which had mobilised large numbers against inequality, the austerity programme and the trebling in university top-up fees.

The fourth condition was the FPTP electoral system and its implications for political mobilisation (discussed in Chapter 1). The excitement, enthusiasm and fervour unleashed by the Corbyn campaign was part of a more general pattern of grass-roots left-wing insurgency, especially among the young, occurring throughout Western Europe. In other European countries, this insurgency was channelled into new radical left-wing parties such as Syriza in Greece, Podemos in Spain and La France Insoumise in France. In the UK, although multiple left-wing bodies have sprung up over the years, their growth, at least in electoral terms, has always been severely inhibited by FPTP. In consequence, many have seen in the Labour Party the only realistic option to promote their causes. With Corbyn's candidature, a window of opportunity was opened, and it made tactical and strategic sense for those whose energies elsewhere were poured into new parties to be, in the UK, directed towards radicalising Labour.[23]

Corbyn's predicament

As the journalist Owen Jones commented, 'no leader of any major political party has assumed office with odds so stacked against them while simultaneously being so unprepared as Jeremy Corbyn in September 2015'.[24] Of the four major centres of power in the party, the PLP, the Shadow Cabinet, the NEC and the party machine, none were under his control and, from the outset, he faced multiple and severe managerial challenges, with only limited resources to overcome them.

By far the greatest and most draining was a parliamentary party no more than 10 per cent of whose members could be said to be in any way sympathetic. Most MPs reacted with horror, consternation and dismay to Corbyn's election, seeing him as both ideologically hopelessly obsolete and electorally disastrous. Throughout his leadership, the PLP constituted a hotbed of seething rebelliousness; never before had a leader of a party been elected in the UK with such a sliver of support among MPs. From the outset, Corbyn confronted a crisis of legitimacy. Initial objections that the contest was in some way illicit soon vanished, and opponents gave up disputing it. But they continued to contest Corbyn's legitimacy because he did not command the confidence of the PLP and because he was deemed to be unelectable. This unwillingness to accept Corbyn's right to rule manifested in weak discipline in Parliament, constant hostile media briefings on an alarming scale and at times intemperate public criticism.

Corbyn also, and again throughout his leadership, had troubles managing his Shadow Cabinet. Although the leader now had the right to select whom he pleased, and he did pick loyalists such as John McDonnell and Diane Abbott to senior portfolios (Shadow Chancellor and Shadow Home Secretary), his base in the PLP was so exiguous that he had no option but to invite MPs from outside the hard left to fill most Shadow Cabinet positions. Some senior figures such as Andy Burnham and Hilary Benn were prepared to serve, others were not. Even the more cooperative did not expect the leadership to last and, as became evident, were simply biding their time for an opportunity to replace him.

Equally, he lacked a majority on the NEC, a debilitating weakness from the perspective of party management. Though 'less flamboyantly oppositional than the PLP majority', Murray later wrote, the Executive 'was hardly more accommodating to the elected Leader'.[25] The fact that it took Corbyn two-and-a-half years before he won a secure majority on the NEC was to prove fatal, because it was the governing body of the party responsible for overseeing its internal operations, including candidate selection, leadership elections, discipline and rule changes. It was also the body to which the party machine was accountable. Crucially, this was run at its highest reaches by officials, including the General Secretary Iain McNicol, who harboured the most severe doubts about the new leader. We discuss the consequences of this in a later chapter, but suffice it to say here that the leader could rely neither on its commitment nor on its loyalty. Not the least of the managerial challenges Corbyn faced was that, until he had a majority on the NEC and appointed a more supportive General Secretary, he could not replace recalcitrant party officials by loyalists. All this created multiple problems of party management.

A leadership team was hastily assembled. Those who played a significant part in party management included John McDonnell, Corbyn's closest parliamentary ally and, as Shadow Chancellor, a key member of the leadership team. He was unusual on the Corbyn left in having practical experience of the problems of governing, as the GLC's (controversial) chair of finance and deputy leader in the early and mid-1980s, and then Chief Executive of the Association of London Authorities. Much more theoretically minded than Corbyn, in 2006 he cited as his 'most significant intellectual' influences Marx, Lenin and Trotsky, which did little to reassure the great majority of his fellow Labour MPs. Indeed, with his abrasive manner, he had a reputation as the 'hard man of the left' and was widely feared, though respected for his ability and intelligence. However, it is worth noting here that as he began to contemplate the prospects of actually being in government, McDonnell began to develop a more flexible streak. 'Proximity to power', the editor of the *New Statesman* wrote, had 'begun to change McDonnell, softening his ideological rigidities, late in his career. His understanding of the nuances and complexities of politics has deepened.'[26] This, as we shall see, influenced the stance he took over both antisemitism and Brexit and brought him into conflict with others in the leadership team.

A second key player was the long-serving *Guardian* journalist Seumas Milne, who was appointed Director of Strategy and whom Corbyn rated hugely and trusted completely. Calm and unruffled in manner and usually convivial, he was extremely knowledgeable about international affairs and widely admired for his intelligence. But, as soon became evident, he lacked many of the qualities of an effective party manager. He was often disorganised, was frequently unpunctual, often sauntering in late to meetings nibbling at a pastry and with a disturbing habit at times of simply vanishing. Despite being Director of Strategy, he imparted little sense of strategic direction. Though a long-time member of the Labour Party, he lacked any roots in its traditions, values and ethos; his strongest affinities had been with the pro-Soviet faction 'Straight Left' of the Communist party. He then became a major figure within the StWC, and he was a vitriolic critic of the US and the North Atlantic Treaty Organization (NATO). He was widely seen as rigid and dogmatic in outlook; not surprisingly, he was deeply unpopular with most Labour MPs.[27] But such was his influence with the leader that some decisions ended up being taken after 'snatched conversations' in Milne's office.[28]

Andrew Murray was a close friend and ally of Milne's and shared his brand of hard-line communism – he joined the Labour Party only in 2016. He had spent most of his life in the trade union movement, latterly as chief of staff to Len McCluskey, an unusual career path for a scion of the Scottish aristocracy (grandson of Baron Rankeillour). He was also a leading figure within the StWC, where he had worked closely with Corbyn. He was highly regarded within the leadership as a thoughtful, measured and experienced operator, and his judgements were more nuanced than other senior Leader of the Opposition's Office (LOTO) members, as we shall see in the issue of antisemitism. However, his involvement was interrupted, and hence his influence reduced, by bouts of ill health. Like Milne, though his principal interest (aside from relations with the unions) tended to be in matters of foreign policy, in practice his remit was a wide-ranging one.

Simon Fletcher, responsible for trade union liaison under Miliband, became Corbyn's first chief of staff and subsequently Director of Campaigning. He had earned his spurs as an advisor to the London mayoral candidate Ken Livingstone. He favoured a pluralist approach to tackling the leadership's extremely taxing managerial problems, advocating a broader political base encompassing elements from the soft left and centre-right of the party. However, his advice went unheeded and he resigned from the Leader's Office (known as LOTO during the Corbyn years) in frustration in March, having already been replaced the previous year by Karie Murphy as chief of staff.

Karie Murphy, whom we have encountered briefly in her earlier persona as an aspiring Labour candidate for the Falkirk constituency, was appointed first as Executive Director of the Leader's Office in February 2016 and shortly after as chief of staff. She was resolute, experienced and efficient, with the rare ability to propel the notoriously indecisive Corbyn into taking a decision. She was utterly loyal to him, brisk, energetic and with a no-nonsense style. But she was also ruthless, and those whom she alienated charged her with being overbearing and unyielding, 'with undertones of menace'; those who crossed her did so at their peril.[29] She was the only person in LOTO whose influence matched that of Milne. Her relationship with McDonnell was, however, often strained – they often took opposing positions on management matters – and by 2019, broke down completely.

Len McCluskey, head of Unite, was the hub of the Unite nexus, also comprising Murphy, Murray and Jennie Formby, first a senior NEC member and then, in 2018, General Secretary of the party. Unite was, as we have noted, Labour's largest affiliate; as well as commanding a large block of delegates at Conference and strong representation on party committees, it also supplied funds, staff and resources for the often harassed and over-stretched leadership team. As Labour's largest industrial affiliate, Unite was a pillar of the Corbyn leadership and also the main point of liaison with other major but less well-disposed unions, UNISON, GMB and USDAW. Forceful and assertive in style, McCluskey's relations with others within the Corbyn camp, notably senior Momentum figures such as Jon Lansman, were at times strained. Throughout the Corbyn years, McCluskey and Unite accumulated a degree of influence in the party unrivalled since the days of Transport & General Workers Union's Jack Jones in the 1970s.

The size, influence and scale of operations of LOTO has grown over the years as more funds have become available.[30] But uniquely under Corbyn, virtually none of its members had experience in managing the Labour Party, indeed, with one or two exceptions, of managing *any* large organisation. Most LOTO members were recruited from the ecosphere of the radical left, with little experience or understanding of the party, its ethos and its traditions: the two worlds had hardly intersected.[31] As a result, they lacked the contacts and tacit knowledge which could be very helpful in discharging managerial roles. In the first months of the leadership, according to McCluskey, the office was 'chaotic, staff felt desperate, morale was through the floor, and discipline had broken down'.[32] Matters later improved, but only patchily. This had a disabling effect, since LOTO's remit encompassed the whole range of party activities. It operated as the nerve centre of the leader's operation, including strategy, organisation, communications and tactics. Crucially, its formal executive role in major managerial issues, including discipline, candidate selections and rule enforcement, was limited, since these lay within the jurisdiction of the party apparatus and the NEC. This meant that cooperation between the two was essential but was rarely forthcoming: the two sets of officials differed too much in political formation, outlook and priorities, and, as we discuss in detail in Chapter 8, the relationship was never good and more often adversarial rather than collaborative.

The row over Syria

The first few months of the Corbyn leadership were a period of uneasy calm which ended abruptly with the first open rupture within the party, very significantly over a matter of foreign policy. In the autumn of 2015, the terrorist organisation ISIS (Islamic State of Iraq and Syria) made major territorial gains in Syria, and Britain, following the US lead, decided in response to launch air strikes. But when a resolution was tabled in Parliament authorising UK participation, both the Shadow Cabinet and the PLP were split, with a majority in favour of endorsing government policy. Corbyn, however, was adamantly opposed to Royal Air Force deployment; as an anti-militarist, he was always a critic of the use of force in international conflicts; as an anti-imperialist, he was utterly opposed to Western interventions in the Global South; and, perhaps most important of all, he had an extremely jaundiced view of American intentions and behaviour in the world. On all these matters Corbyn was completely at odds with most Labour MPs, most of his Shadow Cabinet and, not least, with his Shadow Foreign Secretary, Hilary Benn, the son of Tony but – unlike Corbyn – not a Bennite. Benn and others argued forcefully that the UK had a responsibility to help its closest ally to repel the incursions of a murderous terrorist organisation already guilty of the slaughter of many innocent civilians.

A Wilson would have sought to blur the issue, search for compromises and suggest ambiguous and possibly vacuous formulations to provide some means of averting an outright schism. Corbyn opted for a very different and much more centralist approach. He cited a recent Conference decision stating that military action in Syria must meet four conditions: explicit United Nations (UN) authorisation; a comprehensive plan for humanitarian assistance; assurances that the bombing was exclusively targeted at ISIS; and priority to diplomatic efforts to end the war in Syria: conditions which plainly had not been met. He insisted (controversially) that this decision was binding upon the PLP. He then decided to raise the stakes and mobilise the party membership to secure compliance with the Conference resolution. He persuaded the NEC to order an electronic ballot of party members to ascertain their views: results showed that 75 per cent backed his position. Corbyn's critics were infuriated by what they saw as inadmissible pressure, protesting that the Conference had no right under party rules to instruct MPs how to vote. Rather than trying to hammer out some form of compromise, Corbyn's defiant response was to issue a three-line whip – which provoked uproar in the PLP and threats of mass resignations from the Shadow Cabinet.

Rather than narrowing divisions, Corbyn had widened them; rather than mollifying critics, he had enraged them. He had converted a dispute into a crisis, but he lacked the means to resolve it in his favour. Such was the size of the rebellion that he was forced to retreat; he reluctantly accepted an unprecedented arrangement. It was agreed, firstly, that Labour MPs would not be whipped and, secondly, that he would open the Commons debate expounding his position while Benn, an enthusiastic advocate of air strikes, would close it: Corbyn's lack of authority and the chasm that split the party was laid bare to all, and embarrassingly so. The spectacle of the Shadow Foreign Secretary making a powerful speech brazenly defying the leader maddened many of Corbyn's supporters, who clamoured for Benn's dismissal in a 'revenge reshuffle'.

This was the first major clash since Corbyn's election and was an indication to all of the degree to which Labour was fractured. It also ended ambiguities about the new leadership management style: it would be centralist rather than pluralist with its insistence on compliance with the majority will, as determined by the leadership and Conference mandates. It was the first open demonstration of the mutual ill-will, mistrust and in some cases loathing that was beginning to infect the party. The episode confirmed the views of those in LOTO who held that the leadership's critics could not be placated and that the priority must be to bring the PLP to heel, and of those in the PLP that accommodation with the leadership was impossible and plans must be put in motion to overthrow it.

But for the moment, there was the distraction of the referendum on continued membership of the EU, where, in theory at least, both wings of the party were in agreement in favour of campaigning for a Remain vote.

Brexit and the 'chicken coup'

As it transpired, the shock outcome of the referendum in June 2016 in favour of leaving the EU demolished any prospect of a modus vivendi within the party. We discuss this in detail in Chapter 6, but the key point here is that many distraught Labour MPs attributed the result to Corbyn's half-hearted and tepid campaigning for a Remain vote: in the words of Phil Wilson MP, chair of the Labour In for Britain group, Corbyn had intentionally undermined the Labour Remain campaign, and this was 'the final straw for many MPs'.[33] Rumours began to spread of a coup being organised by Hilary Benn. In fact, plans to find some means of removing Corbyn had been in preparation for months,[34] but the planners' hand was forced by Corbyn's prompt decision to sack Benn. This set in motion, as had been arranged, a sequence of resignations on the part of most members of the Shadow Cabinet. The next step was the calling of a motion of no confidence in Corbyn at a meeting of the PLP on 28 June 2016: it passed by the huge margin of 172 votes to 42. Such a public repudiation of a leader was (at least since Ramsay MacDonald's time) unprecedented, and Corbyn's resignation was seen as inevitable; it seemed inconceivable that a Leader of the Opposition who had so publicly and completely forfeited the confidence of his MPs could survive. And, indeed, Corbyn was tempted to resign.

But MPs had grossly underestimated the wave of fury that inundated the party, which was not confined to the Corbynite left. McCluskey gives some flavour of what many felt. What came to be known as the 'chicken coup' was, he wrote in his autobiography, 'one of the most extraordinary and shameful episodes in the history of the Labour Party'. He added: 'What despicable, spineless people they were [...] a vicious, disreputable, right-wing PLP.'[35] Crucially, the launchers of the 'chicken coup' had overlooked the fact that nothing in Labour's rules required a leader to resign in such circumstances. Buoyed by vociferous support within the constituency parties, Corbyn decided to stay and fight. 'We will not allow the democracy of our movement,' John McDonnell thundered, 'to be subverted by a handful of MPs who refuse to accept Jeremy's mandate.'[36]

Aware of how difficult it would be to beat the Islington MP in an open contest, NEC members and party officials sought a means to exclude him from the ballot by claiming that the rules stipulated that all candidates, including Corbyn, would require the nominations of 15 per cent of the PLP, which he had no chance of gaining.[37] The rules were ambiguous, but it was a highly provocative move and, after a protracted session, the NEC, on which the Corbynites were still in a minority, ruled by eighteen to fourteen that he should automatically be on the ballot. This decision was legally challenged but was upheld by the High Court.[38]

Foiled in this, another step was taken to impede Corbyn. By the casting vote of the party Chair, the Executive ruled that new recruits who had been members for less than six months – who party headquarters knew were overwhelmingly pro-Corbyn – should be ineligible to vote in the election. Party officials then decided to engage in a 'validation' exercise not only of recent but also of current members; social media were trawled to determine whether there were any grounds on which those who seemed likely to vote for Corbyn could be excluded. The *Forde Report* later commented that this was 'improper' and 'by and large a factionally slanted exercise, designed and carried out with a startling lack of transparency'.[39] As it transpired, it was to have little effect.

Nothing better demonstrated the PLP's demoralisation than the unwillingness of any figure of note to challenge Corbyn for the leadership. Eventually, the little-known and uninspiring Owen Smith bravely stepped into the breach, only to be crushed by Corbyn by 61.8 per cent to 38.2 per cent, with an unprecedented 506,438 votes cast on a 77.6 per cent turnout. Corbyn vanquished his opponent in every category – members (59 per cent), registered supporters (70 per cent) and trade union affiliates (60 per cent); and all this without the 150,000 members who had joined the party during the last six months.[40] A poorly planned and haphazardly executed attempt to oust the leader had boomeranged.

After his second victory, Corbyn reshuffled his front bench, promoting more of his supporters, but since they were so thin on the ground he had no option but to draw his net more widely, for example by appointing Emily Thornberry as Shadow Foreign Secretary, Keir Starmer as Shadow Brexit Secretary and Nia Griffiths as Shadow Defence Secretary, none of them part of the Corbyn left. Corbyn's mandate had been emphatically replenished and his supporters were elated, but the fundamentals of the situation had not changed: an unreliable Shadow Cabinet, a still deeply disgruntled PLP and a party machine over which he exercised little authority.

The 2017 election: a moral victory?

The real fear of much of the PLP was less of the policies a Corbyn government might follow in office – that seemed a very remote prospect – than of losing their seats in an election which they knew would not be long delayed. In April 2017, the Tories won the Copeland by-election, the first time a government had snatched a seat from the opposition since 1981; the next month, Labour performed very poorly in the May local elections. The polls were giving the Conservatives leads of over 20 per cent, while Corbyn's personal polling was 'catastrophic'.[41] The temptation to call a snap election became too strong for the Prime Minister, Theresa May, to resist, and the date was set for 8 June 2017.

The atmosphere in Labour circles was one of the utmost apprehension, gloom and despondency, and many feared a wipe-out. As a result, Southside's (party HQ's) preferred strategy was to protect as many vulnerable Labour seats as possible; LOTO, in contrast, wanted a more offensive strategy. Labour's 2017 manifesto was the boldest the party had presented for some time. It called for a reinvigorated and expanded role for the state in managing the economy, including ambitious public investment projects and an active industrial policy. It promised to balance current spending, with additional expenditures funded by higher taxes on the more affluent, including a 50 per cent higher rate of income tax. Recent reductions in corporation tax would be reversed and an Excessive Pay Levy would be charged on firms paying salaries of more than £330,000, while much firmer steps would be taken to combat rampant tax avoidance.[42] Nobel prize-winning economist Joseph Stiglitz described Labour's economic proposals as 'carefully thought-out [...] based on taxing those at the top and ensuring that corporations pay what they should'.[43] The manifesto also pledged a significant boost in NHS spending and the reversal of privatisation and outsourcing. Other commitments included a higher minimum wage, extended free childcare and much greater legislative protection to those in insecure and precarious employment. The huge and completely neglected issue of care for older people would be addressed by the establishment of a National Care Service. The Royal Mail, the railways, water and energy would be brought back into public ownership, while university tuition fees would be abolished. On the thorny issue of Brexit, as we explain in Chapter 6, Labour adopted a stance of 'calculated ambiguity'.[44]

The results of the election were wholly unexpected. Far from being decimated, it was Labour's best performance since 2001, gaining no less than 3.5 million votes, boosting its share of the poll by 9.5 percentage points to 40 per cent, winning thirty-six more seats and securing the biggest swing to the party since the celebrated election of 1945. The government had lost its overall majority. All this was achieved 'despite Corbyn's own obvious limitations, a right-wing press that hounded him from day one, and even worse, right-wingers in the parliamentary Labour party who never ever accepted his legitimate mandate'.[45] The result demolished the almost universally endorsed claim that a Labour Party led from the left could never enlarge its share of the vote. Labour's impressive advance occurred at a time when sister parties in France, Germany and elsewhere were undergoing a precipitous decline. Those who claimed that their major objection to Corbyn was that he was unelectable were proved to be wrong.

The outcome of the 2017 election provided an opportunity for the leadership, negotiating from a position of strength, to widen its support base in the PLP. According to Karie Murphy and McDonnell, it did seek to do so. 'Was there a window of opportunity after the 2017 election to broaden out, to bring more people in?' McDonnell asked. 'Yes,' he responded, 'and we tried that as much as we possibly could,' but too few were prepared to reciprocate.[46] Others, however, denied that any such effort was made, including Jon Lansman, who maintained that the leadership's failure to reach out was 'a terrible mistake'.[47]

The balance of evidence suggests that Lansman was closer to the truth, and that insofar as some, like McDonnell, were prepared to incorporate others, it would be very much on their terms. Three major considerations seem to have influenced the leadership calculations. The first was that Corbyn, who was temperamentally very averse to sacking people, was very unwilling to remove from the front bench people who had served him loyally and replace them by others who had not. The second and more important reason was that the Corbyn left felt thoroughly vindicated by the huge growth in the Labour vote. This, they convinced themselves, was primarily due to the popularity of the manifesto (plus Corbyn's campaigning skills). Many on the hard left had long argued that if presented with a radical manifesto by a leadership seriously committed to delivering it, many voters would rally behind it. In this reading of the election, such factors as Mrs May's notoriously wooden and robotic performance, poor Tory campaign organisation and her sensible but unpopular policy on adult social care were ignored. That so much could be achieved by a radical manifesto suggested to them that a yet more radical one could mobilise even more support: it never appeared to occur to them that very few voters have more than a passing and superficial familiarity with the content of party manifestos. Now, surely, was not the time, so the argument went, for compromising with those always sceptical of the Corbyn project.

The third reason probably scuppered any prospect for a deal: the belief, which rapidly became an article of faith within the Corbyn camp, that Labour would have won the election if senior figures at party HQ had not deliberately sabotaged the campaign. These officials, it was alleged, concealed information from LOTO, leaked negative stories and acted throughout in a half-hearted and lackadaisical manner. They even, quite illicitly, ran a covert and unauthorised parallel campaign in which resources were switched from winnable seats to those being contested by right-wing candidates – the so-called 'Ergon House' operation. They had anticipated that a heavy Labour defeat would force Corbyn's ejection and – it was asserted – they were visibly distraught when this failed to materialise.[48] The *Forde Report* was later to confirm the existence of the 'Ergon House' operation, in clear breach of party rules,[49] but it rejected the Corbynite contention that senior officials had failed to commit themselves to the election campaign, nor did it accept that the Ergon House operation had a significant effect on the election result.[50] Notwithstanding, the belief that Labour would have found itself in government if the campaign had not been subverted by party HQ became part of the official Corbynite narrative.

The election, a seasoned party observer commented, had offered an opening for an accommodation, but 'neither side were looking for a compromise. Jeremy certainly wasn't, nor Seumas nor the party establishment.'[51] The Corbynite left were exultant – 'an intoxication from which Corbynism never sobered up'.[52] They felt on the right side of history. As a result, as one advisor judged, 'Corbynism became more and more insular'.[53] By the second half of 2017, with cleavage lines palpably hardening and polarisation intensifying, the Murphy/Milne belief that precedence must be given to tighter control of the party largely drove the leadership's managerial calculations. Here an indispensable role was played by Momentum.

Momentum, party transformation and the Democracy Review

Formed in October 2015, Momentum was led by Jon Lansman, a veteran of left-wing politics and a highly capable and experienced political organiser. Having managed Corbyn's successful leadership campaign, he and others sought to harness the energies, the idealism and enthusiasm of its many voluntary workers to form a structured faction to sustain the new leadership.

Critics on the party's right professed to see in Momentum a twenty-first-century reincarnation of the Militant Tendency.[54] The comparison was profoundly misleading. Militant was a highly disciplined, tightly controlled and sectarian Trotskyist organisation committed to using 'entryist' tactics of burrowing deep within the party to gain control of slices of it. Momentum was none of these; it was neither monolithic nor very cohesive; instead, it was an often unstable alliance between disparate groups with varying priorities.[55] It was divided from the outset between the 'movementists', who saw Momentum as a spur for the transformation of Labour into a mass, campaigning social movement, and the 'institutionalists' led by Lansman, who wanted to focus on reshaping and consolidating control of the party through contesting internal party elections.[56] It was this second view that largely prevailed.

Momentum was adept at using new communications technology (the importance of which is detailed in Chapter 1) to channel and coordinate the activities of Corbyn sympathisers, to disseminate information and tactical advice and to circulate so-called 'model resolutions' for consideration by Conference. Crucial to Momentum's activities was its compilation of a comprehensive database of supporters within the party, owned not by Momentum but by a company set up and controlled by Lansman. Unlike ginger groups on the party right, which received generous donations from rich businessmen, Momentum was financed by membership dues and contributions. This enabled it to hire a full-time staff in London and a network of organisers in the regions. At its peak, it had about 40,000 members with a presence in many CLPs.[57]

For the leadership and for Momentum, the absolute priority was control over the NEC, which, as we have pointed out, was the major repository of managerial powers: together they agreed slates of candidates in contests for the NEC and other key party bodies. They proved successful. In 2017, the Momentum slates won all six NEC constituency seats and registered major gains in elections to the CAC, responsible for the conduct of Conference business, and the NCC, charged with upholding party rules and discipline. In 2017, Conference approved an NEC proposal to expand the number of NEC constituency seats to nine, all of which were won by the Momentum slate in elections in early 2018. The number of Corbynite CLP delegates to party Conference also swelled, and by 2017 constituted a clear majority.[58]

The wider goal was Labour's metamorphosis into a mass, membership-driven campaigning party. The chosen instrument was the Democracy Review, launched at the 2017 party Conference and led by Corbyn's political secretary, Katy Clark. Its task was to explore 'how our hugely expanded membership becomes a mass movement which can transform our society'.[59] To the right, this was a mask to conceal the real purpose: an 'unparalleled power grab' by the hard left.[60]

The Democracy Review conducted an extensive consultative exercise and received 11,425 submissions from local Labour parties, trade unions, socialist societies and individual Labour Party members.[61] But the outcome justified neither hopes nor fears. The most significant changes included enlarging the constituency section of the NEC from six to nine seats and the trade union section from twelve to thirteen. In addition, it proposed restoring to the NEC its traditional policy-making rights, which had been transferred to the NPF in 1997. There were also a large number of often sensible suggestions, but of a rather minor and unexceptional character.[62] Lansman found the report 'deeply, deeply disappointing'.[63] None of Momentum's radical expectations had been met; one of its NEC members,

Darren Williams, complained that most reforms had either been 'kicked into the long grass or killed off altogether'.[64]

What occurred to derail the project tells us a good deal about the Corbyn leadership's management of the party. Firstly, the lack of strategic thinking and planning. Little thought appears to have been given to precisely what the leadership was seeking to achieve and how, and what steps needed to be taken to navigate the proposals through the party's decision-making process. This required a substantial degree of support from the unions, but three of the four largest unions, GMB, UNISON and USDAW, had little interest in radical change and the fourth, the more sympathetic Unite, was not prepared to break ranks with the others on the issue.[65] Nor was the leadership of one mind. Corbyn himself did favour democratisation of the party, but was not a man for detail, which he left to others. The decisive voice on this, as on other issues, was Corbyn's powerful chief of staff, Karie Murphy, who was resolved from the outset that LOTO would not relinquish any of its powers. As Michael Chessum, a leading Momentum member, observed, the Corbyn leadership 'displayed all the internal management practices of a conventional Labour party leadership rather than a mass movement'; as a result, there was no meaningful democratisation.[66]

However, on one issue, a significant change was made. Under existing rules and with the present composition of the PLP, the prospects of a Corbynite left replacement securing nominations from 15 per cent of parliamentarians were meagre: no MP was likely to repeat the mistake of nominating someone they had no intentions of voting for. LOTO wanted to make it easier to secure nominations, both by lowering the threshold of nominations and by extending nomination rights to the CLPs and affiliated bodies. The Democracy Review accordingly proposed and Conference approved the following changes: nomination by 10 per cent of parliamentarians and nomination by 5 per cent of CLPs; or nomination by at least three affiliates (at least two of which should be trade union affiliates) comprising 5 per cent of the affiliated membership.[67] Beyond this, the much-heralded Democracy Review was a damp squib. Furthermore, the most contentious issue, reform of the candidate selection rules, was dealt with outside the framework of the Review process.

Candidate selection

The struggle for power in the Labour Party has often revolved around selection rules since the institution of mandatory reselection and then its replacement by the 'trigger ballot' procedure. For years, left-wing organisations like CLPD and more latterly Momentum had campaigned for the reinstatement of mandatory – or what came to be dubbed 'open' – reselection on the grounds that it was more democratic and would foster greater accountability of MPs to those who selected them. But ultimately, as all knew, it was about power. The Corbynite camp was well aware that as long as its base in the PLP was so weak, its hold on the party would be shaky and insecure. Hence a mechanism was required which could expedite the process of altering the political complexion of the PLP while at the same time inducing existing MPs to show more loyalty to the leader by making them more vulnerable to rank-and-file pressure.

Most Labour MPs adamantly opposed open reselection, not least because Momentum had embedded itself in so many constituency parties. Corbyn-sceptic MPs reported being told by Corbynite members in their constituencies that their behaviour was being scrutinised; one Momentum group issued a 'deselection hit list' of forty-nine MPs.[68] But there were also practical objections: mandatory reselection would consume time, energy and resources, distracting both members and regional officials from campaigning and electioneering.[69]

Initially, LOTO worked closely with Momentum in mobilising support for Conference resolutions demanding open selection, though it had to await the capturing of an NEC majority in early 2018 before being able to instigate rule changes. Prospects for securing open selection at the 2018 party Conference, dominated by the Corbyn left, seemed very encouraging, but then, very suddenly and unexpectedly, the campaign stalled largely due to opposition from within both the leadership and the unions. Two senior figures, John McDonnell and Andrew Murray, were very anxious that pressing ahead might precipitate mass defections on the scale of the early 1980s (which had seen the formation of the SDP) or even greater. McDonnell feared that as many as seventy might quit, which was 'incredibly dangerous' and 'even threaten[ed] the existence of the Labour Party'; the reform, in short, could be utterly counter-productive.[70]

Many within the unions shared McDonnell's assessment and were also unhappy that open selection would reduce the role assigned to them by the trigger mechanism. Although mandated by Unite's conference to back the reform, McCluskey decided to form a common front with UNISON, GMB and USDAW and opt for a compromise scheme which made it easier to activate the trigger.[71] Under the existing system, a majority of *all* branches (party or affiliated) had to vote for a contest. The new system, firstly, lowered the threshold so that 'If either one third or more of party branches, or one third or more of affiliated branches, indicate that they wish a selection to take place, a selection shall proceed'; secondly, it reduced the aggregate half to one third or more of either party branches, *or* affiliated organisations; and thirdly, it disaggregated the votes and counted the party branches and affiliated branches separately. This meant, in other words, that as long as one third in either section voted for a contest, it would go ahead.[72]

Momentum was dismayed, and there were furious exchanges between its leaders and McCluskey and McDonnell. Using old-style managerial stratagems, the leadership kept resolutions calling for mandatory reselection off the agenda, which meant that the only options available to delegates were the status quo or the leadership's compromise. Notwithstanding, Momentum urged delegates to reject the compromise: 90 per cent of CLP delegates voted to reject the order of business to allow open selections to be debated, but they were outnumbered by the unions, who voted by 97 per cent to uphold it. One observer noted that 'there was a shocked silence in the hall. The machine had just collided head-on with the movement.'[73] Trade union votes then assured the passage of the compromise scheme, leaving both Momentum and most MPs (who objected to facilitating reselection) deeply resentful.

But, with the compromise agreed, in July 2019 Momentum launched a drive urging CLPs with sitting MPs to allow selection contests to take place by 'triggering' them.[74] Very few CLPs took any notice. Six Labour MPs were 'triggered' (almost all because of local factors), and of these, two, Margaret Hodge and Diana Johnson, were reselected by their local parties, one was abandoned and three were automatically readopted because of the calling of the general election. All of Corbyn's most outspoken critics navigated the process with ease, because – as was often overlooked – most members are very reluctant to eject their MPs even when they disagree with them. Finally, the unexpectedly large number of seats made vacant because of either retirement or defections meant that these seats became the real selection battleground for the 2019 election.

However, the indirect effects were more significant and detrimental. Firstly, the very posing of the threat of mandatory reselection further inflamed feelings in the PLP against Corbyn. And secondly, huge amounts of time and energy were consumed in shoring up their positions on the part of those who feared deselection.[75] As the soft left frontbencher Angela Rayner protested, 'anyone who talks about deselecting any of my colleagues, quite frankly, they need to think about who are the real enemy here'.[76]

High tide

Whatever the setbacks, generally speaking, the tide appeared to be flowing strongly in favour of the leadership by the opening of 2018. Twice Corbyn had been elected with hefty majorities, the party had nearly won the 2017 election and, at long last, the leadership had full control of the NEC. The General Secretary Iain McNicol knew his position was untenable and resigned. McCluskey used his muscle to propel Jennie Formby, a senior official in Unite, into the vacant post, in the process forcing another potential candidate, Jon Lansman, to retire from the contest. Formby's appointment opened the sluice gates to sweeping changes in Southside personnel, where most senior officials were replaced by Corbynites. The leadership also tightened its hold over the NEC by ensuring that its key sub-committees were chaired by its members. The soft left Ann Black, previously elected on the left-wing Grassroots Alliance slate and widely regarded as an extremely diligent and fair-minded chair of the Disputes Committee, was ousted in favour of the far less qualified but utterly loyal Christine Shawcroft; she was also dismissed from the Grassroots Alliance slate and (temporarily) lost her NEC seat. By this time, a distinct management style had emerged, as intense and controlling as anything under New Labour; as one Corbyn sympathiser later recalled, LOTO had acquired a reputation for 'secrecy, authoritarianism and narrow-mindedness'.[77]

But confidence and morale within the Corbyn camp were high, its opponents in the party despondent. The weather was set fair: instead, almost immediately, the leadership was engulfed in a double crisis: over Brexit and antisemitism. The following two chapters explore these in turn.

Notes

1 Rowena Mason, 'If Jeremy Corbyn wins leadership Labour faces "annihilation", says Tony Blair', *Guardian*, 13 August 2015.

2 Len McCluskey, 'Blairism is dead and buried. Jeremy Corbyn is the future', *Observer*, 13 September 2015.

3 Owen Jones, *This Land: The Story of a Movement* (London: Allen Lane, 2020), p. 47.

4 Interview, Jon Lansman.

5 Stephen Bush, 'Jeremy Corbyn "on course to come to" in the Labour leadership election', *New Statesman*, 15 July 2015.

6 Tony Blair, 'Jeremy Corbyn's politics are fantasy – just like Alice in Wonderland', *Observer*, 30 August 2015.

7 Gary Younge, 'Corbyn victory energises the alienated and alienates the establishment', *Guardian*, 14 September 2015.

8 Toby Helm, 'Demoralised, dejected and defeated, Labour faces a fight for its very life', *Observer*, 19 July 2015.

9 Paul Krugman, 'Labour's dead center', *New York Times*, 14 September 2015; Terry Macalister, 'Joseph Stiglitz: Unsurprising Jeremy Corbyn is a Labour leadership contender', *Observer*, 26 July 2015.

10 Patrick Wintour, 'Anger after Harriet Harman says Labour will not vote against welfare bill', *Guardian*, 13 July 2015.

11 George Eaton, 'Labour's week of crisis: The inside story', *New Statesman*, 15 July 2015.

12 Thomas Quinn, 'The British Labour Party's leadership election of 2015', *The British Journal of Politics and International Relations*, 18:4 (2016), 772.
13 Wintour, 'Anger after Harriet Harman says'.
14 Michael Chessum, *This Is Only the Beginning: The Making of a New Left, from Anti-Austerity to the Fall of Corbyn* (London: Bloomsbury Academic, 2022), p. 180.
15 Bryan Gould, 'We can't fight the electorate', *Guardian*, 21 July 2015.
16 Peter Dorey and Andrew Denham "'The longest suicide vote in history": The Labour Party leadership election of 2015, *British Politics*, 11:3 (2016), 272.
17 Andrew Gamble, 'After New Labour: The Corbyn surge and the future of social democracy in Britain', *Policy Network*, 24 September 2015.
18 Krugman, 'Labour's dead center'.
19 Andrew Murray, *The Fall and Rise of the British Left* (London: Verso 2019), p. 153.
20 Discussed at length in Chessum, *This Is Only the Beginning* and in Andy Beckett, *The Searchers: Five Rebels, Their Dream of a Different Britain, and Their Many Enemies* (London: Penguin, 2024).
21 Chessum, *This Is Only the Beginning*, p. 155.
22 *Ibid.*, p. 84.
23 Emmanuelle Avril, 'The "movementisation" of the Labour Party and the future of labour organising', in Emmanuelle Avril and Yann Béliard (eds), *Labour United and Divided from the 1830s to the Present* (Manchester: Manchester University Press, 2018), pp. 254–70.
24 Jones, *This Land*, p. 62.
25 Andrew Murray, *Is Socialism Possible in Britain?* (London: Verso 2022), p. 96.
26 Jason Cowley, 'Who is the real John McDonnell?', *New Statesman*, 5 September 2018.
27 Peter Wilby, 'The thin controller', *New Statesman*, 16 April 2016.
28 Jones, *This Land*, pp. 103, 107; Interview, Simon Fletcher.
29 Jones, *This Land*, p. 116.
30 Martin Forde (chair), *The Forde Report* (London: Labour Party, 2022), p. 29.
31 *Ibid.*, p. 31.
32 McCluskey, *Always Red* (New York: OR Books, 2021), pp. 235, 237.
33 Phil Wilson, 'Corbyn sabotaged Labour's Remain campaign. He must resign', *Observer*, 26 June 2016.
34 See Reg Race, *Goodbye to the Working Class* (Canterbury: The Conrad Press, 2021). Race had been a Bennite MP from 1979 to 1983 and was a key organiser of the anti-Corbyn planning.
35 McCluskey, *Always Red*, pp. 247, 252.
36 John McDonnell, 'Jeremy Corbyn is not standing down – 172 Labour MPs cannot drown out democracy', *New Statesman*, 29 June 2016.
37 Interview, Karie Murphy.

38 Tom Quinn, 'From the Wembley Conference to the "McDonnell Amendment": Labour's leadership nomination rules', *Political Quarterly*, 89:3 (2018), 81.
39 Forde, *The Forde Report*, pp. 44–5.
40 Heather Stewart and Rowena Mason, 'Labour leadership: Jeremy Corbyn wins convincing victory over Owen Smith', *Guardian*, 24 September 2016.
41 Jones, *This Land*, p. 133.
42 Peter Dorey, 'Jeremy Corbyn confounds his critics: Explaining the Labour Party's remarkable resurgence in the 2017 election', *British Politics*, 12:3 (2017), 131–4.
43 Joseph Stiglitz, 'Austerity has strangled Britain. Only Labour will consign it to history', *Guardian*, 7 June 2017.
44 Ben Jackson, 'The politics of the Labour manifesto', *Political Quarterly*, 88:3 (2017), 343.
45 Neal Lawson, 'Keir Starmer, you have a golden opportunity. Now try a bit of Corbynism', *Guardian*, 8 June 2022.
46 Interviews, John McDonnell; Karie Murphy.
47 Interview, Jon Lansman.
48 Labour Party, *Leaked Report. The Work of the Labour Party's Governance and Legal Unit in Relation to Anti-semitism, 2014–2019* (London: Labour Party, 2020), p. 117; Jones, *This Land*, pp. 135–6; Forde, *The Forde Report*, p. 54.
49 Pogrund and Maguire also concluded that in the 2017 campaign senior party staff had acted 'as if they were a law – and organisation – unto themselves', something unprecedented in Labour's history. Gabriel Pogrund and Patrick Maguire, *Left Out: The Inside Story of Labour under Corbyn* (London: Bodley Head, 2021), pp. 36–7.
50 Forde, *The Forde Report*, pp. 66–7.
51 Interview, former senior party official.
52 Chessum, *This Is Only the Beginning*, p. 180.
53 Christine Berry, 'Political economy and Labour's factionalism', *Renewal*, 29:2 (2021), 26.
54 For example, Wilson, 'Corbyn sabotaged Labour's Remain campaign'; Toby Helm and Alex Hacillo, 'Secret tape reveals Momentum plot to seize control of Labour', *Observer*, 19 March 2017.
55 Avril, 'The "movementisation" of the Labour Party'.
56 Bradley Ward and Marco Guglielmo, 'Pop-socialism: A new radical left politics? Evaluating the rise and fall of the British and Italian left in the anti-austerity age', *The British Journal of Politics and International Relations*, 24:4 (2022), 694; Adam Klug, Emma Rees and James Schneider, 'Momentum: A new kind of politics', *Renewal*, 24:2 (2016), 39; Chessum, *This Is Only the Beginning*, pp. 63, 145, 162.
57 Ashley Cowburn, 'Momentum: Corbyn-backing organisation now has 40,000 paying members, overtaking Green party', *Independent*, 4 April 2018.
58 Ewen MacAskill, 'Labour Conference: Most grassroots delegates support Corbyn, poll finds', *Guardian*, 18 September 2017.

59 Labour Party, *Democracy Review* (London: Labour Party, 2018), p. 10.
60 Emma Bean, 'A "factional power grab" or giving power to the members? Labour movement reacts to sweeping party reforms', *LabourList*, 20 September 2017, labourlist.org
61 Labour Party, *Democracy Review*, p. 10.
62 *Ibid.*, pp. 79–80; 81–3.
63 Interview, Jon Lansman.
64 Luke Akehurst, 'The rule changes going to Conference – and what they mean for Labour', *LabourList*, 20 September 2018, labourlist.org
65 *Ibid.*
66 Chessum, *This Is Only the Beginning*, p. 196.
67 Labour Party Rulebook, 2019. Chapter 1, Clause II. 2B.
68 Robert Ford, Tim Bale, Will Jennings and Paula Surridge, *The British General Election of 2019* (London: Palgrave Macmillan 2021), p. 111.
69 Ann Black, 'Mandatory reselection? If it ain't broke, don't fix it', LabourList, 17 September 2018, labourlist.org.
70 Interview, John McDonnell. As it happened, seven MPs did desert the party in early 2019, alongside three Tories, to form Change UK, but this was a manageable number (explained in Chapter 6).
71 McCluskey, *Always Red*, p. 365.
72 Luke Akehurst, 'How Labour's trigger ballot system works', *LabourList*, 12 August 2019, labourlist.org
73 Steve Hudson, 'If you've got a problem with open selections, Len, speak to the members', *LabourList*, 27 September 2018, labourlist.org
74 Sienna Rodgers, 'Momentum launch drive for open selections across the country', *Guardian*, 12 July, 2019.
75 Interview, Ann Black.
76 Emma Bean, 'Rayner and Starmer condemn deselections', LabourList, 9 July 2017, labourlist.org
77 Jeremy Gilbert, 'Acid Corbynism for beginners', in Martin Perryman (ed.), *Corbynism from Below* (London: Lawrence and Wishart, 2019), p. 87.

6

Party management and the entangled fracture lines of Brexit

Brexit has unleashed demons that cannot be restrained.

Michael Chessum[1]

The new shape of an old demon

This chapter starts with a puzzle: given the overwhelmingly anti-Brexit stance of the PLP, the TUC and the pro-EU grass-roots membership, Brexit should not have become a problem at all for Labour. How, then, did the Corbyn leadership end up making this issue one of the two most damaging stumbling blocks[2] of their time at the helm of the party, and one that all but sank their project? A focus on party management provides a key entry point to unpick this enigma. Labour was of course not alone in being torn over Brexit. Experts have commented on the fact that Brexit was an issue which cut across ideological lines within the two main parties, rather than pitting left against right, or the government against the opposition, thus eroding cohesion within both the Conservatives and Labour. In Labour, the manner of Corbyn's rise to the head of the party (detailed in Chapter 5) reactivated tensions which had been dormant, setting the leader, the membership and the unions against the more centrist MPs, tensions which crystallised early on around Brexit. Over time, Brexit ended up dividing Corbyn's inner circle and mobilised the grass roots – torn between supporting Corbyn and fighting Brexit – against his preferred line. As such, Brexit constituted not only a source of conflict between the different centres of authority in the party but also 'a genuine fissure within the Corbynite coalition'.[3]

It must be recalled here that Corbyn was elected leader in 2015 following a general election in which David Cameron had promised a referendum: that a campaign would take place and that the party leadership would have to engage with the issue was by no means an unexpected development (although the result of the referendum was). Yet there was a lack of anticipation on the part of the leadership – incidentally shared by all the players, including those who supported Brexit, and it is clear that no one in the Labour leadership had contemplated the implications of a Leave vote.

The crisis unfolded in a number of stages, each posing its specific challenges, and it is important to distinguish the situation at the time of the referendum from what followed. During the campaign, Corbyn, under pressure from the wider 'movement' – in fact a complex array of small groups each jostling for the leader's ear – opted for a 'Remain and Reform' position, whatever that precisely meant. After the victory of Leave, a wholly unprepared leadership confronted the fact that the Leave vote had uncovered major existing fault lines in Labour's electoral coalition: an intractable conundrum for the party (whose vote was split), the unions (whose members had voted Leave) and many MPs in Leave constituencies.

The Brexit timeline between the referendum and the 2019 general election falls into three main moments – followed by the Starmer postscript. The first phase revolved around the 'in/out' debate, during which the issue flared up. The second phase saw the issue subside a little, Labour managing to put Brexit on the back burner, with the debate now seemingly revolving between soft/hard Brexit, until a few months after the 2017 general election. The third phase, as the realities of Brexit were becoming more and more apparent and pressure was growing to reverse Labour's initial post-referendum position of respecting its result, was marked by increased polarisation over a possible second referendum advocated by the newly created cross-party People's Vote campaign. The Labour leadership's focus on playing on Conservative divisions prevented the formulation of a clear position which might risk uniting the government against it. We therefore need to be cautious of blanket statements, as attempts to resolve the problem were made and opportunities existed. But, at each turn, the choices the leadership opted for only worsened its predicament.

A study of events from a party management perspective, looking at the centrifugal effect of Brexit on the different centres of authority and at Corbyn's attempts to manage and balance different groups with their varying priorities and preferences, helps explain why his pursuit of a compromise position failed. In this chapter, we look at the different areas of party management: membership, unions, MPs and Shadow Cabinet, leadership/LOTO and attempts at forging consensus. Importantly, the chapter shows that the leadership's weaknesses were compounded both by the binary nature of the issue of Brexit itself and by the entrenched factionalism which had emerged out of the New Labour years.

The effect of the binary nature of Brexit was that it precluded a nuanced approach – it was impossible to hold that any two things could be true at once. The deceptively simple terms of the IN/OUT referendum hid the fact that the Leave option was in fact going to be a highly complex process – essentially an unknown destination, since neither those who called the referendum nor the two main parties in their campaigns seriously contemplated the Leave option. There was a misperception in the electorate (and more widely) that the two options were somewhat equivalent, which led to the illusion of two equally viable projects. Although there were in fact many positions along the Leave–Remain spectrum, the approach taken by all the main players favoured the kind of binary thinking in which fuzzy rationality could not provide a guide, but emotional clarity could. The referendum thus opened – in Labour as in the population at large – a new cultural axis, with new Leave and Remain identities, in place of the mildly positive indifference which had prevailed until then.

Labour and Europe: conflicting traditions and polarisation

We start with a very brief overview of Labour's trajectory regarding the EU, in order to better understand the situation which Corbyn inherited. The complex relationship between Labour and Europe is not the object of this chapter, but it is nonetheless useful to take a look at the backstory so as to point to the existence of a variety of opinions – which then became polarised around the issue of Brexit. Matt Beech, using Bulpitt's typology[4] to sum up the competing traditions of thought within Labour – Eurosceptics, Euro-pragmatists and Euro-enthusiasts – shows how these traditions had found advocates on both wings of the party. Just as the Labour left has contained Eurosceptics (such as Michael Foot, Barbara Castle or Tony Benn) as well as Euro-enthusiasts (Stuart Holland and Diane Abbott among them), the right had comprised critics (including Ernest Bevin, Hugh Gaitskell, Peter Shore,[5] Frank Field, Kate Hoey and Gisela Stuart) as well as strong advocates of the European project (Roy Jenkins, who resigned from the party in 1980 over Europe and unilateralism, Roy Hattersley, Tony Blair, Gordon Brown, Harriet Harman, David Miliband). Similarly, Euro-pragmatists had sat on both wings of the Labour Party, with Richard Crossman and Harold Wilson (at least initially) on the left, and Tony Crosland, James Callaghan and Denis Healey on the right.[6]

Looking at the trajectory and rebalancing between these traditions, the direction of travel is that of a Europeanisation of the party resulting from the dynamics of the integration process and the UK becoming increasingly enmeshed in the EU.[7] This process of Europeanisation is seen in the integration of UK Labour MEPs of the European Parliamentary Labour Party (EPLP; dissolved in 2020) into the European groups of Socialists and Democrats, and the role granted to them in Labour Party structures (the leader of the EPLP – the latest one of whom was Richard Corbett, from 2017 – had a seat on the NEC and sat on Shadow Cabinet meetings). In fact Labour is still a full member of the Party of European Socialists, together with thirty-two other parties.[8]

Although Europe had caused major rifts in the past, from the 1960s and especially around the time of the 1975 referendum, culminating in the 1981 party split, the dominant perspective, since the 1990s with the adoption of the 1992 Maastricht Treaty, was one of indifferent acceptance, where belonging to the EU was largely taken for granted – at odds with the dominant narrative of the Conservative press (which has also been widely documented). Press hostility to the EU is taken to be one of the main reasons for Labour's timidity in making a better case under Blair, who displayed his commitment to Europe shortly after his 1997 victory by going on a bike ride in Amsterdam alongside other European leaders, but who quickly toned down his enthusiasm and gave up on any idea of the UK adopting the single currency. Bulmer, for example, stresses the paradox which lay at the heart of the high tide of Euro-enthusiasm under New Labour, which simultaneously embraced the constructive approach of 'utilitarian supranationalism' and a strategy to 'reduce the domestic electoral salience of the EU'.[9] This was already evident from the 1997 manifesto, with its commitment to 'lead reform' in the EU, while isolating the single currency from the election campaign through the promise of a referendum,[10] largely because of disagreement between Blair and Brown over the issue, with Brown's strong opposition eventually scuttling any possibility of joining.

The New Labour government's constructive approach towards the EU ran the risk of turning into an electoral liability, since the more Eurosceptic Conservative Party was better aligned with the median voter. And since polls indicated that the saliency of the issue of Europe was more prominent among those who had negative views of the EU, 'New Labour had an overall electoral incentive to turn European policy into a "low-salience issue"'.[11] Nor did the government attempt to shift public preferences by challenging the press narrative. As a result, Eurobarometer data showed that 'the eurosceptic trend in British public opinion that originated in the early 1990s was not reversed during New Labour's tenure'.[12]

More precisely, the New Labour approach consisted of attempts by the Blair government '(1) to *defuse* the European policy cleavage between the Labour Party and the Conservative Party, (2) to *depoliticise* its decision-making on European issues, (3) to *delegate* the final responsibility for decision-making to the public and (4) to *defer* controversial decisions to some future date'.[13] Some of these strategies – especially those of delegating and of deferring – were to have a momentous impact. Using a referendum pledge to contain the saliency of the EU was thus contingent upon the concomitant strategy of deferring controversial European policy decisions,[14] since the intense polarisation and politicisation of domestic debate that comes with referendum campaigns would be certain to spur an upswing in the public saliency of the issue. The dangers associated with strategies designed to contain – rather than reverse – anti-EU sentiment were to be fully revealed with the 2016 referendum.

The arc of travel of the trade unions prior to the referendum is a significant factor too. The TUC and most unions had opposed Britain's membership in the 1975 EEC Referendum, on the basis that the developing European single market threatened sectoral and national bargaining structures.[15] But trade union policy towards the EU underwent a significant shift from the late 1980s, an evolution which needs to be set in the context of a decline in union membership, density and collective bargaining. In this context, the EU has appeared to offer some protection for the unions and their members, a perception reinforced when Jacques Delors, then President of the Commission, in a momentous speech to the TUC in 1988, offered the prospect of collective bargaining at the European level, which swung the unions more firmly behind the EU. British unions have hence been described as 'pragmatic Europeans'.[16]

During the 2016 referendum campaign,[17] the TUC, including the three main unions (Unite, UNISON, GMB, who collectively represent some 3.7 million members), took a clear stance against Brexit. USDAW was also vigorously opposed to Brexit. Only three smaller unions (the Associated Society of Locomotive Engineers and Firemen [ASLEF]; the Bakers, Food and Allied Workers Union; the Rail, Maritime and Transport Workers Union [RMT]), representing under 150,000 members between them, declared themselves in favour of exiting the EU;[18] in a joint statement, they stated that 'The EU is anti-worker and cannot be reformed'. The RMT, the largest of the three (with 80,000 members), was the only major union to call for its members to vote Leave during the referendum campaign, arguing that the EU constituted a threat to collective bargaining and workers' rights.

With the victory of Brexit, the TUC found itself in a paradoxical situation not unlike that faced by Labour generally; although, overall, 60 per cent of union members had voted Remain, among the most disadvantaged categories of the population the majority had voted Leave. The TUC immediately expressed their concern regarding two main issues: the prospect that British social legislation, largely based on European directives, might be dismantled; and the negative consequences of the loss of free access to the single market on growth, employment and wages. After Theresa May, on 29 March 2017, triggered Article 50 of the European Treaty which sets the terms for a member state to leave, the TUC adopted a guidance document in September 2017,[19] which was completed and clarified at the September 2018 Congress,[20] whereby the delegates outlined three priority objectives: the defence of workers' rights, barrier-free trade with the EU and guarantees for people and for trade with regard to Ireland and Gibraltar. The TUC also highlighted the fact that an estimated 2.5 million jobs would be lost in the event of the UK leaving the single market and the customs union. On immigration, the TUC was at pains to stress its benefits for the UK economy and society while stating that the 'government must address the genuine concern of working people about the impacts of migration on stretched public services, transport and housing'.[21] The TUC's strategy was to point the finger at budget cuts, not immigrants.

Conflicting perceptions of the Labour electorate and the problem in the 'heartlands'

Corbyn's management of Brexit was guided by his wish to align the party with Labour's 'heartlands', but tensions at all levels of the party resulted from conflicting interpretations of the consequences for Labour of the Leave vote.[22] While the Labour leadership and some MPs (mainly in Leave seats) declared that the referendum result should be accepted, others pointed out that in Leave constituencies a majority (58 per cent) of Labour voters had voted to remain, which seemed to confirm the view that fear of Labour Leave voters had been overestimated: they would vote Labour even if the party's position on Brexit changed, since their main concern were issues such as the NHS and the railways.[23] Indeed, when the debate shifted, around the time of the 2017 general election, to that of a soft or hard Brexit, or even a No Deal Brexit, it seemed that Labour was managing to unite voters in urban areas, from the young and economically precarious to the liberal professional classes, while also winning the support of sufficient numbers of Leave voters to hold on to most of its heartlands.[24] In the run-up to the December 2019 election, data collected by the British Election Study also indicated that the best strategy for Labour was to pitch itself to Remain voters.[25] Therefore the perception that Labour needed to prioritise the Leave vote was widely taken to be mistaken; this was the conclusion that John McDonnell reached. But the importance of the Leave vote was then reinforced by the 2019 election result and the dramatic collapse of the 'Red Wall', although, as seen in Chapter 1, the weakening of the Labour vote in these areas pre-dated debates on the EU. Labour had been alerted to the significance of a long-term erosion of its working-class vote since the 1990s.

The diametrically opposed interpretations of the lessons to be drawn from the referendum vote were based on a selective understanding of the data, each side accusing the other of being unwilling to accept the poll findings because they did not suit their politics.[26] In the Corbynite Leave camp, tensions did not just boil down to electoral considerations, as both Seumas Milne and Andrew Murray were strong believers of Lexit. Yet the crux of the matter was not so much one of a specific stance on Brexit but more one of how to handle the constituencies which had voted Brexit: 'it was much more about the handling of it than the belief in whether you are pro or anti. People for whom Brexit was really difficult tended to be in Brexit seats and felt that we were not listening to the seats that voted for Brexit, even if they were themselves Remainers. [...] The irony is, it used to roughly correspond to left–right divisions, but the issue cut right through the Corbyn left, it totally divided it.'[27]

Within Corbyn's inner circle, the key issue tended to be over different calculations as to whether it was better to risk alienating Leave or Remain voters. As Tom Quinn argues, Corbyn's caution, at least initially, was arguably 'more in step with Labour voters as a whole'. Few in the party were representing the one third of Labour supporters who had voted to leave. Yet, 'to dismiss their significance, as Remainers sometimes do, [was] astonishingly complacent'.[28] Emily Thornberry, at a 2019 Labour Party

Conference fringe meeting, made the case that if it did not take a clear position, Labour would lose a lot more Remainers, whose policy issue was Brexit, than Leavers, whose interests would be better served by a Labour government anyway: the Remain vote in Leave seats were the party's ballast, as the only guaranteed vote.[29] Pike and Diamond sum up the web of contradictions at the heart of Brexit for the Labour leadership: 'from the standpoint of the majority of Labour people (though not all), the Brexit agenda was a Conservative one, driven by politicians who prioritised restricting migration'.[30] Yet within the more 'traditional' parts of the Corbyn coalition, Brexit was viewed as something 'heartland' seats had voted for, a constituency of voters Labour could not betray.

Managing an undisciplined PLP and the collapse of collective responsibility

The shock of the result upon the PLP cannot be underestimated, generating feelings of disbelief and even distress. Brexit seemed to have happened almost by accident, triggered by a referendum called by a Conservative Prime Minister who did not even support the idea. On the day of the referendum, 23 June 2016, Remain had a ten-point lead, and most people went to bed thinking there was no chance Brexit would win. Whether or not they had secretly wished for a Leave victory, the Labour leadership was not prepared for this result and had not even drafted a response to it.[31] As a result, when Corbyn was doorstepped by journalists in the morning, he briefly stated that the party must respect the vote and then said in his first TV interview that Article 50 should be invoked, giving the impression that this was what he had expected and wanted all along. Yet McDonnell explains that Corbyn's use of the word 'now' was meant as a logical consequence of the vote, and not as a need to rush.[32] He argues that accepting the referendum result quickly was a way to testify to the credibility of a future Labour government: 'I worked on the basis that "the result is not what we wanted, but it's the result". So we're going to have to get on and demonstrate, if we were in government, what we'd be doing is trying to protect the economy as best we could. So we had to get on with the job and try and get some form of deal that got the best out of a very bad job, unfortunately.' In terms of party management, this was a seriously misguided strategy.[33]

Such a reaction failed to resonate with the huge emotional impact of the result for the overwhelming majority of the party (PLP, staff and grass-roots members) and two-thirds of Labour voters.[34] This partly explains why the referendum result generated such a backlash against the Corbyn team inside the party in the blame game which followed, with fingers pointing at Corbyn as the one who had single-handedly made Brexit possible. This view found one of its strongest expressions in Mandelson's comments, in a 2016 BBC documentary, that Corbyn had deliberately sabotaged the Remain campaign.

The emotional shock meant that many felt that the result should be overturned: the referendum itself, and especially the campaign which had led up to it, seemed to leave the whole process open to accusations of having been undemocratic and manipulated by dark forces. Arguments were made that the referendum was consultative only, that the outlandish claims made by the Leave camp had not been called out. Yet, with the Conservatives in government, and with the Labour Party itself being split to an extent – although the vast majority were in favour of Remain, a significant minority of MPs were not – the Labour leadership opted for accepting the result and getting on with it, with a view among some in the Shadow Cabinet to possibly be tactical about it, with a consultation on a deal further down the line.[35] The strategy consisting of exploiting the deep divisions on the issue within the Conservative Party seemed a sound one at the time.

From this point on, the PLP displayed historical levels of indiscipline on the issue of Brexit, illustrating a complete breakdown of collective responsibility. In the context of the referendum result, the result was the focus of the PLP's anger, as well as a lever to oust the leader. McDonnell recalls being warned very early on by Rosie Winterton, Labour's chief whip at the time, that if the Brexit result went wrong – i.e. if the referendum came out in favour of Brexit – this would be the trigger for a major coup against Corbyn, on the basis that there was a build-up of people talking to the media, arguing that the Labour leader wasn't doing enough in the Brexit campaign.[36] The party quickly descended into a sort of open warfare.

For Corbyn's supporters, such as McDonnell, Brexit gave hardcore opponents of the leader the opportunity of linking up with others who simply felt disoriented as a result of the Brexit vote. So, opposition within the PLP resulted from an alliance of dissenters who were never going to accept Corbyn's leadership with others who were emotionally distressed at the Brexit result and wanted to believe that it could be reversed. McDonnell's view is that Brexit was instrumentalised to bring down Corbyn: 'certainly the Brexit issue was used as a device by the most sectarian of the Parliamentary Labour Party to find Jeremy as the scapegoat to further their ambition of removing him from the leadership. If it hadn't been Brexit, they would have tried to find some other issue.'[37] But Corbyn was able to see off the leadership challenge, thanks to his standing among the party's grass roots.

In 2017, the leadership fought the election on an anti-austerity platform and successfully resisted attempts by Theresa May to frame it in terms of the Brexit debate. This opened a window of opportunity for the leadership post-2017, when it could have taken the time to define a clear line on Brexit. Some semblance of cohesion was restored in the vote on triggering Article 50 (where MPs were whipped to support and only about fifty people voted against or abstained), which seemed to vindicate the cautious and nuanced approach to the topic. But, displaying again a tragic lack of strategic thinking, the leadership pushed the issue to the side rather than tackling it head-on.

Such a position was in fact not sustainable. A nuanced approach required keeping the different groups on side. But Corbyn was not good at bringing together conflicting views and being decisive in stating what the majority view was so as to be able to impose a particular line; there was no consequence for voting against the whip (as was the case of Jon Trickett and Ian Lavery). Such a lack of guidance is bound to have contributed to the breakdown of party discipline in the Shadow Cabinet and among MPs at large. By the beginning of 2019, Brexit had become the dominant issue at play, subsuming all others. At this point, the task of managing party splits over Brexit had become an impossible one.

Managing a divided LOTO

One of the big question marks of the debate on Labour's position on Brexit revolved around Corbyn's own views. Seen from the outside, and particularly in the eyes of the hostile media, his stance was a combination of indecisiveness and disingenuousness. Yet, according to people who worked closely with him, it was an exaggeration to consider that Corbyn was fundamentally anti-EU: he could be said to be Eurosceptic – sharing, with most on the hard left at the time, the Bennite view of the EU as a 'capitalist club' – but not on a par with more strident voices such as Kate Hoey or Gisela Stuart. He did not actually seek to actively aid the UK's exit from the EU. His main weakness was an inability to 'read the room' and to register the emotional nature of the issue – which, it must be recalled, was something completely new in the UK, where there had been no affective attachment to the idea of Europe prior to the referendum.

At odds with the binary terms of the referendum, Corbyn's 'remain and reform' position was striving for nuance: he considered that the EU had positive aspects (it could be used to coordinate across Europe on a number of key issues such as tax avoidance, the environment or workers' rights) and more negative ones, such as the directives against public ownership which stood in the way of a socialist programme. The problem was that such positioning was inappropriate in this particular context, in response to a Leave campaign focused almost exclusively on emotional language and arguments, where the EU was construed as an oppressor from which the UK needed to liberate itself. Corbyn's inadequacy in articulating the pro-EU party line lay largely in the fact that he did not feel strongly about the issue, something which put him out of step with party sentiment, both among MPs and the grass roots.[38]

How much the Corbyn leadership was divided on the issue is open to debate, and very conflicting accounts of what went on at the heart of LOTO are to be found in Oliver Eagleton's chapter on Brexit in *The Starmer*

Project,[39] which was criticised by Andrew Fisher for an account which, in his view, exaggerated divisions within the leadership and 'unintentionally infantilises Corbyn'.[40] Insiders such as John McDonnell and Katy Clark insisted in interviews that even if there existed a range of views on Brexit within LOTO, from a soft Brexit position to revoking Article 50, these were not irreconcilable stances: it was more a matter of degree.

Before the shades of opinion within the leadership congealed into a clear split between the Brexit 'hardliners', such as Karie Murphy and Seumas Milne, who considered that Labour should not deviate from its initial stance of respecting the outcome of the referendum,[41] and those who later moved to supporting the People's Vote campaign, there was a perception in much of LOTO that achieving a Labour government was far more important that staying in or leaving the EU: the once-in-a-lifetime chance of a socialist government needed to be seized, as it might never come back. Indeed, the circumstances of Corbyn's rise to power had been a combination of unintended consequences never to be repeated.

But, as the People's Vote campaign gathered pace in July 2019, John McDonnell was believed to have been urging Corbyn to sack his two most senior aides, Murphy and Milne, who were still opposed to Labour committing to backing Remain in a second referendum. The eventual departure from the Leader's Office, in October 2019, of Murphy and other key aides (such as political secretary Amy Jackson), blamed for the damaging Brexit row that had dominated the Labour Conference in Brighton and the failed putsch against Tom Watson, left Corbyn increasingly isolated within the Shadow Cabinet, with McDonnell now rumoured to have the support of a majority of his colleagues.

An insider's leak to *The Times*[42] gave an account of the meeting held on 15 October 2019 during which his senior colleagues openly defied Corbyn and called for Labour to back a second referendum on Boris Johnson's deal. Allies of McDonnell, such as Shadow Business Secretary Rebecca Long-Bailey, were now pushing Corbyn to move to an unambiguously pro-Remain stance. In an interview for *The Andrew Marr Show*, Long-Bailey said that she would back a second confirmatory referendum on a Johnson deal, thus contradicting Corbyn's stance, and suggested that 'many colleagues' were of a similar opinion. According to a Corbyn loyalist MP quoted in the same *Times* article, this was proof that McDonnell was 'flexing his muscles to show that he is the one calling the shots.'

Yet John McDonnell himself kept downplaying talks of civil war, telling for example the *Today* programme on BBC Radio 4: 'do not mistake democracy for division. It isn't – what we're having is an honest debate.' At the same time, he was explicit in supporting the notion that no future deal could be better than Britain staying in the EU, in contradiction to Corbyn's stance. So, while stating that talk of a split was a 'myth'[43] and being generally reluctant to acknowledge differences of opinion with Corbyn even when they were blatant, McDonnell also acknowledged that he and Corbyn did 'disagree on things', adding that this was because Corbyn was in a different position from him because, as party leader, he had a duty to 'build consensus'. But the Shadow Chancellor's changed approach on Brexit was bound to have had a strong influence on Corbyn's reluctant acceptance of the second referendum as a means to pacify an increasingly restless party.

Managing the grass roots: 'Love Corbyn Hate Brexit'

That Corbyn alienated the membership and sections of Momentum is one of the most puzzling aspects of his management of Brexit. Upon his second victory in 2016, Corbyn had pledged to give more say to the membership. With a 2018 YouGov poll showing that some 90 per cent of Labour members would vote to stay in if there were a new referendum, and 86 per cent would back a public vote on the outcome of Brexit negotiations, Europe turned out to be the biggest test of 'member power'.[44] The annual Conference was the arena where the growing discrepancy between the leadership and its grass-roots base was played out publicly.

In 2017, Momentum had managed to head off embarrassment for Jeremy Corbyn by blocking a vote on Brexit at the annual Conference, whipping delegates against prioritising a Brexit debate.[45] But in the following conferences, in 2018 and 2019, the party tore itself apart over the issue of Brexit and the second referendum. Indeed the 2018 annual Conference was the scene for a 'tug-of-war over whether the party should endorse a second referendum on a Brexit deal', putting Corbyn 'in the uncomfortable position of being out of step with his most ardent supporters', and throwing up 'important questions about power in the party and the Corbyn project, as well as Brexit'.[46] Over 140 Brexit motions – a record for any single issue – were submitted to the Conference by local parties and unions,[47] virtually all of these either calling for the party to oppose Brexit or/and pushing for a public vote on any deal. Many wanted Labour to make support for a public vote explicit in its next manifesto.

Yet the leadership instead came up with a muddled motion calling for a general election or, if this was not achieved, a public consultation; it was unclear whether this would include an option to remain in the EU. The carefully worded compromise motion, presented during the debate on the morning of 25 September 2017, was designed to manage internal divisions by setting out a sequence of steps, including a public vote option. It proposed 'full participation in the Single Market', the idea that 'Labour MPs must vote against any Tory deal failing to meet these [the 6 tests] tests in full', and, crucially: 'If we cannot get a general election Labour must support all options remaining on the table, including campaigning for a public vote'. The motion did not explicitly refer to Remain as an option, despite the fact that the membership backed this. It was voted overwhelmingly.

One key player in this vote was Momentum, who decided just before the Conference not to take a position on Brexit and did not whip delegates either way on any motion about a 'people's vote', agreeing instead to launch a consultation of members on Brexit later in the year. In the event, the results of Momentum's Brexit consultation, which was open for ten days on Momentum's digital democracy platform and completed by more than 6,500 members, published on 5 November 2018, showed that only 17 per cent of respondents did not support a public vote, and that 41 per cent were in favour in all circumstances, with an extra 28 per cent supporting it as an option if there was no general election, and 12 per cent only if there was no election.[48]

At the following Conference, in September 2019, Labour's internal divisions were magnified, as the party could again not agree on the wording of a Brexit motion to be presented to Conference. Party activists submitted ninety motions on Brexit, with 90 per cent of these being 'anti-Brexit'. Although Corbyn had come out in favour of a public vote before the Conference, he now proposed that Labour's position during a future referendum should remain neutral, a position which would eventually be carried by the Conference on 23 September, despite strong opposition. Behind the scene, the role of Momentum was once again crucial: it was decided during a phone meeting on the Monday morning, after pressure was exerted by the Leader's Office, to support the leadership's position and reject the motion which proposed taking a clear Remain stance, a move which was publicly opposed by Jon Lansman, who said he was 'incredibly disappointed with the process by which the NEC statement on Brexit was produced [...] there was no meeting, no discussion, no consultation with the membership'.[49]

In the end, the Conference had to vote on two contradictory motions, one demanding a public vote with Labour campaigning for Remain, which was supported by CLPs, the other supporting the position put forward by the NEC, which also mandated a public vote but gave no indication as to Labour's position in any referendum, a manoeuvre which was vigorously opposed by some delegates, many of whom were seen wearing 'Love Corbyn Hate Brexit' T-shirts.[50] The NEC statement proposed holding a one-day conference to decide. Keir Starmer stated in his speech that 'in 2016 millions of people wanted change. They told us the system was not working. We need a fundamental shift. We have to defend them, and we will. A radical Labour government.' A delegate urged that 'we cannot tell Brexit voters that they are stupid and that they are racist'.[51] Observing the debate and the reactions it generated, it was very difficult to see how the two camps could come to a compromise position, with anti-Corbyn delegates in very combative mood, waving 'Stop Brexit' placards and heckling. When a supporter of the NEC-backed composite echoed the call for a special conference to decide, a group of young pro-Remain attendees on the balcony shouted back that 'this is the democratic conference!' and 'you are at a conference now. Decide now!' The impression was that of a party in disarray and lacking clear direction.

The voting process over the two Brexit motions was very confusing. On composite 13, which the leadership opposed, after a show of hands seemed to show that it had been carried, Wendy Nichols, in the chair, stated that General Secretary Jennie Formby, sitting next to her, had seen more clearly that it was rejected. Refusing to grant a card vote, she then called another show of hands and announced it as lost, to a prolonged outcry in the room. NEC veteran Ann Black wrote that although she believed that the chair's decision had been correct, the voting process seemed to break Conference decision-making rules, since it contradicted the Delegates' Report which stated that 'Where a show of hands is unclear a card vote can be taken having been either requested by delegates or by the decision of the Chair'. She concludes on this episode, writing that 'There were strong views on all sides, but once the debate had been framed as a vote of confidence in the leader, it was bound to end as it did.'[52]

The divisions played out at Conference again illustrate the tensions caused by the nature of the Brexit issue. The hotly contested NEC statement insisted that 'Brexit is dividing our country; let's not let it divide our party'. A pro-Corbyn CWU delegate regretted that the toxic populist issue of Brexit had 'drowned out many of the debates we should be having today'. He stressed that 'Labour can unite the country'.[53] But in the eyes of Remain activists and MPs, the party was trying to use the NEC to crush democratic debate and silence the views of a clear majority of party members. In the words of Clive Lewis, Shadow Treasury Minister: 'This move is just plain wrong. How can this be defended? We, the left, took over the leadership of this party promising internal democracy, promising a new kind of politics. And yet here we are, with a leadership apparently determined to shut down democratic debate on the crucial issue of the day, probably relying on union bloc votes to outvote the members.' One Momentum activist was quoted as saying: 'In Liverpool we will see whether we really have become a party of the members. Or are we still one of party management?'[54]

The role of the unions

The 2019 Brexit Conference vote pitched Corbyn, Momentum and some of the biggest unions, including Unite and the GMB, against much of the party's membership, Shadow Cabinet ministers such as Emily Thornberry and UNISON. Ultimately, the leadership relied on the trade union bloc votes – still wielding 50 per cent of the total Conference share – to overcome the mass membership and to push through Corbyn's policy agenda on Brexit. In the Economy, Business and Trade debate at that conference, Len McCluskey had 'implored' the Conference to 'keep your eyes on the prize' – a Corbyn-led government – and to give Corbyn the support he needed.[55] Thus the trade unions held the balance of power, with Unite, the GMB and CWU backing the leader's position, while UNISON and the Transport Salaried Staffs' Association (TSSA) opposed it, and 'saved Corbyn from defeat in the face of widespread opposition from Remain activists'.[56]

In September 2017, a few months after the general election, at a time when the party was in upbeat mood, Corbyn was hopeful that he had moved the party to a 'jobs-first Brexit' position 'that maintains and develops workers' rights, and consumer and environmental protections and uses powers returned from Brussels to support a new industrial strategy'.[57] Yet TUC General Secretary Frances O'Grady was putting pressure on Corbyn to soften the Labour Party's Brexit position by insisting that staying in the Single Market was the best way to protect British workers. The three main unions (Unite, UNISON, GMB) were comforted in their stance by the publication, in September 2018, of the results of a survey carried out among their members, which indicated that over two-thirds wanted a new referendum and a majority wanted to remain within the EU (61 per cent vs 35 per cent opposing opinions for Unite and UNISON; 55 per cent vs 37 per cent for GMB).[58] Crucially, the survey also indicated that they considered that priority should be given to preserving trade rather than controlling immigration (65 per cent vs 27 per cent for Unite; 68 per cent vs 22 per cent for UNISON; 58 per cent vs 32 per cent for GMB). These results showed that the positions of the members of these three unions had significantly changed since the Brexit vote. As a result, Corbyn, who had previously ruled out keeping Britain in the Single Market after Brexit, softened his position significantly. Concerned that the unions would undermine the party's agenda for change if they backed a referendum on the EU exit deal, Labour announced at the 2019 TUC conference that the party had adopted 'A Manifesto for Labour Law: towards a comprehensive revision of workers' rights'.[59]

Even if they agreed on the main objectives, the unions played complex games during the period, which ended up with the House of Commons rejecting Theresa May's proposals multiple times. Their attitudes reflected differences in orientations, but also, and more importantly here, the links that their respective leaders had with the Labour Party leadership and the support they were prepared to provide to Corbyn's oscillating strategy. Indeed the major unions had been hostile to Brexit in 2016, but in 2019 they were among the main supporters of Corbyn, whose position in this debate, as we have seen, was deeply ambiguous. The debate mainly revolved around the desirability of a second referendum, which was supported by some of the anti-Brexit unions, while others, such as Unite, were prepared to support the process of exiting the EU to go ahead in return for the government's commitment to maintain workers' rights.[60]

After the disastrous European elections, there was again a very small window of opportunity to make Labour's stance clear. In the end, after a meeting with Corbyn, the five major unions – Unite, UNISON, GMB, USDAW and CWU[61] – adopted a common text on 8 July 2019 which defined the position that the Labour Party should adopt in two hypothetical scenarios:[62] the text required a popular vote on any solution put forward by the government. The complex compromise could be reached partly because the unions all agreed that the No Deal option was to be avoided at all costs. But even if this unexpected compromise put an end to the open conflict between the unions, it sent mixed messages to trade union members and to voters at large. Overall, Corbyn's efforts to keep the unions on board delayed any decision being made regarding clarifying Labour's stance on Brexit.

In the summer of 2019, as Corbyn came under huge pressure to fully support a second referendum and back staying in the EU, he met the leaders of twelve affiliated trade unions, including GMB, UNISON, ASLEF, USDAW and, crucially, Unite, whose boss Len McCluskey had been resisting a shift in the party's position. On 8 July, it was announced that a surprise consensus had been reached and that union leaders had agreed that the party would demand a referendum on any deal struck between the Conservative government and the EU, and would back Remain (albeit with the caveat that Labour could still support leaving the EU under a Brexit deal of its own). The document read that 'The Labour Party should confirm that whatever deal is negotiated by the new Tory prime minister or an exit based on no deal should be put to the people in a public confirmatory vote.' It said such a referendum should offer the choice of the Tory position (either a deal or no deal) versus Remain, and that 'in this event the Labour party should campaign to remain in the European Union.'[63] This 'surprise consensus' was seen as quite a coup for Corbyn and a means to force any remaining sceptics within the Shadow Cabinet to agree to the new position.[64] A *Guardian* article the following day[65] considered this to show that 'The wider Labour movement seems to have successfully asserted itself against the leader's closest advisers', but asked, is it 'too little too late?'

Doggedly pursuing compromise? The 'constructive ambiguity' approach

One question which dominates discussions of Labour's position on Brexit is how deliberate the lack of clarity was. Was Corbyn seeking inspiration from Harold Wilson, who had succeeded in positioning himself as a broker between contending camps when managing party splits over the same issue in the early 1970s? This would grant some intentionality to his careful use of language in the period running from the referendum campaign to the 2019 general election and would reflect more than a mere will to evade the issue of Brexit. It could be interpreted as an attempt at using the discursive strategy of 'constructive ambiguity' to manage the issue of Brexit, while trying to advance in other areas of policy.[66] John McDonnell explains that he met very early with Hilary Benn to talk about Brexit and the Labour Party's role in the campaign: 'I took the Harold Wilson view that there would be differences of view within the Labour Party and therefore we should allow those differences to be aired and people to campaign on the different sides as they saw fit'.[67] And although he describes him as quite hardline in wanting a very strong pro-European campaign, he says that Benn did concur that there could be differences of view, even though there was a Labour Party position.

Writing in 2018, after the 2017 general election and before the 2019 election, at a period when caution and strategic ambiguity seemed to work, Patrick Diamond asserted that 'despite a long track record of principled opposition to the European Union (EU), Corbyn has acted prudently on Europe since becoming leader, paying attention to the need to preserve party unity and shore up Labour's electoral coalition,' 'The position that Corbyn has adopted on the Brexit negotiations is redolent of Harold Wilson's approach in the early 1970s.'[68] This echoed Labour strategist Steve Howell's judgement that 'Corbyn has, much to the frustration of some, doggedly pursued an attempt to unite people across the Brexit divide through a deal that protects trade and standards. And this now puts him in a position akin to Wilson's as someone who can credibly act as an honest broker in giving people a final say.'[69]

The June 2017 'victory in defeat' election result (Labour lost, but gained thirty-six seats) allowed the leadership to brush over the detail of the result, which showed problems mounting in Leave constituencies and in the heartlands, and take it as a vindication of the leadership's strategy of ambiguity. Labour fought the election on a promise to preserve 'the benefits of the single market and the customs union'. The relative goodwill generated by the result – which stemmed from the idea that a Labour victory was not completely impossible – presented a window of opportunity which the leadership did not take advantage of, and Labour strategists continued to favour ambiguity as their preferred tactic.

But the lull was short lived. The compromising stance faced two main new challenges: Boris Johnson's simplistic claim to 'get Brexit done', which, as the 2019 general election showed, had a very strong appeal to the public, and the launch, in April 2018, of the cross-party and multi-organisation People's Vote campaign, with Tom Baldwin – former Director of Communications for Miliband – becoming its director in June. Its most obvious achievements were the large marches in October 2018 and March 2019, where an estimated one million people – making it one of the biggest marches in British political history – marched through London to demand a People's Vote.[70] This contributed to entrenching the idea of a second referendum, further splitting opinion within the party around uncompromising opinions.

Indeed Tom Baldwin realised that some of the MPs involved in the campaign were mobilising to create a breakaway party, with huge financial resources being mobilised to that end.[71] John McDonnell in particular was very worried that the People's Vote and then the Independent Group was going lead to a repeat of the SDP scenario, and ostensibly devoted considerable time and effort to keeping People's Vote MPs on side, making sure key campaigners – such as Alastair Campbell – were seen to meet him in his office or in Portcullis House.[72] Having calculated that the number of defectors could have gone up to seventy at one point, and believing that such a move would be supported by some of the liberal media, he considered it an existential threat to the Labour Party.

McDonnell's efforts paid off and averted a split, but a succession of leaks to the media give an idea of how deep the divisions ran among the PLP in the last few months of the Corbyn leadership. The Shadow Cabinet meeting of 25 June 2019, which took place shortly after the party had haemorrhaged votes in the European Parliament elections, coming third behind the Liberal Democrats, was leaked to HuffPost journalist Paul Waugh, who wrote a piece describing the atmosphere at the meeting as 'heated'.[73] The meeting took place in the context of Unite making it clear to Corbyn it would not back a second referendum on 'any' Brexit deal and Corbyn explaining that further consultation with trade union bosses was needed before any decision could be made. John McDonnell warned that the current lack of clarity was causing severe damage to morale among party members and voters who supported Corbyn: he likened the party's position on Brexit to 'a slow-moving car crash'. According to the leaked information, other frontbenchers pushing for a change of policy included Diane Abbott, who stressed that the discontent among the mass of party members was now widespread, Emily Thornberry, who said 'we need a decision today – this is about leadership', and Keir Starmer, who stated 'We can't have half a policy' and also stressed that backing a referendum would instantly prompt the next question of which side the party would take in that referendum – and it had to clearly campaign for Remain.

On the other side, Corbyn's move to delay a decision was backed up by Party Chair Ian Lavery and Shadow Cabinet Office Minister Jon Trickett. Unite was accused of being the main culprit for the delay, even though the GMB union, which had pushed hard for a public 'confirmatory ballot', was not yet ready to campaign for Remain in a referendum, while UNISON General Secretary Dave Prentis made it clear that he wanted a decision to be taken quickly. Thus not only were there tensions between those who were primarily concerned about bringing the unions on board and those urging for a quick resolution – Phil Wilson MP, who had led attempts in the House of Commons to get a new referendum, lamented that 'we have to listen to muddle, confusion and the sound of the can being kicked listlessly down a never-ending road' – but there also were disagreements between the unions, who could not agree on a compromise position.

By 2019, what could have been perceived as a clever attempt at reconciling antagonistic positions and keeping the party – and the country – united, hoping 'to appear as the magnanimous and unifying leader who respects the will of the people (and of the party) and who wants to heal a bitterly divided country',[74] had become untenable. Corbyn's 'three-pronged approach to Brexit' (a Labour government would negotiate a new withdrawal agreement; it would then hold a referendum with the option to Remain; and the official position of the party would be agreed three months after the general election) was at odds with party sentiment, still lacked clarity and 'fuel[ed] the suspicion that Corbyn's alleged neutrality [was] nothing of the sort'.[75] This left him open to accusations that he was ignoring the voices of the majority of Labour MPs, members and voters, as well as many in the Shadow Cabinet.

The missed opportunity of soft Brexit?

There is an argument that, rather than seeking to contest the democratic nature of the referendum, Labour should have moved on from the shock of the result and started to make the case for a soft Brexit early on. Instead, over time, positions solidified into not accepting the result rather than mitigating it, which led to the worst possible outcome from a Remain perspective: a hard Brexit. Increased polarisation hid the fact that many nuances existed within the PLP, and meant that the option of soft Brexit, arguably the best realistic option, was set aside, since people would simply not agree to sit down and discuss the options. Why the party leadership was unable to foster a climate of compromise and consensus is key to understanding how Brexit played such a major part in sinking the Corbyn project.

The series of indicative votes in Parliament played out to kill any soft Brexit solution.[76] MPs were presented with five options: Theresa May's withdrawal agreement, a no-deal Brexit, staying in the Customs Union, staying in the Single Market, and the so-called Common Market 2.0 idea. Although some of the options were highly compatible, some Labour MPs remained entrenched in supporting their preferred option, at the exclusion of any other, however close. The result of such intransigence was that all five options were rejected. As a procedural fix for a political problem, the 'indicative votes' were therefore a failure, since MPs refused to compromise and settle for an acceptable Brexit deal. It must be pointed out that this uncompromising attitude applied in particular to Remain MPs. This is because, as Rutter and Menon explain, to achieve a second referendum, 'it was as important for the People's Vote crowd as it was for the ERG [European Research Group] Brexit ultras to kill off the idea of a soft Brexit'.[77] Labour arch-Remainers such as David Lammy and Ben Bradshaw thus played their part in ensuring that various soft Brexit compromises were defeated.

In other words, soft Brexit was something that all sides could agree to disagree with. More particularly, a political mindset which prizes adversarialism over collaboration could not come to terms with the compromising approach required for a soft Brexit option to be viable, even if this was the only realistic avenue for an eventual form of reintegration into the EU down the line. And so it was that while what most Labour MPs really wanted to achieve was to stop Brexit, they unintentionally contributed to delivering a hard Brexit, which was the preferred outcome of only the twenty-eight members of the Conservative ERG faction.[78] Johnson's Withdrawal Agreement Bill was approved by the House of Commons on 22 October 2019 on its second reading with the backing of nineteen Labour MPs who broke a three-line whip to vote with the government.[79] It was the first time any Brexit deal had secured a majority, after Theresa May had lost three votes. After he lost a timetable motion, making it impossible to proceed in time for the 31 October deadline, Johnson proposed an early election to take place on 12 December.

The degree of factional strife and the largely artificial polarisation over Brexit precluded the finding of any common ground, thus squeezing out the soft middle option. Yet, two years after the 2019 election, poll analysis was showing that attitudes towards Brexit had started to change, the soft Brexit option now a position closest to the wishes of the majority of Labour voters. As the true cost of Brexit is being felt, this trend continues to grow. John Curtice's analysis of polling data in the summer of 2024 led him to conclude that 'Labour might feel that while their supporters might want a closer relationship with the EU than the party is offering, at least they are likely to back any specific steps that might be taken over the next five years towards softening Brexit'.[80]

Brexit post-Corbyn

How much Brexit played a part in the 2019 general election defeat is a moot point. The Brexit section of Labour's manifesto was based on the policy adopted at Conference of negotiating a softer Brexit deal and putting it to the people in a referendum with the option to Remain. Most people's attention was fixed on the fracturing effects of the issue on the Conservative Party, believing that they would incur damaging electoral consequences. This can partially be taken to account for the Labour leadership's failure to reach a compromise with Theresa May, which was blamed on her intransigent stance: there is a view that Corbyn in fact had been 'content to allow the chaos of Brexit to persist as long as it creates the possibility of achieving his own overriding aim: forcing a general election'.[81] Yet there is no doubt that the ambiguity, a forlorn attempt to keep Leave voters on side, in fact cost the party a great number of Remain voters. Indeed, according to internal party figures, 'the total support lost [just] to the Liberal Democrats equalled that lost to the Conservatives and Brexit party combined'.[82] Added to the votes lost to the Greens, the SNP and Plaid Cymru, overall, Labour lost more votes to Remain parties than to Leave parties, even if this was not evenly distributed.

Starmer's own trajectory since becoming party leader has undergone a remarkable turnaround, from his involvement with the People's Vote campaign, to stating, as Prime Minister, that he would not seek to rejoin or even sign up to the Single Market, the Customs Union or freedom of movement. Eager to pitch himself and a future Labour government as responsible and legitimate, Starmer dropped all attempts to counter or even temper Brexit: 'By December 2020, just as McSweeney was warning that Leave voters were still wary of the Labour Party, Starmer was all but confirming that he would whip his MPs to make Boris Johnson's Brexit happen – the very last thing that would have been expected of him a year earlier.'[83] Even if this caused the biggest rebellion Starmer had to face, with thirty-seven Labour MPs refusing to vote for the deal, the strategy was clear: in the words of Rachel Reeves, 'the politics are such that we cannot win an election if we don't get behind Leave'.[84] This raises the question of how much of Starmer's stance under Corbyn had been driven by tactical considerations, paving the way for his intended bid for the leadership. As party leader, Starmer has striven to brush the toxic issue of Brexit under the carpet. In early 2023, he even embraced the 'take back control' Brexit slogan, saying that he wanted to turn Brexit 'into a solution',[85] and stated just before the 2024 general election that he ruled out rejoining the EU, the Single Market or the Customs Union.

For now, Starmer therefore backs a 'twin track' strategy of building closer security ties with the EU while ruling out the Single Market, Customs Union and free movement,[86] a timid approach which is likely to cause problems in terms of party management. London mayor Sadiq Khan expressed his frustration, saying, 'there will need to be a conversation about whether we have a better future inside the EU or outside of it'.[87] Despite a series of polls in 2024 and 2025 showing that close to 60 per cent of Britons, including a majority of Leavers, would now vote to rejoin the bloc even if this meant a return to free movement,[88] Starmer will not make the case for rejoining the EU. Starmer's Brexit silence has meant that it has not constituted a management issue overtly, mainly because the prospect of winning power overrode all else. But the relationship with the EU and the problems caused by Brexit are bound to resurface. The electoral quandary is still there, albeit hidden by the huge swing to Labour. Even though the results of the 2024 general election and subsequent polls show Reform as Labour's main overall competitor, in January 2025 voting intention surveys nevertheless confirmed the idea that Labour is 'losing more voters to the Greens and Lib Dems than to Reform'.[89] There is also a contradiction between Starmer's growth policy and his stance on not joining the Single Market or Customs Union, since most economists agree that failing to do so would place a serious drag on the UK's growth prospects. Donald Trump's presidential election victory on 5 November 2024 and the return of tariffs are bound to force a shift in the UK government's position. Brexit is thus very likely to be a recurring feature of Starmer's premiership.

Conclusion

Brexit was never going to be an easy issue for the Labour Party. It turned out to be one of the biggest tests of party management. Although the EU had arguably motivated the party split in 1981, and strong disagreements had existed under Wilson, it was not expected to create such deep divisions in the 2010s. Corbyn and his team failed to foresee the importance the issue would take and the damage it could cause their project. This was because the party's main attitude to Europe had been one of indifferent acceptance, with only a very limited fringe actively against and a limited group enthusiastic about it, while the bulk of the party was mildly critical of the EU. Brexit brought to the fore divisions which had been mostly dormant. The nature of the issue was such that it cut across the party, separating Corbyn from his grass roots and dividing LOTO.

'Corbyn's leadership was partly destroyed by Brexit, by the remorseless attacks of its internal and external opponents, and by its own severe mistakes.'[90] The leadership, whose mindset on the issue belonged to another era, did not analyse the situation correctly and failed to react quickly enough, thus disappointing the Remainers and failing to persuade the Leavers. The priority for the Corbyn leadership was to achieve a Labour government. In trying to secure this objective, they placed themselves in an acrobatic position designed to reconcile the two stances. Despite later claims that absolute clarity on the topic was the only possible route, this compromise position was seen as viable by many at the time. The mark of a good politician is often seen as being able to convey different messages to different people. In addition, Labour's broad church approach had in the past made it possible to accommodate a range of varied opinions on some topics.

But Brexit was a different kind of issue which polarised opinion in ways not seen before (partly because the decision was made through a referendum). Entrenched factionalism precluded the attitude necessary to reach a compromise, even at the cost of a Labour defeat. Thus Brexit posed very specific managerial problems which the Corbyn leadership were not equipped to solve, both because of their mindset and worldviews and because of their lack of experience of leadership. Corbyn was not able to arbitrate between the various centres of power and legitimacy in the party: members and unions were equally important in his view; he was subjected to contradictory forces from within LOTO; and was unable to make an executive decision to choose and stick to one line. In this context, neutrality was interpreted as acceptance or even as a cowardly means to let Brexit happen, which contradicted Corbyn's image as 'authentic'. Is there room for nuance in party leadership?

It may now be pointless to wonder whether things could have gone differently under another leader. The fact that the PLP felt no loyalty to Corbyn was certainly a major hindrance: the post-referendum 'coup' to oust him would have been unlikely to happen to another leader. Brexit thus acted both as a cause per se and as a proxy to disagreement with the Corbyn leadership in general. There was no will to compromise, in fear that this would help him.

At the same time as the Brexit imbroglio, the controversy over antisemitism was reaching crisis point, and the two fed into each other, dissipating trust and the inclination to compromise. The split over Brexit within the Corbyn camp was paralleled by a similar split over managing antisemitism, as we see in the next chapter, with a broadly similar alignment.

Notes

1 Michael Chessum and Caroline Flint, 'Should Labour be campaigning for a fresh vote on Brexit?', *Guardian*, 16 December 2018.
2 The other being antisemitism, explored in Chapter 7.
3 Tom Quinn, 'Behind the Brexit vote, Labour remains dangerously divided', *The Conversation*, 26 September 2018, theconversation.com
4 James Bulpitt, 'Conservative leaders and the "Euro-ratchet": Five doses of scepticism', *Political Quarterly*, 63:3 (1992), 258–75.
5 Although Peter Shore, for a time a staunch unilateralist who also promoted a nationalistic approach, is notoriously very difficult to place on the Labour left–right spectrum, and despite the fact that he was for a period close to Benn, his position came to be increasingly associated with the right. See Kevin Hickson, Jasper Miles and Harry Taylor, *Peter Shore: Labour's Forgotten Patriot* (London: Politico, 2020).
6 Matt Beech, 'Brexit and the Labour Party: Europe, cosmopolitanism and the narrowing of traditions', in Mark Bevir and Matt Beech (eds), *Interpreting Brexit. Reimagining Political Traditions* (Basingstoke, Palgrave Macmillan, 2022), pp. 37–54.
7 Philip Daniels, 'From hostility to "constructive engagement": The Europeanisation of the Labour Party', *West European Politics*, 21:1 (1998), 72–96.
8 pes.eu

9 Simon Bulmer, 'New Labour, new European policy? Blair, Brown and utilitarian supranationalism', *Parliamentary Affairs*, 61:4 (2008), 617.
10 *Ibid.*, p. 615.
11 Kai Oppermann, 'The Blair government and Europe: The policy of containing the salience of European integration', *British Politics*, 3 (2008), 157.
12 *Ibid.*, p. 160.
13 *Ibid.*
14 Bulmer, 'New Labour, new European policy?', p. 175.
15 See Ian Fitzgerald, Ron Beadle and Kevin Rowan, 'Trade unions and the 2016 UK European Union referendum', *Economic and Industrial Democracy*, 43:1 (2022), 388–409, DOI: 10.1177/0143831X19899483
16 Richard Hyman, *Understanding European Trade Unionism: Between Market, Class and Society* (London: Sage, 2001).
17 See Fitzgerald, Beadle and Rowan, 'Trade unions and the 2016 UK European Union referendum'.
18 RMT Press Office, 'Joint Union statement supporting a Leave vote'.
19 TUC, 'General Council statement on Brexit', 10 September 2018.
20 TUC, 'Risks 864 – 1 September 2018', 29 August 2018.
21 *Ibid.*
22 Emmanuelle Avril, 'Labour and the interplay of Brexit and electoral politics', *Journal of Contemporary European Studies*, 29:3 (2018), 335–50, DOI: 10.1080/14782804.2020.1846505
23 John Curtice, 'Is Labour's Brexit dilemma being misunderstood?', *UK in a Changing Europe* (2017), ukandeu.ac.uk
24 Andrew Harrop, 'Labour's Brexit dilemma', *Fabian Society*, December 2017, fabians.org.uk
25 Edward Fieldhouse, 'Labour's electoral dilemma', *British Election Study*, 10 October 2019, britishelectionstudy.com
26 Interview, Karie Murphy.
27 Interview, Dianne Hayter.
28 Tom Quinn, 'Behind the Brexit vote, Labour remains dangerously divided', *The Conversation*, 26 September 2018, theconversation.com
29 Personal notes from Conference.
30 Karl Pike and Patrick Diamond, 'Myth and meaning: "Corbynism" and the interpretation of political leadership', *British Journal of Politics and International Relations*, 23:4 (2021), 663–79, DOI: 10.1177/1369148121996252
31 Owen Jones, *This Land: The Struggle for the Left* (London: Penguin, 2020), pp. 179–80.
32 Interview, John McDonnell.
33 *Ibid.*
34 Interview, Ruth Lister.
35 *Ibid.*
36 Interview, John McDonnell.

37 *Ibid.*
38 Therefore the view that Corbyn was pig-headed on this issue and digging his heels in, secretly praying for Brexit and manoeuvring to get there, is misguided. Interview, Andrew Fisher.
39 Oliver Eagleton, *The Starmer Project: A Journey to the Right* (London: Verso 2022).
40 Andrew Fisher, 'Don't play the blame game', *Labour Hub*, 24 May 2022, hub.labour.org.uk
41 Interview, Karie Murphy.
42 Oliver Wright, 'Jeremy Corbyn isolated as shadow team defy him over new Brexit vote', *The Times*, 14 October 2019.
43 Jessica Elgot, 'Unions agree Labour should back Remain in referendum on Tory deal', *Guardian*, 8 July 2019.
44 Toby Helm and Daniel Boffey, 'Jeremy Corbyn "vindicated" as he pledges more power to Labour members', *Guardian*, 25 September 2016.
45 Sienna Rogers, 'Momentum to take no position on Brexit at Labour Conference', *LabourList*, 1 September 2018, labourlist.org
46 Quinn, 'Behind the Brexit vote'.
47 Sienna Rogers, 'Will Labour Conference change the party's Brexit policy?', *LabourList*, 21 September 2018, labourlist.org
48 Momentum, Members' Consultation on Brexit Results, 5 November 2018.
49 Rowena Mason and Ben Quinn, 'Labour rows over Brexit worsen before crucial votes at conference', *Guardian*, 23 September 2019.
50 Personal notes from Conference.
51 Personal notes from Conference.
52 Ann Black, 'Annual Conference', *Ann Black on the Record*, September 2019, annblack.co.uk/annual-conference-september-2019 [consulted 23 March 2025].
53 Personal notes from Conference.
54 Toby Helm, 'Corbyn faces clash with Labour members over second EU referendum', *Guardian*, 22 September 2018.
55 Personal notes from Conference.
56 Christopher Massey, 'Labour Conference pitted unions against members on the two biggest issues of the day', *The Conversation*, 2019, theconversation.com
57 Jeremy Corbyn, Speech to TUC Congress, 12 September 2017.
58 Peter Kellner, 'Two thirds of UNISON members polled said they would support a second public Brexit vote', *Guardian*, 8 September 2018.
59 Institute of Employment Rights (IER), 'A Manifesto for Labour Law: Towards a comprehensive revision of workers' rights' (Liverpool: IER, 2016). The policies included key recommendations made by the IER in its Manifesto for Labour Law, such as: the establishment of a Ministry of Labour (renamed a Ministry of Employment Rights); the restoration of sectoral collective bargaining; the repeal of the Trade Union Act 2016; Real Living Wage; equal rights for all

workers from day one; ban on zero-hour contracts; an independent Labour Inspectorate (renamed a Workers' Protection Agency); workers on company boards.

60 See James Pickard, 'UK union leaders "at war" over Brexit', *Financial Times*, 6 February 2019; Kevin Schofield, 'Trade unions split over whether Labour should back Remain in second EU referendum', *PoliticsHome*, 24 June 2019, politicshome.com.

61 In September 2018, the RMT warned the TUC against the idea of a campaign for a second referendum which would effectively call into question the 2016 referendum vote.

62 Jessica Elgot, 'Unions agree Labour should back Remain'; Iain Watson, 'Labour affiliated unions agree Brexit vote stance', *BBC News*, 8 July 2019.

63 'Labour affiliated unions agree Brexit vote stance', *BBC News*, 8 July 2019.

64 Elgot, 'Unions agree Labour should back Remain'.

65 Gaby Hinsliff, 'Labour is finally backing a second referendum. Is it too little, too late?', *Guardian*, 9 July 2019.

66 Stephen Bell, 'Do we really need a new "constructivist institutionalism" to explain institutional change?', *British Journal of Political Science*, 41:4 (2011), 883–906, DOI: 10.1017/S0007123411000147; Vivian Schmidt, 'Discursive institutionalism: The explanatory power of ideas and discourse', *Annual Review of Political Science*, 11:1 (2008), 303–26, DOI: 10.1146/annurev.polisci.11.060606.135342

67 Interview, John McDonnell.

68 Patrick Diamond, 'Brexit and the Labour Party. Euro-caution vs. Euro-fanaticism? The Labour Party's "constructive ambiguity" on Brexit and the European Union', in Patrick Diamond, Peter Nedergaard and Ben Rosamond (eds), *The Routledge Handbook of the Politics of Brexit* (London: Routledge, 2018).

69 Steve Howell, 'Brexit: Corbyn is following in Wilson's pragmatic footsteps', 19 September 2019, https://www.steve-howell.com/labours-approach-to-brexit-echoes-wilsons-pragmatism/ [consulted 23 March 2025].

70 Six million people signed an online petition to stop Brexit but this did not result from a People's Vote initiative.

71 Quoted in Jones, *This Land*, p. 190.

72 Interview, John McDonnell.

73 Paul Waugh, 'Jeremy Corbyn faces backlash as he postpones decision on second Brexit referendum', *Huff Post*, 25 June 2019.

74 Eunice Goes, 'Labour and Brexit: Corbyn's "neutrality" on a second referendum is not neutral', *LSE Blogs*, 23 September 2019, https://blogs.lse.ac.uk

75 *Ibid.*

76 Maddy Thimont Jack, 'Parliament once again rejected all Brexit options', Institute for Government, 2 April 2019, https://www.instituteforgovernment.org.uk

77 Jill Rutter and Anand Menon, 'Who killed soft Brexit?', *Prospect*, 9 November 2020.

78 For a thorough analysis of Labour's failure to achieve soft Brexit, see Tom Quinn, 'Why was there a hard Brexit? The British legislative party system, divided majorities and the incentives for factionalism', *Political Studies*, 72:1 (2022), 227–48, DOI: 10.1177/00323217221076353

79 Labour rebels were: Kevin Barron, Sarah Champion, Rosie Cooper, Jon Cruddas, Gloria De Piero, Jim Fitzpatrick, Caroline Flint, Mike Hill, Dan Jarvis, Emma Lewell-Buck, John Mann, Grahame Morris, Lisa Nandy, Melanie Onn, Stephanie Peacock, Jo Platt, Ruth Smeeth, Laura Smith and Gareth Snell.

80 John Curtice, 'What do Labour voters want Starmer to do about Brexit?', *UK in a Changing Europe* (blog), 2 July 2024, https://ukandeu.ac.uk

81 Craig Berry, 'Why Jeremy Corbyn secretly hopes his Brexit talks with Theresa May will fail', *The Conversation*, 9 April 2019, theconversation.com

82 Labour Party, 'General Election 2019 What happened? Initial top-level findings in relation to demography and geography', Unpublished Labour NEC document, 27 January 2020, cited in Paul Mason, 'Labour after Corbyn', Friedrich-Ebert-Stiftung, April 2020, https://library.fes.de/pdf-files/bueros/london/16782.pdf [consulted 21 March 2025].

83 Patrick Maguire and Gabriel Pogrund, *Get In: The Inside Story of Labour under Starmer* (London: The Bodley Head, 2025), p. 158.

84 *Ibid.*, p. 159.

85 'Starmer makes "take back control" pledge to voters', *BBC News*, 5 January 2023.

86 'Labour's Brexit conundrum', *The Week*, 18 April 2024.

87 'London mayor Sadiq Khan hints at Brexit disconnect with Keir Starmer', *Independent*, 20 August 2024.

88 See for example, Peter Walker and Jon Henley, 'Majority of Brexit voters "would accept free movement" to access single market', *Guardian*, 12 December 2024. This confirms a two-year-long trend, as detailed by John Curtice, 'Five years on: Why have public attitudes to Brexit changed?', *UK in a Changing Europe*, 31 January 2025, ukandeu.ac.uk

89 Luke O'Reilly, 'Labour losing more votes to Greens and Lib Dems than Reform', *LabourList*, 14 January 2025, labourlist.org

90 Owen Jones, 'Brexit and self-inflicted errors buried Labour in this election', *Guardian*, 18 December 2019.

7
Corbyn and the crisis over antisemitism

> I'm not sure there has ever been anything like the Labour antisemitism crisis in the history of British politics. It was ferocious and relentless and extraordinarily painful for people on all sides.
>
> Len McCluskey[1]

No issue had a greater polarising effect on the Labour Party between 2015 and 2019 than the alleged 'crisis of antisemitism'. Its impact dwarfed all other issues in the sheer vehemence and ferocity it unleashed and in the harm it inflicted on the party. On the one hand, there were those who alleged that antisemitism completely permeated the party while the Corbyn leadership at best looked on indifferently, at worst actually connived at it. On the other hand, there were those who insisted that the whole problem was wildly exaggerated and 'weaponised' in a cynical drive to demolish the party's left-wing leadership.

As well as causing turmoil in the party, the antisemitism crisis attracted a torrent of immensely damaging publicity. One report found that between 15 June 2015 and 31 March 2019 there were no less than 5,497 newspaper stories on the topic, nearly all negative, as well as very extensive coverage on television and on social media. The effect was to firmly implant in the public mind an impression of Labour as a party harbouring people with deeply unsavoury sentiments.[2] 'A prolonged drip feed' about the chaotic events, Owen Jones recalled, 'helped fundamentally change the British public's sense of Corbynism from something positive and hopeful to something poisonous and sinister.'[3] In this chapter, we investigate how the problem arose, the course it took, its magnitude and the reasons why it proved to be unmanageable.

Labour and Israel

Crucial to understanding the character of the antisemitism crisis was its entanglement with the highly emotive matter of the Israel–Palestinian question. From very early in its history, Labour had affirmed its sympathy for a Jewish state in Palestine, increasingly emphatically so as persecution of the Jews intensified. However once in power from 1945, and under the direction of Labour's powerful Foreign Secretary, Ernest Bevin, the new government altered its stance. Its priority was the preservation of Britain's imperial hegemony in the Middle East, and this was seen to require friendly relations with existing Arab states. According to the historian Ben Pimlott, Bevin had 'little sympathy for the aspirations of the Jews',[4] and he only very reluctantly, under intense American pressure and in response to the intractability of the conflict, delivered the matter for resolution to the UN. The UN proposed the partition of Palestine and the creation of both a Jewish and an Arab state. The UK abstained in the UN vote, but with both the US and the USSR voting for it, the plan passed, and, after the first of many wars, the state of Israel emerged triumphant in 1948.

From the 1950s onwards, Labour exhibited growing enthusiasm for the new Jewish state, reinforced by its ideological affinity with the Israel Labor Party, the dominant political force in Israel's first few decades. In the 1940s, Labour left-wingers, such as Richard Crossman, Michael Foot and Ian Mikardo, were among the keenest advocates of the formation of a Jewish state and castigated Bevin's handling of the issue.[5] But from the 1970s, criticism of Israel became increasingly common on the left. This was in response to a range of interconnected developments, such as the proliferation of illegal settlements on the West Bank, the multiplying violations of Palestinian rights in the occupied territories and the punitive and what were seen as disproportionate Israeli reprisals to terrorist incursions. Two leading leftists previously sympathetic to Israel, Eric Heffer and Tony Benn, resigned from the PLP group the Labour Friends of Israel, in protest against Israel's invasions of Lebanon and its opposition to Palestinian statehood.[6] However, the Labour left still firmly upheld Israel's right to exist and live in peace and security. For example, when Tony Benn was invited in 1984 by the Labour Movement Campaign for Palestine to agree that Israel was an 'ally of imperialism', he riposted: 'I am in favour of a Jewish state, and I believe the Jews are entitled to have security in Israel. I don't believe that a criticism of individual items of policy can be used to see Israel destroyed.'[7] Furthermore, the balance of opinion in the party, especially on the dominant centre right and within the leadership, remained strongly pro-Israel.[8] However, by the 1980s and 1990s, sympathy for the Palestinian cause had so increased as to become 'the default position' for many on the liberal and social democratic left, even 'a defining marker of what it means to be progressive'.[9] Though only small numbers on the far left and mostly outside the party questioned the Jewish state's right to exist, the pro-Israel consensus in the party had largely dissolved.

In 2010, Ed Miliband became Labour's first Jewish leader. By this time, criticism of Israel from the left was causing unease, anger and resentment within the Jewish community. In July 2014, in response to frequent rocket attacks, Israel launched a full-scale invasion of Gaza, causing more than 2,100 Palestinian deaths, as compared with 73 deaths of Israelis. Though Miliband supported Israeli airstrikes, he regarded their land incursion as a gross over-reaction. He stated that 'I cannot explain, justify, or defend the horrifying deaths of hundreds of Palestinians, including children and innocent civilians.' The effects would be 'more Palestinian suffering, more hatred and more recruits to the ranks of terrorist groups like Hamas'.[10] Miliband's comments provoked a furious response from the Jewish community. Its leading organ of opinion, the *Jewish Chronicle*, admonished him for his 'knee-jerk criticism of a nation defending itself from terrorism'.[11] Reports soon circulated that Jewish donors, regarding the party as 'too toxic for them', were deserting it. Miliband further infuriated Jewish opinion when, in October 2014, he whipped his MPs to support a motion calling for unilateral recognition of a Palestinian state.[12] Shortly before the 2015 general election, a poll commissioned by the *Jewish Chronicle* reported that only 22 per cent of Jewish voters intended to vote Labour, as compared to 69 per cent for the Tories. Almost three-quarters stated that Miliband's stance on Israel was an important factor in determining their vote.[13]

Corbyn's arrival

None of this augured well for the Jewish response to Corbyn's election. Miliband had emphasised his admiration for Israel, declaring that 'for me', Israel was 'the homeland for the Jewish people' and 'a sanctuary' for Jews fleeing persecution.[14] His successor, in contrast, had a long record as an uncompromising critic of Israel and a passionate champion of the Palestinian cause. In the 1980s he was a supporter of the Labour Movement Campaign for Palestine, which demanded the eradication of Zionism and the creation of a 'democratic, secular state' in its place.[15]

Even before Corbyn's election, the *Jewish Chronicle* cited 'overwhelming evidence' of his association with 'Holocaust deniers, terrorists and some outright antisemites'.[16] Any hopes that Corbyn's relationship with the official Jewish community would be anything other than extraordinarily difficult were torpedoed when Corbyn stated that he was sympathetic to the boycott, divestment and sanctions campaigns against Israel. Most Jewish organisations saw the campaign as simply an effort to delegitimate and undermine Israel, and their opposition to it was uncompromising.[17]

Dave Rich, the head of policy at Community Security Trust, a Jewish organisation that monitors antisemitism, was soon reporting 'an incessant stream of party members, activists, and officials propagating antisemitic tropes'.[18] This included accusations of antisemitism in the Oxford University Labour Club. In response, the party commissioned an investigation by Baroness Royall which, reporting in June 2016, uncovered some disturbing findings about antisemitic conduct in the club. Allegations of antisemitism then began to multiply. In April 2016, it was revealed that Naz Shah, Parliamentary Private Secretary to Shadow Chancellor John McDonnell, had posted a map showing Israel superimposed on the United States, suggesting Israel's population should be relocated there and adding some derogatory remarks about 'Zionists'. After some hesitation, the party suspended her; she later apologised for her action and the matter was considered closed.

Much more damaging for the party was the declaration by Ken Livingstone, the very high-profile former mayor of London and a long-standing ally of Corbyn, defending Shah, followed by the bombshell claim that Hitler had been 'sympathetic to Zionism', an obvious effort to tar the Jewish state by association with Nazism. The Jewish community was incandescent, and the incident attracted massive and very negative media coverage. Under intense pressure, Corbyn expressed 'very grave concerns' about Livingstone's 'grossly insensitive' language, and he was suspended pending investigation. The investigation was long and protracted, and itself became a cause of controversy, as we shall see below.

The next row implicated the Corbyn left more directly. Jackie Walker (who is both Black and Jewish), a vice-chair of the recently established pro-Corbyn group Momentum, asserted in September 2016 that Jews were among 'the chief financiers of the sugar and slave trade' and had contributed materially to the 'African holocaust'.[19] Again, Jewish organisations as well as people in the party were incensed, and, after a party investigation, she was suspended from the party – but a campaign by pro-Corbyn forces succeeded in having her reinstated. Further dubious comments by Walker on Holocaust Memorial Day led to the launching of a second investigation. Momentum removed her as vice-chair, deeming her remarks 'ill-informed, ill-judged and offensive', but denied they were antisemitic and continued to oppose her expulsion.[20] The case dragged on until Walker was finally expelled from the party in March 2019 for 'prejudicial and grossly detrimental behaviour against the party'.

Alongside these heavily publicised cases were many others. Corbyn attempted to defuse what had now become a major managerial problem by inviting the barrister and human rights campaigner Shami Chakrabarti to investigate antisemitism in the party. Other members of the inquiry were Professor David Feldman, the director of the Pears Institute for the Study of Antisemitism at Birkbeck College, and Baroness Jan Royall. The rapidly compiled Chakrabarti report found evidence of 'ignorant attitudes', and of an 'occasionally toxic atmosphere' with 'the word "Zionist" used personally, abusively or as a euphemism for "Jew"', but it concluded that allegations were exaggerated and Labour was not 'overrun by antisemitism'.[21]

Initial response to the report was positive. Jeremy Newmarket, chair of the Labour-affiliated Jewish Labour Movement (JLM), described it as setting 'a gold standard for tackling racism and antisemitism', while Jonathan Arkush, president of the Board of Deputies of British Jews, the main representative body of official Jewry, stated his appreciation of 'the careful way in which Shami Chakrabarti has engaged with our community', addressing 'our concerns with commendable speed'.[22] But the tone of the comment then changed, with the inquiry being dismissed as a whitewash, and Chakrabarti's credibility was not helped by her acceptance of a Labour peerage shortly afterwards. A report by the cross-party Home Affairs Select Committee, published a little later in 2016, argued that Chakrabarti had not appreciated the full gravity of the situation, adding that Corbyn's ineffectual responses risked 'lending force to allegations that elements of the Labour movement are institutionally anti-Semitic'.[23]

However, the issue itself went into abeyance, overshadowed by the seismic 2016 Brexit referendum, the 'chicken coup' and the 2017 general election. In fact, matters seemed to improve. In September of that year, Conference approved a rule change, sponsored by the JLM and agreed with Corbyn, making antisemitism a specific disciplinary offence. Luke Akehurst, a prominent commentator from Labour's right, welcomed 'the way in which the leadership has engaged with the Jewish Labour Movement'.[24]

Then, in March 2018, a full-blown crisis erupted, with explosive accusations that Corbyn himself was an antisemite. This was triggered by a claim by the prominent young Jewish MP Luciana Berger that, in 2012, Corbyn had approved a mural by an American graffiti artist, Mear One, which contained very obvious antisemitic caricatures. Corbyn had signed a protest against the decision by the Tower Hamlets (Labour) mayor, Lutfur Rahman, to remove the mural, citing freedom of expression. Berger declared that she had raised the issue with Corbyn's office on several occasions but received no response, at which point she went public.[25] For whatever reason, Jewish community leaders decided on a comprehensive assault on the Labour leadership. Jonathan Arkush and Jonathan Goldstein, two senior figures, denounced Corbyn's attitude both to Israel and to the Jewish people as deriving from 'the far left's obsessive hatred of Zionism, Zionists and Israel', emanating from 'a conspiratorial worldview in which mainstream Jewish communities are believed to be a hostile entity, a class enemy'.[26]

Over the spring of 2018, a rash of other claims about Corbyn's antisemitism flooded the airwaves. These included his description of representatives of Hamas and Hezbollah – two organisations which articulated antisemitic memes and were committed to Israel's destruction – as 'friends'; his comparison of Israel with Nazi Germany at a Holocaust Memorial Day event in 2010; his association around the same time with a campaigner for Palestinian rights who was also a Holocaust denier; and his comment in a speech in 2013 that Zionists 'don't understand English irony', with the word 'Zionist' allegedly used as a coded reference to Jews.[27] The former chief rabbi, Jonathan Sacks, described this comment, luridly, as the most offensive remark by a British politician since Enoch Powell's 'Rivers of Blood' speech.[28] These and other examples, critics alleged, formed a clear pattern: Corbyn's politics were saturated by deep prejudices against Jews. Indeed, in August 2018, Marie van der Zyl, president of the Jewish Board of Deputies, in a truly extraordinary outburst, proclaimed that Corbyn had 'declared war on the Jews'.[29]

Corbyn vehemently denied all the charges as crude misrepresentations and distortions (for example, he had used the word Zionist literally, not as a code word for Jews); at worst, he had been guilty of misjudgements, but always in good faith. The most serious charge was over the mural. Corbyn's own response was that he had only glanced at the mural over the phone and just assumed it was anti-capitalist and didn't want it censored.[30] He came under relentless pressure to offer public apologies, but he resisted on the grounds that this would simply give credence to the accusations levelled at him. Eventually, he did release a statement conceding that the mural was 'deeply disturbing and antisemitic' and apologised for the 'pain and hurt to our Jewish community' – but only after the LOTO communications team had prodded him to sharpen up an initially bland statement.[31]

However, he did seek to mend fences by writing a conciliatory letter to the Jewish community leaders in which he acknowledged that the problem of antisemitism had been too tardily addressed.[32] But the statement cut no ice, and relations remained frigid; Jewish groups even organised a rally outside Parliament in protest over antisemitism in the party, attended by around fifty MPs, one of whom, David Lammy, was threatened with deselection. Then, almost immediately, the party became embroiled in the most damaging row yet over antisemitism.

The controversy over the IHRA's definition of antisemitism

In July 2018, three Jewish newspapers, the *Jewish Chronicle*, the *Jewish News* and the *Jewish Telegraph*, published identical front pages with a chilling declaration: since Corbyn's election as leader, 'The stain and shame of antisemitism has coursed through' the Labour Party and the arrival of a Jeremy Corbyn-led government would pose an 'existential threat to Jewish life in this country'.[33] What shocking antisemitic act precipitated this?

In 2016, the International Holocaust Remembrance Alliance (IHRA)[34] adopted a definition of antisemitism as 'a certain perception of Jews, which may be expressed as hatred toward Jews', and to this definition were attached eleven examples of antisemitic behaviour. In December the same year, the NEC's Equalities Committee adopted a complaints procedure which incorporated the agreed IHRA definition with all of its constituent examples (this we henceforth call the 'IHRA formulation'). Then, on 17 April 2018, the Antisemitism Working Group, newly established by Labour's National Executive, adopted a Code of Conduct which included the IHRA definition but excluded two of the examples: one 'denying the Jewish people their right to self-determination (e.g., by claiming that the existence of a State of Israel is a racist endeavour)' and the second 'applying double standards by requiring of it [Israel] a behaviour not expected or demanded of any other democratic nation'. Corbyn had insisted that these two examples be excised on the grounds that they could be exploited to vilify anti-Zionist opponents of Israel as antisemites.[35]

In their joint editorial, the three Jewish newspapers ascribed these omissions to 'a cynical exercise in Jew hatred' and then labelled the party as 'institutionally antisemitic'.[36] The party, not surprisingly, was stunned by the ferocity of this response. Head of Momentum and NEC member Jon Lansman (who is Jewish) reminded critics that the exclusion of the proposition condemning Israel as a 'racist endeavour' was the *only* substantive area where Labour's code differed from the IHRA.[37] Furthermore, Labour's code did avow its belief in the Jewish people's right to self-determination, adding that 'to deny that right is to treat the Jewish people unequally and is therefore a form of antisemitism'.[38]

In fact, doubts about the value of the IHRA formulation extended well beyond Labour's leadership. In 2016 David Feldman had warned that there was a danger that it placed the onus on Israel's critics to demonstrate they were not antisemitic.[39] To the former Court of Appeals judge Sir Stephen Sedley, the formulation was worded in such a way as to construe 'everything other than anodyne criticism of Israel as anti-Semitic'.[40] Geoffrey Robertson QC, an eminent human rights barrister, found it 'imprecise, confusing and open to misinterpretation and even manipulation'.[41] And the definition's main drafter, Kenneth Stern, a prominent US lawyer, explained that his main aim in creating the formulation was for data classification purposes: 'the definition', he added, 'was not drafted, and was never intended, as a tool to target or chill speech'.[42]

In short, on the *substance* of the issue – that the IHRA formulation with all examples included could be used to delegitimate criticism of Israel – the leadership had a plausible and even persuasive case, and one arguably borne out by what was to happen under Starmer. But from a *managerial* perspective, the manner in which Corbyn dealt with the matter was maladroit and ham fisted. Corbyn had made no real effort to consult with people of standing within the Jewish community, or with the official party affiliate, the JLM, confining his contacts to the totally unrepresentative and bitterly anti-Israel Jewish Voice for Labour (JVL).[43] The optics, a senior aide later recalled, were 'terrible': at a time when he was being accused of antisemitism, Corbyn was claiming the right to judge what was antisemitic and what was not.[44]

A wiser leader would have realised that the overriding priority should have been to smother what was plainly a toxic controversy as soon as possible. Instead, Corbyn's intransigence meant that Labour's antisemitism crisis dominated the media schedules the whole summer of 2018, with a deluge of extremely damaging publicity portraying the party in the worst possible light. Senior figures in the leadership were exasperated and angry at what they saw as quibbling about the wording of the definition imperilling the whole Corbyn project. John McDonnell, Shami Chakrabarti and Andrew Murray all complained.[45] Paul Mason, a Corbyn-sympathising journalist, was terse when consulted: 'sign the goddamn IHRA definition right now!'[46] Labour's Director of Policy, Andrew Fisher, agreed: 'For God's sake, vote for it!'[47]

By autumn 2018, the leader's position had become untenable. The PLP overwhelmingly approved a motion calling for the IHRA formulation to be adopted and – in a direct show of defiance to the leadership – voted to write it into its own Rulebook, with both Starmer and McDonnell signalling their agreement. Furthermore, the NEC (now with a pro-Corbyn majority) favoured full implementation. Even then, Corbyn dug in his heels in a last-ditch action when he presented the September 2018 NEC with addendums reiterating the right to condemn Israel as racist. But he could not muster enough votes, and the formulation was finally agreed.[48]

By this time, a rift had opened between Corbyn and McDonnell, and worse was to follow. Increasingly upset by his stance over antisemitism, senior Jewish MP Margaret Hodge confronted Corbyn and, in a rage, accused him of 'making Labour a hostile environment for Jews', denouncing him as an antisemite.[49] An infuriated Corbyn demanded a public apology, which Hodge refused point blank; the following day, she was notified that she was under investigation and could be disciplined. McDonnell warned that this would be a public relations disaster and Corbyn seemed to agree, but then reversed his position. When the Shadow Cabinet met on 23 July, an apoplectic McDonnell was 'gripped by an almost biblical temper' at the decision to proceed with action against Hodge. Proceedings against Hodge were dropped – but not before 'the most profound breach between Corbyn and McDonnell the Project would ever experience' had occurred; the relationship between the two never fully recovered.[50]

This final episode confirmed what the prolonged row over the IHRA definition had made plain: Corbyn's lack of the skills, the instincts and the sensitivities required to manage the party effectively. As one key aide reflected, he had 'just entrenched the problem much, much deeper. I think that really, for me, was the point where it became unmanageable, because we'd lost all respect.'[51]

The EHRC, *Panorama* and the general election

The year 2018 was horrendous for Labour, but worse was to follow. As Labour was reeling before an avalanche of bad publicity, two more lethal blows were delivered. In May 2019, to Labour's huge embarrassment, the Equality and Human Rights Commission (EHRC) announced that it was launching an investigation into complaints of anti-Jewish discrimination in the party – taken as prima facie evidence that something was seriously amiss. Then in July 2019, a documentary entitled 'Is Labour Anti-Semitic?' was broadcast by the BBC's long-established *Panorama* programme, presented by the veteran broadcaster John Ware. Its conclusions could not have been less palatable. Relying upon interview testimony from former senior party HQ officials and leaked documents, including a large cache of e-mail exchanges between LOTO and HQ's Government and Legal Unit (GLU), the documentary claimed, firstly, that antisemitism was rife within the party and, secondly, that efforts by GLU officials to tackle it had been deliberately impeded by senior LOTO staff.[52] The party assailed the *Panorama* programme as 'a seriously inaccurate, politically one-sided polemic, which breached basic journalistic standards, distorted and manipulated the truth and misrepresented evidence to present a biased and selective account'. It described the whistle-blowers as 'former disaffected employees' who had 'both personal and political axes to grind'.[53]

Whatever the truth, the documentary unloosed yet another tsunami of dire publicity for the party.

The timing could not have been worse, as the next election was clearly drawing near and the *Panorama* programme helped to set the way in which 'Labour's antisemitism crisis' was framed. Weeks before the election, the *Jewish Chronicle* warned its readers that the impact of a Labour electoral victory would be 'almost unimaginable for our community [...] the prospect is truly frightening'.[54] Then, in a highly unusual intervention in the election campaign, the chief rabbi, Ephraim Mirvis, accused Corbyn of allowing a 'poison sanctioned from the top' to take root in the Labour Party, causing 'justified anxiety 'amongst British Jews at the prospect of a Corbyn government':[55] a truly devastating indictment. The direct impact of Labour's alleged antisemitism on voters may not have been substantial, but it did feed a sense that there was something deeply unpleasant, even repellent, about the party, and certainly contributed to the extraordinarily low esteem in which Jeremy Corbyn was held.

Conflicting narratives

A striking feature of the whole controversy was the existence of two radically opposing narratives. A narrative 'refers to the ways in which we construct disparate facts in our own worlds and weave them together cognitively in order to make sense of our reality'.[56] Nothing testified to the depth of the fracture over antisemitism than the fact that the protagonists of each deployed radically opposed narratives and appeared to be inhabiting different mental universes. In what follows, we first present what we may call the anti-Corbyn narrative, then the pro-Corbyn narrative, and finally seek to reach some conclusions about both the scale of antisemitism in the party and the leadership's response to it.

The anti-Corbyn narrative was presented most exhaustively in evidence submitted to the EHRC inquiry in 2019 by the JLM,[57] though our account also draws upon other sources. The submission stated that the JLM had 'received extensive evidence of Party employees, agents and members both posting generalised antisemitic content online and directly targeting antisemitic abuse at individual Jewish members'.[58] Having documented multiple examples of anti-Jewish comments, the JLM claimed that the party, rather than eradicating the problem, had engaged in '(i) denial; (ii) discrediting of victims; (iii) defence of perpetrators; (iv) cover ups; and (v) active victimisation of those calling out antisemitism'. Its most serious and sweeping charge was that the party had become 'institutionally antisemitic'.

Not surprisingly, given their much higher public profile, particular attention was given to the experience of Jewish MPs, in particular Louise Ellman, Luciana Berger, Margaret Hodge and Ruth Smeeth. As early as September 2016, the *Observer* had reported that Corbyn had ignored mounting evidence of abuse directed at these MPs and that persistent appeals from the beleaguered MPs for support had been ignored.[59] Matters had deteriorated to such an extent that in April 2018 the House of Commons held a debate on antisemitism. Luciana Berger, Margaret Hodge and Ruth Smeeth all told the House that they had been targets of 'a torrent of anti-Semitic abuse' and 'vicious anti-Semitic tweets' from the left as well as the extreme right. All had been accused of being 'Israeli agents', 'Mossad operatives' and instruments of global Zionism. Berger judged that antisemitism was 'now more commonplace, more conspicuous and more corrosive within the Labour party'.[60] Later, Margaret Hodge recollected that in her many years of activity in the party, she had experienced 'nothing as debilitating and horrible as the time spent battling antisemitism'.[61] To add insult to injury, the leadership had responded by charging these MPs with gross exaggeration.[62] This takes us to the crux of the case against the Corbyn leadership: it made no determined effort to repel the antisemitic tide and at times actually abetted it; in Hodge's words, under Corbyn, 'permission was given for antisemitism to spread from the fringes to the mainstream'.[63]

The term 'the Corbyn narrative' is in fact a little misleading because, as we shall see, it contained two distinct storylines which at times contradicted each other, reflecting substantial differences within the Corbyn camp. Initially, the dominant approach, and one that remained very influential throughout, was that the issue had been 'weaponised'. In April 2016, for example, Richard Kuper, spokesperson for the pro-Corbyn Jews for Justice for Palestinians, contended that the scale of antisemitism complaints indicated 'a coordinated, willed and malign campaign to exaggerate the nature and extent of antisemitism as a stick to beat the Labour party'.[64] Claims by Labour MPs that they were being hounded because they were Jewish were fabrications; their constituency parties objected to them because they were right wing and openly disloyal to the leader.[65] Antisemitism, in short, was being imagined and exploited quite deliberately and cynically to divide, disrupt and demoralise the party.

However, especially from early 2018, the Corbyn leadership shifted position. In his letter to Jewish leaders in March 2018, Corbyn acknowledged that the problem of antisemitism was real and that the party had been slow in responding. But he insisted that the responsibility for this lay not with the leadership but with the party HQ. The full exposition of this narrative had to await the leaked publication of a report compiled by pro-Corbyn officials in April 2020, which presented a lengthy, very detailed and heavily documented defence of the Corbyn leadership's handling of antisemitism. It was originally intended as evidence to be submitted by the party to the EHRC, though, on legal advice, it was not submitted. Because of the circumstances of its publication, it came to be known as 'the Leaked Report'. Much of what follows in this section draws heavily on the report and the documents contained within it.

Its point of departure was that, constitutionally, responsibility for addressing complaints about antisemitism lay with party HQ (Southside), specifically the GLU, which was charged with conducting investigations, holding hearings and formulating charges. Cases warranting serious disciplinary action would then be referred to the NEC (usually its Disputes Panel) or the NCC for determination. The crucial point in the Corbyn narrative was that none of the relevant bodies – the party HQ, the Disputes Panel, the NEC or the NCC – had pro-Corbyn majorities until March 2018; prior to this date, 'LOTO and Jeremy Corbyn himself had little to no oversight over the disciplinary process'.[66] LOTO conceded that it did intervene at times – reluctantly – but only to cajole GLU staff to act, sometimes to little avail.[67] 'We asked time and again for swift and competent management of complaints, and the implementation of the Chakrabarti Report,' Karie Murphy insisted, 'but there were always excuses.'[68] Far from frustrating the GLU drive against antisemitism, LOTO cited detailed evidence of indolence, inefficiency and negligence on the part of its senior officials.[69] For example, in February 2018 Corbyn wrote to McNicol, complaining that 'the current processes are far too slow to meet the volume of disciplinary cases the party has to deal with', and leaving the impression that antisemitism was not being taken seriously enough.[70]

In short, blame for procrastination, complacency and outright incompetence in the handling of antisemitism lay unambiguously with the GLU officials.[71] Senior Corbyn figures adduced four reasons for this failure. Firstly, the party's disciplinary procedures and resources could not cope with the sheer volume of complaints. Secondly, they blamed incompetence, negligence and mismanagement within Southside.[72] Thirdly, there was a 'lack of motivation to take disciplinary action when there were not factional gains to be made'. Fourthly, by dragging out proceedings as much as possible, they sought to cause Corbyn maximum embarrassment in the PLP and media by creating the impression that he was either unwilling to act firmly over antisemitism or even antisemitic himself.[73]

The final point was that serious improvements to eradicate antisemitism occurred only after the Corbyn left secured a majority on the NEC in early 2018 and McNicol was replaced by the Corbynite Unite official Jennie Formby; only then did the party seek to improve its cumbersome disciplinary system. The outcome, the leadership claimed, was a rapid acceleration in the number of antisemitism cases processed, complaints resolved and numbers expelled and in other ways sanctioned.[74] As Karie Murphy, the leader's chief of staff, contended, 'antisemites were removed from the Labour party more quickly, transparently and effectively than ever before'.[75]

The prevalence of antisemitism

It is important here to appreciate that the principal function of a political narrative is not to lay bare the facts as objectively and rigorously as possible but to persuade: to select and arrange aspects of a perceived reality in such a way as to promote a given interpretation. What Schon and Rein call 'rhetorical frames' are designed to portray situations in such a way as to enlist support for and legitimate a particular point of view; they are political devices, and this applies to both the narratives we have surveyed.[76]

Both sides, in effect, were narrating stories to achieve political goals, and both made sweeping claims they failed to, indeed could not, corroborate. Here, Martin Forde QC made a crucial point: it was impossible to quantify the extent of antisemitism without a survey of a representative sample of constituency parties, and this had never been conducted.[77] Feldman, Gidley and McGeever, in a rare academic study, made a similar point: that the incidence of antisemitism within the party was impossible to ascertain without much more evidence.[78] It follows from what we have said that any conclusions we reach, based as much as possible on non-partisan sources, must necessarily be preliminary, cautious and provisional.

The EHRC report, published in 2020 after Corbyn's resignation, claimed to have compelling evidence of an 'intimidating, hostile, degrading, humiliating or offensive environment' for Jews.[79] Unfortunately, the evidence was not included in the report.[80] The EHRC's remit was a legal one, whether the Equality Act had been breached, and thus did not include assessing the scale of antisemitism in the party, though it did note that the cases it covered did not represent 'the full extent of the issues we identified within the files in our sample; it represents the tip of the iceberg.'[81] Similarly, Feldman, Gidley and McGeever argued that the number of official complaints understated the real level of antisemitic incidents because many members who had experienced or witnessed antisemitic statements probably did not bother to use official channels to report them.[82] They concluded that the cases processed by the party were not an accurate reflection of the 'volume of antisemitic ideas, stereotypes and narratives circulating among Labour members.'[83]

All this raises the question of what exactly constitutes evidence of antisemitism. Waxman, Schraub and Hosein usefully distinguish between people who are overtly antisemitic (with a coherent racist ideology) and those who draw upon a '"cultural reservoir" of stereotypes, myths and narratives that can be easily and unwittingly drawn upon by people who are not personally antisemitic'.[84] There were definite examples of the former among party members, recalled one senior Corbyn advisor, and some of it was 'horrific, and it shocked me. I'd never come across any of that before. I can genuinely say, not within the party.' It often took the form of conspiracy theories about the power of Jewish finance – what the German socialist August Bebel had called 'the socialism of fools'.[85]

But the latter type was far more common. The bulk of antisemitism complaints, according to Jon Lansman, who, as an NEC member, attended many hearings in which hundreds of allegations were heard, did not involve people who adhered to coherent, or deeply held, antisemitic views but who drew upon Waxman, Schraub and Hosein's 'cultural reservoir' of traditional antisemitic tropes.[86] This was particularly to be found among pro-Palestine campaigners who, as Andrew Fisher observed, 'in their outrage, exuberance, whatever you want to call it, said some pretty horrific things, or slipped, sometimes just slipped into antisemitic language, loose language'.[87] In an article he drafted for the *Evening Standard*, Andrew Murray deplored the expounding on the left of ideas which depicted capitalism and imperialism 'as the product of a conspiracy by a small shadowy elite only a step from hoary myths about "Jewish bankers" and "sinister global forces"'.[88] In August 2018, Harry Hayball, appointed by Jennie Formby as a senior governance officer, reported that 'there are large numbers of Momentum/Labour members publicly commenting about Rothschild-Zionists controlling the world'.[89] Such ideas began to circulate on Labour-oriented websites in a way that had never occurred prior to 2015.[90]

Much attention, both in the EHRC report and in wider comment, was focused on the antisemitic invective targeted at Jewish Labour MPs, and we have already referred to their allegations. We can take as case studies the more fully documented experiences of Louise Ellman and Luciana Berger. Corbyn's chief of staff, Karie Murphy, claimed that no occasion arose when any Labour MP provided LOTO with credible evidence of significant antisemitic abuse in their constituencies.[91] This comment has any credence only if one wholly discounts the testimonies of the MPs themselves and the evidence they supplied.

Louise Ellman was the long-serving MP for Liverpool Riverside. She had enjoyed good relations with her constituency party until a major influx of new recruits following Corbyn's election, which quintupled its total membership. A minority of these had backgrounds in the Militant Tendency and other far-left groups, and these figured disproportionately among regular attenders at all-membership constituency meetings. Relations between the MP and her opponents then rapidly deteriorated, with Ellman complaining to party HQ about antisemitic abuse. At the same time, an anonymous dossier was distributed alleging far-left infiltration of the Labour Party in Liverpool.[92] The party launched an investigation into the CLP in October 2016, which reported later in the year. The report uncovered a bitterly divided and polarised party, with the MP persistently subjected to inquisitorial interrogations of her stance on the Israel–Palestine conflict. Critics claimed that Jews who were ardent supporters of Israel were 'Zio-fascists', that ISIS was a Zionist creation and that 'Zionists' 'deserve to feel uncomfortable' in CLP meetings. This investigation concluded that 'whilst there is not an endemic antisemitism problem within the CLP, there have been incidents where criticism of Israel has been framed in language which could be deemed anti-Semitic'.[93] The CLP was put under 'special measures', but no disciplinary action against individuals was taken, and Ellman's position weakened when the sympathetic Iain McNicol was replaced by the much less helpful Jennie Formby.[94] In autumn 2019, a motion of no confidence in the MP was tabled for discussion on Yom Kippur (the Day of Atonement), the holiest day in the Jewish calendar. Shortly after, lamenting that under Corbyn a Jewish member had been 'bullied, abused and driven out' of the party, Ellman resigned from the party.[95]

Luciana Berger had been MP for another Liverpool seat, Wavertree, since 2010, and her relations with her party turned sour after pro-Corbyn elements gained control of the party in 2016. She had been Director of Labour Friends of Israel between 2007 and 2010, and many activists were vehement critics of Israel. She served in a junior position as mental health spokesman in Corbyn's Shadow Cabinet from 2015 to 2016, where, according to both Lansman and Murray, she had been one of the most cooperative and diligent of frontbenchers.[96] Her relationship with her pro-Corbyn CLP lurched into a crisis after she publicised the 'Mear One' mural case (discussed above). Right-wing extremists had already been gaoled for sending hate messages to Berger, but she was now confronted with 'an increasingly violent, hostile language' from local Labour members.[97] Examples included 'caricatures of her with a hooked nose, sometimes featuring Stars of David soaked in blood'.[98] She received no help from the national party. 'That the party did not reach out to support her more,' Andrew Murray later wrote, 'is a rebuke to all of us.'[99] By February 2019, the situation had deteriorated irretrievably and, along with other Labour MPs, Berger left the party to form the short-lived Independent Group of MPs.[100]

One cannot extrapolate from the experience of Ellman and Berger and, indeed, Smeeth and Hodge, general conclusions about the scale of antisemitism in the party. Here the crucial point is that no hard or compelling evidence was ever presented to corroborate claims that antisemitism was 'endemic' or 'ubiquitous' in the party, and certainly not that it was 'institutionalised' in the strictly Macpherson sense.[101] As previously noted, this would have required a programme of research into membership attitudes that was never commissioned or undertaken. But it does not follow that antisemitism was not a major managerial problem. As one senior figure with access to all the party's documentation explained, 'if you start counting numbers, you probably don't get very many. But that's not the point. The point is that many party members in the constituency parties and elsewhere were in effect hounded because of being Jewish and being made to feel responsible for the actions of Israel or the plight of the Palestinians.' He added: 'It was pervasive in the party, in the sense that there were enormous numbers of cases all the time.'[102] The crucial issue was that, whatever its precise dimensions, antisemitism on any significant scale had never previously surfaced in the Labour Party: the inference must be that those guilty of such behaviour were recruits who had joined the party during and after Corbyn's election and in response to it. Lansman spelt out the essential point: 'I never expected to find antisemitism in the Labour party, and I did find it. I found it in appalling ways in the stuff that I saw in disciplinary cases [as an NEC member].'[103]

LOTO intervention in the disciplinary process

If, given the present state of evidence, no definitive finding about the precise magnitude of antisemitism in the party is possible, what of the crucial allegation that LOTO actively obstructed efforts made by the party apparatus to root out antisemitism? According to the JLM submission, the leadership's response, including denial and cover-ups, 'established an atmosphere of impunity and, indeed, encouragement for agents and members of the Party to direct abuse at those challenging antisemitism.'[104] One of the EHRC's main findings was that LOTO had regularly intervened in the party's disciplinary and complaints process, though constitutionally it had no right to do so. It accepted that in some cases intervention by LOTO 'catalysed action'; however, it judged that the key issue was not the outcomes but 'the inappropriateness of political interference'. This, the EHRC commented, 'put Jewish members at a particular disadvantage compared to non-Jewish members' and hence such interference 'amounted to unlawful indirect discrimination against its Jewish members in breach of the Equality Act 2010'.[105] Indeed, there was a 'culture within the Party which, at best, did not do enough to prevent antisemitism and, at worst, could be seen to accept it'. In short, antisemitism 'could have been tackled more effectively if the leadership had chosen to do so'.[106]

The most thorough and authoritative investigation into these competing claims was provided by the *Forde Report*, and it appeared, at first glance, to exonerate the Leader's Office. It stated that it had received no 'clear and convincing documentary evidence that there was a systematic attempt by the elected leadership to interfere unbidden in the disciplinary process in order to undermine the party's response to allegations of antisemitism'. Furthermore, there was clear evidence that when LOTO *did intervene* – it did so at the express invitation of Southside officials.[107] For this reason, the *Forde Report* was greeted by the hard left as total vindication of the Corbyn leadership. But there were important caveats. The *documentary* record, Forde stressed, could be misleading, noting the 'numerous' non-documented 'examples of LOTO pressure and interference' that were submitted by witnesses to his inquiry.[108] These examples referred to telephone calls and face-to-face conversations between LOTO and senior Southside officials which left no paper trail, for reasons not hard to fathom: both LOTO and Southside were notoriously leaky. 'It would be hard for us,' Forde wrote, 'to comprehend the cumulative effect [on GLU officials] of difficult NEC meetings, telephone calls, in person confrontations and so on which have been described to us [but which] rarely manifested itself in writing.' It also accepted that requests for formal written sign-offs by LOTO 'were seen by many GLU staff as a necessary means of pushing those invisible pressures into the open.' Furthermore, Southside operated in an environment where they were constantly harassed by radical left media platforms assailing 'right-wing bureaucrats' for their 'smear tactics' over antisemitism and for conducting 'witch-hunts' against Corbyn supporters.[109]

Situations, in short, could be ambiguous. Take, for example, the Livingstone case. To recall, in April 2016 he made the highly inflammatory assertion that 'before he went mad,' Hitler had been well disposed to Zionism, an obvious attempt at guilt-by-association. GLU officials brought charges of antisemitism to the NCC, and the former mayor was suspended pending a full investigation. But matters then dragged on, with Southside and LOTO blaming each other for delays. By February 2018, the issue was still unresolved, with GLU insisting upon quick action, else Livingstone's suspension would automatically end. The Leaked Report claimed that LOTO was continually prodding GLU officials to bring the Livingstone case to a conclusion and take appropriate disciplinary action.[110] There is no doubt that Corbyn was genuinely angry with the former mayor,[111] but he had been an ally for many years, and evidence from other sources suggests he was reluctant to expel him. Indeed, Corbyn's senior aide, Seumas Milne, pressed for Livingstone to be cleared on the grounds that his claims were historically accurate, while Corbyn-affiliated media platforms such as *The Canary* and *THE SKWAWKBOX* (often briefed by LOTO) regularly excoriated Southside officials for defaming Livingstone.[112] There is also evidence that, far from procrastinating, McNicol and GLU pushed for a second Livingstone suspension, but that LOTO blocked action until Corbyn's preferred outcome, that Livingstone resign from the party, could be arranged.[113] Whatever the truth, plainly there was LOTO involvement – and inevitably so, given Livingstone's status.

Three other cases are worth noting. The first concerned the pugnacious and combative Corbynite MP for Derby North, Chris Williamson, who, over the years, insisted that allegations of anti-Jewish racism were a 'dirty lowdown trick', weaponised for 'political ends', and that the party had been far 'too apologetic' in not contesting them.[114] In February 2019 he was suspended pending investigation: that same month, Corbyn defended Williamson as 'a very good, very effective Labour MP, not antisemitic in any way'.[115] The case was referred by GLU in June 2019 to the NEC Disputes Panel (which by then had a Corbynite majority). It found that Williamson had engaged in conduct which was 'grossly detrimental to the Party' and 'may reasonably be seen to involve antisemitic sentiments, stereotypes and actions' – but it then decided he should be reinstated with a formal warning; according to Owen Jones, Karie Murphy had objected to moves to discipline the errant MP. But this prompted an outcry from the Jewish community and the media, and, with an election imminent, in November 2019, the NEC felt it had no option but to refuse to endorse Williamson as a Labour candidate, in effect deselecting him.[116]

A second example of LOTO involvement in the complaints process involved Alan Bull, a member of Peterborough CLP with connections to the Corbyn left. Steps had been taken by GLU to expel him on the grounds that he had asserted the Holocaust was a hoax. The hard left veteran Christine Shawcroft, who had replaced Ann Black as Chair of the NEC's Disputes Panel, insisted that Bull's suspension be reversed, arguing that Holocaust denial could be 'taken out of context'. However, the case was leaked and the resulting uproar compelled Shawcroft to resign from the Disputes Panel, and Bull was expelled. The third case involved Glyn Secker, secretary of the anti-Zionist JVL (hence Jewish) and a close Corbyn ally.

The GLU had judged Secker's anti-Zionism so intemperate – he had told a rally that the Zionist Federation had 'embraced' the neo-fascist English Defence League and claimed that Israel was helping to finance ISIS – that on 7 March 2018 the decision was taken to suspend him. However, Secker was a Corbyn ally and, in an e-mail on 10 March, Milne told GLU to take no further action against him.[117]

According to the BBC journalist John Ware, 'the Secker case marked the moment when [Emilie] Oldknow [Director of Governance, Membership and Party Services] decided she'd had enough' and she resolved that, in future, GLU would refer all future cases to LOTO for their written sign-off.[118] In her EHRC submission, Oldknow claimed that Seumas Milne, Karie Murphy and Amy Jackson [Corbyn's political secretary] regularly challenged recommendations to discipline members charged with antisemitism, creating 'an extremely pressurised environment to work in'.[119] For this reason, the decision was made to involve LOTO so that they would be forced to take responsibility for disciplinary decisions.[120]

However, it would be wrong to infer from this that LOTO always resisted the disciplining of those found guilty of antisemitism; much seemed to depend upon whether the accused had Corbynite affiliations. Equally, there is evidence that at times GLU *was* slow in processing complaints and was indeed pushed by LOTO to act with more urgency. Whether factional reasons influenced their behaviour cannot be ruled out, but it was also the case that Labour's complaints system – and this was too often overlooked – simply often could not cope: 'no complaints system in any political party on earth could have tackled that tsunami of complaints that deluged the GLU after Corbyn became leader'.[121] Most complaints were about social media activities, which required checking the accounts of those accused, a hugely time-consuming task at a time when there were multiple demands on Southside officials. Not surprisingly, the system jammed. There were other systemic problems. As the lawyer David Renton pointed out, there was 'a complete lack of clarity as to how to investigate efficiently and fairly, for Labour made itself not merely the "judge" of the process, but also the "prosecutor" and the "investigating officer"'.[122] The dysfunctionality was exacerbated by the very poor relations between LOTO and Southside; thus, in some cases, 'wires were crossed, interventions were misunderstood, and individuals were unfairly maligned'.[123] Bottlenecks, poor decision-making and inconsistencies were, in the circumstances, inevitable, and, Forde concluded, 'were not necessarily attributable to any individuals acting in bad faith'.[124]

Understanding the leadership's conduct: (1) the ambiguities of Jeremy Corbyn

Few would dispute the conclusion that the antisemitism crisis was mishandled by the Corbyn leadership, and in the rest of the chapter we seek to explain why. We explore two key factors: Corbyn's role and the fraught issue of the Israel–Palestine conflict. Part of Corbyn's poor management of the issue reflected his manifold weaknesses as a leader: he was notoriously indecisive, preferred to duck issues rather than face them and indeed at crucial times disconnected himself from what was happening and withdrew into himself; he could also be stubborn and self-righteous.[125] When distressed, as he was profoundly so over what he regarded as totally unfounded accusations of antisemitism,[126] he became defensive and prickly. But there were other factors at work.

For a start, there was always a tension between Corbyn's speeches, scripted by aides, and his personal views. Angela Rayner stated that Corbyn had a 'blind spot' about antisemitism. The evidence that this 'blind spot' was anti-Jewish sentiment was always thin and unconvincing,[127] so we have to look elsewhere for an explanation. Normally a 'kind and empathetic' person, Renton noted, when interviewed over antisemitism, Corbyn 'ended up looking surly and defensive. He came across as having no emotional intelligence on the issue at all.'[128] In addition, he was always uncomfortable and ill at ease in meetings with mainstream Jewish organisations, such as the Board of Deputies and JLM, and was in general reluctant to engage with representatives of the Jewish community (beyond JVL).[129]

For example, there were informal contacts with Lord Levy, a prominent Jewish figure and previously a donor to the Labour Party, who initially sought to be helpful. Corbyn showed no interest in meeting with him, nor with his more left-wing son, Daniel, an expert on the Israeli–Palestinian conflict and former advisor to the Israeli government who was a staunch critic both of the Israeli occupation of the West Bank and also of the Jewish communal leadership's 'deeply counterproductive rhetoric about Corbyn'.[130] As the Corbyn-sympathising journalist Owen Jones put it, he was 'exactly the sort of constructive, thoughtful voice' to whom Corbyn should listen, but the latter showed no willingness to do so.[131]

How can we account for this attitude? One reason was his close association with a group of long-standing Jewish friends with backgrounds in radical left politics. In 2017 they had formed the pro-Corbyn but zealously anti-Israel Jewish Voice for Labour; two of the three members of Corbyn's 'kitchen cabinet' for dealing with antisemitism were senior JVL members.[132] Their insistent advice was that antisemitism in the party was being magnified out of all proportion and ruthlessly exploited by his enemies inside and outside the Labour Party. Lansman warned Corbyn that JVL was 'totally detached and disconnected' from the Jewish community, and utterly unrepresentative of Jewish opinion, and pleaded with him to widen his circle of contacts within the Jewish community, but unavailingly.[133] In April 2018, Momentum, under Lansman's leadership, called for acknowledgement that anti-Jewish bias was 'more widespread in the Labour party than many of us had understood even a few months ago'.[134] Lansman and McDonnell both pressed upon Corbyn that support for the Palestine cause could be combined with greater sensitivity towards Jewish opinion. But this advice more often than not fell on stony ground.[135]

Many in Corbyn's inner circle and in the wider Corbynite camp totally disagreed with Lansman and McDonnell and demanded that he stand firm. They included, as well as JVL and Jews for Justice for Palestinians, Seumas Milne and Karie Murphy, and most radical left media platforms such as *SKWAWKBOX*, *The Canary*, *Jacobin* and, to some degree, *Novara Media*: indeed, most of the Corbynite commentariat. Their message was simple and unequivocal: the bulk of accusations of antisemitism were both mendacious and malicious, gross exaggerations designed specifically to blacken Corbyn's reputation and stigmatise all criticism of Israel.[136]

Corbyn was instinctively more sympathetic to this advice and more likely to accept it.

Why? Corbyn, his senior aide Andrew Murray considered, found it difficult to map antisemitism onto his understanding of racism. Racism was characterised by economic exploitation, systematic discrimination at work, in housing and education, and continual police harassment; it was also a matter of colour and of colonial repression. The life of the generally affluent and integrated Jewish community did not fit easily into this picture. Corbyn was very empathetic with 'the poor, the disadvantaged, the migrant, the marginalised', Murray noted, 'but the Jewish community in Britain was relatively prosperous'. This, he concluded, is 'where the failure to understand comes in – that, actually, antisemitism has different aspects to other forms of racism'.[137]

So far we have focused on the thinking, goals and priorities which influenced the conduct of the Corbyn leadership as well as other protagonists. But to fully understand why the conflict over antisemitism effectively became so utterly disruptive, we have to contextualise it in the long-standing Israel–Palestine conflict and the extraordinary strength of feeling it aroused on all sides.

Understanding the leadership's conduct: (2) antisemitism and the Israel–Palestine conflict

Strong criticism of Israel had always provoked the fury of many within the Jewish community, as Miliband found out to his cost. But the terms of debate changed fundamentally after 2015 as the result of the influx into the party of significant numbers from radical left organisations, including the StWC, the Palestine Solidarity Campaign and the Socialist Workers Party for whom, as Milne put it, Palestine had become 'the great international cause of our time'.[138] What they challenged was not simply Israel's conduct, but its right to exist.

In fact, Labour's official position over the Israel–Palestine issue, which was a two-state solution, did not change much, and it is very probable that the majority of Corbynite MPs favoured this. But within the wider Corbynite coalition, especially among those who ran media platforms and more generally contributed to the debate, probably a majority did not, instead preferring 'a single democratic Palestinian state' into which, presumably, Israel would be dissolved. The very fact that their voice tended to be the loudest had a profound effect, since most official Jewish community organisations appeared to have assumed that this represented the real Corbynite agenda.

The problem here was that the collision between the more radical section of the Corbyn left and the pro-Israel camp (the majority of the PLP) was as deep seated as it is possible to imagine, as it was rooted in fundamentally different ways of understanding the world. These can be conceptualised in terms of 'cognitive maps'. Cognitive maps help to navigate complex realities. By influencing 'what we attend to, what we perceive, what we remember and what we infer' they impart order and intelligibility to what might otherwise seem to be a whirlwind of bewildering events, actions and impressions.[139] A cognitive map tells people, for instance, what a conflict is about, what the major issues are, the motives of the protagonists and the appropriate responses. As a result, where people adhere to radically divergent responses, they literally look at the world in different ways.

Most Labour Party members in the past deployed a cognitive map which visualised the discord between Israelis and Palestinians as a clash between two peoples, each with legitimate claims to self-determination. The cognitive map to which much of the Corbynite left adhered can best be described as the 'settler state' thesis of Israel's origins and character. This viewed Israel as a European settler state, a product of Western colonial expansion, which had dispossessed or subjugated and immiserated most of the native Palestinian population.[140] Israel, according to Novara Media's Aaron Bastani, was 'founded on racism, massacres and the intentional displacement of an entire people'.[141] By its very nature, it was repressive, exploitative and (as many added) inherently racist, anchored in the complete denial of the rights of the native population. But not only was it a European import; it was a bastion of American imperialism, the recipient of a vast flow of military aid and dollars, a capstone of the exploitative global order, Washington's bridgehead in the Middle East. It lacked any real democratic legitimacy. It was from this perspective that Corbyn had greeted Hamas and Hezbollah as friends, partners in the struggle against imperialism, and committed, in his words, to 'bringing about long-term peace and social justice and political justice in the whole region'.[142]

Not all those within the Corbyn camp accepted the 'settler colonial state' thesis – for example, John McDonnell and Jon Lansman did not.[143] Nor did Len McCluskey, who wrote that if 'I had been a young Jewish man at the end of the Second World War, I would have fought and if necessary died to create the State of Israel as a safe haven for Jews after the horror of the Holocaust'[144] – but the key point here is that those who formed the public face of Corbynism generally propounded the thesis; and perhaps it was what many of Corbyn's enemies, viewing the world through their own cognitive maps, wanted to hear.

Advocacy of the thesis per se is not antisemitic, and there is no reason to believe that many of its adherents were antisemitic. The problem for the party was that, for the great majority of the Jewish community and, indeed, many MPs and party members, nothing was more provocative than comparing Jewish survivors of, or those fleeing from, persecution to Israel as just another wave of white intruders 'ethnically cleansing' the natives. It seemed oblivious, Owen Jones observed, to the 'two thousand years of blood libel, scapegoating, pogroms, expulsions and murder, culminating in an attempt to exterminate every single Jew on the European continent by industrialized, bureaucratic means'.[145] And astonishing little account was taken by exponents of the thesis of the profound impact of the Holocaust upon the Jewish psyche and the passionate allegiance to Israel as the ultimate sanctuary to which it gave rise. Even when anti-Zionism did not transmute into antisemitism, the fervency with which it was propagated was bound profoundly to antagonise the Jewish community, including most of Labour's Jewish members.

This was compounded by the fact that Israel was often presented as uniquely culpable in the world. At the party's 2018 Conference, Ivor Gaber, a veteran left-wing journalist and broadcaster, noted that while Corbyn was politely applauded when denouncing atrocities against the Rohingya people by the Myanmar government and against the Yemini people by the Saudis, 'when it came to condemnation of Israeli bombing of Gaza, the cheers turned to visceral yelps of approval'.[146] Attention paid within Labour left circles to serious human rights abuses in countries such as Syria, Saudi Arabia and the Sudan was 'minuscule compared with the obsessive attention that is paid to the Israel/Palestine dispute'.[147]

The fact that Corbyn, out of conviction as well as defensiveness, was not prepared to disown advocates of the settler colonial state thesis inevitably alienated many within the party, on the right, the soft left and indeed even, as we have seen, some Corbynites. The same was true of his obduracy over the IHRA formulation. To Corbyn, animated by the ethic of conviction, what mattered most in making major decisions was listening to one's conscience and standing by one's principles – whatever the consequences. He was, Karie Murphy noted, 'phenomenally loyal' to the Palestinian cause,[148] and upon this he was very reluctant to compromise. But the final factor that rendered the conflict over antisemitism intractable was, as we shall see in the next chapter, that it was viewed through a heavily factionalised prism.

Notes

1 Len McCluskey, *Always Red* (New York: OR Books, 2021).
2 Greg Philo and Mike Berry, *Bad News for Labour: Antisemitism, the Party and Public Belief* (London: Pluto 2019), pp. 1, 7.
3 Owen Jones, *This Land: The Story of a Movement* (London: *Allen Lane, 2020),* p. 255.
4 Ian Nelson, 'The British New Labour Party and Political Zionism: Continuity of an Essential Dilemma' (PhD thesis, University of Durham, 2009), p. 134.
5 See also, for example, the pamphlet by two left-wing MPs, William Warbey and Lyall Wilkes, *Palestine: The Stark Facts and the Way Out* (London: Narod Press, 1948).
6 Aneira J. Edmunds, 'The British Labour Party in the 1980s: The battle over the Palestinian/Israeli conflict', *Politics*, 8:2 (1998), 111–18.
7 Quoted in David Feldman, 'Anti-Zionism and antisemitism in Britain', in *Proceedings, International conference 'Antisemitism in Europe today: The*

phenomena, the conflicts', 8–9 November 2013 (Berlin: The Jewish Museum, 2014), p. 3.

8 Edmunds, 'The British Labour Party in the 1980s', pp. 114–15.

9 Dave Rich, *The Left's Jewish Problem: Jeremy Corbyn, Israel and Anti-Semitism* (London: Biteback, 2016).

10 Liam Hoare, 'Ed Miliband has a very Jewish problem', *Times of Israel*, 14 August 2014.

11 Leader, 'Israel's true friends', *Jewish Chronicle*, 24 July 2014.

12 At a dinner for the Jewish charity the Community Security Trust, a fundraising video featuring Miliband was 'greeted with loud and widely joined-in booing'. Robert Philpot, 'Jews against Miliband', *Spectator*, 18 April 2015.

13 *Ibid.*

14 Hoare, 'Ed Miliband has a very Jewish problem'.

15 Rich, *The Left's Jewish Problem.*

16 Leader, 'The key questions Jeremy Corbyn must answer', *Jewish Chronicle*, 12 August 2015.

17 Interview, Andrew Fisher.

18 Dave Rich, 'The etiology of antisemitism in Corbyn's Labour Party', *Israel Journal of Foreign Affairs*, 12:3 (2018), 357–65.

19 Jessica Elgot, 'Momentum likely to oust Jackie Walker over Holocaust remarks', *Guardian*, 29 September 2016.

20 Julia Rampen, 'Momentum removes Jackie Walker from vice chair post after anti-semitism controversy', *New Statesman*, 4 October 2016.

21 Shami Chakrabarti, *The Shami Chakrabarti Enquiry* (London: Labour Party, 2016), pp. 1, 12.

22 Ian Hernon, *Anti-Semitism and the Left* (Stroud: Amberley, 2020), p. 165; Jonathan Arkush, Board of Deputies of British Jews, 'Response to the Chakrabarti Report', 30 June 2016.

23 House of Commons Home Affairs Committee, *Antisemitism in the UK* (London: House of Commons, 2016), pp. 45–6.

24 Luke Akehurst, 'We will fight and fight again against the "McDonnell amendment"', *LabourList*, 21 September 2017, labourlist.org

25 Gabriel Pogrund and Patrick Maguire, *Left Out: The Inside Story of Labour under Corbyn* (London: Bodley Head, 2021), p. 100.

26 Heather Stewart and Kevin Rawlinson, 'Jewish leaders accuse Jeremy Corbyn of "siding with anti-Semites"' *Guardian*, 26 March 2018.

27 Jakob Guhl, '"Everyone I know isn't antisemitic": Antisemitism in Facebook pages supportive of the UK Labour Party', in Monika Hübscher and Sabine von Mering (eds), *Antisemitism on Social Media* (London: Routledge, 2022), pp. 57, 60.

28 Pogrund and Maguire, *Left Out*, pp. 123–4.

29 Lee Harpin, Board President: 'It's like Jeremy Corbyn has declared war on the Jews', *Jewish Chronicle*, 22 August 2018.

30 Interview, Andrew Fisher.

31 David Renton, *Labour's Antisemitism Crisis* (London: Routledge, 2021), p. 96.

32 Jeremy Corbyn, '"I will always be your ally in the fight against antisemitism" – Corbyn's letter to Jewish leaders', *LabourList*, 26 March 2018, labourlist.org

33 Kevin Rawlinson and Pippa Crerar, 'Jewish newspapers claim Corbyn poses "existential threat"', *Guardian*, 26 July 2018.

34 The IHRA was an intergovernmental body established in 1998, to which thirty-one countries, the UK included, belonged.

35 Labour Party, *Leaked Report. The Work of the Labour Party's Governance and Legal Unit in Relation to Anti-semitism, 2014–2019* (London: Labour Party, 2020), p. 610; Pogrund and Maguire, *Left Out*, pp. 108–9.

36 Rawlinson and Crerar, 'Jewish newspapers claim Corbyn poses "existential threat"'.

37 Jon Lansman, 'Labour's antisemitism code is the gold standard for political parties', *Guardian*, 12 July 2018.

38 Labour Party, *Leaked Report*, p. 610.

39 David Feldman, 'Will Britain's new definition of antisemitism help Jewish people? I'm sceptical', *Guardian*, 28 December 2016.

40 Stephen Sedley, 'Defining Anti-Semitism', *London Review of Books*, 39:9 (4 May 2017).

41 Quoted in Anthony Lerman, 'Labour should ditch the IHRA working definition of antisemitism altogether', *Open Democracy*, 4 September 2018, opendemocracy.net

42 Ruth Gould, 'The IHRA definition of antisemitism', *Political Quarterly*, 91:4 (2020), 825, 826. Renton, *Labour's Antisemitism Crisis*, p. 20.

43 Pogrund and Maguire, *Left Out*, pp. 107–8; Interview, Jon Lansman.

44 Interview, Andrew Fisher.

45 Jones, *This Land*, pp. 38, 240, 244; Andrew Murray, *Is Socialism Possible in Britain?* (London: Verso, 2022), pp. 127, 129.

46 Pogrund and Maguire, *Left Out*, p. 118. 'Are we saying' Corbyn's senior policy advisor Andrew Fisher expostulated, that 'we're going to define Antisemitism better than an international panel of Jewish academics agreeing with it – it's just a fucking idiot thing to do.' Jones, *This Land*, p. 238.

47 Interview, Andrew Fisher.

48 Pogrund and Maguire, *Left Out*, pp. 243–4.

49 *Ibid.*, p. 112.

50 *Ibid.*, pp. 118, 115.

51 Interview, Andrew Fisher.

52 Pogrund and Maguire, *Left Out*, pp. 239–43.

53 Kevin Schofield, 'Labour goes to war with BBC over Panorama probe into anti-semitism in party', *PoliticsHome*, 11 July 2019, politicshome.com. Linking

commentary in the documentary was provided by Dave Rich and Alan Johnson (not the MP), both harsh critics of Corbyn's stance on antisemitism and close to Israel. Pogrund and Maguire, *Left Out*, p. 243.

54 Leader, *Jewish Chronicle*, 1 November 2019.

55 'General election 2019: Chief Rabbi attacks Labour anti-semitism record', *BBC News*, 26 November 2019.

56 Molly Patterson and Kristen R. Monroe, 'Narrative in political science', *Annual Review of Political Science*, 1 (1998), 315–31.

57 The Jewish Labour Movement was originally entitled Poale Zion, Hebrew for 'workers of Zion', a socialist organisation committed to the establishment of a Jewish homeland in Palestine, which affiliated to the Labour Party in 1903 and was renamed in 2004.

58 Jewish Labour Movement, *Antisemitism in the Labour Party. Submission to EHRC* (2019), p. 6.

59 'Editorial on the Labour leadership election', *Observer*, 25 September 2016.

60 Hansard, HC (series 5) vol. 639, 'Anti-Semitism' (17 April 2018). Smeeth was particularly graphic, giving some examples – 'a snapshot' of typical antisemitic tweets she had received with pro-Corbyn hashtags: 'Poke the pig – get all Zionist child killer scum out of Labour'; 'Ruth you are a Zionist plant, I'm ashamed you are in Labour. Better suited to the murderous Knesset!' *Ibid.*

61 Margaret Hodge, 'Antisemitism in the Labour Party was real and it must never be allowed to return', *Guardian*, 29 October 2020.

62 Jewish Labour Movement, *Antisemitism in the Labour Party*, pp. 16–17.

63 Hodge, 'Antisemitism in the Labour Party was real'.

64 Quoted in Ben White, 'Shifty antisemitism wars', *Open Democracy*, 22 April 2016, opendemocracy.net

65 Asa Winstanley, *Weaponising Anti-Semitism: How the Israel Lobby Brought Down Jeremy Corbyn* (New York: OR Books, 2023), pp. 211–13.

66 Labour Party, *Leaked Report*, p. 848.

67 *Ibid.*, pp. 306, 329. For example, an internal LOTO briefing on 12 December 2017 expressed concern that the Chakrabarti Report had not been fully implemented and called upon the NEC to act 'swiftly and decisively' to resolve antisemitism cases. *Ibid.*, p. 336.

68 Interview, Karie Murphy.

69 Labour Party, *Leaked Report*, pp. 14, 268. It provided copious examples, drawn from the written records, of repeated instances of Holocaust denial and the use of extremely offensive language about Jews which it claimed GLU ignored. *Ibid.*, pp. 271–7.

70 *Ibid.*, pp. 397–8.

71 *Ibid.*, pp. 223–8.

72 On this, the EHRC agreed. It uncovered examples of 'inaction or a failure to investigate', that delays in progressing complaints were common' and

that 'a significant number of complaints relating to antisemitism were not investigated at all'. Equality and Human Rights Commission, *Investigation into Antisemitism in the Labour Party* (October 2020), pp. 7, 71, 95.

73 Labour Party, *Leaked Report*, pp. 303, 556; interview, Karie Murphy. Three senior officials seen as especially culpable were: John Stolliday, GLU Director 2016–18, Sam Matthews, Head of Disputes 2016–18, and Emilie Oldknow, the Director of Governance, Membership and Party Services 2015–18. *Ibid.*, pp. 239–40.

74 *Ibid.*, pp. 285, 567, 749. The changes included expanding the party's capacity for conducting investigation, more thorough investigations, clearer guidelines on disciplinary matters and tougher sanctions. *Ibid.*, pp. 17–18, 749; Forde, *The Forde Report*, pp. 95–6.

75 Jessica Elgot and Heather Stewart, 'Jeremy Corbyn ramps up plans to expel antisemites from party', *Guardian*, 23 July 2019.

76 Donald Schon and Martin Rein, *Frame Reflection* (New York: Basic Books, 1984), p. 32.

77 Personal notes from Compass webinar, 23 March 2023.

78 Ben Gidley, Brendan McGeever and David Feldman, 'Labour and antisemitism: A crisis misunderstood', *Political Quarterly*, 91:2 (2020), 417.

79 Equality and Human Rights Commission, *Investigation into Antisemitism in the Labour Party*, p. 29.

80 We have, however, been able to obtain access to some documents supplied to the EHRC.

81 *Ibid.*, p. 8.

82 Gidley, McGeever and Feldman, 'Labour and antisemitism', p. 417.

83 David Feldman, Ben Gidley and Brendan McGeever, 'The EHRC report shows how difficult building real anti-racist politics will be', *Guardian*, 3 November 2020.

84 Don Waxman, David Schraub and Adam Hosein, 'Arguing about antisemitism: Why we disagree about antisemitism, and what we can do about it', *Ethnic and Racial Studies*, 45:9 (2022), 1817.

85 Interview, Andrew Fisher.

86 Interview, Jon Lansman.

87 Interview, Andrew Fisher.

88 Andrew Murray, *Is Socialism Possible in Britain?* (London: Verso 2022), pp. 130–1. Similarly, Ian Saville, a founder-member of Jewish Voice for Labour, drew attention to the 'abundance of conspiracy theorists' on the Corbynite left. Ian Saville, 'Antisemitism and the left – some lessons to learn', Labour Hub, 15 October 2021, hub.labour.org.uk

89 Quoted in Labour Party, Leaked Report, p. 766.

90 Guhl, '"Everyone I know isn't antisemitic"', p. 63.

91 Interview, Karie Murphy.

92 Joe Thomas, 'Labour to investigate claims of anti-semitism and entryism within Riverside branch', *Liverpool Echo*, 27 October 2016.
93 Ben Westerman, *Report to the NEC on Liverpool Riverside CLP* (London: Labour Party, 2016).
94 Letter from Louise Ellman to the authors (2021).
95 Lee Harpin, 'MP Dame Louise Ellman quits Labour, saying antisemitism is now "mainstream" under Jeremy Corbyn', *Jewish Chronicle*, 16 October 2019. Ellman rejoined Labour in 2021.
96 Renton, *Labour's Antisemitism Crisis*, p. 118; Murray, *Is Socialism Possible in Britain?*, p. 165.
97 Murray, *Is Socialism Possible in Britain?*, pp. 133, 135.
98 Jewish Labour Movement, *Antisemitism in the Labour Party*, p. 8. Eventually two of Berger's left-wing abusers were convicted of offences against her. Renton, *Labour's Antisemitism Crisis*, p. 134.
99 Murray, *Is Socialism Possible in Britain?*, p. 165.
100 Berger subsequently rejoined the Labour Party.
101 This was the claim made by Jewish Labour Movement, *Antisemitism in the Labour Party*, p. 46. The 1999 *Macpherson Report* was an inquiry into the murder of a young black man, Stephen Lawrence, and identified major failings in the Metropolitan Police, including what it called 'institutional racism'. The report defined institutional racism as: 'The collective failure of an organisation to provide an appropriate and professional service to people because of their colour, culture or ethnic origin. It can be seen or detected in processes, attitudes and behaviour which amount to discrimination through unwitting prejudice, ignorance, thoughtlessness and racist stereotyping which disadvantage minority ethnic people.' W. Macpherson, *The Stephen Lawrence Inquiry*, Cm 4262 (London: Stationery Office, 1999), para. 6.34.
102 Interview, party insider. Forde judged as antisemitic pressure on Jewish members to respond to criticism of the Israeli government simply because they were Jewish.
103 Sienna Rodgers, 'Exclusive: Lansman "wasn't happy" with Corbyn response to EHRC report', *LabourList*, 11 November 2020, labourlist.org
104 Jewish Labour Movement, *Antisemitism in the Labour Party*, p. 16.
105 Equality and Human Rights Commission, *Investigation into Antisemitism in the Labour Party*, pp. 55, 70.
106 *Ibid.*, pp. 6, 101.
107 Forde, *The Forde Report*, pp. 50–1.
108 *Ibid.*, p. 52.
109 *Ibid.*, p. 51.
110 Labour Party, *Leaked Report*, p. 377.
111 Interview, Andrew Fisher.

112 Renton, *Labour's Antisemitism Crisis*, pp. 57–9. For a detailed exposition of the Milne view see Winstanley, *Weaponising Anti-Semitism*.
113 Labour Party, *Leaked Report*, p. 377; Jones, *This Land*, p. 223; John Ware, 'Rewriting history: Corbyn's Labour Party, antisemitism and "Panorama"', *The Article*, 18 October 2022.
114 Nichola Mairs, 'Jeremy Corbyn defends ally Chris Williamson against antisemitism claims', *PoliticsHome*, 1 February 2019, politicshome.com
115 *Ibid.*; Renton, *Labour's Antisemitism Crisis*, pp. 160–1.
116 Equality and Human Rights Commission, *Investigation into Antisemitism in the Labour Party*, p. 78; Jones, *This Land*, p. 251; Renton, *Labour's Antisemitism Crisis*, p. 156.
117 Renton, *Labour's Antisemitism Crisis*, p. 127; John Ware, 'Rewriting the history of the Corbyn years', *Fathom*, September 2023.
118 Ware, 'Rewriting the history of the Corbyn years', citing Oldknow's submission to the EHRC.
119 Quoted in *Ibid.*
120 John Ware, 'Exposed: Lies of the Corbynites' leaked dossier', *Jewish Chronicle*, 10 September 2020.
121 Ware, 'Rewriting the history'.
122 Renton, *Labour's Antisemitism Crisis*, p. 214.
123 Forde, *The Forde Report*, p. 52.
124 *Ibid.*, p. 40.
125 Robert Ford, Tim Bale, Will Jennings and Paula Surridge, *The British General Election of 2019* (Basingstoke: Palgrave Macmillan 2021), p. 136.
126 Interview, Karie Murphy.
127 Geoffrey Alderman, a respected professor of politics and a pillar of the Jewish establishment, who knew Corbyn personally, stated that 'the grounds for labelling him an anti-Semite simply do not exist'. Geoffrey Alderman, 'Is Jeremy Corbyn really anti-semitic?' *Spectator*, 8 May 2019. Andrew Murray pointed to Corbyn's campaigning over many years against antisemitism and his praise for the work of the Holocaust Memorial Trust. Murray, *Is Socialism Possible in Britain?*, p. 119.
128 Shane Burley, 'Britain's Labour antisemitism controversy, revisited: An interview with David Renton', *Jewish Currents*, 27 August 2021, https://jewishcurrents.org/britains-labour-antisemitism-controversy-revisited [consulted 12 August 2025].
129 Interview, Jon Lansman. Pogrund and Maguire, *Left Out*, pp. 115–16.
130 Daniel Levy, 'The Jewish community must not become a sacrificial pawn in Labour's war', *Prospect*, October 2018.
131 Jones, *This Land*, pp. 232–3.
132 Renton, *Labour's Antisemitism Crisis*, p. 103.
133 *Ibid.*, p. 104; Interview, Jon Lansman. Lansman's own views shifted, particularly when, as a member of the NEC's Disputes Panel, he encountered 'appalling'

examples of antisemitism, adding that he personally 'had lots of antisemitic abuse'.

134 Jessica Elgot, 'Labour antisemitism more widespread than thought, Momentum says', *Guardian*, 2 April 2018.

135 Renton, *Labour's Antisemitism Crisis*, pp. 34, 213; Interview, Jon Lansman.

136 See, for example, Daniel Finn, 'Crosscurrents Corbyn, Labour and the Brexit crisis', *New Left Review*, 118 (July–Aug 2019); Winstanley, *Weaponising Anti-Semitism*. According to Stern-Weiner, far from being complicit over antisemitism, 'Corbyn and his advisors erred in the opposite direction […] they supported the suspension or expulsion of members on the flimsiest of grounds.' Jamie Stern-Weiner, 'Anti-semitism and the British Labour Party', Jewish Voice for Labour, 10 August 2020.

137 Pogrund and Maguire, *Left Out*, pp. 120, 121.

138 Quoted in Rich, *The Left's Jewish Problem*.

139 Martha Augoustinos and Iain Walker, *Social Cognition: An Integrated Introduction* (London: Sage, 1995), pp. 32–3.

140 John McIlroy, 'British Labour and the challenge of Israel–Palestine', *Capital & Class*, 37:3 (2013), 491–5.

141 Aaron Bastani, 'Labour's obligation to peace between Israel and Palestine starts by rejecting the IHRA examples', *Novara Media*, 17 August 2018.

142 Quoted in David Hirsch, *Contemporary Left Antisemitism* (London: Routledge, 2018), p. 43.

143 Interviews, John McDonnell; Jon Lansman. Lansman pointed out that most Jews who arrived in Israel did so as refugees whom no other country would take. George Eaton, 'Jon Lansman: What the left gets wrong about Israel', *New Statesman*, 8 November 2023.

144 McCluskey, *Always Red*, p. 310.

145 Jones, *This Land*, p. 213.

146 Ivor Gaber, 'Anti-semitism: The touchstone issue for the new Labour leader', *Political Quarterly*, 91:1 (2020), 71.

147 Ivor Gaber, 'Why the EHRC report into anti-semitism in the Labour Party is about so much more than anti-semitism in the Labour Party – A personal view', *Political Quarterly*, 92:3 (2021), 139–40.

148 Interview, Karie Murphy.

8
Corbynism: mission impossible

> The Labour party was 'far closer to extinction as a major party' than ever before because, for the first time in its history, Labour is in real danger of a permanent domination by the unrepresentative and unelectable left.
>
> Roy Hattersley[1]

In 2018, the *New Statesman* declared that the Corbyn left 'has hegemonic control of the wider movement, the Unite super-union, most of the membership and the key rule-making institutions such as the National Executive Committee. What it doesn't yet control is the PLP, but that will change over time.'[2] A former party official echoed these judgements: the Corbyn leadership had 'seized control of every stratum of the party' and had tightened its grip 'to an extent that no previous leadership has achieved.'[3] In this concluding chapter on the Corbyn experiment, we present a very different thesis: Corbyn's control over the party was always precarious, unstable and beleaguered. It was an edifice built on weak foundations.

We have argued that the capacity of Labour leaders to exert tight managerial control over the party varies according to three conditions: institutional integration under the primacy of the leader in party management; its underpinning by a pattern of concurrent majorities spanning all centres of decision-making; and an experienced and capable cohort of party managers. The effectiveness of party management varies according to the magnitude of managerial challenges, in turn a function of the scale and severity of internal conflicts and cleavages. In what follows, we argue, firstly, that none of the three conditions of effective managerial control existed and, secondly, that the scale of the managerial challenges was overwhelming.

Managerial control capability

Under Corbyn, institutional integration was replaced by institutional dislocation and embedded conflict as rival wings of the party controlled different centres of power and decision-making. 'The fundamental sociological law of political parties', Michels declared, was: 'Who says organization, says oligarchy.'[4] But, in Corbyn's case, for a crucial two and a half years, control over the party machine eluded him. It was 'impossible to overstate', Owen Jones later wrote, 'the enmity of top Southside officials' and their 'all-encompassing hatred' of the Corbyn leadership and their engagement in 'a wrecking operation'.[5] This wore a central theme of the Corbynite left's master narrative: the project failed because it had been sabotaged by factionally minded senior party officials.[6] There was, according to James Meadway, economic advisor to McDonnell, a 'persistent, slow-burn attempt to undermine the elected leadership of the Labour party by a small (but influential) minority of its staff that began as soon as Corbyn entered office'.[7] 'In the catechism of party duties,' Michels wrote, 'the strict observance of hierarchical rules becomes the first article,' the necessary conditions of a functioning bureaucracy.[8] According to Murphy, in contrast, many of Corbyn's 'requests [were] thwarted or disregarded' by Southside, many of whose officials, Murray added, were 'disgruntled apparatchiks merely pretending to work'.[9]

Party officials vehemently denied this narrative, dismissing it as a rationalisation to mask LOTO's own ineptitude, incompetence and complete lack of realism. As loyal and impartial servants of the party, they tried their best to work with LOTO, which, however, rebuffed all efforts to improve relations. Indeed, they were treated with mistrust and hostility, threatened with dismissal and often harangued by Corbynite staffers and websites; they were the scapegoats for the leadership's own failings.[10]

The whole debate about the role of Southside and the party apparatus has thus been enveloped in huge controversy, where even basic facts are contested. However, there are two studies which do provide detailed and reliable accounts of the relationship between LOTO and Southside. One is a well-sourced book by two *Sunday Times* journalists based on numerous interviews with key players. It corroborates the claim that most of those who held senior positions in the party HQ were 'aggressively and openly opposed' to the Corbyn leadership.[11] It described senior officials such as Patrick Heneghan, Director of Elections, Campaigns and Organisation, John Stolliday, Director of the Governance and Legal Unit, and Emilie Oldknow, Director of Governance, Membership and Party Services, as intransigent opponents of the Corbyn left leadership with a 'visceral loathing' for the leader himself; their behaviour could be 'openly mutinous'.[12] Southside, Pogrund and Maguire concluded, became 'the last bastion of New Labour within the party's structures [...] impervious to reform'. Senior officials 'had no intention of relinquishing their hold on the party machine'.[13]

The most thorough and authoritative investigation into the LOTO/ Southside schism was conducted by the *Forde Report*, set up by Starmer in 2020, which had access to a mass of documentation, witness statements and interview material. Its point of departure was that a historically unprecedented rupture had occurred between the leadership and the party organisation. Corbyn's election saw officials 'come into direct conflict with the Party's elected leadership for the first time; [...]. This gave rise to a new type of conflict, in which each faction had its hands on at least some of the Party's operational levers of power.'[14] The party machine is formally accountable to the General Secretary and the NEC and not the leadership: this provided shelter to senior Southside officials, many of whom, according to Forde, regarded the politics of the Corbyn leadership quite simply as 'unacceptable'.[15] An extreme manifestation of this was the abusive, scurrilous and expletive-plated language at times used by these officials, as revealed by the so-called Leaked Report, compiled (illegally) by Corbynite officials from WhatsApp groups in 2019. Forde unambiguously rejected assertions by former party officials that the 'at times shockingly disparaging and derogatory' extracts quoted in the Leaked Report were 'cherrypicked and selectively edited', concluding that 'in the main the messages represent the tone and contents of the discussions about Jeremy Corbyn, his staff, and the Party's Left in the SMS WhatsApp groups'.[16]

However, Forde by no means fully endorsed the sabotage narrative.[17] There was 'some justification' for the perception that LOTO was antagonistic, 'and we do not doubt that the intense pressure many of them have described to us was genuinely felt'; this was 'amplified and exaggerated' through social media 'echo chambers'. As a result, some officials 'lost perspective' and concluded that they inhabited 'a conflict zone in which otherwise unacceptable conduct could be justified'.[18] In short, if they felt they were operating in a hostile environment, one well-informed observer noted, it was at least in part because 'Jeremy always regarded Southside officials and regional officials as the enemy'.[19]

Fully accounting for the behaviour of Southside officials requires exploring their role conceptions. The role of party officials has always been a complex and ambivalent one. Pre-Blair, party officials saw themselves as the 'civil servants' of the party, charged with performing their duties in an impartial manner, though – as with civil servants – this always had to be balanced with loyalty to their 'political masters': the NEC, and, more ambiguously, the leadership.[20] However, as we have seen in Chapter 2, during the New Labour years the Blair leadership fostered an important shift in how those charged with managerial responsibilities conceived their roles and functional responsibilities.[21] They were encouraged to redefine themselves as political organisers charged with advancing the 'New Labour project', and their success in doing so became a criterion for advancement.[22] This role conception persisted after 2010 as the party machine exhibited the propensity of most organisations to recruit from among the like-minded. The result, Forde concluded, was an 'ideological homogeneity [that] prevented HQ from collectively fulfilling a neutral "civil service" role', rendering a clash with the Corbyn leadership as more or less inevitable.[23] The key point here is that senior Southside staff felt that in their lack of wholehearted commitment to the leadership, they were serving the *real interests of the party* because they believed Corbynite politics were rendering the Party unelectable.[24] It did not follow that relations between LOTO and Southside were entirely and always uncooperative, but they became increasingly so.

Until McNicol could be removed, the leadership could not instigate the clear-out of Southside that it desperately wanted. The outcome was an impasse – a semi-paralysed party. Not surprisingly, new hires became flashpoints of contention, with LOTO seeking to appoint the politically reliable, and senior officials resisting.[25] All this came to a head in the clash over the community organising scheme. As we have seen in Chapter 4, Arnie Graf had been brought over from the US by Miliband to introduce the idea of hiring community organisers, though nothing substantial had materialised, in large part because of opposition from party staff. Corbyn's plan was much more ambitious and far reaching: the recruitment of a new breed of community organisers as part of Labour's transformation from being an electoral machine into 'a gigantic lever of popular mobilisations, championing the causes of all sectors of the oppressed'.[26]

The proposal was vehemently resisted by the party apparatus, even by those (such as McNicol) who had been sympathetic to the Graf/Miliband initiative. Partly this was for practical reasons: critics claimed that the new type of organiser would cause unnecessary duplication and friction. But the main objection was that they saw the scheme as factionally motivated, to tighten the Corbynite grip on the party.[27] As a result, 'neither side were willing to compromise'.[28] In his written submission to the Forde Inquiry, Jeremy Corbyn bemoaned the fact that though he stressed that community organising was a priority, the proposal 'met with nothing but obstruction and delay from Head Office and most of the Regional and national offices of the Party'.[29] As a result, virtually no progress was made until Jennie Formby's arrival as General Secretary.[30]

The Community Organising Unit was immediately launched, with forty staff members hired, mainly in marginal constituencies. Officially under the joint authority of LOTO and party regional offices, the unit was (as Southside had feared) in practice run by the former, working closely with local Momentum groups and recruited mainly from among its activists.[31] Not surprisingly, relations between the new organisers and regular officials were poor, with the Labour Together report highlighting 'a failure of integration and coordination between community organising and other campaign work' and much infighting as one of the biggest problems of the 2019 campaign.[32] According to Forde, it became 'a totemic issue' in which both sides were intransigent and for both of whom the 'best possible electoral outcome was a secondary concern'.[33]

Not all the conflict between LOTO and Southside was overt. The Labour Party has always been prone to the practice of leaking and anonymous briefings by politicians and officials. Under Corbyn, this became endemic and extended to the leaking of confidential documents and discussions. The effect, as *Forde* reported, was profound. It 'undermined [the party's] operational effectiveness, since it inhibited colleagues' ability to communicate freely and frankly and sowed ever deeper mistrust'.[34] The outcome was both to reinforce the leadership's bunker mentality and to erode the quality of decision-making, as increasingly decisions were taken in secret, with insufficient consultation with relevant officials who were not trusted with sensitive documents, and hence often on the basis of inadequate information. As the veteran journalist Steve Richards noted, 'The people in Corbyn's office behave like paranoid neurotics partly because they have lots to be paranoid about.'[35]

The infirmities of leadership

Under New Labour, Minkin wrote, there was 'no denying the skills, commitment and, at times, audacity of those who led and managed the party,'[36] and the same, it could be added, under Starmer. The contrast with the Corbyn years is striking. No incoming team in Labour's post-war history was so utterly unprepared and poorly qualified to discharge the responsibilities of leadership and management than Corbyn's. Though matters later improved, LOTO's serious and pervasive systemic failures were never really repaired. There was no clear chain of command, no precise remits and no clarity in assignment of responsibilities, coupled with inadequate internal communications and little coordination.[37] Decisions, once made, were not infrequently unpicked. One party manager described the process: 'what would happen was, you'd have a meeting at noon, and something would be decided. And then there'd be another meeting at, say two, and something slightly different would be decided, and then you'd have another meeting at four, basically about the same thing. And it would be a different position again; and at times it was not even clear what we were trying to do.'[38] The *Forde Report*'s judgement was bleak: the leadership operation 'was unstructured and at times chaotic, with a lack of clear decision-making and reporting lines' and 'with no policy direction, no messaging'.[39] This was about as far from Michels's hierarchically ordered and smooth-running party bureaucracy as can be imagined.

It did not help that LOTO, as we have noted previously, was recruited mainly from the ecosphere of the radical left: very few of its staff had any experience of working for the Labour Party. Their lack of familiarity with party rules, conventions, norms and practices frequently impaired their ability to discharge their managerial tasks effectively.[40] Murphy's appointment as chief of staff brought more order into decision-making, but at a heavy cost. Her assertive, brusque and what some saw as her autocratic style led to mounting unrest and disaffection. At the close of 2018, twenty-four LOTO staffers signed a letter of complaint.[41] The charge sheet was long, detailed and damning, and concluded with a call for a 'wholesale change in the culture of the office'.[42] Matters did not appear to improve. Then, in September 2019, Andrew Fisher, Senior Policy Advisor, threw a bombshell into the proceedings by suddenly resigning. The e-mail explaining his resignation, which was soon leaked, was candid and brutal. After chronicling a wide array of failures and weaknesses, he concluded by declaring: 'None of these things individually would be enough to make me leave. [...] But they are a snapshot of the lack of professionalism, competence and human decency which I am no longer willing to put up with daily.'[43] It was a devastating indictment by a top LOTO official.

Ultimate responsibility lay with the leader. Blair had been a highly adept and ruthlessly skilled party manager, and this set the tone of party management during his thirteen years as leader. Corbyn was a complete contrast. No Labour Party leader has ever had fewer aptitudes for leadership or been equipped with so few of the relevant skills, acumen and experience for political management. According to the sympathetic Owen Jones, he had a 'pathological aversion to conflict' which led to 'a destabilising inability to take decisions'.[44] He was unable to chair meetings effectively, which as a result 'lacked structure or focus, his own contributions tended to meander and the outcomes were frequently inconclusive'.[45] As one staffer recalled, 'things take so long, things don't happen because they go into a black hole and disappear'.[46] 'Jeremy simply wasn't a leader,' Jon Lansman, who observed him frequently, reflected. 'He didn't have a plan, nor did he prioritise developing one and wasn't in control of what happened around him.'[47]

A vital leadership skill is performative: the ability to present oneself as a credible leader and potential Prime Minister. But Corbyn confronted unique disadvantages. He inhabited a hugely inhospitable media environment in which his every step was subjected to withering scorn: a 'laser-sharp scrutiny from journalists desperate to exploit every minor stumble'.[48] In their analysis of national newspapers in the months prior and after his election in 2015, a London School of Economics team found that Corbyn was regularly referred to as 'loony', 'insane,' 'Marxist', 'extremist' and 'unpatriotic', descriptions validated by highly selective reporting and the outright distortion and misrepresentation of his actual words.[49] In another report published in 2016, the Media Reform Coalition found that the BBC, in covering Corbyn, regularly breached its own political neutrality rules, frequently using pejorative language as well as relying heavily on hostile sources.[50] Indeed Michael Lyons, former chair of the BBC Trust, citing 'some quite extraordinary attacks on the elected leader of the Labour party', wondered whether 'some of the most senior editorial voices in the BBC have lost their impartiality on this'.[51] Leading Corbynite figures, in short, encountered a ferocity of criticism that exceeded anything that British politics had ever before witnessed. The matter was made worse by the fact that the voracious appetite of much of the media for belittling stories about Corbyn and his allies was generously fed by his enemies.

But not all was the invention of Corbyn's media enemies. Corbyn was the perennial back-bench dissident and never really learned that the expectations of a leader are radically different. He displayed a propensity for maladroit and poorly thought through actions and pronouncements. These included his (very extensively publicised) failure to sing the national anthem at a memorial service to commemorate the Battle of Britain in September 2015, or to wear a poppy on Remembrance Day. His fretful and irritable TV interview style also did not help. One observer familiar with the inner workings of the party at the time noted that 'Corbyn didn't take seriously enough what it means to be a leader of a political party and how to deal with the hostility towards him in the parliamentary party. He tried to recreate the party in his image but didn't think about what sort of tools he needed to do so.'[52]

The chaotic character of party management in the final period of Corbyn's leadership can be illustrated by one single episode: the attempt to remove Labour's Deputy Leader, Tom Watson. Watson (elected in 2015) was a thorn in the side of the leadership, endlessly conspiring against it behind the scenes and widely suspected to be a source of copious leaks. However, he could not be sacked from the Shadow Cabinet, since he was a member ex officio as elected Deputy Leader. In September 2019, Corbyn finally lost patience and, in a rare outbreak of fury, told his inner circle that he wanted him ejected from the Shadow Cabinet; his device for achieving this was abolishing the role of Deputy Leader.[53]

But the plan was hurried, impulsive and ill prepared, and not all within the leadership, notably McDonnell, agreed with it. Abolition of the Deputy Leadership required a rule change which had to be tabled at and approved by the NEC and then voted on by the – imminent – annual Conference. Notwithstanding, the Corbynite leaders on the Executive, Jon Lansman and Andi Fox of the TSSA union, decided to submit to the NEC a request that its standing orders be suspended to allow for the proposed rule change. But the chair, a UNISON representative and decidedly not a Corbyn stalwart, ruled that Lansman's motion was out of order. A vote was called to overturn the chair's decision, but narrowly failed to obtain the requisite two-thirds majority; Lansman then tabled an identical motion for the following morning's NEC on the eve of Conference. By then, predictably, there was uproar in the party at what was so patently a sleight of hand, and, unsurprisingly, a fierce backlash from the PLP ensued. It transpired that even simple preparatory steps, such as securing the approval of key players such as UNISON and the GMB, had not been taken. In a much-publicised comment, Watson accused LOTO of attempting 'a drive-by shooting'. LOTO then backed down, and Lansman withdrew his motion.[54]

The whole episode presented a case study of how not to manage a party. By his ill-advised suggestion, Corbyn had stirred a hornets' nest, then prevaricated, and eventually retreated in response to an outcry. The cohesion of the leadership had weakened further, the schism within the party worsened, an overwhelmingly hostile press crowed in delight and Watson's position actually strengthened. Maximum damage had been caused for no gain whatsoever. And there was a sting to the tale. The spectacular collapse of the coup against Watson shook Corbyn's confidence in Murphy's judgement and emboldened those, especially McDonnell, determined to oust her. With Corbyn's agreement, he asked Bob Kerslake to conduct another review, and the three agreed that Murphy should be removed, with a new role in Southside as a consolation prize. But the enduring image was of a party in disarray.

In short, far from a hierarchical, Michelsian-style oligarchy, tightly controlled by a cohesive elite, Labour under Corbyn was a deeply fractured organisation with a poorly organised and divided leadership struggling to gain a grip on the party. The importance of the long delay before it gained command over the NEC, and hence over the party machine, cannot be overstated; integrated and effective managerial control became an impossibility. Nothing better illustrated the limits of managerial control than the failure to assert control over the candidate selection process for the 2019 election, in stark contrast with what was to happen under Starmer, as detailed in Chapter 10.

The leadership had been caught unprepared by the calling of the 2017 election. Rather more groundwork was in place for the 2019 election. In Chapter 5 we have already reviewed the alteration to the rules governing the 'triggering' of sitting Labour MPs and their very limited impact. For a variety of reasons, including the delaying effect of the reorganisation of constituency boundaries, by the autumn of 2019, many candidates had yet to be adopted. In October, the NEC introduced a new fast-track system for vacant (due to retirement or defection) Labour seats and those considered to be winnable ones, with more power over longlisting assigned to the NEC and regional executive committee members.[55]

Concern was expressed by those on the right of the party that these truncated procedures would enable the NEC to exclude from the longlists politically unreliable candidates, but in fact there was little evidence of this occurring.[56] Of the twenty-six new candidates elected in 2019, seventeen joined the SCG, half the group's membership in 2021, despite a significant Momentum presence in most CLPs.[57] This was a definite improvement on previous years, but, given the strong Corbynite presence in most CLPs, less than might have been anticipated – and the contrast with what was to happen under Starmer is startling. Why was this? Firstly, a key role in selections has always been played by Regional Directors in promoting candidates favoured by the leadership. Few within the regional machinery of the party had much sympathy for the Corbyn project, and the leadership was not in a position to replace most of them until too late. The second point is that the leadership felt cross-pressured when contemplating revising selection procedures. Although the new fast-track procedures did allow for a more active NEC role, it remained a limited one, and proposals to strengthen it were rejected on the grounds that it was undemocratic and because the left had long been a defender of CLP autonomy; the NEC under Starmer was to be much less inhibited and much more indifferent to the rights of local parties.[58]

In the two previous chapters, we analysed the two most serious and formidable managerial problems the leadership confronted: Brexit and antisemitism. Now we propose to dig a little deeper and shed more light on why they proved so intractable. In Chapter 2, we identified four variables which can operate either to exacerbate the impact of internal divisions or to help temper them by acting as conflict shock-absorbers: legitimacy, ideological coherence, strategic convergence and normative order. In each case, as we shall see, these variables operated in such a way as to aggravate the impact of conflicts dividing the party while minimising the leadership's capacity to mitigate and contain them.

Managerial challenges: (1) the crisis of legitimacy

Leaders, to entrench themselves, can rely upon persuasion, patronage and ingrained loyalty, but the most stable and reliable mechanism is legitimacy, the belief that leaders have the right to rule, members the obligation to comply. The precondition for legitimacy is agreement over the basic rules and principles that validate the way power is structured and exercised, and decisions are made. The essential basis for Corbyn's legitimacy was that he had been democratically elected not once but twice, both times with a thumping majority. For many MPs, this did not suffice. As far as one can gather, they queried Corbyn's legitimacy on two grounds. The first was that he was completely unable to command the confidence of his own party in Parliament, without which no Prime Minister could govern. The second was his lack of personal fitness, by which was meant both that he possessed few or any of the qualities which the role of Prime Minister demanded, and he was unelectable, that is, he was not seen by most voters as a credible Prime Minister. Labour's impressive showing at the 2017 election seemed to suggest otherwise, but the moment did not last, as Corbyn's ratings collapsed soon after. Polling conducted in October 2019 gave Corbyn the lowest score of any Leader of the Opposition since records began.[59]

Whether or not these beliefs were justified was beside the point, which is that most MPs held them. They felt under no real obligation to accept Corbyn's authority or even respect it, resulting in a permanent crisis of legitimacy. This unwillingness to accord Corbyn legitimacy was manifested in two main ways. Firstly, by open defiance: at regular weekly PLP meetings, Corbyn was met by a degree of abuse, McDonnell recalled, that 'would not be tolerated in any other organisation.'[60] He was also the target of repeated and often very harsh public criticism by his MPs. Secondly, more covertly, there was the perpetual and incessant leaking and negative briefing, with endless stories in the media about Corbyn's political failings and personal blemishes. Combined with very weak discipline, the result was that the party under Corbyn presented an image to the voters as hopelessly divided and therefore incapable of governing.

Managerial challenges: (2) the breakdown of ideological consensus

'It is doubtful', Easton wrote, 'whether any political system could survive long under the oscillation between polar extremes in value orientations on the part of different segments of the politically relevant members.'[61] This applies equally to political parties. One might have anticipated that polarisation in the Labour Party in this period would have manifested itself most sharply over core economic and social policies. But they did not, in large part because Corbyn's many opponents in the PLP never believed there was any real possibility of his being in a position to implement these policies – so why bother to debate them?

Leaving aside the issue of the EU, already fully explored, matters of foreign policy were different because they raised fundamental questions of British security and patriotism. If voters reached the conclusion that Labour could not be relied upon to defend the realm or was unpatriotic, severe and lasting damage could be inflicted. Added to this was a third factor: on key international questions, even more than domestic ones, the gap between the Corbyn left and the right of the party was so wide as to be insurmountable. As Owen Jones observed, 'for many of Corbyn's enemies within the Labour Party, it was his foreign policy positions more than his domestic policies which rendered the Labour leader illegitimate'.[62] Murray agreed: 'The PLP majority would not die in a ditch to keep the water industry in private hands, but the alliance with Washington, the right and capacity to intervene militarily wherever necessary, and the solidarity of NATO – those were different matters.'[63] It was not coincidental that the first clash in the party under Corbyn was over foreign policy – the Syrian intervention.

On the surface, this is puzzling, since Corbyn *did* compromise: firstly, he agreed to the retention of Britain's allegedly 'independent' nuclear deterrent and to continued NATO membership, though (along with Milne, Murray and many other senior aides) in both cases only because he knew he could never win Conference majorities to abandon them.[64] As a result, the changes in Labour's stance on global politics under Corbyn were relatively modest. Yet, below the surface agreement were the most profound fractures: sharply conflicting ways of making sense of the world, or, as we have called them in the previous chapter, cognitive maps.

The central organising theme in the Corbynite cognitive map of global politics was the Marxist theory of imperialism. Corbynism's anti-imperialism, Murray averred, 'was not a specialist side-show relating to foreign policy, but the core to remaking British society around a vision for social and economic transformation'.[65] Indeed, he acclaimed Corbyn's arrival to the Labour leadership as 'the expression of the advance of anti-imperialist politics' and his project to 'challenge the imperial world order'.[66] At the centre of the imperialist world order, according to this reasoning, lay the US. The US was driven by economic imperatives to seek fresh markets, sources of raw material and profitable outlets for capital investment: in other words, to prey upon the weak and vulnerable in the Global South.[67] It followed that, irrespective of which party controlled the presidency, the US was by its very nature imperialist and expansionist;[68] and to this impulse could be ascribed a whole sequence of Western military interventions in Iraq, Serbia, Syria, Libya, Sierra Leone and elsewhere.

It is worth distinguishing this approach to the US from that held by both the Labour right and soft left. For the Labour right, the Anglo-American axis and the Atlantic alliance that underpinned it formed the cornerstone of any conceivable Labour foreign policy. The Labour Foreign Secretary Ernest Bevin had been a key architect of the Atlantic Alliance in 1949, and loyal membership of NATO and close alignment with US policy were the bedrock principles of the party's approach to international issues ever since. The soft left, always more sceptical of Atlanticism, favoured a more nuanced and discriminating appraisal of the US global role, praise where it lived up to its own democratic principles, and criticism when it embarked on aggressive actions to subvert or overthrow governments in the pursuit of narrow, selfish interests. This lay at the root of the dissent articulated by the soft left Foreign Secretary Robin Cook over the Iraq war, which prompted his resignation from the government in 2003.

The radical left schema, in contrast, stressed structure rather than agency: the inherently imperialist character of US policy. In this bipolar view of the world, one could align either with the imperialist camp led by the US or with the 'progressive' and 'anti-imperialist' forces arrayed against it. This helps to explain why so many on the Corbyn left felt such affinity and sympathy for what many saw as the Palestinian dimension of the worldwide struggle against imperialist aggression and exploitation.

More puzzling was the attitude taken by Corbyn, Milne and Murray (though not by McDonnell) towards Russia. There was, of course, a long tradition of pro-Sovietism on much of Labour's hard left. After the collapse of the Soviet Union and its slippage into right-wing authoritarianism, positive attitudes lingered, partly because of the reflex response to crises which almost invariably blamed US and NATO expansionism, and partly because Russia was seen as a powerful counterweight to US global domination, in Milne's words, providing 'some check to unbridled US power'.[69]

Thus, as early as 2008, Milne attributed Russia's encroachment into Georgia to Moscow's defensive response to 'ever tighter encirclement of Russia by a potentially hostile power'.[70] In 2014, Russia's first invasion of Ukraine was, in Corbyn's view, 'not unprovoked': the 'root of the crisis' lay in 'the US drive to expand eastwards'.[71] When Ukraine's corrupt and repressive regime led by the pro-Russian Viktor Yanukovych was overthrown after mass protests, Milne saw this as 'an entirely unconstitutional takeover' designed 'to pull Ukraine decisively into [NATO's] orbit and defence structure'. Putin's absorption of Crimea and incursion into eastern Ukraine was 'clearly defensive', for 'no Russian government could have acquiesced in such a threat from a territory that was at the heart of both Russia and the Soviet Union'.[72] The responsibility for 'thousands of dead, hundreds of thousands of refugees, indiscriminate shelling of civilian areas' plainly lay with the West and its Ukrainian clients.[73] A similar indulgence was displayed to other autocratic regimes seen to be part of the 'anti-imperialist camp', such as Cuba, Venezuela and Nicaragua, Iran and Syria: for example, both Corbyn and Milne claimed that no reliable evidence existed to corroborate reports of the use of chemical weapons by the Assad regime.[74]

To most in the PLP and, indeed, to a fair chunk of the membership, such beliefs were totally unacceptable, indeed beyond the pale. Their doubts, reservations and misgivings were crystallised in the single most catastrophic error made by Corbyn as leader. In early March 2018, the news broke out that Sergei Skripal, a former Russian intelligence officer who had defected to the West and was given asylum in Britain, and his daughter Yulia, had been poisoned in Salisbury. Within days, the security services reported that, since Novichok, the nerve agent used to poison the Skripals, was manufactured only in Russia, the evidence pointed overwhelmingly to Putin's culpability – but not to Corbyn's satisfaction. In the House of Commons debate, he called for a 'robust dialogue with Russia' and proposed despatching a sample of Novichok to Moscow so it could 'run its own tests'.[75] To make matters worse, Milne in his lobby briefing expressed scepticism about the intelligence finding, commenting that there was 'a history in relation to weapons of mass destruction and intelligence which is problematic, to put it mildly'.[76]

The bulk of the PLP was appalled. As Pogrund and Maguire commented, 'That Corbyn was unwilling to even condemn what evidence suggested was an act of chemical warfare carried out on British soil in broad daylight by a hostile power, was all the evidence that the PLP needed that their opposition to him was justified.'[77] Open mutiny followed, with both the Shadow Foreign and Defence Secretaries, Emily Thornberry and Nia Griffiths, publicly distancing themselves from Corbyn's stance. Unbelievably, Corbyn seriously considered disciplining them, but an angry McDonnell bluntly told Corbyn that he agreed with Thornberry and Griffiths and indeed with the Prime Minister.[78] Inevitably, Corbyn had to back down, but the political consequences of the Skripals incident were profound and far reaching. The right-wing press exulted with multiple headlines such as 'Corbyn, the Kremlin stooge' and 'Putin's puppet'.[79] Corbyn's personal ratings crashed, and the party was tarred. Every negative preconception about Corbyn, his utter unreliability on security matters, his gullibility, his naivety about Britain's foes and his lack of patriotism seemed to be conclusively confirmed. As Murray later recollected, until this point the party was 'doing all right in the polls' and the PLP was 'quiescent'. Now all confidence in the leader dissipated within the PLP.[80]

The row over the Skripals' poisoning was significant, less in itself than in what it revealed about opposing worldviews; the gap between Corbynite anti-imperialism and mainstream Atlanticism was so wide as to be unbridgeable. And by further intensifying the polarisation process, it helped to demolish any lingering hope of a modus vivendi between the two contending blocs.

Strategic fractures: the ethic of conviction versus the ethic of power

Divisions over policy and ideology were compounded by another fundamental source of disagreement: conflicting notions of what Labour was *for*. We have traced the conflict between the ethics of power and of responsibility during the Miliband leadership. The Corbynite left (or much of it) adhered to a third ethic, the ethic of conviction, one previously confined to the margins of Labour politics. The ethic of conviction, as we have seen, was composed of two key components: the notion of politics as a calling, and a 'monist' approach to truth and reality.

Politics as a calling holds that politics is a serious activity only to the extent that it is concerned with principles or service to a cause. This is undoubtedly how Corbyn and many of his lieutenants and advisors saw their role. Corbyn saw himself as, above all, a conviction politician: in a world of murky motives, opportunism and shady dealings, he had, throughout his long political life, shown himself to be a man of unflinching principle and unbending integrity. Politics as a calling did not rule out compromise or a willingness to show flexibility and adjust one's position to hard realities. We have already noted the major concessions Corbyn made over British nuclear weapons and NATO membership, while, as we have seen, the long, protracted negotiations over Brexit were all about accommodating as many viewpoints as possible. Nor was it correct to say (as many of its critics did) that Corbynism exhibited a bland disregard for what the voters actually wanted. Corbynites like Lavery and Trickett so strenuously opposed any commitment to a second Brexit referendum because they argued (rightly, as it transpired) that it would alienate voters, especially in the North and Midlands. They also pointed out, citing polling evidence, that many of the policies proposed in both the 2017 and 2019 manifestos were individually quite popular. But such compromises were acceptable only to the extent that they did not imperil – or could even be construed to advance – the cause as a whole: on fundamental principles, there could be no equivocation. The idea that these principles should be shed because focus groups showed them to be unpopular was, for Corbynites motivated by the ethic of conviction, to trivialise politics, empty it of meaning and detach it from the real fabric of people's lives.

The second facet of the ethic of conviction was a tendency towards 'monism', or a claim to have privileged access to some undisputed truths, both moral and ideological. Such an attitude fostered a sense of rectitude and what the former Labour minister Alan Johnson called a spirit of 'finger-wagging certitude'.[81] In effect, many Corbynites found it difficult to cope with the unsettling vision that other points of view were as legitimate as one's own. As the left-wing barrister and writer Dave Renton observed, 'What many of my fellow leftists seemed to lose during Labour's crisis was the sense that people could disagree with you, and just *disagree with you* […] without needing to imagine bad faith or the assistance of any foreign power.'[82] A typical example was Stern-Weiner's detailed dissection of the aims of those who made allegations about antisemitism: it simply excluded the possibility that they might be *genuinely* worried about antisemitism.[83] As Neal Lawson, head of the soft left group Compass, observed, 'the very characteristics that made [the Corbyn left] so attractive in 2015, their moral certainty, their conviction, the lack of taint, now threaten them. Because the flip side is a politics that can't compromise, when necessary, that finds it hard to trust and reach out, to build alliances, to admit it might have got something wrong – when the common narrative they want to push is that they were instead always right.'[84]

Monism also encouraged a combative, even intolerant, style of discourse. A former Momentum enthusiast who worked for the Corbynite Party Chair, Ian Lavery, recalled an 'atmosphere of fear and intolerance' where 'blind faith' replaced healthy debate, in which even a 'minor infringement of a very rigid world view' was routinely castigated and anybody who was not on the hard Left was dubbed 'right wing'.[85] The assumption of a single truth and the 'correct line' – so endemic in the politics of the radical left – engendered a spirit of what William Hazlitt called an 'inquisitorial watchfulness'[86] towards those who might deviate – and this extended to the Corbynites' own ranks. For example, in July 2016 the Corbynite journalist Owen Jones wrote a blog expressing serious reservations about the leadership which caused fury within LOTO; he later recalled, 'I was hauled into the office by of one of the most prominent leaders of the labour movement, who demanded, bluntly: "What the fuck do you think you're doing? You've practically resigned from the left and need to find a way back."'[87] Even McDonnell became an object of suspicion. For example, left-wing commentator Oliver Eagleton attributed his advocacy of 'greater compromise with the Right' to his vanity, his propensity for 'knee-jerk decisions without thinking through their consequences and a tendency to buckle under pressure'[88] – but never to genuine conviction. All this fostered a black-and-white view of the world, a culture, as a leading activist put it, in which it was 'not possible to have an honest disagreement with the party leadership [...]; you could either defend Jeremy or betray him'.[89]

Between the ethics of conviction and of power, there was no overlap, no point of convergence, no possibility of compromise. They offered two such diametrically opposed conceptions of the Labour Party and its role, indeed utterly opposed views about the proper limits and scope of politics as a practical activity, that the pressure this placed upon Labour's cohesion became almost unbearable. The inevitable consequence of this, as well as other sources of contention, was the disintegration of normative order in the party.

Normative disorder

Shared behavioural norms contribute to sustaining cohesion by regulating and smoothing relationships within a party. In Labour's case, we have singled out three key norms: loyalty, solidarity and civility. The extent to which they were shared and, hence, the degree of normative order, has varied over time, largely as a result of two main factors: changes in the composition of the membership and the severity of schisms within Labour's ranks.

As we have noted, Corbyn's candidature and election witnessed a surge of new recruits into the party. The majority of these were idealists, but among the most vocal and active were those reared in the dogmatic and often intolerant culture of far-left parties and the radical social movements they influenced, notably the StWC. This influx was so large and so sudden that normal socialising mechanisms had insufficient time to take effect. Equally important were the ideological presuppositions and precepts that the more doctrinaire, with their formative experiences in radical left parties, brought with them. These drew heavily on elements of Marxism, especially its thesis that class conflict underpinned all politics, reinforcing those on the hard left who had always subscribed to it. Notions of class conflict were applied to Labour's internal politics, giving rise to a binary division between 'the left' or 'the socialists' (themselves), the custodians of the 'real' interests of the working class, and 'the right' (sometimes called 'the centrists'), who favoured working-class incorporation into the existing capitalist social order. It followed that Labour's internal politics registered the clash of opposing class interests, and although truces could be reached and deals struck, for example at election times, ultimately the objectives of the rival wings were irreconcilable.[90] This view was by no means held or held in entirety by all, especially not by the more pragmatic Corbynites such as McDonnell, ironically one of a minority who defined themselves as Marxists.

This adversarial approach to Labour politics combined with other elements of the ethic of conviction to demolish any feelings of solidarity in the party with others with differing views, and hence any sense of Labour as a political community. The right of the party heartily reciprocated: thus the Blairite *éminence grise*, Peter Mandelson, described the Corbynite belief system as a 'far-left ideology' which emphatically lay 'outside the party's historical mainstream'.[91] As Murray concluded, seldom if ever had there been a time in Labour's history 'when its principal factions have been so estranged from each other, really bound together by nothing except a mutual loathing and a determination to obliterate their internal opponents'.[92]

The consequence of the decomposition of the norms of loyalty and solidarity was to sap or even debilitate the operation of the third norm, civility, which stipulated that debate be conducted in a reasonable and restrained manner. This was most notably the case in those CLPs most affected by the entry of activists schooled in far-left sectarianism.[93] A senior party manager summed up the new temper of debate in this way: 'It always had to be a fight; it was always quite confrontational. That was the playbook.'[94] Tessa Milligan, later chair of the soft left group Open Labour, described her own experiences: 'I have been harassed, defamed, threatened, bullied, deceived, followed, photographed without my knowledge, racially abused (I am Jewish), demeaned as a young woman […] All in the name of political warfare.'[95]

These manifestations of normative disorder were most pronounced in the old Militant strongholds in Merseyside. For example, in Liverpool and in the adjacent Merseyside seat of Wallasey, Lewis Goodall found 'a culture of bullying and intimidation [was] gripping parts of the Labour Party […]. Politics, all round, has become coarser.' Factionalism had become 'all-consuming', with many convinced that the other side was 'not only wrong but immoral'.[96] Similarly, the investigation into Liverpool Riverside, previously discussed, uncovered a 'toxic atmosphere' with much 'heckling, jeering and baying' of speakers, threats and abuse, with members of the Corbynite left 'demonstrating little regard for other members'.[97] A later report disclosed evidence of 'bullying, factionalism, misogyny and dysfunction' in the Liverpool party as a whole.[98] This even infected the internal politics of the Corbyn left. By 2019, Michael Chessum recalled, the atmosphere within his local left group had become 'toxic', with growing intolerance of any dissent and an obsession with factional advantage.[99]

A major role was played, as we have seen, by the radical left 'digital outriders', the new media platforms which proliferated in this period, including *THE SKWAWKBOX*, *The Canary*, *Novara Media*, *Jacobin* and *New Socialist*, key agencies for transmitting Corbynite messages. Often strident and polemical in tone, these tended to be the most visible and vocal representations of Corbynism. *THE SKWAWKBOX* and *The Canary*, in particular, the most virulent of these platforms, had close links with Corbyn's chief of staff, Karie Murphy and other LOTO officials.[100] For such platforms, Lansman wrote, there was 'no grey zone between us and our enemies, no openness not only for compromise or tactical retreat but also for adjustments to presentation or framing of our case in order to win over waverers or disarm opponents. You're either with them or you are the enemy.'[101] These 'digital outriders' did much to contaminate the public conversation within the party. The right, especially the Blairites, reciprocated, and could be as splenetic and intemperate as the Corbyn left; as a result of which a vicious circle of intensifying invective took hold.[102]

Though it is difficult to establish with any precision the magnitude and scale of this factionalism, Labour Together, in its 2019 election post-mortem study, reported that many of its 11,060 respondents complained of a fractious, hostile and unwelcoming atmosphere in their parties. Many CLPs were 'consumed by highly factional battles over motions and internal elections', findings broadly corroborated by a 2021 Fabian Society survey.[103] The barrister Adam Wagner, who was hired by the Jewish Labour movement to submit evidence to the EHRC's inquiry, drew a parallel with the Mid-Staffordshire hospital inquiry, in which he had been professionally involved. In both cases, investigations uncovered 'a breakdown of civility, humanity and empathy', a situation where 'everybody's out to get everybody else. There's no trust.'[104]

Mission impossible

The proposition that the Corbyn leadership ever ruled supreme over the party is a myth. The scale of opposition it faced in both the PLP and the party apparatus was formidable and ultimately insurmountable. Subject to remorseless attacks from the bulk of media outlets, struggling always to get its message across, exposed to destabilisation from the party's right wing, it is difficult to avoid the conclusion that the Corbyn project was, in the words of one LOTO staffer, 'mission impossible'.[105] If the preservation of a reasonable degree of internal cohesion and robust internal governance is a measure of effective party management, Corbyn's managerial strategy failed spectacularly – a failure which contributed to its devastation at the polls in 2019. The new leadership could only have survived by adopting a more pluralist and inclusive approach to political management; only through building a wider coalition could it have established a firmer base in the party. But the inevitable corollary of such an approach would have been a dilution of its programme, its principles and its aspirations to control the party, a step that most Corbynite leaders were unwilling to take: for then it would have ceased to be the Corbyn project.

Notes

1 Roy Hattersley, 'Labour is far closer to extinction now than in the 1980s', *New Statesman*, 26 September 2016.
2 Jason Cowley, 'Who is the real John McDonnell?', *New Statesman*, 5 September 2018.
3 Bob Westerman, 'The inner workings of British political parties' (London: Constitution Unit, 2020), pp. 31, 33.
4 Robert Michels, *Political Parties: A Sociological Study of the Oligarchical Tendencies in Modern Democracy* (New York: Free Press, 1962), p. 365.
5 Owen Jones, *This Land: The Story of a Movement* (London: *Allen Lane, 2020*), pp. 65, 70.
6 Labour Party, *Leaked Report. The Work of the Labour Party's Governance and Legal Unit in Relation to Anti-semitism, 2014–2019* (London: Labour Party, 2020), pp. 37, 57.
7 James Meadway, 'I witnessed Labour staff working to undermine Jeremy Corbyn's leadership', *Novara Media*, 2 September 2020.
8 Michels, *Political Parties*, p. 72.

9 Interview, Karie Murphy; Andrew Murray, *Is Socialism Possible in Britain*? (London: Verso 2022), p. 95.
10 Interview, former senior party official.
11 Gabriel Pogrund and Patrick Maguire, *Left Out: The Inside Story of Labour under Corbyn* (London: Bodley Head, 2021), p. 36.
12 *Ibid.*, pp. 5, 14, 46–7, 174.
13 *Ibid.*, p. 36.
14 Martin Forde (chair), *The Forde Report* (London: Labour Party, 2022), p. 29.
15 *Ibid.*, pp. 28, 113.
16 *Ibid.*, pp. 34, 25–6.
17 We have already discussed two specific Corbynite allegations over Southside's obstruction: attempts to block Corbyn's re-election by manipulation of the rules and procedures and by deliberately sabotaging Labour's electoral campaign in 2017.
18 Forde, *The Forde Report*, p. 34.
19 Interview, former senior party official.
20 Lewis Minkin, *The Blair Supremacy: A Study in the Politics of Labour's Party Management* (Manchester: Manchester University Press, 2014), p. 133.
21 This does not apply to officials occupying politically less sensitive roles, such as organising conferences or routine administration of the rules.
22 Minkin, *The Blair Supremacy*, pp. 155–6.
23 Forde, *The Forde Report*, p. 76.
24 *Ibid.*, p. 113
25 Andrew Murray, *Is Socialism Possible in Britain?* (London: Verso 2022), p. 95.
26 James Schneider, 'A world to win and a planet to save', *Open Democracy*, 11 January 2021, opendemocracy.net
27 Forde, *The Forde Report*, p. 113; Andrew Murray, *The Fall and Rise of the British Left* (London: Verso 2019), p. 185.
28 Forde, *The Forde Report*, pp. 58, 60.
29 *Ibid.*, p. 58.
30 Interview, Karie Murphy.
31 Robert Ford, Tim Bale, Will Jennings and Paula Surridge, *The British General Election of 2019* (Basingstoke: Palgrave Macmillan 2021), pp. 113–14.
32 Labour Together, *General Election Review 2019* (Labour Together, 2020), p. 111, labourtogether.uk
33 Forde, *The Forde Report*, p. 60.
34 *Ibid.*, p. 56.
35 Steve Richards, 'Labour's rebels, unable to get their act together, are part of the problem', *Guardian*, 22 July 2016.
36 Minkin, *The Blair Supremacy*, p. 707.
37 Interview, Katy Clark.
38 *Ibid.*

39 Forde, *The Forde Report*, pp. 31, 29.
40 *Ibid.*, p. 31.
41 Pogrund and Maguire, *Left Out*, p. 157; Jones, *This Land*, p. 124.
42 Pogrund and Maguire, *Left Out*, p. 160.
43 *Ibid.*, p. 264.
44 Owen Jones, 'Only an honest conversation about the Corbyn era will help us learn from it', *Guardian*, 17 September 2020.
45 Jones, *This Land*, p. 97.
46 *Ibid.*, p. 104.
47 Interview, Jon Lansman.
48 Len McCluskey, *Always Red* (New York: OR Books, 2021), p. 235.
49 Bart Cammaerts, Brooks DeCillia and João Magalhães, 'Journalistic transgressions in the representation of Jeremy Corbyn: From watchdog to attack dog', *Journalism*, 21:2 (2020), 197–206. Even a random Google search of the coverage by the *Sun*, Britain's largest-selling daily, of Corbyn, uncovers such epithets as hapless, pathetic, clueless, gaffe-prone, cringeworthy, unpatriotic and extreme.
50 Media Reform Coalition, '*Should he stay* or *should he go? Television* and *online news coverage* of the *Labour Party* in *crisis*', *Media Reform Coalition*, July 2016, mediareform.org.uk
51 Rowena Mason, 'BBC may have shown bias against Corbyn, says former trust chair', *Guardian*, 12 May 2016.
52 Interview, Ruth Lister.
53 Pogrund and Maguire, *Left Out*, pp. 236–7.
54 *Ibid.*, pp. 256–9.
55 Sienna Rodgers, 'Exclusive: New selection process agreed by Labour's ruling body', *LabourList*, 8 October 2019, labourlist.org
56 Frances Perraudin and Kate Proctor, 'Labour accused of "control-freakery" over candidate selections', *Guardian*, 18 October 2019.
57 Sienna Rodgers, 'Labour gained just one seat – but many more fresh faces', *LabourList*, 16 December 2019, labourlist.org
58 Rodgers, 'Exclusive: New selection process.
59 Jonathan Freedland, 'The question for Labour: Why are you sticking with Jeremy Corbyn?', *Guardian*, 25 October 2019.
60 Interview, John McDonnell.
61 David Easton, *A Systems Analysis of Political Life* (New York: John Wiley and Sons, 1965), p. 196.
62 Owen Jones, *This Land*, p. 108.
63 Murray, *Is Socialism Possible in Britain?*, p. 48.
64 All major unions, including Unite, supported retaining British nuclear weapons, as much for industrial as any other reasons.
65 Murray, *Is Socialism Possible in Britain?*, p. 218.
66 *Ibid.*, pp. 94, 216.

67 *Ibid.*, pp. 94, 88, 164.
68 Murray, *The Fall and Rise of the British Left*, p. 163.
69 Peter Wilby, 'The thin controller', *New Statesman*, 16 April 2016.
70 Seumas Milne, 'This is a tale of US expansion not Russian aggression', *Guardian*, 14 August 2008.
71 Jeremy Corbyn, 'NATO belligerence endangers us all', *Morning Star*, 17 April 2014.
72 Seumas Milne, 'It's not Russia that's pushed Ukraine to the brink of war', *Guardian*, 30 April 2014.
73 Seumas Milne, 'The demonisation of Russia risks paving the way for war', *Guardian*, 4 March 2015.
74 Ibrahim Azeem, *The Prospective Foreign Policy of a Corbyn Government and its U.S. National Security Implications* (Washington, DC: Hudson Institute, 2019), p. 19; Seumas Milne, 'An attack on Syria will only spread the war and killing', *Guardian*, 27 August 2013.
75 Pogrund and Maguire, *Left Out*, p. 78.
76 Jones, *This Land*, pp. 109–10.
77 Pogrund and Maguire, *Left Out*, p. 79.
78 *Ibid.*, pp. 82–3.
79 Jones, *This Land*, p. 110.
80 Pogrund and Maguire, *Left Out*, p. 81.
81 Alan Johnson, *The Long and Winding Road* (London: Corgi, 2017), Kindle edition.
82 David Renton, *Labour's Antisemitism Crisis* (London: Routledge, 2021), p. 114.
83 Jamie Stern-Weiner, 'Antisemitism and the British Labour Party', Jewish Voice for Labour, 10 August 2020.
84 Neal Lawson, 'The anti-semitism crisis shows the Labour leadership needs to get better at listening', *Open Democracy*, 2 August 2018, opendemocracy.net
85 James Matthewson, 'Progressive Pragmatism', *Compass*, 2020. https://www.compassonline.org.uk/wp-content/uploads/2020/09/ProgressivePrag_JM_FINAL-2.pdf [consulted 23 March 25].
86 William Hazlitt, *On the Pleasure of Hating* (Digiread.com, 2010).
87 Jones, *This Land*, p. 115.
88 Oliver Eagleton, *The Starmer Project* (London: Verso, 2022), p. 113.
89 Michael Chessum, *This Is Only the Beginning: The Making of a New Left, from Anti-Austerity to the Fall of Corbyn* (London: Bloomsbury Academic, 2022), p. 191.
90 Michael Calderbank, 'How likely is a Labour Party split?' *Red Pepper*, 4 August 2016; Simon Hannah, *A Party with Socialists in It* (London: Pluto, 2018), p. xvi; Daniel Finn, 'The Forde Report has exposed the rotten foundations of Keir Starmer's leadership', *Jacobin*, 22 July 2022.

91 Peter Mandelson, 'Labour is a broad church – Jeremy Corbyn is turning it into a narrow sect bound for the abyss', *Guardian*, 31 December 2015.
92 Murray, *Is Socialism Possible in Britain?*, p. 222.
93 Lewis Goodall, *Left for Dead? The Strange Death and Rebirth of the Labour Party* (London: Collins, 2019), p. 232; Ben Cooper and Andrew Harrop, *More to Do: Unequal Experiences of Labour Party Membership* (London: Fabian Society, 2021), fabians.org.uk; Interview, Peter Hain.
94 Interview, Rosie Winterton.
95 Tessa Milligan, 'The Forde report shows how Labour cannot remain a factional seesaw', *LabourList*, 21 July, 2022, labourlist.org.
96 Goodall, *Left for Dead?*, pp. 231–2.
97 Labour Party, 'NEC investigation into Liverpool Riverside', 2016. (Document in possession of the authors.)
98 Sienna Rodgers, 'Exclusive: Labour Liverpool report finds local bullying, misogyny, toxic culture', *LabourList*, 20 July 2021, labourlist.org.
99 Chessum, *This Is Only the Beginning*, pp. 189–90.
100 Renton, *Labour's Antisemitism Crisis*, p. 56; Interview, Ruth Lister.
101 Quoted in Renton, *Labour's Antisemitism Crisis*.
102 Jeremy Gilbert, 'Why wouldn't they be reconciled? Corbyn's leadership and the recalcitrance of the Parliamentary Labour Party', *Political Quarterly*, 92:2 (2021), 208.
103 Labour Together, *General Election Review 2019*, pp. 101, 102; Cooper and Harrop, *More to Do*.
104 Adam Wagner, 'Labour's institutional antisemitism – Corbynism: The post-mortem', Apple Podcast, Episode 1, 2020.
105 Interview, Katy Clarke.

9

Labour under Starmer: taking back control

> I have no spur
> To prick the sides of my intent, but only
> Vaulting ambition, which o'erleaps itself
> And falls on th'other.
>
> *Macbeth*

The consolidation of managerial control

Keir Starmer inherited a fractured, bitterly divided and intensely polarised party reeling from a devastating electoral defeat, with fewer MPs than in any election since 1935. Five years later, Labour elected the second-largest number of MPs ever in its history and had achieved in one parliamentary term what it had taken three after the equally disastrous 1983 defeat. One reason for Starmer's triumph, according to the leader, was that he had totally and irrevocably transformed the party bequeathed by Corbyn a few years earlier. This chapter seeks both to chronicle and account for this transformation.

The election to replace Corbyn was conducted in an amicable spirit. Two of the contenders, Keir Starmer and Lisa Nandy, were associated with the soft left of the party, and the third, Rebecca Long-Bailey, with the Corbynite or (as we shall now call them) the hard left. The result was never in much doubt as Starmer coasted to victory with a percentage of the poll roughly equal to that obtained by Corbyn in 2015. Long-Bailey,

Table 9.1 Leadership election 2020 results

Section	Rebecca Long-Bailey	Lisa Nandy	Keir Starmer	Total
Affiliates	16,970 (22.31%)	18,681 (24.56%)	40,417 (53.13%)	76,068
Members	117,598 (29.29%)	58,788 (14.64%)	225,135 (56.07%)	401,521
Registered supporters	650 (5.00%)	2,128 (16.36%)	10,228 (78.64%)	13,006

Source: Labour Party

in contrast, secured only half the vote won by Corbyn less than five years previously (Table 9.1). Starmer won because he was seen by dispirited and demoralised party members as a much more credible, competent and electorally appealing leader than his predecessor; because he offered radical policies; and because he presented himself as a unifier.

Strengthening managerial control capability

The scale of the challenge the victorious Starmer encountered was daunting, indeed colossal. The party was battered, racked by mutual suspicions and repugnance, the deep wounds inflicted by years of fierce infighting still festering. However, on the plus side, he had assembled a formidable coalition of support encompassing the right of the party, the soft left and, indeed, a large slice of the Corbyn left; and the size of his triumph had conferred upon him a powerful democratic mandate. The very fact that his political experience was relatively limited could be considered an advantage because he had relatively few enemies.

Starmer had emphasised his determination to heal Labour's wounds, and these and other pronouncements suggested he would adopt a pluralist approach to party management. When asked which Labour leader over the last half-century he most admired, he cited Harold Wilson because of the way he 'actually managed to hold bits of the party together […] he was spinning plates left, right and centre, but he actually steered through it pretty well'.[1] Whether he ever intended to adopt a pluralist strategy is doubtful, for it increasingly became evident that all his instincts were centralist and controlling; ruthlessness and single-mindedness were characteristics constantly applied to him by his biographer, Tom Baldwin.[2]

According to one shrewd and experienced participant in Labour's internal struggles, there were 'basically three nodal points of power that form a triangle in the Labour Party, and if you control all three, you can drive the party in the direction that you want it to go in: the Leader and the Leader's Office, the General Secretary and the NEC'.[3] Starmer controlled the first, and his priorities were, in order to reconstitute a New Labour-style centralised managerial regime, to secure control over the other two.

The first was the easiest – the summary removal of the Corbynite General Secretary Jennie Formby, who was told to resign. She was replaced as General Secretary in May 2020 by David Evans, a highly experienced and skilled organiser, having served during the Blair era first as a Regional Secretary (1995–99) and then as Assistant General Secretary (1999–2001). His election by the NEC was a clear intimation of the resumption of New Labour's approach to party management. This was confirmed by appointments to key managerial roles of others who shared the same background and outlook as Evans, the two most important of whom were the 'two Matts'. Matt Pound was formerly National Organiser for the Labour right-wing ginger group Labour First and played a key role in the Starmer leadership campaign. He was then successively Head of Political Organising (April 2020–March 2022), Senior Advisor (until March 2024) and Political Director for Elections. Matt Faulding, a senior figure in another right-wing pressure group, the more Blairite Progress, became primarily responsible for overseeing candidate selections;[4] later, in 2023, he was appointed to the important position of PLP Secretary.[5] All three were centralisers and disciplinarians by temperament, right-wing Labour by political inclination and uncompromisingly hostile to the hard left. They also proved themselves to be highly capable, talented and uninhibited about deploying managerial power to their fullest extent.

Completing the quad of top party managers was Morgan McSweeney, appointed by Starmer as his chief of staff in April 2020. He had been employed in Labour HQ's rapid rebuttal unit during the Blair years and had worked for the Labour leader of Lambeth Council, Steve Reed, where he demonstrated his organisational skills in the successful bid to oust the hard left from control of the local party. He then collaborated with Jon Cruddas in the triumphant campaign to repel the British National Party in Barking and Dagenham. After organising Liz Kendall's doomed bid for the leadership in 2015, he was in 2017 appointed director of the recently formed Labour Together organisation.

Initially, Labour Together was a broad-based body seeking to build bridges in the party, but, under McSweeney, it was transformed into a bridgehead for the overthrow of the Corbynite regime. Wealthy businessmen sympathetic to Labour were approached for funding. The most important were Martin Taylor, a hedge fund manager who had made a fortune as founder of Nevsky Capital, 'a £1.5bn fund launched in the Cayman Islands known for investing in Russian companies such as Gazprom';[6] and Trevor Chinn, a businessman and philanthropist who had donated generously to Labour in the Blair/Brown era. This funding enabled McSweeney to commission extensive research into the party membership. Its key finding was that many who had voted for Corbyn were not ideologically hard left but, rather, soft left idealists, disenchanted by Labour's equivocations over austerity, and could therefore be peeled away by a platform that combined radical policies with professional and inclusive leadership. Appealing to them was to become Starmer's winning formula.

Sometime in 2019, McSweeney concluded that the politician best placed to block a Corbynite succession was Keir Starmer, and, from this point, the two worked closely together, with the Irishman appointed his campaign manager and then chief of staff. (After September 2021, he became Director of Campaigns until October 2024, and then resumed his role as chief of staff, this time to Prime Minister Starmer.) Described by Cruddas as a 'brilliant organiser' and election campaigner,[7] he was by instinct and inclination a managerial disciplinarian. His politics were unambiguous: he detested the hard left, felt it had no legitimate place in the party and favoured an all-out war to crush it.[8] According to his friend Nick Forbes, a former leader of Newcastle City Council, he 'doesn't have room for compromise with the hard Left. He thinks they need to be eradicated from the party because they are so dangerous'.[9] He proved to be adroit, highly resourceful and audacious.

With the recruitment of a talented team of political managers, the next step was to take command over the NEC. Starmer inherited an Executive with a pro-Corbyn majority, but of its thirty-nine members, the leader appoints the three front bench representatives, and, if one adds the leader's own vote, this meant an immediate swing away from the Corbyn left, yet not enough to give him a reliable majority. There were three crucial NEC by-elections in April 2020, two in the constituency section and one for the BAME representative; helped by the Corbyn left's inability to agree on a common slate, the right-wing Labour First slate won all three seats. Notwithstanding, David Evans's winning margin in the NEC election for General Secretaryship was a relatively slim twenty votes to sixteen. The job was far from completed.

In the run-up to the 2020 NEC elections, the Executive altered the voting system for electing its constituency members from FPTP to a single transferable vote, which guaranteed a fairer spread of opinion. Two major slates competed for the members' vote: the hard left alliance Grassroots Voice (whose major component was Momentum) and the new group Labour to Win, an umbrella body linking together Labour First and Progress. The Grassroots Voice slate won five of nine CLP representatives, plus the youth and disabled posts, that is, seven out of the eighteen being contested: a further loss of support on the NEC but still testimony to its continuing support in the constituencies. The overall outcome was that Starmer could rely on the unequivocal support of twenty members, normally supplemented by four others. As a result, the leadership gained control over the NEC's powerful Officers' group, to which many of the NEC's responsibilities were delegated, and which previously had a left majority.

During his campaign for the leadership, Jon Cruddas wrote, Starmer 'preached the language of factional reconciliation and internal pluralism'.[10]

But his practice was radically different, for, as noted, key party managers were steeped in the New Labour ethos of centralised party management. They had been traumatised by the victory of Corbynism, which, they were convinced, had been a near-death experience for the party, and so they were implacable in their determination to prevent a recurrence. They concluded that the earlier generation of Blairites had been too complacent and too tolerant, and this had allowed the hard left to escape from Mandelson's 'sealed tomb'.[11] What was required was more centralisation, tighter discipline and less concern with political accommodation. As one of Starmer's aides put it: 'There's a tradition of Labour leaders trying to maintain unity by tolerating every strand of opinion in the party, but that approach is crippling.'[12] In a memorandum written in April 2021, he wrote that 'prizing unity above all else leads us to look inwards and away from our voters. We overvalue its importance, and this narrows our thinking and shrinks our electoral appeal.' He advised an end to the 'self-regard of endless internal conversations'. Labour's electoral revival pivoted on convincing voters that Labour had irrevocably broken with Corbyn; provoking opposition from the hard left and then pulverising it was the best way to demonstrate this.[13]

Starmer was quick to avail himself of the opportunities that Corbynite mistakes furnished him. In June 2020, Rebecca Long-Bailey, the sole Corbynite in the Shadow Cabinet, shared on Twitter an article by Maxine Peake in which the actress claimed that American police officers had learned the harsh techniques that had led to the death of George Floyd from the Israelis. The claim was inaccurate, but Starmer also insisted that it was antisemitic. When Long-Bailey foolishly refused Starmer's request to delete her tweet, she was immediately sacked.[14] Later in the year, three junior Corbynite frontbenchers provided the grounds for their own instant dismissal by defying a three-line whip.[15] And shortly after, as we see below, Corbyn conveniently offered himself as a sacrificial lamb.

But before Starmer could take further steps to tighten his grip on the party, two events intervened: the deepening crisis over COVID (which we briefly touch upon below), and the publication in October 2020 of the much-awaited EHRC report on antisemitism in the party.

Unfinished business: antisemitism, the EHRC report and the disciplining of Jeremy Corbyn

The antisemitism crisis had already resurfaced with the publication in April 2020 of the so-called 'Leaked Report' referred to in Chapter 8, with its very detailed defence of the Corbyn leadership's handling of antisemitism complaints; its most explosive conclusions were that the scale of antisemitism had been wilfully exaggerated in a determined bid to destabilise the Corbyn leadership, with action against antisemitism deliberately stymied by Southside to maximise Corbyn's embarrassment. The report was widely disseminated on hard left social media platforms and other outlets as a full exculpation of the Corbynite record over antisemitism. The result was uproar in the party.

However, as soon became evident, the report had relied upon illegally obtained data (such as the scraping of personal WhatsApp accounts). An angry Starmer directed the NEC to launch an inquiry into the leaking of the report and the identity of those responsible. Its terms of reference were to determine the accuracy of the report's major allegations, the circumstances in which the report was commissioned and written, and its purposes; the structure, culture and practices of the party organisation, including the relationship between senior party staff and the elected leadership of the Labour Party; and to make recommendations as to how any problems identified should be tackled. These were very broad terms of reference, and precisely why the NEC anticipated an early delivery of the inquiry's report is unclear, as two years were to elapse before it was published. The investigating team chosen by the NEC comprised four members: the chair, Martin Forde QC, a senior barrister, Baroness Debbie Wilcox, former leader of Newport City Council, Lord Larry Whitty, a former Labour General Secretary, and Baroness Ruth Lister, a social policy professor and chair of the soft left organisation Compass:[16] all were very independent minded.

Six months after the Leaked Report, the EHRC published its own report. The impact was as explosive as the Leaked Report's, but its conclusions were dramatically different. As we have already seen, they were forthright and unequivocal in condemning the Corbyn leadership and finding it in clear breach of the Equality Act. It made a series of recommendations, the most important of which were that the Labour Party should:

- establish a comprehensive procedure 'setting out how antisemitism complaints will be handled and how decisions on them will be made';
- engage with Jewish stakeholders to establish 'robust principles and practices to tackle antisemitism';
- provide education and practical training, in consultation with Jewish stakeholders, for all individuals involved in the antisemitism complaints process and for all those found to have engaged in antisemitic conduct;
- 'Implement clear rules and guidance that prohibit and sanction political interference in the complaints process'; and 'put in place long-term arrangements for independent oversight of the complaint handling process';[17]
- formulate an action plan which would require EHRC approval within six weeks.

The report was greeted by the JLM and the many other critics of Corbyn's handling of antisemitism as a total vindication. It was also welcomed in other quarters too, including by the soft left mayor of London, Sadiq Khan, and the Corbyn-leaning Scottish Labour leader Richard Leonard.[18] Even the SCG MPs called for the party to unite 'behind the implementation of the EHRC's recommendations', although not all members of the group were prepared to sign the statement.[19]

But one person was quite unrepentant. Jeremy Corbyn continued to insist that obstruction by Southside had been principally to blame for any failings in tackling antisemitism and that 'the scale of the problem was also dramatically overstated for political reasons by our opponents inside and outside the party, as well as by much of the media'.[20] Corbyn's response provided an opportunity for Starmer, which he seized with alacrity. He declared that 'if there are still those who think there's no problem with antisemitism in the Labour Party, then, frankly, you are part of the problem too. And you should be nowhere near the Labour Party either.'[21] The party announced that, in view of Corbyn's failure to retract his statement, he had been suspended both from the party and from the PLP pending investigation.[22]

Corbyn's suspension was an extraordinary move: no former Labour leader has been disciplined since Ramsay MacDonald was ejected in 1931 for forming a coalition with the Tories. The hard left was furious and demanded his immediate reinstatement. An NEC Disputes Panel (just two of whose four members were Corbyn supporters) decided that Corbyn's offence merited only a formal warning and therefore restored his membership. Protracted negotiations between senior officials and key Corbyn aides then took place to agree a form of words in which Corbyn would refine his immediate response in such a way that the leadership found acceptable. It appeared that an agreement had been reached, but JLM, the Jewish Board of Deputies and the high-profile MP Margaret Hodge (who threatened to resign) responded with fury to any hint of a compromise, and the leadership backed away. Instead, Starmer instructed the party's chief whip that Corbyn was to remain suspended from the PLP.[23] This meant that, unless the whip was returned, Corbyn would be ineligible to stand as a Labour candidate in the next election. This was probably what the leadership wanted all along.[24]

The decision was immediately denounced by the SCG. Len McCluskey called it 'a vindictive and vengeful action' and accused Starmer of bad faith in reneging on a deal which he claimed had been negotiated to bring Corbyn back into the fold.[25] In January 2022, left-wing members presented a motion to the NEC describing the move as 'deeply divisive' and calling for an immediate end to Corbyn's suspension from the PLP, but this was defeated by twenty-three votes to fourteen.[26] 'Had Jeremy shown appropriate contrition for what happened on his watch,' the right-wing NEC member Luke Akehurst stated, 'or merely stayed silent, he could have continued on the Labour backbenches.'[27] But, in fact, according to a party source, even if he had been prepared to apologise 'unequivocally, unambiguously and without reservation', the whip would not be restored.[28] Removing Corbyn had become a symbol of the party's transformation, and allowing him back would be politically highly inconvenient and was never really considered.

In the meantime, in December 2020, the NEC unanimously agreed a draft plan in line with EHRC recommendations. Its main elements included the establishment of an independent antisemitism complaint handling process, full consultation with the Jewish community and delivering antisemitism training for all staff.[29] Appropriate rule changes were approved by the NEC in September 2021 by eighteen votes to eight. They were adopted by that year's Conference by 74 per cent to 26 per cent, while the new disciplinary procedures (discussed below) were agreed by 62 per cent to 38 per cent, with Unite abstaining on both motions.[30] In February 2023, the EHRC announced that Labour had fully complied with all its recommendations; Starmer responded by stating that this showed the progress Labour had made in 'tearing out antisemitism by its roots'.[31] With the problem of antisemitism, it seemed, finally resolved, the leadership could now focus fully on its project of party reform. Instead, Starmer faced a crisis in his leadership.

Starmer: crisis and recovery

No sooner had Starmer settled into the leadership than the COVID pandemic struck. Though investigations were later to demonstrate that the government's response was thoroughly incompetent, ineffective and muddled, Boris Johnson actually benefited in the short term, and for the two or so years of Starmer's leadership Labour trailed worryingly behind the Tories in the polls, while his personal ratings were consistently poor. Then, in a further blow, in a by-election in May 2021, the party lost the once-solid seat of Hartlepool, which had survived the crumbling of the so-called 'Red Wall' in December 2019, with a swing to the Conservatives of 16 per cent; Labour also shed hundreds of seats at the local elections. Rumours began to circulate that Blairites were considering a challenge to Starmer.[32] A further by-election then followed for another once safe northern Labour seat, Batley and Spen. If Labour had lost, then Starmer would certainly have faced a challenge from the right; indeed, he considered resigning.[33] In the event, Labour scraped through, holding the seat by only 323 votes, and the leader survived.

These events prompted a major rethink about how to manage and overhaul the party. Advised by Evans and McSweeney, Starmer concluded that the pace of change had been too slow to register with the public and too much concern had been displayed with preserving party unity.[34] For key party managers, including McSweeney and Evans, the time had arrived to address structural problems in the party, notably what was considered to be the excessive power of the party membership. Members – and a fortiori the activists – were seen as 'dangerously left wing', failing to reflect the views of the electorate, particularly that segment, the 'Red Wall' voters, which the party was targeting. Under existing rules, the reasoning ran, there was too much accountability to the rank and file, which encouraged ambitious MPs and frontbenchers to pay too much heed to their views and not enough to those of the voters. Proposed rule changes to be presented to the 2021 party Conference in Brighton were therefore designed to weaken accountability mechanisms, thereby enhancing the autonomy of the PLP.[35]

The object, the party briefed, was 'to shake up party rules in ways that would sharply cut the influence of the membership'.[36] In fact, many of the NEC's rule changes were not contentious and will not be discussed. The more controversial ones were as follows:

- doubling the nomination threshold for party leadership contenders from 10 per cent of the PLP to 20 per cent (Starmer had wanted 25 per cent but was persuaded to lower it to 20 per cent). This would render it virtually impossible for a hard left candidate to ever again qualify;
- abolishing the category of 'registered supporters' in leadership elections, which it was believed had disproportionately benefited the left;
- raising the bar for 'triggering' a selection contest, making it more difficult to challenge a sitting MP;
- transferring the right to compile selection longlists from local parties to the NEC and Regional Executive Committees;

- introducing a probationary system for new recruits to the party by establishing a period of 'provisional membership';
- requiring that, in the future, local parties could no longer affiliate with any group without the prior permission of the NEC;
- the establishment of a new complaints and disciplinary procedure.

A package containing the first three reforms was approved by Conference, though by the less than convincing margins of 53.67 per cent to 46.33 per cent, and, since the majority of CLP delegates voted against by 53 per cent to 47 per cent, only because of union backing. The role of the unions had, in fact, been crucial. Generalising about 'the union bloc vote', as many commentators in the media do, grossly oversimplifies the complexity of the relationship between the leadership and the major affiliated unions, each of whom had their own interests, policies, constitutional constraints and internal politics. Of the four major unions, USDAW was the most supportive. The leaders of UNISON and GMB, the Scots Christina McAnea and Gary Smith, were also sympathetic and predisposed to back any moves that further curtailed the influence of the hard left, but the former had to take account of a powerful left-wing current on the union's executive, while the latter was reluctant to act unilaterally. Unite, under its new General Secretary, Sharon Graham, was the least sympathetic and highly unlikely to back the rule changes. Neither UNISON nor Unite were convinced about either the value or the timing of the reforms, which meant that party managers had to spend much time and effort persuading, exhorting and arm-twisting the two unions. According to one senior party insider, 'It went down to the wire, we only won because UNISON backed us at the last minute,' adding that 'If we'd lost, then Morgan [McSweeney] would have been sacked, Matt [Pound] would have been, Keir probably would have faced a coup.'[37] Embarrassingly, Conference endorsed David Evans's appointment as General Secretary only after a personal appeal in a speech which elicited some booing from the Conference floor,[38] and even then, 47 per cent of the constituency vote was cast against him.[39]

The party's briefing in fact exaggerated the scale of change; only some of the constitutional changes had a significant effect on the balance of power in the party (see the following chapter). Furthermore, even before the Conference had opened, the leadership had been forced to retreat over the one really radical rule change, scrapping OMOV and restoring the electoral college. This, it was calculated, would remove any prospect of the party ever again electing a left-wing leader with so little support in the PLP. Since the bulk of CLP delegates would almost certainly reject it, this change required the backing of all three pivot unions, UNISON, GMB and USDAW. However all three bristled at the way the rule changes had been placed before them with little prior consultation and negotiation. A meeting of the Trade Union and Labour Party Liaison Organisation, the trade union liaison body which links together all affiliated unions, refused to accept the leadership proposal, and the leadership, with no realistic prospect of Conference endorsement, had no option but to withdraw it. The unions, party managers should have known, could not be taken for granted.[40]

Overall, it was a difficult, unruly and turbulent Conference, the most fractious, Ann Black reported, since she began attending conference in 1995, with much ill-tempered shouting and heckling both for and against the platform[41] – something confirmed by the observations of one of the authors (Emmanuelle Avril) of Conferences since 1992. NEC muscular chairing – most notably by Margaret Beckett, Mark Ferguson and Wendy Nichols – was attacked by left-wing delegates for being partisan, and there were multiple complaints of flagrant violations of the rules. On the one hand, a tempestuous Conference suited the leadership, as it could be presented as facing down the left and bringing the party to heel. But, on the other hand, in so doing, it had had to rely heavily on the unions, an awkward position for a leadership which claimed to represent the will of the members. The process of party transformation, it seemed, was far from complete.

But there were heartening signs that the Corbyn tide was ebbing. In the absence of reliable data, it is very difficult to trace with real precision the shifting balance of opinion in the constituencies, but various proxies can be used, such as votes for the constituency section of the NEC and other important committees and voting by Conference constituency delegates. Labour to Win captured four out of nine constituency seats for the biennial NEC elections. In voting for the constituency section of the influential CAC, the left-wing Grassroots Voice and Labour to Win each obtained two seats, with the latter's score of 46 per cent the best the Labour right had achieved in any CAC or NEC election since 2015. The vote for constituency members of the NCC was even more encouraging, with Labour to Win candidates gaining two seats from Momentum; overall, Labour to Win notched up 51 per cent of the vote and Momentum 49 per cent, which was down from 70 per cent in 2019 and 80 per cent in 2018. If we take the second proxy, voting by Conference constituency delegates on contentious issues, Momentum's hefty majority in 2019 had shrunk to around 40 per cent in 2021, falling probably to less than 25 per cent in 2022 and 2023.[42] Elections at the 2023 party Conference saw Labour to Win secure all five constituency places on the NCC and both constituency members of the CAC.[43] The right further strengthened its position at the 2024 Conference. By then, of the thirty-nine members of the NEC, twenty-seven were supportive of the leadership, and not all the others were consistent opponents. In the elections for the NPF, the results were even more striking, with Labour to Win-backed candidates gaining fifty out of fifty-five seats.[44] The message was unmistakable: the hard left was shrinking, and rapidly.

How can we account for this? There were three possible factors: turnover of membership, differential mobilisation by rival organisations and changing rank and file opinion. All certainly played a part, but the first was probably the weightiest. Analyses of membership often overlook the sheer scale of membership turnover; a surprisingly high proportion of members leave the party every year, either for political reasons or simple loss of interest. During the Corbyn years, as we have seen, there was a huge upsurge in membership, probably well over 300,000 once we take account of the not insignificant numbers (we have no exact figures) who quit because of Corbyn. The reverse then occurred under Starmer. At the time of the 2020 leadership election, membership stood at 552,835, falling to 512,000 at the start of 2021, to 434,000 in 2022, to 407,328 in 2023 and to 366,604 in March 2024.[45] However, again, these are net figures. Since Starmer's election, one very well-informed insider who compiles his own data calculated that around 120,000 new members joined or rejoined the party, so that the numbers who left the party, mostly in protest against Starmer, might have been more than a quarter of a million (again, no exact figures are available).[46]

The second factor was the respective mobilising capacity of the rival factions. A key point to bear in mind here is that the relatively high turnouts for leadership elections are never matched by those for the NEC (and other party committees). For example, only 27 per cent of members voted in the 2020 NEC elections.[47] By 2024, turnout had fallen to a meagre 12.9 per cent.[48] This meant that the various party ginger groups played a vital role in mobilising the vote. It is easy to overlook the sheer amount of hard work – endless telephone calls, e-mails and text messages, encouraging and motivating and so forth – and huge stamina required to secure the election of one's favoured candidates. Much effort was expended by both camps on compiling, arranging and analysing a mass of information to build up reliable databases of potential supporters.[49]

To recall, the two major players in presenting slates were Labour to Win (combining Labour First and Progress) and Grassroots Voice, of which Momentum was by far the largest component.[50] After Labour's debilitating performance at the polls in 2019, followed by Starmer's election, confidence, energy and optimism drained from Momentum. Its membership fell, its presence in constituency parties contracted, and it became increasingly riven by internal disputes. An internal faction hostile to Lansman won control of the organisation in 2020 and he was summarily dropped from the Grassroots Voice slate for the NEC, thereby losing his place on the Executive; in this way, the Corbyn left dispensed with the services of their most capable and gifted organiser.[51]

Lansman's removal (he ceased to play any significant part in Momentum) left the field open to his counterpart on the right, Luke Akehurst, equally experienced and talented and with a comparable grasp of Labour's internal politics. In the more conducive climate under Starmer, the right displayed greater mobilising prowess than the hard left. In this, it was greatly aided by two major assets. Firstly, Labour to Win (and like-minded bodies such as Labour Together) was much more lavishly funded, mainly by wealthy business donors, and therefore could recruit many more full-timers than the fading hard left. The increasing role donors and money are now playing in the internal politics of the party has been a major, if underpublicised, factor in Labour's internal politics and one much welcomed by its beneficiaries.

Secondly, and more important still, the right worked hand in glove with officials both in the Leader's Office and, especially, in party HQ. For example, a group called 'Project Ex' was established as a clandestine operation which brought together Luke Akehurst, party staffers McSweeney and Pound, and a former senior official, Roy (now Lord) Kennedy (others were later added). With access to official party records, they assembled a huge amount of data about the party membership with a comprehensive spreadsheet of names, numbers and e-mail addresses. Old ideas about party officials as Labour's impartial 'civil servants' were totally jettisoned as General Secretary David Evans 'gave their work his official imprimatur. "We have to do this," he told a meeting of Labour's regional directors.' For example, the party's 'entire bureaucracy' was deployed to compile the spreadsheet of delegates to the 2021 Conference, spelling out their political outlook and views in granular detail. 'Reliable' delegates could then be encouraged, with some being assigned to convincing doubters to vote 'the right way'.[52] The transformation in the culture of the party machine instigated by New Labour had been completed: officials in politically sensitive roles were there to serve the leadership, and not the party as a whole.

Thirdly, changes were also occurring in the political outlook and preferences of the rank and file, and especially more active party members, though again, hard data are in short supply. Interestingly, the key organisers of both the Corbyn left and the right, Lansman and Akehurst, agreed that neither of their wings of the party ever commanded the allegiance of the majority of party members; insofar as these could be labelled, they were broadly soft left in outlook.[53] They were idealists, but rarely doctrinally minded, caring deeply about poverty and inequality, firmly committed to core Labour values but also strong party loyalists often immersed in electoral campaigning and not unaware that, to win, compromises had to be made – precisely the type of members identified by the research commissioned by Morgan McSweeney and targeted for the Starmer leadership campaign.[54]

Over the years, many soft left activists who had enthusiastically voted for Corbyn in 2015 and 2016 gradually became alienated by the combative style, hectoring tone and sectarianism of many Momentum cadres. They resented constant pressure to deselect councillors and MPs and disliked the more aggressive and divisive spirit they introduced into party meetings. They also resented Momentum's organisational practices: caucusing before every meeting, always voting as a bloc and showing little disposition to collaborate with others. As a result, many of those whom we have loosely called soft left began making common cause with the apparently more inclusive right-wing Labour groups.[55] Some of those who joined the party because of Corbyn – the idealists and not the ideologues – underwent a socialisation process not unlike the generation of the 1980s (see above), finding for themselves a niche within the party and gradually imbibing its norms (such as loyalism and civility), its traditions and its ways of thinking.[56]

The combination of these factors meant that the composition, outlook and priorities of activists in 2024 were very different from those which prevailed in 2019. Furthermore, whatever their reservations over policy, few members disputed that Starmer's hefty majority in 2020 conferred upon him a powerful democratic mandate: his right to rule and their obligation to show loyalty. This movement of opinion manifested itself in changed behaviour patterns at Conference. In contrast with the tumultuous, defiant and bad-tempered 2021 conference, those in the following three years were far more sedate and respectful, with (usually) smartly dressed delegates responding to speeches by Starmer and other senior party figures with due respect and deference, punctuated by enthusiastic ovations. Attendance by hard left delegates at increasingly tightly managed Conferences dwindled, and criticism was largely confined to the margins of hard left fringe meetings. As the *Guardian* wrote of the 2023 Conference,

'After years of Labour conferences being overshadowed by factional rows, this year's event in Liverpool passed by with barely a hitch.'[57]

The new complaints and disciplinary system

The first major batch of rule changes adopted by the 2021 Conference was primarily concerned with leadership election and candidate selection; the second set, more far reaching though overlooked by most commentators, involved a complete overhaul of the party's complaints and disciplinary procedures. The EHRC report had required the party to 'put in place long-term arrangements for independent oversight of the complaint handling process, to make sure that standards are monitored and enforced, and adequate resources are in place'. The NEC responded with an 'Action Plan' submitted to Labour's 2021 Conference. The rule changes were placed into two categories: those mandated by the EHRC, adopted by 74 per cent to 36 per cent, and more wide-ranging alterations to disciplinary procedures, passed by 62 per cent to 38 per cent.[58] In what follows, we analyse the main features of the revised disciplinary system.

Under the new system, investigating complaints remained the responsibility of the General Secretary and GLU officials, with recommendations passed to the NEC (normally its Disputes Committee, now entitled the NEC Complaints and Disciplinary Sub-Committee), which determined whether a disciplinary offence had occurred and, if so, what sanctions should be imposed. Where, however, oral as well as written evidence was required, responsibility was transferred to a new body, the Independent Complaints Board (ICB, see below). Rather confusingly, the NCC retained a responsibility for disciplinary matters presented to it by CLPs or the NEC, as well as the right to impose sanctions, though not in cases that involved a protected characteristic.[59] The NEC could also refer disciplinary matters to the NCC or the ICB.[60]

In pursuance of EHRC recommendations, three new offences were introduced: conduct prejudicial to 'protected characteristic', and the committing of 'proscribed' and 'prohibited' acts. The term 'protected characteristics' referred to matters of race, religion, ethnicity, sexual orientation and so forth as defined in the Equality Act 2010.[61] 'Proscribed Acts' referred to membership of, or support for, any other political party. 'Prohibited Acts' were more encompassing, including membership of, or support for, any political organisation 'that the NEC in its absolute discretion shall declare to be inimical with the aims and values of the Party', and threatening or abusive behaviour.[62] The rationale for these distinctions is not immediately obvious.

In each case, responsibility for determining whether an offence had been committed lay exclusively with the NEC, though with a right of appeal. Previously, the NCC operated as Labour's court of appeals, but it was elected, and experience since 1986 showed that political considerations influenced its judgements. Under the new system, the NCC retained its right to hear appeals in certain cases, but two new bodies were established. The Independent Review Board (IRB) was entrusted with the responsibility for reviewing disciplinary decisions by the NEC, especially those involving 'protected characteristics'. It was also empowered to review 'any aspect of the Party's disciplinary decisions, procedures, systems, policies, practices or processes'.[63] The ICB was responsible for reviewing protected characteristic cases that required witnesses and oral evidence, and membership appeals against expulsion or suspension by the NEC, and for acting as a final court of appeal for any cases that the NEC may refer to it.[64]

Unlike the NCC, IRB and ICB members were appointed and not elected. The membership of the IRB comprised six qualified lawyers, while the ICB was composed of twelve members, four of whom were to be lawyers, four human resources professionals and four from the party. Another new body, the Standing Recruitment Committee, was responsible for selecting these members.[65] The SRC consisted of six members, all politicians of standing, mostly with an ethnic minority (including Jewish) background. Members of the SRC, in turn, were appointed by the party's General Secretary.

It was, by any token, a complex, opaque and even convoluted process, scarcely, if at all, intelligible to the ordinary party member.

We have noted the EHRC's insistence on a complaints and disciplinary process insulated from political interference. In September 2022, the NEC issued a rather curious document laying down a protocol to establish 'the parameters that govern the involvement of the Labour Party's leadership in the Labour Party's disciplinary processes'. While the process must be wholly independent, according to the protocol, 'interaction' and 'conversations' between the leadership and party officials conducting investigations were permissible where the integrity of the process and 'the reputation of the Labour Party' was affected. Apparently, such 'interactions' or 'conversations', the protocol reassured, would not 'affect the outcome of the complaint'.[66] The experience of the Diane Abbott case (see below) suggested otherwise.

Discipline in practice

The Starmer leadership saw a revival in the use of the power of proscription on a scale not seen for decades. Even prior to the acceptance of the new disciplinary code, under existing rules, the NEC in July 2021 had proscribed four groups – Socialist Appeal, Labour in Exile Network, Labour Against the Witchhunt, and Resist – on the grounds that they were 'not compatible with Labour's rules or our aims and values'. More specifically, Socialist Appeal was banned on the grounds that it was a successor organisation to Militant, the other three because of the stance they took on antisemitism.[67] In March 2022, three more bodies were proscribed: Labour Left Alliance, Socialist Labour Network and the Alliance for Workers' Liberty (AWL). AWL was proscribed on the long-established grounds that it was a separate organisation with its 'own programme, principles, policy, distinct and separate propaganda'; Socialist Labour Network because it was a merger, in January 2022, of the already proscribed Labour Against the Witchhunt and Labour in Exile Network; Labour Left Alliance because it was closely linked to proscribed organisations.[68] Membership of proscribed bodies carries with it the penalty of automatic expulsion from the party.[69] This also applies to those deemed to be supporters, with 'support' being defined, *inter alia*, as participation in events organised by or writing for or selling a publication produced by a proscribed organisation.[70]

Accusations were made that alleged support for a proscribed organisation was being used to conduct 'McCarthyite purges',[71] though Ann Black reported in April 2023 that only around three hundred members had been expelled on these grounds.[72] But the importance of proscription should not be underestimated. According to one (anonymous) Labour official, proscriptions were 'absolutely key because it sent a message that if you're in any way affiliated with them, this is not the party for you'.[73] It was, in short, an attempt to build a barrier between Labour and radical left organisations to prevent the influx of members of the latter into the former that had occurred under Corbyn.

Proscription was responsible for only a minority of expulsions, many of which resulted from clearing a backlog of antisemitism cases. For example, in 2022, NEC member Luke Akehurst reported that as of June, NEC panels had heard 1,026 cases, of which two-thirds related to antisemitism; of these, some form of disciplinary action was taken in 87 per cent of cases.[74] One radical left organisation very much in the crosshairs of the leadership was JVL, many of its members friends of Jeremy Corbyn, which, strangely, was not proscribed. [75] As of July 2022, forty-seven of its members, including its entire executive committee, had been expelled or suspended, many on grounds of antisemitism,[76] which meant that quite a high proportion of members expelled for this reason were Jewish.[77]

This raised the thorny question of what constituted antisemitism. The party, it was recalled, had accepted the full IHRA formulation, and this was further elaborated in an NEC document that supplied sixteen guidelines to determine whether views could be construed as antisemitic. Of these, only two were controversial, taken directly from the IHRA: denying the Jewish people the same right to self-determination as any other people, and 'applying double standards by requiring more vociferous condemnation of such actions from Jewish people or organisations than from others'.[78] In some cases (e.g., Jeremy Corbyn), the claim that the problem of antisemitism had been exaggerated and weaponised was added as an example of antisemitism, though this never figured in any rules or protocols. Whether fervent anti-Zionism should be construed as evidence of antisemitism remains a contentious matter.

The much more energetic use of the power of proscription was accompanied by other measures to limit the discretion and assert greater control over the activities of CLPs and other party units. We have already noted the adoption of a rule at the 2021 party Conference forbidding CLPs from affiliating with any outside group without the prior permission of the NEC. It was activated in May 2023, when party HQ wrote to constituency parties with a list of bodies listed as ineligible for local affiliation. The list included: the Palestine Solidarity Campaign, Labour Campaign for Nuclear Disarmament, StWC, JVL, Health Campaigns Together, and the Campaign Against Climate Change Trade Union Group.[79]

The NEC also became more assertive in regulating the matters CLPs were permitted to discuss. For example, in 2020, CLPs were directed that they were not allowed to table motions protesting against Corbyn's suspension.[80] Labour's Head of Internal Governance, Fraser Welsh, warned that the party would 'not hesitate to take appropriate action […] where our rules and guidance are not adhered to, or standards of behaviour fall below that which we expect';[81] and in fact officers in several constituency parties were disciplined for failing to comply with the NEC directive.[82] In the absence of research, it is not possible to determine how constraining such directives were on CLP rights and activities, but they were plainly part of a systematic effort to impose tighter controls over the party on the ground.

The submission of and response to the *Forde Report*

The long-awaited *Forde Report* was finally published in July 2022, after repeated delays. The leadership had wanted and initially anticipated a forthright condemnation of Corbyn's mishandling of the antisemitism crisis and a full endorsement of its reforms to the disciplinary system. It received neither. As we have seen, Forde's judgements over antisemitism and the factional struggle in the party were nuanced, balanced and evidence based. Why the Starmer leadership should have expected a more compliant inquiry panel, having appointed four independent-minded people, is a puzzle, but it was intensely irritated by the panel's conclusions.

Most relevant for our present purposes is that the *Forde Report* expressed reservations about the fairness and adequacy of the new disciplinary code and highlighted four problems. The first was the fact that the NEC was afforded 'absolute discretion' in determining whether a political organisation was 'inimical with the aims and values of the Party' and should therefore be proscribed. Forde found this clause too general and suggested instead that the NEC should establish 'fair and transparent' criteria for proscription. The second was the use of the vague term 'support' in deciding whether a member's involvement in a proscribed body justified automatic termination of membership. The third was the retrospective application of proscription, which seemed to conflict with a long-established legal principle, and the fourth reservation was the use of administrative suspension, which too often appeared to be indeterminate in length.[83] The NEC decided that none of these objections had any real merit. The report also contained other notable criticisms of the leadership, in particular the operation of the so-called 'hierarchy of racism', in which prejudice against Black people and Muslims received less attention than anti-Jewish prejudice, an issue that surfaced in the treatment of Diane Abbott (see below).

Initially, the leadership tried to put a positive gloss on Forde, but its real feelings were evinced by its treatment of the report and its compilers. Since the NEC had commissioned the report, the authors had assumed that they would have the opportunity to report back to it. But they were never invited to present the report to the NEC and discuss its recommendations. NEC member Ann Black had initially been led to believe that Forde had refused to meet the NEC and only subsequently discovered 'that there was no consensus in favour of inviting him'.[84] Not surprisingly, given the amount of work, time and energy the four had devoted to preparing the report over two long years and in the face of numerous obstacles (some placed there by the leadership), the inquiry team were pretty angry.[85]

In March 2023, a clearly frustrated Martin Forde decided to go public, first in an interview with Al Jazeera and then more fully in a Zoom conference convened by Compass (whose chair, it may be recalled, had been

Forde committee member and Labour peer Ruth Lister). After reprimanding 'opposing factions' for cherry-picking his report 'in support of their factional view', he complained about the 'hierarchy of protected characteristics', criticised the lack of transparency about sanctions and lamented the party's decision not to establish a separate legal directorate to oversee its disciplinary system.[86] Eventually, the NEC did, after some pressure and prodding, make a serious effort to implement most (though not all) of the report's many recommendations.

But there was an extraordinary coda. In June 2024, details about a remarkable exchange of correspondence between Forde and the NEC emerged. Lawyers acting on Labour's behalf wrote to the eminent barrister after his Al Jazeera interview, accusing him of making 'highly prejudicial' comments about the party, questioned his professional conduct, and warned that it was 'considering all of its options'. In an interview with the *Independent*, after rejecting the accusations as 'baseless', Forde expressed surprise at the letter's 'tone and content, because I thought I had a sufficiently good working relationship with the general secretary'. He added: 'I'm a private individual; they can't silence me. I fundamentally object to people saying to me, "You don't know how to behave as a professional." I'm afraid that Black professionals get it all the time.'[87] The party did not respond and took no further action.

Managerial centralism in action

Forde's critical report reflected a growing unease and anger within the party about the managerial regime installed by Starmer. Hard left commentators predictably complained of 'an unrivalled offensive against the left' and 'a flood of suspensions on spurious grounds'; the left had been 'hammered with an iron fist with no concern for Party rules or natural justice'.[88] But such sentiments were not confined to the hard left. In July 2023 the long-standing and much respected soft left NEC member, Ann Black, wrote that disquiet about the operations of the disciplinary system 'extends beyond the usual suspects, and loyal mainstream members see them as continuing the factional behaviour so deplored in the Forde report'.[89] Equally, she expressed concern about the much more interventionist and partisan role being played by party officials in seeking to influence decisions at selection meetings, at the annual Conference and at regional conferences.[90] She drew attention to an office paper submitted to the NEC, which stated that staff were expected 'to take a steer from the leadership in all their dealings and therefore cannot remain neutral and objective'.[91] This was a clear repudiation of the once-hallowed 'civil service role'. In the concluding section of this chapter, we consider two case studies, those of Neal Lawson and of Diane Abbott MP, which, we suggest, afford considerable insight into the character, dynamics and limitations of Starmerite managerial centralism.

The case of Neal Lawson

Neal Lawson was a veteran of Labour's soft left. A senior figure in the Labour Co-ordinating Committee in the 1980s and 1990s, he was also, in the early 1990s, a speechwriter for Gordon Brown. Subsequently, he has been the long-standing head of the soft left pressure group Compass, which for years has campaigned energetically for a progressive alliance between Labour, the Greens and the Lib Dems. A contributor to many progressive publications, he was described by the eminent sociologist Zygmunt Bauman as 'one of the most insightful and inventive minds on the British political stage'.[92]

In June 2023, Lawson (by then a Labour member for forty-four years) received a curt letter from the party telling him he had been suspended. The letter reminded him that two years previously (in May 2021) he had retweeted a Lib Dem MP's call to back Green candidates in local Oxford elections.[93] Lawson's offence, according to an NEC insider, was that he had – unwittingly, as it happens – endorsed an alliance between the Greens and the Lib Dems designed to remove sitting Labour councillors. He apparently compounded his guilt by failing to 'publicly show any contrition' and apologise.[94]

Precisely why this somewhat minor misdemeanour was unearthed only after two years and used to suspend Lawson requires some explanation. Why single out a high-profile political figure with very good access to the media and many friends in the Labour Party for what appeared to be a trivial offence, if an offence at all? But Lawson had become an irritant. This was less because of Compass's campaigning for an anti-Tory 'progressive alliance' than for his pungent critique of Starmer's managerial regime. He had on a number of occasions, in the *Guardian* and elsewhere, upbraided the leadership for squeezing out internal party democracy, constantly meddling in parliamentary selections and bullying critics into submission.[95] It was time to make an example of him.[96]

The action provoked widespread protests throughout the party. Lawson's friend and ally Jon Cruddas did not mince words, describing the suspension and possible expulsion of Lawson as 'unprecedented in Labour history – the most right-wing, illiberal faction in the party has been handed control to decide who is and is not a member. They are settling scores and are clearly embarked on a witch-hunt – not just of the Corbynite left but of mainstream democrats within the party such as Neal.' Lawson's sin was that he was an outspoken champion of pluralism and tolerance within the party.[97]

While it may have been a misjudgement, it was a consciously chosen, deliberate act, a shot across the bows, intended as a warning of the dire consequences that might befall anyone who stepped too far out of line.[98] And in this, it may well have worked.[99] As Lawson reflected, people like himself had access to barristers and to sympathetic editors of national newspapers. But what of members who did not?[100] Not the least significant aspect of the episode was that it appeared to corroborate many of Forde's criticisms. The proper procedures had decidedly not been followed, either in the filing and processing of the complaint or in its investigation. Lawson was never informed about the precise nature of the charges against him. And, despite the fact that the rules stipulated that the case involving suspension should be heard within a finite time, and that it involved a simple matter in which the facts were not in dispute, Lawson received no communication from the party for almost eighteen months.[101] Until, that is, he received an e-mail informing him that he had been found 'not guilty'.[102]

The case of Diane Abbott MP

Diane Abbott was a much more high-profile and controversial figure than Lawson, an MP since 1987 (and now 'Mother of the House' as the most long-serving female member), a pacesetter as the first Black woman MP, a contender for the Labour leadership, a champion of many causes, a senior figure in the Corbyn leadership and a parliamentarian who had received more abuse, including death threats, than any other member.

In April 2023, she wrote a letter to the *Observer* in which she stated that Jews (alongside the Irish and Travellers), though they had 'undoubtedly experienced prejudice', had never 'experienced racism in the same way as black people'. This amnesia over the recent history of Jews (and the Irish and Travellers) elicited condemnation from right across the party. Margaret Hodge called her comment 'deeply offensive and deeply depressing', while Jon Lansman labelled them 'disgraceful', adding that 'racism is not a competition'. Abbott immediately 'wholly and unreservedly' apologised, but by then Labour had suspended her from the PLP for her 'deeply offensive' words, pending an investigation.[103] John McTernan, Tony Blair's former political secretary, called Abbott's apology 'swift and appropriate', reminded people that she had been the butt of 'vile racist abuse throughout her career', and urged her reinstatement.[104] The party insisted that the investigation must take its course.

The investigation proceeded at a snail's pace. In September 2023, five months having elapsed, Diane Abbott castigated it as 'fraudulent'. The proper procedures were not being followed, and the inquiry was 'now run entirely out of the Labour party HQ'. Furthermore, she complained, 'the Labour apparatus has decapitated the elected leadership of the constituency party to install its own, handpicked personnel and replace me as the candidate prior to the next election'.[105]

The matter seemed simple and straightforward: whether the wording of Abbott's *Observer* letter contained antisemitic sentiments. The party, as we have seen, had published a series of criteria to judge whether comments were antisemitic and, if applied, the conclusion seems inescapable: Abbott's words may have been very foolish, but were not antisemitic. Yet the investigation continued in its leisurely and stately pace, with Starmer insisting that the matter was being dealt with by a 'wholly independent disciplinary process' and therefore was entirely out of his hands.[106] As the general election crept ever nearer, the suspicion grew that the inquiry would still be 'incomplete' when the election was called, leaving a whip-less Abbott ineligible to stand as a Labour candidate. And indeed there were reports of various Labour politicians manoeuvring for selection for the soon-to-be-vacant seat of Hackney North and Stoke Newington.

But in May 2024, as the election campaign got underway, the party's whole case was demolished by a BBC *Newsnight* report which revealed Labour's investigation had in fact been completed in December 2023, with a recommendation that the MP be given a formal warning and be required to do an online antisemitism course (which she had completed in February 2024). The matter had then been passed to the chief whip, who, according to PLP standing orders, was required to reach a final decision within three months – which he had not.

All this was deeply embarrassing. The left-wing NEC member Jess Barnard tweeted, 'What a farce. So for five months, Starmer has been sitting on Diane's resolved case, running the clock down apparently with one aim – to push her out [...] What happened to those independent processes called for by the EHRC?'[107] Pressure for allowing the MP back into the PLP also came from other quarters of the party, including Angela Rayner and even Ed Balls. The leadership hastily decided to restore the whip to Abbott, and reports circulated that a compromise had been arranged, with Abbott, now back in the PLP, allowed to make a 'dignified exit'. However the deal spectacularly imploded after an anonymous source briefed journalists that, whatever happened, Abbott would have been barred from standing again.[108]

By this time, the whole issue had become hugely controversial, threatening to derail Labour's campaign. Unite and a band of smaller unions demanded that Abbott be allowed to stand, and Martin Forde KC declared that the way the issue had been handled was 'utterly shambolic' and 'deeply disturbing'.[109] To compound the embarrassment, a whole galaxy of celebrated and distinguished Black figures, including Sir Lenny Henry, David Harewood, Jackie Kay, Adrian Lester and Gary Younge, signed a letter describing Abbott's treatment as 'vindictive'; and demonstrating 'a determination to humiliate her. Coming from a community where discrimination is a daily reality, we know unfairness when we see it.' It was, they concluded, an example 'of the systemic racism highlighted in the Forde report'.[110]

Furthermore, observers noted that MPs on the right of the party, for example MP Neil Coyle, found to have made racist comments, had been swiftly reprieved.[111] In truth, the leadership's position was becoming unsustainable. Senior figures, none of them with sympathies that were remotely Corbynite, such as Anas Sarwar, Sadiq Khan, Wes Streeting and Yvette Cooper, expressed discomfort with the way the affair had been managed, while deputy leader Angela Rayner stated bluntly, 'If Diane wanted to stand again, I don't see any reason why she can't.'[112] By this time, it was plain that the NEC had no option but to endorse her as a Labour candidate.

Starmer had for months insisted that the investigation had not been completed, which the *Newsnight* story showed was plainly not true. He had been equally adamant that he had played no role whatsoever, which was equally plainly not true. Even the sympathetic journalist Polly Toynbee commented that 'Starmer appearing on TV, denying it was up to him and giving no reason for the interminable delay, lacked honesty – and it showed'.[113]

Though this was generally overlooked, the whole affair raised fundamental questions about the integrity of Labour's new disciplinary system. The leadership's behaviour had clearly contravened a cardinal EHRC principle: independence from political pressures. If the leader (or, rather, those acting on his behalf) had intervened in a so extensively publicised case, how credible was the assertion that it had not intervened in others? The new system had failed to afford any protection against systemic political interference. It was, Black concluded, not only 'incomprehensible' and 'labyrinthine', it was 'not independent':[114] the very principle that, above all, the system was meant to uphold.

Discipline in the PLP

So far, we have largely focused on management of the extra-parliamentary party. What of the PLP? During the Corbyn years, many of its members had seethed with the spirit of rebellion and defiance; parliamentary discipline seemed, at times, to have disintegrated. The contrast with the behaviour of the parliamentary party under Starmer until October 2023 was striking. Of course, the major reason for this was that most MPs were hugely relieved at Corbyn's departure and, in general, happy with Starmer's leadership. The only sustained source of dissent was from the hard left, and Starmer rapidly made it clear that his tolerance was limited. In February 2022, eleven SCG members signed a statement over the outbreak of the war in Ukraine, drafted by the StWC, which held NATO's 'eastward expansion' as in part responsible for the Russian invasion. To Starmer, this was a challenge to his authority and also to his determination, after the equivocations of the Corbyn years, to realign Labour categorically with the US and NATO. The errant MPs were bluntly instructed to remove their names from the letter or be suspended from the PLP; all complied. As a party spokesperson explained: 'With Keir Starmer's leadership there will never be any confusion about whose side Labour is on – Britain, NATO, freedom and democracy – and every Labour MP now understands that.'[115] Traditionally, the threat of expulsion from the PLP is activated following a serious offence, such as defying a three-line whip, and even then, for the first offence, a warning is generally issued. The leadership was in effect signalling that a much tougher disciplinary regime was now in place.[116]

By October 2023, the PLP was presenting an image of unity and harmony, in stark contrast with the fractiousness on the Tory benches. Then, on 7 October 2023, Hamas launched a bloody incursion into Israel, massacring 1,200 people, mostly civilians, often with extreme brutality, and taking large numbers of hostages. This elicited an almost universal wave of revulsion and much sympathy for Israel in the party (with a few exceptions on the outer fringes of the hard left). But the balance of sympathies soon reversed, as the mounting toll of casualties (many women and children) caused by the full-scale Israeli invasion of Gaza became evident.[117]

It was unfortunate for Starmer that one of his first interventions over the Israel–Gaza conflict and, in time, the most heavily publicised, contained ill-judged comments: in response to a question, he appeared to agree that Israel 'has the right' to cut off power and water supplies in Gaza, comments that went viral online. Eventually, Starmer rowed back, claiming that he had been misinterpreted, but his words were not forgotten, returning with a vengeance during the general election campaign.

In the meantime, a major fracture in the party opened over demands for an immediate ceasefire to end the carnage in Gaza. Starmer rejected them on the grounds that a ceasefire would freeze the status quo, leaving Hamas solidly embedded in Gaza, and so capable of launching further bloody attacks on Israel. But many, both in the PLP and the wider party, vehemently disagreed, with calls for an immediate ceasefire emanating from all quarters of the party. They included Labour's two senior mayors, Sadiq Khan and Andy Burnham, and its Scottish leader, Anas Sarwar, as well as many council leaders (e.g., in Leeds, Sheffield, Leicester and Glasgow) and a very large number of Labour councillors.[118] More discreetly, advocates of a ceasefire included senior Shadow Cabinet members such as David Lammy, the Shadow Foreign Secretary, Lisa Nandy, Yvette Cooper and Shabana Mahmood, the most senior Muslim in the leadership.[119] There was also a rising swell of protest in the PLP, and by early November no less than seventeen members of Labour's front-bench team ignored collective responsibility and publicly appealed for an immediate ceasefire.[120] The rebellion gathered pace. Fifty-six Labour MPs, over a quarter of the membership of the PLP, defied the whips and voted for an SNP amendment to the King's Speech demanding a ceasefire; eight frontbenchers avoided dismissal by resigning. It was by far the largest PLP rebellion that Labour had yet suffered under Starmer.[121]

The leadership seized the opportunity to withdraw the whip from two more hard left MPs, Andy McDonald and Kate Osamor, the former for using the expression 'from the river to the sea',[122] the latter for describing, on Holocaust Memorial Day, Israeli actions as genocidal.[123] Both later apologised for their comments and had the whip restored.[124] But the party briefed that the chief whip was 'losing patience' with MPs who made 'controversial comments about sensitive topics like the war between Israel and Hamas',[125] and elected representatives of the party were barred from attending or speaking at pro-Palestinian rallies, though no action was taken against those who did so.[126] But, given the sheer scale and breadth of the revolt, tough disciplinary action against the rebels was simply not feasible.

As one Shadow Cabinet member cautioned, the issue had 'united MPs on the left, right and centre of the party'.[127] Furthermore, the leadership was well aware that many MPs were under intense pressure from party members and constituents, mainly but not solely Muslims; nor could they ignore the fact that a majority of the British population agreed with the clamour for an immediate ceasefire. One MP warned that 'we are haemorrhaging Muslim votes massively, enough to lose seats if there was an election tomorrow'. There were over four million Muslim voters, and around 80 per cent normally backed Labour, a sizeable slice of its electorate; in twenty constituencies, more than 30 per cent of the electorate was Muslim.[128]

On the other hand, party strategists noted that most Muslims lived in solid Labour seats, so even if some deserted the party, they calculated, the electoral risks were low. Instead, the priority was to reassure its key target demographic, patriotically minded former Labour voters in the 'Red Wall', who were not seen as too bothered about events in Gaza. So, Starmer continued to resist pleas to call for a ceasefire, instead urging a 'humanitarian pause', a stance applauded by Labour Friends of Israel and JLM, though by few others. Reviving the party's traditional Atlanticism, he believed that the party must cleave as closely as possible to the US stance. His stubbornness also reflected his centralist philosophy of party management. The responsibility of the leader was to lead; compromise signalled weakness and vacillation, which would only damage both himself and the party.[129] But, given the intransigence of the egregious Benjamin

Netanyahu, with his pledge to 'eliminate Hamas' whatever the cost in civilian lives, this stance was not sustainable, and by February 2024 Starmer finally agreed to call for an immediate ceasefire. Tension in the party gradually abated, and the issue was then overtaken by the calling of the election.

As the election results were announced, it became evident that the leadership had been too sanguine about the electoral fall-out: a very large swathe of the Muslim electorate had deserted the party, four Labour MPs, including the senior frontbencher Jonathan Ashworth, lost their safe seats to pro-Gaza independents, and the rising star of the party right, Wes Streeting, came within five hundred votes of losing his.

Notes

1 Patrick Maguire, 'Keir Starmer: The sensible radical', *New Statesman*, 31 March 2020.
2 Tom Baldwin, *Keir Starmer: The Biography* (London: William Collins, 2024), passim.
3 Interview, party insider.
4 Baldwin, *Keir Starmer*, p. 329.
5 Stephen Bush, 'The lady or the tiger: How candidate selections work', *Financial Times*, 28 May 2024. To confuse matters there was a third Matt in the Starmer inner circle, Matt Doyle, the party's Director of Communications.
6 Gabriel Pogrund and Harry Yorke, 'The secretive guru who plotted Keir Starmer's path to power with undeclared cash', *Sunday Times*, 12 November 2023. It later transpired that McSweeney had somehow overlooked reporting over £700,000 to the Electoral Commission, as required by electoral law; as a result, Labour Together was fined in 2021 for breaches of the law.
7 Interview, Jon Cruddas.
8 Patrick Maguire and Gabriel Pogrund, *Get In: The Inside Story of Labour under Starmer* (London: Vintage, 2025), pp. 85, 173.
9 Rachel Wearmouth, 'Morgan McSweeney – Labour's power broker', *New Statesman*, 16 November 2022.
10 Jon Cruddas, *A Century of Labour* (Cambridge: Polity Press, 2024), p. 226.
11 Interviews, Jon Cruddas; Neal Lawson.
12 Jim Pickard and George Parker, 'Keir Starmer's ruthless remaking of the Labour Party', *Financial Times*, 7 June 2023.
13 Baldwin, *Keir Starmer*, p. 30.
14 *Ibid.*, p. 293.

15 *Ibid.*, p. 294.
16 Sienna Rodgers, 'Terms of reference set by Labour NEC for investigation into leaked report – full text', *LabourList*, 28 April 2020, labourlist.org.
17 Equality and Human Rights Commission, *Investigation into Antisemitism in the Labour Party* (October 2020).
18 Andrew Kersley, 'How the labour movement has reacted to the EHRC antisemitism report', *LabourList*, 29 October 2020, labourlist.org.
19 Elliot Chappell, '18 Socialist Campaign Group MPs sign call for Corbyn reinstatement', *LabourList*, 5 November 2020, labourlist.org
20 Jessica Elgot, 'Jeremy Corbyn rejects overall findings of EHRC report on antisemitism in Labour', *Guardian*, 29 October 2020.
21 Sienna Rodgers, 'Labour suspends Jeremy Corbyn from the party pending investigation', *LabourList*, 29 October, 2020, labourlist.org
22 Elliot Chappell, '"I don't want a civil war," Starmer says in wake of Corbyn suspension', *LabourList*, 30 October 2020, labourlist.org
23 Maguire and Pogrund, *Get In*, p. 142.
24 *Ibid.*, p. 149.
25 Heather Stewart and Jessica Elgot, 'Labour in fresh turmoil as Starmer refuses to restore whip to Corbyn', *Guardian*, 18 November 2020.
26 Sienna Rodgers, 'Labour leadership wins key NEC votes on Corbyn whip and selections changes', *LabourList*, 25 January 2022, labourlist.org. Criticism was not confined to the hard left, with former Tory cabinet minister Rory Stewart contending that the treatment of Corbyn had been unduly punitive. Rivkah Brown, 'Rory Stewart slams Keir Starmer for "disgusting" treatment of Jeremy Corbyn', *Novara Media*, 11 September 2023.
27 Luke Akehurst, 'Why I voted for the NEC motion to block Corbyn's candidacy', *LabourList*, 29 March 2023, labourlist.org
28 Aletha Adu, Pippa Crerar and Jessica Elgot, 'Jeremy Corbyn will never stand for Labour again, say senior figures', *Guardian*, 14 November 2022.
29 Labour Party, *Action Plan: Driving out Antisemitism from the Labour Party* (London: Labour Party, 17 December 2010).
30 Sienna Rodgers, 'Starmer passes EHRC rule changes and internal party reforms at conference', *LabourList*, 26 September 2021, labourlist.org
31 Labour Party, 'Keir Starmer responds to EHRC announcement', 15 February 2023.
32 Baldwin, *Keir Starmer*, p. 311.
33 Interview, Jon Cruddas.
34 Aaronovich, 'Eight years' hard labour', podcast, *Tortoise Media*, Episode 6, 14 December 2023.
35 Pickard and Parker, 'Keir Starmer's ruthless remaking'. This was effectively the first Conference of Starmer's leadership; the previous year's had taken place in abbreviated form online because of COVID.
36 *Ibid.*

37 *Ibid.*
38 Labour Party, CAC Report, September 2021.
39 Personal notes from Conference.
40 Elliot Chappell and Sienna Rodgers, 'Starmer set to "take suggestions" on rule changes ahead of conference', *LabourList*, 22 September, 2021, labourlist.org
41 Ann Black, NEC Report, September 2021.
42 Katie Neame, 'Every rule change at Labour conference 2022: What it means and how it passed', *LabourList*, 30 September 2022, labourlist.org.
43 Luke Akehurst, 'Labour First Conference round-up', 11 October 2023, labourfirst.org
44 Tom Belger, 'Labour NEC election results as the left lose rep on ruling body and first ever "Labour Women" rep elected', *LabourList*, 18 September 2024, labourlist.org
45 Eleni Courea, 'Four in five Labour members back Keir Starmer, polling shows', *Guardian*, 2 April 2024. One has to be very careful about membership estimates, since some figures include those in arrears and some (e.g., by Ann Black in her NEC reports) do not.
46 Interview, party insider.
47 Sienna Rodgers, 'What we can learn from Labour's 2020 NEC results', *LabourList*, 14 November 2020, labourlist.org
48 Interview, Ann Black.
49 Interviews with senior activists.
50 There was also a much slower and poorly resourced soft left group, Open Labour. Compass did not involve itself in internal Labour elections.
51 Interview, party insider. The disenchantment was mutual and Lansman drifted towards a more soft left position.
52 Maguire and Pogrund, *Get In*, pp. 217–19.
53 Interviews, Jon Lansman; close observer of the party. The paradox was that there was only one soft left representative on the NEC's constituency section, Ann Black, though from 2020 she gained the highest number of votes; precisely why this is so has never been properly researched.
54 Based on the participant observations of both authors over many years and on interviews with close observers of the party.
55 Interviews, Ann Black; party insider. This is confirmed by personal discussions with a range of ordinary CLP members.
56 Interview, Terry Ashton.
57 Pippa Crerar, Peter Walker and Kiran Stacey, 'On a tight leash', *Guardian*, 12 October 2023.
58 Labour Party CAC report, September 2021.
59 Labour Party Rulebook, 2022, Clause IX 2a.
60 *Ibid.*, Chapter 1, Clause VIII, 3, f.; Chapter 6, Clause I A–D.
61 *Ibid.*, Chapter 2, Clause II.

62 *Ibid.*, Chapter 2, Clause I, 4B, C 5B, C.
63 *Ibid.*, Chapter 1, Clause X, 4A, B.
64 *Ibid.*, Chapter 1 Clause XI, 2.
65 *Ibid.*, Chapter 1, Clause X 2; Clause XI, 10 A, B.
66 Labour Party, *Labour Party Protocol* (London: Labour Party, 2022), pp. 3–4. The rather ambiguous constitutional grounding for this provision was Chapter 1.VII.1.A.v of the Rulebook.
67 Sienna Rodgers, 'Battle between leadership and Labour left intensifies amid proscription plans', *LabourList*, 18 July 2021, labourlist.org
68 Sienna Rodgers, 'Labour NEC bans three more groups "not compatible" with party rules or values', *LabourList*, 29 March 2022, labourlist.org
69 People who participated in groups *prior to their proscription* were automatically expelled, which seemed to breach the principle that legal sanctions should not be retrospectively applied but actually saved much time and effort.
70 Rodgers, 'Battle between leadership and Labour left', 18 July 2021.
71 Jon Trickett, 'Labour must end the purges, cast aside McCarthyism and move on', *Labour Outlook*, 6 July 2023.
72 Ann Black, 'Corbyn, Forde report, selections appeals and local elections – Labour NEC report', 3 April 2023.
73 The source added that this 'has absolutely been a deliberate strategy to change the membership'. Eleni Courea, 'Four in five Labour members back Keir Starmer, polling shows', *Guardian*, 2 April 2024.
74 Luke Akehurst, 'A party transformed: How UK Labour is ripping left antisemitism out by the roots', *Fathom*, October 2022. For full details see the Labour Party website, labour.org.uk/resources/complaints
75 It is unclear why it was not proscribed.
76 John McDonnell MP, 'A letter to Keir Starmer and David Evans', *Labour Hub*, 27 July 2022, hub.labour.org.uk
77 This included Jewish Voice for Labour co-founder, the outspoken Naomi Wimborne-Idrissi, who was elected to the NEC in 2022 but almost immediately, on her suspension, ejected: a very rare case of the Executive expelling one of its members. Katie Neame, 'Wimborne-Idrissi removed as NEC member following expulsion from party', *LabourList*, 16 December 2022, labourlist.org
78 Labour Party, *Labour's Antisemitism Policy* (London: Labour Party, 2023).
79 Carol Turner, 'Labour CND condemns ban on CLP affiliations', *Labour Hub*, 12 May 2023, hub.labour.org.uk
80 Elliot Chappell, '18 Socialist Campaign Group MPs sign call for Corbyn reinstatement', *LabourList*, 5 November 2020, labourlist.org
81 Quoted in SKWAWKBOX, 'Outraged Jewish members accuse Labour of "weaponising" them to kill free speech as party uses "safe space" to threaten CLPs over Corbyn motions', *THE SKWAWKBOX*, 25 November 2020, skwawkbox.org

82 Elliot Chappell, 'Members suspended over leadership no confidence motion that was not heard', *LabourList*, 3 February 2021, labourlist.org
83 Forde, *The Forde Report*, pp. 98–9.
84 Ann Black, 'Corbyn, Forde report, selections appeals and local elections – Labour NEC report', 3 April 2023; 'NEC meeting', *LabourList*, 28 March 2023, labourlist.org
85 Interviews, Ruth Lister; party insider.
86 Katie Neame, 'Forde speaks out about factionalism and the Labour Party's response to his report', *LabourList*, 21 March 2023, labourlist.org
87 Nadine White, 'Labour tried to gag Black lawyer who wrote party's own racism report', *Independent*, 19 June 2024.
88 Mike Phipps, 'On tactics', *Labour Hub*, 5 March 2022; Liam Payne, 'The endgame', *Labour Hub*, 16 February 2023, hub.labour.org.uk
89 Ann Black, 'NEC Reports, Complaints and Disciplinary Sub-Committee', 4 July 2023. Noting that the appeals process had upheld all actions taken by the NEC, Black commented that she was not convinced that an 'appeal process with a 100% rejection rate is a meaningful enhancement of members' rights'.
90 Phipps, 'On tactics'.
91 Black, 'Corbyn, Forde report, selections appeals and local elections'. The same pattern of tighter management surfaced at Annual Conference when, in an attempt to prevent the discussion of a motion criticising the leadership's stance in allowing more private sector penetration of the NHS which would very likely have passed, the NEC overruled a decision by the CAC, which had placed the motion on the order paper. The CAC has always operated as an independent custodian of Conference rights, and this was an unprecedented step.
92 Zygmunt Bauman, 'The European elections, politics and inequality', *Social Europe*, 30 May 2014, socialeurope.eu
93 Neal Lawson, 'There seem to be bullies at the top who don't understand pluralism. They see only true believers and sworn enemies', *Guardian*, 30 June 2023.
94 Interview, party insider.
95 Neal Lawson, 'Labour's manipulation of selection contests reveals its emptiness of purpose', *New Statesman*, 2 December 2022.
96 Interview, Jon Cruddas.
97 Cruddas, who worked as senior advisor to Tony Blair in No. 10 for a number of years, added that this 'would never have happened under New Labour, who accepted the democratic, plural character of the party'. Toby Helm, '"Rightwing, illiberal": Labour MP Jon Cruddas condemns Keir Starmer's "witch-hunt"', *Guardian*, 1 July 2023.
98 Interview, Neal Lawson
99 Interview, Chris McLaughlin.

100 Interview, Neal Lawson.
101 *Ibid.*
102 Neal Lawson, 'After 44 years as a Labour member, I spent 18 months facing expulsion. This is what the party got wrong', *Guardian*, 21 November 2024.
103 Tom Belger, 'Diane Abbott has whip suspended over "deeply offensive" comments on racism', *LabourList*, 23 April 2023, labourlist.org
104 *Ibid.*
105 Aletha Adu, 'Diane Abbott accuses Labour of "fraudulent" inquiry into racism comments', *Guardian*, 17 September 2023; Toby Helm, 'Protest increases pressure on Starmer to restore Labour whip to Diane Abbott', *Observer*, 8 October 2023.
106 Pippa Crerar, 'Diane Abbott's chances of getting whip back appear remote despite Hester row', *Guardian*, 14 March 2024.
107 Labour Hub editors, 'Can Diane Abbott run for Labour? It really is up to Starmer', *Labour Hub*, 28 May 2024, labourhub.org.uk
108 Peter Walker, Pippa Crerar, Jessica Elgot and Sammy Gecsoyler, 'I want to be an MP for as long as possible, Diane Abbott tells supporters', *Guardian*, 29 May 2024.
109 Labour Hub editors, 'Can Diane Abbott run for Labour?'
110 Aletha Adu, 'Leading Black figures criticise Labour's "disgraceful" treatment of Diane Abbott', *Guardian*, 30 May 2024.
111 Archie Bland, 'Thursday briefing. Diane Abbott, Faiza Shaheen and how the Labour Party is changing', *New Statesman*, 30 May 2024.
112 Kiran Stacey, Pippa Crerar and Heather Stewart, '"Purge" of Labour leftwingers must end, Keir Starmer told', *Guardian*, 30 May 2024.
113 Polly Toynbee, 'Memo to Labour amid the Diane Abbott debacle: Stop the pointless rows, stop making enemies', *Guardian*, 31 May 2024.
114 Interview, Ann Black.
115 Jim Pickard, George Parker and Victor Mallet, 'British politicians put on spot by Ukraine invasion', *Financial Times*, 25 February 2022.
116 In February 2022, the left-wing Liverpool MP Kim Johnson was forced to apologise 'unreservedly for the intemperate language I used' or lose the whip for describing Israel as a 'fascist' and an 'apartheid state' Katie Neame, 'Labour MP apologises for comments describing Israel as "apartheid state"', *Guardian*, 1 February 2023.
117 By October 2024, the estimated death toll was well over 40,000, not including thousands more buried in the wreckage of ruined homes, and perhaps twice as many injured out of a population of around 2.2 million.
118 Labour Hub editors, 'Senior Labour MP suspended for speech at Palestine march', *Labour Hub*, 30 October 2023, hub.labour.org.uk
119 Maguire and Pogrund, *Get In*, p. 352.
120 Labour Hub editors, 'Two Labour council leaders: Starmer must go!', *Labour Hub*, 3 November 2023, hub.labour.org.uk.

121 Aletha Adu and Kieran Stacey, 'Keir Starmer faces growing Labour rebellion over stance on Gaza', *Guardian*, 9 November 2023.
122 Critics of the chant claimed that it implied a call for the destruction of Israel, though McDonald vigorously denied he meant this.
123 The same day, as it happened, that the International Court of Justice pronounced such a description as 'plausible'.
124 Nadine Batchellor-Hunt, 'Rebel Labour MPs face final warning over breaking ranks with party line', *PoliticsHome*, 2 February 2024, politicshome.com.
125 *Ibid.*
126 Simon Fletcher, 'Labour and Gaza – consequences of a bad line', 21 October 2023, substack.com
127 Eleni Courea, 'High noon in the Commons on Israel and Gaza', *Politico*, 25 October 2023.
128 *Ibid.*
129 Maguire and Pogrund, *Get In*, pp. 350–1.

10
Starmer and candidate selection

> Perhaps the most visible evidence of Starmer's iron grip on the party is how it goes about choosing election candidates.[1]

No better insight into the realities of power within a party is afforded than by its procedures for selecting its candidates for public office, and it is precisely for this reason that selection rules have been a perpetual source of strife in the Labour Party. In 1995, Norris and Lovenduski suggested that the central question in the analysis of candidate selection in the Labour Party has always been the balance between central control and constituency autonomy, and this will be our primary focus in this chapter.

Early in his leadership campaign, Starmer signalled his disapproval of what he saw as the excessive control over the selection process under Corbyn's leadership. He tweeted on 4 February 2020 that 'The selections for Labour candidates need to be more democratic and we should end NEC impositions of candidates. Local Party members should select their candidates for every election.' Similarly, in 2022, the (pro-Starmer) NEC noted that in the run-up to the 2019 election, 'Local parties were prevented from selecting candidates, in some cases despite the vacancies being apparent for many months and only to have an NEC imposed shortlist or candidate at the last minute.' This, it stated, was 'unacceptable' and would not recur under the new leadership.[2]

In what follows, we first analyse changes to Labour's selection rules and procedures introduced by the new leadership. We then briefly review the more contentious selections (and deselections) that punctuated the

Starmer leadership between 2020 and 2024. This is followed by an analysis of the techniques and mechanisms used by the leadership to influence selection outcomes, and then by some general reflections upon the intensity and effectiveness of central control over the selection process.

Labour's selection rules

Although the final responsibility (in most cases) for selecting a Labour candidate lies with CLPs, the NEC is equipped with two broad framework powers giving it regulatory oversight over the whole process. Firstly, it is charged with ensuring full compliance with the rules and procedures, a role largely delegated to a representative, normally a regional party official who, in addition, must be present at all selection conferences. Secondly, the NEC is empowered to modify selection rules, procedures and guidelines 'as required to meet particular circumstances or to further the stated objectives and principles of these rules'. This includes the right to impose candidates 'where it deems this is required by the circumstances'.[3]

Starmer was well aware that the stakes in the next round of selections would be exceptionally high. Given the number of seats the party would have to win in order to return to government, added to the usual number of retirements, a majority of the PLP would consist of new MPs. Careful consideration of the rules was therefore a matter of real importance, and a series of amendments to the rules and procedures were laid down in a succession of NEC documents issued between 2022 and 2024. The first and the most important was the 2022 report entitled *Procedural Guidelines for Westminster Parliamentary Selections where there is a vacancy*.[4] We concentrate here on two significant innovations, both of which proved to be controversial: enhancing NEC control over the longlisting of candidates for Parliament and instituting a new system of quality control called 'due diligence'.

Longlisting. To be considered for inclusion on a longlist, an aspiring candidate must obtain at least one nomination from local party branches or branches of affiliated organisations, that is, trade unions and so-called 'socialist societies'.[5] Prior to the Starmer rule changes, the responsibility for compiling both a longlist of nominated candidates and a shortlist was entrusted to a Selection Committee consisting of CLP members. The NEC representative was required to approve both longlists and shortlisting; in the case of disagreements with the CLP, the chair of the NEC's Organisational Committee would make the final decision.[6] Under the new rules agreed in 2022, responsibility for longlisting was transferred to a new panel consisting of three to five members, with at least one member from each of the NEC and the relevant Regional Executive Committee, but with *no* CLP representatives. Furthermore, the Organisation Committee chair (virtually always a leadership loyalist) appointed members of the panel. The new rules stated that 'the eventual longlist should usually consist of no less than six prospective candidates, where such candidates meet the criteria'.[7] The reason given for centralising the process and depriving CLPs of longlisting rights – in contrast to Starmer's initial commitment to extending those rights – was that key party goals of gender balance and greater ethnic diversity could not be safely left to CLPs.[8]

'Due diligence.' Under Corbyn, the lack of sufficiently robust competency checks had led to the selection of poorly qualified or otherwise inappropriate candidates; Labour found itself saddled with two MPs who were later convicted of crimes while investigations – usually by Tory researchers or the right-wing press – had also uncovered candidates who had made offensive, antisemitic and other bigoted comments. Under the new rules, due diligence checks would be undertaken prior to longlisting, with reports provided to the panel in order to identify 'skeletons in the cupboard' and weed out the undesirables, thereby saving time and avoiding poor publicity.[9] Under this process, applicants were required to notify party officials of all their social media accounts (if any), and these accounts and published sources were then scrutinised to uncover anything that could cause the party embarrassment or raise doubts about the suitability of a candidate. Where the panel was uncertain whether applicants met the required standards, they would be called to interview.[10]

However, this enhancement of NEC powers was balanced by a number of provisions safeguarding constituency rights. Firstly, constituency-run Selection Committees remained responsible for compiling shortlists, consisting of a minimum of four individuals. Secondly, applicants with at least three nominations from affiliated organisations must be invited to interview for inclusion on the shortlist. Thirdly, any applicant with 'nominations from more than half of eligible Labour Party branches must be shortlisted unless the Panel and the NEC Representative agree there are exceptional circumstances following shortlisting interviews'.[11]

As the selection process got underway from 2022 onwards, allegations began to multiply of excessive and intrusive interference and abuse of the rules by the party machine in the selection (and deselection) of parliamentary candidates, to screen out left-wingers.[12] This was categorically denied by the NEC. To assess these competing claims, we briefly describe those selections (chronologically ordered) that, because of their controversial character, attracted press coverage. We also discuss two other manifestations of central control, the (alleged) central orchestrations of deselections, and the involvement of the party machine in general in the selection process. We then seek to uncover any patterns that emerge that cast light on the intensity and purposes of central control.

Candidate selection cases

Wakefield

Jack Hemingway, deputy leader of Wakefield Council and a Corbyn supporter, was excluded from the longlist after due diligence, apparently on the grounds of his social media posts, particularly his rejection of claims that the party under Corbyn had been 'institutionally antisemitic'. The NEC-controlled panel chose a longlist of just four, hence removing the need for a shortlist. Claiming that the selection had been 'stitched-up', the CLP executive resigned en masse.[13]

Stroud

The Labour leader of Stroud District Council, Doina Cornell, was barred from the longlist, despite being nominated by Unite, the CWU, the Fire

Brigades Union (FBU), the TSSA, ASLEF and USDAW, apparently because of Twitter posts indicating support for Occupy and Palestine Solidarity events. Although the rules stated that the longlist should consist of at least six members (later reduced to four), a longlist of only two was approved, pre-empting the shortlisting stage and leaving the CLP with a very limited choice.[14]

Hastings and Rye

Maya Evans, the deputy leader of Hastings Borough Council, was blocked from the longlist for Hastings and Rye. Labour sources cited three reasons: her involvement with the StWC, her arrest during an anti-Iraq war protest and the decision by the Hastings Labour Group to reach a cooperation agreement with the Greens on the council.[15]

Kensington and Bayswater

Emma Dent Coad had been a left-wing MP for Kensington between 2017 and 2019 and, according to Michael Crick, had built a 'formidable reputation' for her campaigning over the Grenfell fire tragedy in her constituency. She was also the current leader of the Labour group for Kensington and Chelsea Council.[16] The only reason given for her exclusion from the longlist was a social media posting which described Conservative London Assembly member Shaun Bailey as a 'token ghetto boy', for which she later apologised. The NEC also dissolved the constituency's Selection Committee because of alleged leaking and antisemitism.[17]

Milton Keynes

In October 2022, Lauren Townsend, a Milton Keynes councillor nominated by six trade unions (ASLEF, the FBU, the CWU, UNISON and the TSSA), was excluded from the longlist after failing the due diligence process. Townsend stated that among the reasons given for her exclusion were the fact that she had 'liked' a tweet from Nicola Sturgeon saying she had tested negative for COVID, and liked another one by the Novara journalist Aaron Bastani calling Starmer a 'prat'.[18]

Camberwell and Peckham

In October 2022, Maurice Mcleod, a former editor of *The Voice*, Britain's leading Black newspaper, was blocked from the longlist in Camberwell and Peckham. Mcleod, previously a Corbyn supporter, reported that he had been told that he had failed the 'due diligence test' because he had criticised the Labour council's treatment of its residents, 'liked' a tweet by then Green Party MP Caroline Lucas and, while approving the IHRA definition of antisemitism, had objected to some of the examples.[19]

Bolton North East

The shortlisting stage was once again skipped in the selection for the candidate for Bolton North East, since the longlist consisted of only two members. One of the excluded nominees was the chair of Labour North West, Leigh Drennan, a UNISON organiser, despite nominations from Unite, UNISON, the GMB and the CWU and the support of deputy leader Angela Rayner. Drennan had stood for Labour's NEC in 2020 on a Momentum-backed ticket.[20]

Broxtowe

In Broxtowe in the East Midlands, Greg Marshall, who was Labour candidate in 2017 and 2019, failed to be longlisted despite being backed by eight unions. The grounds given to him were Twitter postings in which he had criticised 'unfair suspensions' by the party. Members of the CLP's Selection and Executive Committees resigned in protest.[21]

Wolverhampton

One of the more intriguing of the party's decisions was the exclusion from the longlist for Wolverhampton of an NEC member, the

Momentum-affiliated Mish Rahman. Rahman had been nominated by seven trade unions and affiliated socialist societies – the FBU, the CWU, ASLEF, the TSSA, Unite, the Socialist Education Association and the Socialist Health Association. The NEC issued a statement declaring that 'The public have a right to know that everyone we put forward at election time is of the highest standard.'[22] Ironically, as an NEC member, Rahman has himself served on selection panels charged with the task of evaluating the suitability of Labour candidates.[23] Initially, the grounds for barring him from the selection contest was the allegation that he had opposed the EHRC report into Labour antisemitism, though this was shown to be incorrect. Rahman claimed that the reason for his exclusion was that he had voted against the disciplinary structures introduced after the EHCR report on antisemitism in the party.[24]

Bangor Aberconwy

Dawn McGuinness, a member of Labour's National Policy Forum and a Senedd candidate in 2021, was nominated by Labour's two largest affiliates, UNISON and Unite, but was not included on the longlist for the new Bangor Aberconwy constituency. The reasons given focused on her previous support for Jeremy Corbyn. Two-thirds of the Selection Committee resigned in protest. McGuinness stated that 'In informing me of the decision, Welsh Labour have encouraged me to apply for other seats, implying that they view me as a suitable candidate – but just not for the place where I grew up and live.'[25]

Jamie Driscoll, mayor of North of Tyne Combined Authority

Perhaps the most interesting example of the exercise of NEC powers did not involve Westminster but the position of mayor of the new North East Combined Authority. Jamie Driscoll, the well-regarded mayor of the North of Tyne authority, had steered the negotiations, which had concluded with a £1.4 billion devolution settlement to establish the new authority.

Notwithstanding, he was excluded from the longlist for the new post. Greater Manchester mayor Andy Burnham and Liverpool City Region mayor Steve Rotheram both wrote to the NEC praising Driscoll's 'constructive, non-partisan approach' to his work and reminded the Executive of its 'responsibility to ensure decisions are democratic, transparent and fair. To exclude a sitting mayor from a selection process with no right of appeal appears to us to be none of those things. At the very least, we believe Jamie Driscoll should be entitled to a process of appeal with the ability to put his case to an NEC panel.'[26]

The initial reason for barring Driscoll, who was loosely associated with the Corbyn left, was, according to Baroness Jenny Chapman, a Starmer ally, 'simply guaranteeing the highest quality candidates'.[27] However, Jonathan Reynolds, the Shadow Business Secretary, later pinpointed the fact that in March 2022 Driscoll had shared a platform with the much-lauded film director Ken Loach, who had been expelled from the party for claiming that antisemitism had been weaponised: prohibiting Driscoll from standing was designed to signal that Labour was utterly committed to a 'zero-tolerance' stance on antisemitism.[28] Driscoll had been invited to take part in the event, whose purpose was to discuss with Loach his three films set in the North East, *Sorry We Missed You*, *I, Daniel Blake* and *The Old Oak*. All dealt with issues of poverty, social deprivation and a draconian benefits system; the issue of Israel and antisemitism was never mentioned. Driscoll referred to the fact that he had shared a platform with the Conservative Tees Valley mayor Ben Houchen, asking: 'does that make me a Tory?'[29]

Perhaps the most illuminating comments on the Driscoll affair emanated from Alan Johnson (the academic, not the politician), editor of the staunchly pro-Israel journal *Fathom* and who had in 2019 compiled a major dossier alleging widespread antisemitism under Corbyn. Calling on the NEC to reverse its decision over Driscoll, he cited the following facts: no one had ever accused Driscoll of antisemitism; under his leadership his authority had adopted the IHRA definition of antisemitism; he had been on a JLM training course and worked closely with the Jewish Leadership Council; and he had rejected Loach's views on the 'weaponisation of antisemitism'.

The real reasons for the NEC's decision, Johnson suggested, were the mayor's views on public ownership of the utilities, on privatisation in the NHS and on the right of Labour MPs to join picket lines.[30] Despite these protests, the ban on Driscoll was not lifted.

This list is not necessarily exhaustive since it covers only those cases which were publicised – indeed we know of at least one other instance from personal information which accidentally came to light.

Three points can be made here. Firstly, the NEC rarely provided explanations for precisely why candidates were excluded from longlists or had failed due diligence, and we must rely on the testimony of those so affected and/or reports in the press. Secondly, where surmises can be made about the reasons, they almost invariably referred to expressions of political views and not to the qualities of the candidates. Thirdly, the compiling of very short longlists in many of these cases had the effect of pre-empting the shortlisting stage, therefore reducing the role of CLPs in the selection process, a point we discuss in more detail below.

Candidate deselection cases

Rules governing the deselection of MPs and candidates, as we have seen, have been an endless source of dissension in the Labour Party, but it is worth stressing that deselections have always been rare. Most MPs develop good working relations with their local parties and, even where they differ on major issues, serious attempts to remove a sitting MP occur only when that relationship has broken down.

In the 2021 rule-change package (see above), the threshold needed for a 'trigger ballot', whereby CLPs can compel a sitting MP to undergo a full selection contest, had been raised from a third to a majority of party and affiliate branches, voting separately in a 50/50 electoral college.[31] This was designed to afford MPs more protection against attempts by CLPs to oust them. In the past, where such attempts had been made for political reasons, the pattern had always been that of left-wing CLPs seeking to unseat more right-wing MPs. Under Starmer, however, this pattern was dramatically reversed. Every MP who was 'triggered' was from the Corbynite or hard left of the party and a member of the SCG: Apsana Begum, Ian Byrne, Lloyd Russell-Moyle, Bell Ribeiro-Addy, Zarah Sultana, Sam Tarry and Nadia Whittome. Of these, Ribeiro-Addy, Sultana and Whittome were all reselected without too much difficulty, Apsana Begum after a protracted struggle, Byrne very narrowly after a bitter contest. Tarry was deselected, while Lloyd Russell-Moyle was refused endorsement by the NEC.[32]

Zarah Sultana, Coventry South

Zarah Sultana was selected as candidate in 2019 for Coventry South, a seat which she narrowly won by 401 votes. A staunch member of the Corbyn left, she faced accusations that her selection had been a fix by the 'Corbynite machinery'.[33] In her youth, she had made some inflammatory remarks about Israel for which she later apologised. She was one of the eleven Labour MPs who signed the StWC statement following the Russian invasion of Ukraine, blaming NATO's 'eastward expansion'. In 2021, unrest within her local party led to a move to deselect her; she lost the trigger ballot, and a full selection contest followed. However, she was a high-profile MP and was plainly popular in her constituency party, romping home with 90 per cent of the vote in the local electoral college.[34]

Sam Tarry, Ilford South

Sam Tarry was selected as Labour candidate for Ilford South to replace Mike Gapes, who had quit the party to join the 'Independent Group of MPs', subsequently Change UK. He was backed by both Momentum and many trade unions. But, in a move that caused much rancour, his main rival for the Labour nomination, leader of the local Redbridge Council Jas Athwal, had at the last minute been suspended from the party pending investigation of allegations of sexual harassment and therefore removed from the contest; Tarry was selected.[35] Labour's National Constitutional Committee subsequently cleared Athwal of wrongdoing, and he was reinstated, but the CLP was left deeply divided, with many querying the motivations of those responsible for the complaint against the council leader.

Tarry, who joined the SCG, was appointed in January 2021 as Shadow Minister for Transport. Plainly, the ill feeling among many in his CLP stemming from his original selection had not dissipated, for, in July 2022, most local branches and affiliated organisations – 57.5 per cent to 42.5 per cent in the electoral college – voted to 'trigger' the MP and hold a full selection process. Tarry submitted a dossier detailing allegations of rule-breaking and voter fraud and impersonation, but this was not accepted by party HQ; he also claimed that the party machine was targeting 'socialist and trade union backed candidates' for removal.[36] That same month (July 2022), Tarry, a former official for the rail union TSSA, angered the leadership by appearing on a picket line in a rail dispute and was shortly after sacked from the front bench. The reason, Starmer explained, was that he had given interviews without permission 'and then made up policy on the hoof, and that can't be tolerated in any organisation, because we've got collective responsibility'.[37]

In October 2022, Tarry was triggered and was then defeated in the subsequent selection conference by his erstwhile 2019 opponent Jas Athwal by 499 votes to 361. Both candidates had strong bases within the party membership and among affiliated unions. Athwal was a close ally of senior Labour right-wing frontbencher Wes Streeting, while Tarry had been endorsed by Ed Miliband.[38] The deselected MP once more questioned the integrity of the selection process, in particular the use of electronic votes, and called for an investigation, a request which was refused. Electronic ballots had been counted via an online voting system called Anonyvoter; Tarry was understood to have won 57 per cent of the in-person votes at the selection but only 35 per cent of the Anonyvoter votes, plus some postal votes.[39]

Ian Byrne, Liverpool West Derby

Ian Byrne, a staunch Corbynite, was selected in 2019 in a fractious contest – and only by the incredibly close margin of three votes (222 to 219) – as candidate for the very safe Labour seat of Liverpool West Derby, after the sitting MP, Stephen Twigg, decided to stand down.[40] Many members were angry that the NEC had excluded long-serving local Labour councillors from the longlist, a standard stratagem for removing strong contestants from the race and, as a result – as with Ilford South – the party was left deeply divided. However, Byrne soon established a reputation as an energetic campaigner, having set up Fans Supporting Foodbanks and chaired the Hillsborough Law Now campaign, which campaigned for justice for Liverpool FC fans over the Hillsborough football disaster, an incredibly emotive cause in the city. He had even been received by the pope in the Vatican – a huge honour in the eyes of the many Catholics in the constituency. Critics in the party riposted that he was negligent in his constituency duties, overlooking local concerns in favour of boosting his national profile.[41]

In July 2022, all four branches of the West Derby CLP voted in favour of a fresh selection contest, with reports that the party machine was intervening in a bid to remove one more troublesome left-winger. The contest rapidly soured, with both protagonists claiming breaches of the rules, intimidation and unruly behaviour.[42] Despite his close alignment with the hard left, Byrne received endorsements from influential figures from other sections of the party, including mayors Andy Burnham and Steve Rotheram, as well as Angela Rayner.[43] Byrne narrowly defeated his challenger Anthony Lavelle, a local councillor, by 210 votes to 198, with Momentum claiming that he had 'struck a blow against an out-of-control Starmer machine'.[44]

Apsana Begum, Poplar and Limehouse

Apsana Begum was selected as Labour candidate for the 2019 election for the solid Labour seat of Poplar and Limehouse, with the enthusiastic support of the Corbyn leadership, and after her election joined the SCG. From the outset of her parliamentary career she was mired in controversy, both political and personal. A little prior to her election, it was reported in the press that in 2017 she had shared a social media post that referred to Saudi Arabia's (improbable) 'Zionist masters', for which she later apologised. In July 2021, after a protracted court case, the MP was cleared of charges brought by Tower Hamlets Council of having made fraudulent housing claims. She also fell out with many in her constituency party, who complained about her inaccessibility and inactivity, and in July 2022 the CLP voted to hold a trigger ballot. Begum in response protested that she had suffered both from illness and from a 'sustained campaign of misogynistic abuse and harassment' and that the process to deselect had been 'unjust, undemocratic and unacceptable'. A statement signed by three leaders of left-wing unions, the FBU, ASLEF and the TSSA, called on the NEC to halt the trigger ballot process.[45]

An investigation dragged on for well over a year with no apparent progress. In February 2024, Begum wrote complaining that the long drawn-out process had been 'extremely distressing and damaging to my health'.[46] By the time the election was called, the matter was still unresolved, though it seemed unlikely that the NEC would endorse her. As it happened, her candidature was caught up in the backwash of the Gaza dispute and, especially, the thoroughly mishandled Diane Abbott case, and the NEC, reluctant to instigate another row in London with another non-white MP, hastily voted to endorse her. However, in July 2024 she had the whip withdrawn along with six other SCG members for voting for an SNP amendment to scrap the two-child benefit cap.

Lest we forget: Jeremy Corbyn, Islington North

It had long been clear that Jeremy Corbyn, suspended from the PLP in 2021, would not be readmitted and would therefore be ineligible to stand as a Labour candidate. In March 2023 this was made official. His constituency party, Islington North, had been supportive and was therefore sidelined by the NEC, which took control over the selection for his replacement. As it happened, Corbyn was unexpectedly returned to Parliament as an independent.[47]

Two other members of the SCG, Bell Ribeiro-Addy and Nadia Whittome, both survived the trigger ballot processes and were readopted as Labour candidates and subsequently elected. But there were two unexpected casualties during the run-up to the election.

Lloyd Russell-Moyle, Brighton Kemptown

In late May 2024, Lloyd Russell-Moyle, SCG member and MP for Brighton Kemptown since 2017, stated that he had been administratively suspended by the NEC 'pending investigation following the receipt of a serious complaint last week'. According to Russell-Moyle, the complaint, which was never disclosed and had been made eight years previously, 'was vexatious and politically motivated'. Given that there was no time for an investigation, the effect of the suspension was that he was in effect deselected – which came as a shock to local members, leading many to write letters of protest and to stop campaigning. The NEC exercised its right to impose a candidate, Chris Ward, a Starmer aide, who was elected MP.[48]

Faiza Shaheen, Chingford and Woodford Green

Faiza Shaheen, an economist, had been one of a very small number of left-wingers to have been selected, though, according to Michael Crick, 'the high command put up quite a fight to stop her'.[49] An Oxford graduate from a working-class background, she had also gained a PhD from Manchester University. A recognised expert on inequality, she worked both for the New Economics Foundation, a left-wing think-tank, and the charity Save the Children UK. From 2016 to 2020, she was the director of the trade union-backed Centre for Labour and Social Studies and was a visiting professor at the London School of Economics. She was an extraordinarily well-qualified candidate.

Selected to fight Chingford and Woodford Green in 2019, she nearly defeated the sitting MP, Iain Duncan Smith, very much against the tide. She was then selected to contest the seat again and, despite having recently given birth, threw herself into campaigning and fund-raising. With the election announced, she was abruptly called to an online meeting with three NEC members who presented her with fourteen tweets she had 'liked' over the previous ten years, including one calling for companies trading with Israel to be boycotted, a photo of her standing with Corbyn affirming her commitment to the Palestinian cause and a clip from the Jon Stewart TV show in which the Jewish American satirist had criticised the 'Israel lobby'.[50] (Stewart tweeted in response that 'This is the dumbest thing the UK has done since electing Boris Johnson.'[51]) Party sources maintained that Shaheen's removal would have the effect of reassuring voters of Starmer's determination to repudiate Corbynism.[52] She was replaced as candidate by a senior member of the right-wing pressure group Labour to Win. She decided to stand as an independent, and in the subsequent election, with the Labour vote split, Iain Duncan Smith, despite his very narrow majority, held on to his seat.[53]

While it was difficult (unsurprisingly) to obtain any details about the precise role that the party machine played in these deselection controversies, it was obviously not coincidental that in every case the MPs affected, plus Shaheen, were members of the SCG. Though most survived their 'triggering', these events no doubt had a chilling effect on others, as clearly intended. But it is also worth noting that in almost all cases there was considerable local opposition to those triggered, in some cases (e.g., Tarry and Byrne) because of resentment at the role of the then pro-Corbyn NEC in their initial selection.

The role of the party machine in selections

The cases enumerated above cover only instances of overt and therefore publicised conflict. However, situations may arise where selections are influenced by the centre in such a way that publicity is avoided through 'nondecision-making'. This refers to a process in which power is exerted unobtrusively through manipulating rules, procedures and institutional practices in such a way that desired results can be obtained without any open conflict.[54] We distinguish between two types of 'nondecision-making': the management, or what Minkin called the 'creative' application of the rules,[55] and the mobilisation of influence.

In 1995, Norris and Lovenduski noted the influence of 'those who set, implement and adjudicate over the rules of the game'.[56] In the Labour Party, this is the responsibility of the NEC and its enforcement arm, the party apparatus. Officials have the overall responsibility 'for approving each stage of the selection process, including the election of the selection committee, timetable, and shortlist'.[57] After Blair's election to the leadership, the party's traditional reverence for the rules was replaced by a more 'pragmatic' approach in which rule interpretations and applications were seen as part of the process of delivering the 'right' political ends.[58] With so many senior managerial officials schooled in the techniques and ethos of the New Labour era, it is not surprising that this pragmatism resurfaced under Starmer. We can give two examples of this. Firstly, rules governing the timing of access to membership constituency lists. Gaining early access to these lists is an advantage because it gives beneficiaries more time to contact and persuade members. Crick reports that 'having spoken to a number of those involved in the selection process, anointed or LOTO contenders appear to have a remarkable ability to obtain membership lists before their ordinary rivals'. Equally, Labour has tough spending rules, but these too can be flexibly applied. As Crick comments, 'It's amazing how much some candidates manage to do with their limited budgets.'[59]

More important is what we have called the mobilisation of influence. As Gallagher and Marsh observe, 'real influence may be wielded behind the scenes. The more the process involves backstairs negotiations, the more the room for trade-offs – and the more difficult the task of the researcher to reconstruct the process.'[60] Finding documentation is, therefore, not easy, and those involved in the process are understandably reluctant to divulge information. As a result, any conclusions we reach are hampered by the lack of reliable data and must necessarily be somewhat tentative.

One of the tasks of Regional Directors and their deputies is to gather information about the CLPs in their region, their political orientations, concerns and idiosyncrasies, and they are expected to establish a good working relationship with the chairman, the secretary and other influentials.[61] This information and 'feel for things' can then be used to help those candidates judged to have particular merit.[62] According to a former Regional Director of the London Labour Party, as organisers 'we can nurture new people [...] point them in the right direction, tell them what's possible, maybe even tell them someone appropriate [they might meet]'.[63] An official quoted in a 2020 study summed up his role in selections as introducing favoured candidates to key players, providing them general background about the party, connecting them to influential networks and generally helping them to navigate the politics of the area.[64]

It should be added that Regional Directors have always differed in how they have conceived their roles in the selection process. Some have been (and are) sticklers for the rules and insist on strict impartiality, others were more interventionists. For example, there were reports that the East Midlands Regional Office was quite assertive in promoting preferred candidates, excluding strong local applicants from longlists and selectively leaking membership lists. Similar observations were made about the London Regional Office.[65] Not all these interventions were factional: motivations could include the promotion of gender equality, ethnic diversity and helping the most obviously able. This said, during the New Labour years a test of the organising ability of regional officials was their success in getting 'the right people' selected in winnable seats.[66] It is highly likely that the same applied under Starmer.

But it is important to emphasise that there are limits to what can be achieved. The extent of the influence of regional organisers depends on their relationship with CLPs. They also have to be circumspect, skilled and diplomatic, since local parties can easily be provoked by evidence of too overt and heavy-handed interventions. If an organiser is suspected of trying to 'fix' a selection, this is likely to be counter-productive.[67] Equally, it is important to stress that in most constituencies a selection contest, while highly competitive, is also a consensual process, since, except in the most factionalised CLPs, most members have a common purpose: the picking of a standard-bearer most likely to win the seat for their party.

The final act

In 2022, as noted above, the NEC pledged that it would not repeat the 2019 practice of emergency procedures being used to impose shortlists or shoe-horn candidates at the last minute. Though the 2024 general election was called a few months earlier than anticipated, it had long been awaited and was not (unlike 2017 and 2019) a snap election. However, in many constituencies the selection process was initiated only in November 2023, which left little time for it to be completed using normal procedures. This was in part because of practical reasons: selections required the presence of a regional official, and there were multiple pressures upon their time.[68] In May 2023 a streamlined procedure had been agreed for non-priority seats (which Labour did not expect to win, though, in the event, in a significant number of cases it did) in which shortlisting rights were transferred from CLPs to five-person panels, one each from the NEC and the local Regional Executive Committee, and three from the CLP.[69] Clearly, the NEC had second thoughts, judging that this gave it insufficient control, and in December that year the right to shortlist was assigned to a three-person panel to be appointed by the chair of the Organisation Committee and consisting of two NEC and one Regional Executive Committee members, with no CLP representation.[70] Furthermore, the panel was also allowed to choose a shortlist of one 'where there is only one suitable applicant, or where the statutory timetable makes it impractical to progress to a final hustings meeting'.[71] Ann Black commented that 'exercising unprecedented central control of all selections without sufficient resources has led to unnecessary delays and fewer CLPs getting a choice, with many having candidates imposed for the third successive general election. This is very hard to justify.'[72]

Furthermore, and much more significantly, the calling of the election in May 2024 precipitated a burst of last-minute resignations by sitting Labour MPs, which very conveniently meant that, together with deselections, two dozen eminently winnable seats suddenly became vacant.[73] Because of the tight time-schedule, the Executive (acting, of course, on behalf of the leader) could invoke emergency procedures: a three-person

NEC panel was now empowered to compile a shortlist, conduct interviews and appoint a candidate, with no right of appeal: in a word, total NEC control over the selection process.[74] By an extraordinary piece of good fortune, the NEC had conveniently at hand a list of politically on-message candidates who were available to fill the vacancies. Those parachuted into these seats included Camden Council leader Georgia Gould (daughter of the late Blair confidante Philip Gould); former Rachel Reeves adviser Heather Iqbal; Josh Simons, director of the Starmerite think-tank Labour Together; Torsten Bell, head of the Resolution Foundation; Chris Ward, a former Keir Starmer advisor; TUC head of campaigns and communications, Antonia Bance; senior researcher at shopworkers' union USDAW, Connor Rand; and the well-known journalist Paul Waugh. Perhaps most remarkable of all – indeed quite startling – the NEC, the body which controlled these late selections, selected as candidates six of its own members: James Asser, Gurinder Singh Josan, Luke Akehurst, Nesil Caliskan, UNISON's Mark Ferguson and USDAW's Michael Wheeler. Given that former UNISON official Joanna Baxter had already been selected, this meant that seven pro-leadership members of the NEC (almost 20 per cent of its membership) helped to pick themselves as candidates – an extraordinary break from party tradition.[75]

Quality control or ideological cull?

In bringing the threads together, we can now draw some conclusions about the magnitude, intensity and purposes of central control over the selection process. We use here the concept of 'gatekeepers', that is, 'those who design, interpret and operate the rules and procedures, administer them and adjudicate in disputes'.[76] Gatekeepers included all those officials involved in the selection process in party HQ, the Leader's Office and the various Regional Offices. In this account, we will concentrate on five key gatekeepers. Four were party officials: General Secretary David Evans, Campaign Director Morgan McSweeney and two other senior officials, the two Matts – Matt Faulding and Matt Pound.[77] The formative experiences of all four had been working either for the party machine in the New

Labour years or for right-wing Labour pressure groups like Labour First and Progress. 'Each,' Michael Crick maintained, 'is easily more powerful than most members of the Shadow Cabinet and in combination effectively run the candidate selection operation orchestrated from party HQ,' and each, he concluded, was 'hugely partisan'.[78] The fifth was Luke Akehurst, a senior NEC member, head of Labour First and then of Labour to Win, and someone widely acknowledged as possessing very considerable organisational talents and a profound understanding of Labour's internal politics.

These gatekeepers, with the help of regional officials, operated the two major gateways screening aspiring Labour candidates: longlisting and due diligence. As we have seen, control over longlisting was transferred from the local party to the centre. The initial NEC advice stipulated that 'The eventual longlist should usually consist of not less than six prospective candidates, where such candidates meet the criteria.'[79] However, in July 2022 this was reduced to four, and the minimum shortlist from four to two.[80] A clear pattern emerges from the selection cases we have reviewed: a very short 'longlist', sometimes below the minimum of four. At times, this was the unintended consequence of gender balance, since in most constituencies far more men than women applied.[81] But in other cases it was plainly a control mechanism, since its effect was to render shortlisting – which, to recall, was a constituency prerogative – quite superfluous. In addition, the provision allowing for mandatory longlisting of candidates nominated by trade unions was annulled,[82] and, as our cases showed, candidates with multiple union nominations were blocked from longlists.[83]

The second major gateway was due diligence. There were no written criteria to advise how this task should be implemented. NEC guidelines did state that Westminster candidates 'must be passionate advocates for their communities; be capable of taking Labour's message to the electorate; and ultimately be competent to serve in the next Labour Government'. But there is no evidence that these were used in the vetting process.[84] As one panel member commented, it was more 'an art rather than a science'; relevant criteria were informally agreed, and precedents set, though neither were documented.[85] In practice, the panel members and officials involved had considerable discretion in determining whether any of the comments made rendered an applicant unfit to be a Labour candidate and whether they met appropriate standards.

It seems, as far as one can tell, to have achieved its object of winnowing out the patently unfit. Whether it also lifted the overall calibre of Labour MPs must await further research. But it is difficult to avoid the conclusion that due diligence also operated as a political vetting device. In April 2023, the *Spectator* columnist Katy Balls reported that selections so far had been 'more tightly controlled than at any previous point in the party's history'; it was a New Labour 'restoration'; she quoted one senior official exulting: 'it's a takeover'.[86] By the time the process was completed, hardly anyone on the hard left and very few on the left more broadly had been adopted, despite the hundreds of potentially winnable seats available.[87] This was very plainly the intent. Indeed Matt Faulding, charged with the responsibility for overseeing candidate selections, was instructed to ensure that shortlists only contained those acceptable to the leadership,[88] and undoubtedly the due diligence process took account of this.[89]

In addition to the direct impact of the gatekeepers in filtering out political undesirables, we should also note the indirect impact, or the deterrence effect. How many potential candidates on the left abandoned their pursuit of a parliamentary career because their prospects of success were so slim? This is impossible to quantify, though Crick instanced one case in which aspiring left-wing candidates in Lancashire were told by party officials that applying would be pointless, since they would be excluded by the due diligence stage. 'Such is the strength of the Starmerite machine,' Crick concluded, 'that many on the Left have simply given up trying.'[90]

Restraints on central control

It would, however, be wrong to exaggerate the extent of central control, since there were various structural barriers limiting it. Here we can identify three.

The first is the existence of local centres and circuits of power or influence, especially in Labour's urban strongholds. Senior councillors contemplating a parliamentary career have the advantage of being well known locally and entrenched in local influence networks. The introduction of devolution and of mayoralties has created additional power bases which can operate as platforms for the ambitious seeking a seat in the House of Commons. We should also add, though there has so far been little research in this area, that, as Labour has become more reliant on the votes of ethnic minorities, especially Muslims, so the importance of local religious or communal-based networks has grown.

The second counterweight to central control derives from the party's federal structure. Estimating trade union involvement in candidate selection is difficult in that it is rarely either documented or publicised. Though direct influence at constituency level over the choice of candidates has certainly diminished from the days when selections were determined by constituency General Committees, it remains significant in areas of high unionisation. As we have noted, affiliated trade union branches have nominating rights, and the more nominations a candidate can assemble, the better. Unions can also supply funds, other material sources (e.g., office equipment and space) and useful information and contacts to preferred candidates. However, though an advantage, trade union support, particularly when it derived from the initiative of left-wing local branches rather than from the leadership, did not suffice to overcome opposition from the party apparatus, as we have seen above.

Yet, to assume that trade union power necessarily acts as a counterweight to central control would be to oversimplify: the relationship is often more collaborative than conflictual. This is most plainly the case at the national level. Union members of the NEC, especially those representing UNISON, GMB and USDAW, were embedded in the machinery for regulating selections.[91] By convention, trade union NEC members figure prominently on the NEC officers' group, to which much of the organisational work of the NEC is delegated and where, as one NEC insider put it, 'the real power lies'.[92] Again, by convention, the chair of the Organisation Committee is normally a trade unionist. He or she is responsible for deciding the composition of NEC panels – which must contain at least one trade union member – whose role, as we have noted, has steadily expanded over all stages of the selection process.[93] At an even higher level, senior party officials regularly meet with trade union leaders to discuss the allocation of parliamentary seats to union-backed candidates.[94] These feed through at the regional level, where, historically, Labour's Regional Directors have often worked closely with their counterparts in the larger unions. There is a strong element of reciprocity in these relationships: in return for general political help (e.g., casting pro-leadership votes at Conference), the (larger) unions expect to be rewarded with a share of winnable parliamentary seats.

The third factor is more plainly a constraint. Despite all the funding the party now receives from 'high-value' donors, Labour is still heavily reliant on the unpaid, voluntary work of party members: some members are prepared to devote an extraordinary amount of time, enthusiasm and energy to electioneering: loyalty to the party, as we have constantly stressed, throughout Labour's history has been a major behavioural norm. But there are limits, and the option of exit is always available. Trampling too brazenly and too frequently on the cherished rights of constituency parties to choose their own parliamentary representatives incurs resentment and then alienation and can lead ultimately to defection. The link between constituency campaigning, activism and voter engagement is now well established, and a party that loses too many active members risks weakening ties with its potential electorate.

Notwithstanding these considerations, it remains the case that the effects of new selection rules and the more vigorous exploitation of long-established powers had substantially augmented the ability of selection gatekeepers to filter the flow of candidates. What conclusions can we reach about their goals? These included gender balance, greater ethnic diversity and a higher quality of candidates. But, equally, the leadership wanted on-message MPs who could be relied upon, and its definition of reliability excluded many aspiring left-wing candidates: it was to this end that it deployed its managerial powers to the full.

Notes

1 Jim Pickard and George Parker, 'Keir Starmer's ruthless remaking of the Labour Party', *Financial Times*, 7 June 2023.
2 Labour Party NEC, *Procedural Guidelines for Westminster Parliamentary Selections where There Is a Vacancy* (London: Labour Party, 2022).
3 Labour Party Rulebook, 2022, p. 33. In addition, no selection process is completed until a candidate is endorsed by the NEC. This is normally a formality. Labour Party Rulebook, p. 35.
4 Labour Party NEC, *Procedural Guidelines.*
5 For a full list see https://labour.org.uk/about-us/socialist-societies/ [consulted 23 March 2025].
6 Labour Party NEC, *Parliamentary Selection Procedures* (London: Labour Party, 2019).
7 Labour Party NEC, *Procedural Guidelines.*
8 *Ibid.*,
9 Interview, party insider. As a result of protests from CLPs, the NEC in 2023 agreed to institute a right of appeal for those excluded from English parliamentary longlists on due diligence grounds but only to the NEC. Ann Black, NEC Reports, 28 March 2023.
10 Interview, party insider.
11 Labour Party NEC, *Procedural Guidelines.*
12 Nicholas Watt, 'Keir Starmer's allies purging Labour left, says John McDonnell', *BBC News*, 4 July 2023.
13 Elliot Chappell, 'Exclusive: Labour accused of breaching rules in Wakefield candidate selection', *LabourList*, 13 May 2022, labourlist.org. Here and indeed elsewhere in this chapter we are heavily indebted to Michael Crick's work in meticulously chronicling and analysing the more controversial selection cases.
14 Elliot Chappell, 'Labour council leader excluded from standing as parliamentary candidate', *LabourList*, 8 June 2022, labourlist.org
15 Heather Stewart, 'Starmer allies reject claims leftwingers blocked from standing for Labour', *Guardian*, 1 July 2022.
16 Michael Crick, 'Starmer's ruthless attack on the left: Labour's selection process verges on corruption', *UnHerd*, 2 December 2022, unherd.com
17 Elliot Chappell, 'Former MP blocked from standing as Labour candidate for Kensington', *LabourList*, 17 October 2022, labourlist.org; Aletha Adu, Pippa Crerar and Jessica Elgot, 'Jeremy Corbyn will never stand for Labour again, say senior figures', *Guardian*, 14 November 2022.
18 Katie Neame, 'Councillor blocked from selection argues working-class women "aren't welcome"', *LabourList*, 25 October 2022, labourlist.org
19 Maurice Mcleod, 'Like others on the left, I was blocked from standing as a Labour MP', *Guardian*, 1 November 2022.

20 Katie Neame, 'Labour MP apologises for comments describing Israel as "apartheid state"', *LabourList*, 1 February 2023, labourlist.org
21 Pickard and Parker, 'Keir Starmer's ruthless remaking'.
22 Berny Torre, 'Socialist member of Labour's NEC blocked from standing as MP', *Morning Star*, 18 July 2023.
23 In September 2022, Starmer presented Rahman with a certificate in recognition of his service on the NEC.
24 Rahman was also a graduate of the Bernie Grant Leadership programme, designed to promote BAME representation and the third to be blocked from standing, after Maya Evans in Hastings and Maurice Mcleod in Camberwell and Peckham. Torre, 'Socialist member of Labour's NEC'.
25 Labour Hub editors, 'Dawn McGuinness blocked from standing for Labour', *Labour Hub*, 11 July 2023, hub.labour.org.uk
26 Michael Crick, 'How Keir Starmer betrayed the North East? Purging Jamie Driscoll was a sign of weakness', *UnHerd*, 20 July 2023, unherd.com
27 Helen Pidd, 'Labour mayors say party undemocratic for blocking Jamie Driscoll's candidacy', *Guardian*, 5 June 2023.
28 *Ibid.*
29 *Ibid.* See also Aditya Chakrabortty, 'Notes on a scandal: This is how Starmer's bullies took out Jamie Driscoll – and why it matters', *Guardian*, 8 June 2023.
30 Johnson added that the NEC's decision indicated a 'profound lack of respect' towards the voters of the North East who had elected the mayor. Alan Johnson, 'A good principle misapplied: The case for thinking again about the Jamie Driscoll decision', *Fathom*, June 2023.
31 Labour Party Rulebook, 2022, p. 35.
32 Two other MPs, Claudia Webbe and Jared O'Mara, had been expelled from the PLP for criminal offences.
33 Noa Hoffman, 'Labour insiders say an operation to deselect Corbynite MPs is underway', *PoliticsHome*, 11 November 2021, politicshome.com.
34 *Ibid.*; Kate Knowles, 'Zarah Sultana "thrilled" at reselection as Coventry South MP', *Coventry News*, 12 October 2022.
35 Sienna Rodgers, 'Sam Tarry wins Ilford South selection to replace Mike Gapes', *LabourList*, 22 October 2019, labourlist.org
36 Elliot Chapell, 'Shadow minister and Labour MP Sam Tarry to face full selection process', *LabourList*, 8 July 2022, labourlist.org
37 Katie Neame, Starmer says Tarry was sacked because he "made up policy on the hoof"', *LabourList*, 28 July 2022, labourlist.org
38 Rachel Wearmouth, 'Keir Starmer's sacking of Sam Tarry threatens a new Labour civil war', *New Statesman*, 27 July 2022.
39 Ben Riley-Smith, 'Labour threatened with legal action over "voter fraud"', *Telegraph*, 22 March 2024.
40 Katie Neame, 'Exclusive: Byrne files "official notification" over alleged intimidation', *LabourList*, 17 November 2022, labourlist.org

41 Claire Hamilton, 'Liverpool Labour MP Ian Byrne faces reselection battle', *BBC News*, 14 October 2022.
42 Neame, 'Exclusive: Byrne files "official notification"'.
43 Jack Walton, 'Ian Byrne fights for survival', *Liverpool Post*, 29 October 2022.
44 Katie Neame, 'Ian Byrne's win is unlikely to assuage the left's concerns about this selection round', *LabourList*, 21 November 2022, labourlist.org
45 Jennifer Scott, 'Labour MP Apsana Begum to face trigger ballot from local party', *Sky News*, 5 July 2022; Katie Neame, 'Apsana Begum "triggered" amid "campaign of misogynistic abuse"', *LabourList*, 5 July 2022, labourlist.org
46 Labour Hub editors, '"Unjust, undemocratic and unacceptable" – Apsana Begum hits out at her treatment by Labour's complaints procedure', *Labour Hub*, 2 February 2024, hub.labour.org.uk
47 Sienna Rodgers, 'Labour takes direct control of selection to replace Jeremy Corbyn in Islington North', *PoliticsHome*, 16 May 2024, politicshome.com
48 Daniel Green and Tom Belger, 'Selections drama as Waugh and Starmer allies Akehurst and Simons picked but Russell-Moyle out and Shaheen "at risk"', *LabourList*, 29 May 2024, labourlist.org
49 Michael Crick interview, 'Crick on the "purge" in candidate selections of the Labour left, and the threat to democracy', *Conservative Home*, 23 January 2024.
50 Daniel Green and Tom Belger, 'Faiza Shaheen left shell-shocked by deselection in "purge"' of the left', *LabourList*, 20 May 2024, labourlist.org; Faiza Shaheen, 'I was mistreated – and that's why hundreds of people will no longer vote Labour, they've told me', *Guardian*, 31 May 2024; Emile Lawford, '"I'm no Che Guevara": Faiza Shaheen on running as an independent', *Prospect*, 18 June 2024.
51 Labour Hub Editors, 'It's a purge!', *Labour Hub*, 30 May 2024, hub.labour.org.uk
52 Rachel Cunliffe, 'How the Faiza Shaheen row helps Keir Starmer', *New Statesman*, 30 May 2024.
53 Daniel Green and Tom Belger, 'Labour denies "purge" but union slams "jobs for the boys" as Shaheen deselected', *LabourList*, 30 May 2024, labourlist.org
54 Peter Bachrach and Morton S. Baratz, 'Decisions and nondecisions: An analytical framework', *American Political Science Review*, 57:3 (1963), 641.
55 Lewis Minkin, *The Blair Supremacy: A Study in the Politics of Labour's Party Management* (Manchester: Manchester University Press, 2014), p. 159.
56 Pippa Norris and Joni Lovenduski, *Political Recruitment: Gender, Race and Class in the British Parliament* (Cambridge: Cambridge University Press, 1995), p. 199.
57 Labour Party NEC, *Procedural Guidelines*, p. 2.
58 Minkin, *The Blair Supremacy*, p. 159.
59 Michael Crick, 'Starmer's ruthless attack on the left'.
60 Michael Gallagher and Michael Marsh, *Candidate Selection in Comparative Perspective: The Secret Garden of Politics* (London: Sage, 1988), p. 6.

61 Interview, Terry Ashton.
62 Gerry Hassan and Eric Shaw, *The Strange Death of Labour Scotland* (Edinburgh: Edinburgh University Press, 2012), p. 296.
63 Interview, Terry Ashton.
64 Jeanette Ashe, *Political Candidate Selection* (London: Routledge, 2020), p. 119. See also Minkin, *The Blair Supremacy*, p. 370.
65 Interview, Ann Black; Crick, 'Starmer's ruthless attack on the left'.
66 Minkin, *The Blair Supremacy*, p. 369.
67 Interview, Terry Ashton; Crick, 'Starmer's ruthless attack on the left'.
68 Interview, Ann Black.
69 Labour Party Rulebook, 2022, p. 36; Ann Black, 'Boundary changes, amended selection process, attack ads – Labour NEC report', *LabourList*, 25 May 2023, labourlist.org
70 Labour Party NEC, *Variations to Selection Procedures for Parliamentary Candidates* (London: Labour Party, 2023).
71 *Ibid.*, pp. 1–2.
72 Katie Neame, Daniel Green and Tom Belger, 'Revealed: Member anger as around 100 Labour candidates still not unveiled', *LabourList*, 22 May 2024, labourlist.org
73 Katie Neame, Tom Belger and Daniel Green, 'Late selections in seats where candidates stood down, deselected or not chosen: Full list of new picks as Labour completes full slate', *LabourList*, 5 June 2024, labourlist.org
74 Labour Party NEC, *Emergency Selection Procedures for Parliamentary Candidates* (London: Labour Party, 23 May 2024), labour.org.uk
75 It is worth noting that UNISON and USDAW, two of the four big unions who had worked closest with the Starmer leadership gained two MPs apiece.
76 David Easton, *A Systems Analysis of Political Life* (New York: John Wiley and Sons, 1965), p. 88.
77 Tom Baldwin, *Keir Starmer: The Biography* (London: William Collins, 2024), p. 329.
78 Michael Crick, 'Starmer will regret purging the left', *UnHerd*, 9 June 2023, unherd.com
79 Labour Party NEC, *Procedural Guidelines*.
80 Ann Black, NEC Reports, 19 July 2022.
81 Interview, Ann Black.
82 Ann Black, NEC Reports, 23 May, 2022.
83 Kate Dove, 'Activists, from all wings of our party, should be able to stand before members', *LabourList*, 19 October 2022, labourlist.org
84 Labour Party NEC, *Procedural Guidelines*.
85 Interview, party insider.
86 Jessica Elgot, 'Starmer takes aim at loose cannons with his tight control of Labour selections', *Guardian*, 13 November 2022; Katy Balls, 'The stormtroopers: How Labour centrists took back control', *Spectator*, 29 April 2023.

87 Patrick Maguire and Gabriel Pogrund, *Get In: The Inside Story of Labour under Starmer* (London: Vintage, 2025), pp. 383–4.
88 *Ibid.*, p. 383.
89 Interview, Ann Black.
90 Crick, 'Starmer will regret purging the left'.
91 Interview, party insider. The role, and relationship to the party, of Unite, the Labour Party's biggest affiliate, has tended to differ from the others of the big four unions. Under McCluskey's leadership it was more supportive of Corbyn, but more critical of Starmer as party leader. It has also, more recently, shifted under McCluskey's successor, Sharon Graham, who, though remaining critical of Starmer, has placed a greater emphasis on and devoted more resources to the union's industrial responsibilities.
92 Interview, party insider.
93 Trade unions are also well represented on the Regional Executive Committee, which also, as we have seen, supplies members to longlisting panels.
94 Interview, party insider.

11

The turning away: the management of policy divisions under Starmer

> Presume not that I am the thing I was;
> For God doth know, so shall the world perceive,
> That I have turn'd away my former self;
> So will I those that kept me company.
>
> Prince Hal, *Henry IV*, Part 2

As we noted in Chapter 10, Starmer won the contest for the Labour leadership on a radical platform designed to appeal to as many members as possible. A retreat from some of its pledges was to be expected as the target audience became the electorate at large; what was not expected was that so many of them would be so summarily dropped. Starmer's platform, on which he had contested the leadership, contained many left-wing policies. These included common ownership of rail, the Royal Mail, energy and water, an end to outsourcing in the NHS and in other public services, an increase in income tax for the top 5 per cent of earners, the reversing of cuts to corporation tax, abolition of the punitive benefit sanctions system, a more compassionate immigration policy, a rapid transition to a net-zero economy and the introduction of a swathe of new employment rights and regime. By 2024, only the latter two had (largely) survived Starmer's cull. This, inevitably, provoked tensions and misgivings in the party, though, as we shall show, for a combination of reasons, they were articulated in a restrained and muted manner.

Economic credibility and public spending

The conduct of the Starmer leadership, we shall argue, was largely shaped by the ethic of power, operationalised in terms of the strategic precepts of power accommodation and opinion alignment. These furnished the guidelines that shaped political calculations and policy choices and were applied, as we shall see, with remorseless logic during the years 2020 to 2024.

Labour has for years struggled with public doubts about its capacity to manage the economy effectively and avoid 'profligacy' with the nation's money. For this reason, the leadership judged that regaining a reputation for economic competence was essential for winning the next election. The precept of power accommodation stipulated that this could be achieved only by securing the approval of those powerful forces widely regarded as the authoritative adjudicators of good sense in economic policy: the City, the corporate sector and the mass media. The second precept, opinion alignment, laid down that on matters of high public salience, policies should correspond as closely as possible to the grain of public opinion. When it came to the crucial issues of tax, borrowing and spending, the two maxims, the leadership was convinced, pointed in the same direction: an unrelenting accent on fiscal discipline.

Fiscal discipline could best be demonstrated, the leadership calculated, by the party's adherence to two iron-clad fiscal rules: that current spending should always be covered by tax receipts and that the level of borrowing as a proportion of Gross Domestic Product (GDP) should be on a downward slope over five years. Public anxieties about the party could further be allayed, the leadership believed, by rock-solid pledges to avoid anything other than modest increases in taxation. Hence it pledged not to raise the rates of the four major sources of tax revenue: income tax, National Insurance contributions, VAT and corporation tax, which, in combination, yielded over 75 per cent of all tax revenues. Labour's attachment to these two self-denying ordinances was reinforced by events: the huge spending incurred by the COVID-19 pandemic, the impact of the Russian invasion of Ukraine and the inflationary wave it provoked, and then the effects of the disastrous Truss/Kwarteng budget.

Fiscal discipline meant scaling back spending commitments as far as possible. Making 'painful choices' was, party leaders warned, inescapable, and it soon became evident that the pain would be for the party and those they wished to serve. The Tories' two-child benefit cap had been announced by then Chancellor George Osborne in 2015 and implemented in April 2017; it barred parents from claiming child tax credit or Universal Credit for any third or subsequent child born after April 2017. It had been fiercely castigated by Labour. Shadow Work and Pensions Secretary Jonathan Ashworth had described it as 'one of the single most heinous elements of the system which is pushing children and families into poverty today'; Deputy Leader Angela Rayner had labelled it 'obscene and inhumane'.[1] The cap came to symbolise the harsh and punitive welfare regime established by the Conservatives, so it was widely anticipated that it would be scrapped by a Labour government. According to Paul Johnson of the Institute for Fiscal Studies (IFS), the cap had 'a direct, laser-like effect of increasing child poverty'.[2] The amount of money involved in removing the cap – about £1.4 billion – was small, while its effect would be immediate, bringing 270,000 households out of poverty. But Starmer and Reeves point-blank refused to make any such pledge to scrap it. There were two main reasons for this, both electoral: by standing firm against strong internal party pressure, the leadership was demonstrating that it would not flinch from making 'tough decisions'.[3] If this caused anguish in the party, then 'the more painful the spending thumbscrew, the more convincing to undecided voters'.[4] The second reason was that the cap was popular. According to a YouGov poll conducted in July 2023, it was approved of by 60 per cent of British adults, including a majority of Labour voters,[5] on the grounds that it prevented immigrants and welfare recipients with large families from 'milking the system'. By refusing to end the cap, Labour was signalling that it understood public anxieties about 'welfare abuse'.

Many within the party were dismayed: surely the alleviation of poverty and helping the most distressed was an absolutely core value? Starmer's response was that the party could no longer dwell in its 'comfort zone of promising vast sums of money'.[6] But what, then, of the NHS? The party was constantly hammering home the message that the Conservatives had 'run it into the ground', that it was facing 'an existential crisis': indeed, resolving it was one of the party's much-touted five 'missions'.[7] With an ever-increasing number of older people with complicated health conditions, the rising cost of equipment, drugs and new technologies, and the desperate need to boost pay to combat severe staff shortages, a massive infusion of money seemed to be essential. But Labour's message was that, until the new golden age of higher economic growth with its additional tax revenues, reform would have to do much of 'the heavy lifting'.[8] Precisely what 'reform' meant was never very clearly spelt out. Labour did instance three specific reforms: harnessing information technology and artificial intelligence to create a 'fully digital NHS'; switching the emphasis from cure to prevention by transferring resources from hospitals; and making greater use of private sector facilities. In the real world, none of these would save money, at least not in the short term, or, in the case of relying on private provision, ever. In truth, Labour must have known that an immediate cash injection for the NHS was unavoidable but thought it politically preferable not to say so.

The presumption throughout was that big spending pledges equated in the public mind with higher tax bills, and if the voters caught a whiff of this, they would run a mile. The perception of Labour as a recklessly extravagant party was, the leadership believed, so hard-wired in the popular psyche that the party had to go to extraordinary lengths to dislodge it. Many disputed this interpretation of public opinion, and not only on the left and in the unions. For example, the election guru John Curtice pointed to opinion research showing that most voters were willing to pay more tax to revitalise public services, a finding that was constantly repeated.[9] But embedded in the leadership's mindset was the anxiety that, in the privacy of the voting booth, voters would be swayed by fears of tax rises whipped up by the Tories and the press. 'To understand the brain of Labour's high command,' the *Observer*'s political commentator wrote, 'and to fully appreciate why it so often defaults to a defensive caution, the first step is to grasp how terrified they are of losing an election virtually everyone else assumes the party must win.'[10] Four consecutive defeats, and folk memories of polling leads suddenly evaporating, persuaded the leadership that nothing must be taken for granted. This came to be dubbed the 'Ming vase strategy': don't frighten the voters, listen very closely to what they have to say and take no risks. As Polly Toynbee pointed out, 'Politicians can be economical with the truth, but voters can also be fickle and contrary, wanting public spending but reluctant to pay the price.' After fourteen long years wandering in the wilderness of opposition, could Labour really take that risk?[11] Far better, then, to close down one's vulnerabilities and leave as few hostages to fortune as possible.

The 'Green Prosperity Plan'

By holding the line on social spending, Labour left itself with only one major spending item, its 'Green Prosperity Plan' (GPP). The plan, unveiled with great fanfare by Rachel Reeves at the 2021 party Conference, had a three-fold function. It would show how the party could tackle the looming climate crisis by presenting a policy package designed to substantially reduce the UK's reliance on fossil fuels. It offered a strategy by which the party's 'mission' of accelerated economic growth could be delivered. And it was a policy, indeed almost a philosophy, around which an enthusiastic party could rally.

As originally set out in September 2021, the plan envisaged a Labour government borrowing £28 billion a year to invest in wind, solar and tidal energy, green hydrogen, the construction of electric battery factories, a major home insulation scheme, carbon capture and other environmental projects. The money would be used to create a new state-run company, Great British Energy, with a capital of £8.3 billion, which would invest directly in renewable and nuclear energy and contribute towards energy self-sufficiency.[12] In addition, a Labour government would establish a £7.3 billion National Wealth Fund, a state national investment body which would take equity stakes in potentially high-growth firms, and a Keynesian-style effort to stimulate private investment by higher public outlays.

However, from early 2023, reports began to circulate that Rachel Reeves, Director of Campaigns Morgan McSweeney and Campaigns Coordinator Pat McFadden – three of the most powerful voices in Labour's inner counsels – had serious reservations about the feasibility of the GPP. A variety of factors were adduced: capacity constraints, the competing demands of other spending priorities, the Truss-provoked rise in borrowing costs and worries that the plan was not compatible with Labour's fiscal rules. But perhaps the most serious objection was that the sums entailed opened the party up to the charge that it would have either to raise taxes or increase borrowing to meet the costs. In short, it threatened the 'Ming vase' strategy.

Shadow Net Zero Secretary Ed Miliband fought a strenuous rearguard action, but Starmer swung behind Reeves and her allies. The £28 billion figure disappeared even as an aspiration, and the actual additional spending was gradually whittled down to just £4.7 billion per year. This, the *Observer*'s political commentator commented, was not 'a routine political volte-face' but the shedding of Starmer's 'signature pledge', his 'flagship policy'. The amount Labour was now committed to spending was 'a puny sum'.[13] Many in Labour's ranks, and not only on the left, were disheartened and deflated – though loath to go public.

No turning away: employment rights

The one area of policy where pressures towards policy dilution were (largely) resisted was over Labour's ambitious plans for enhancing employee rights. These involved a raft of policies including giving workers employment rights from day one, ending the qualifying time for unfair dismissal, sick pay and parental leave, banning zero-hours contracts and 'fire and rehire' practices, facilitating union recognition procedures and establishing a 'single status of employees all of whom would be afforded the full protection of employment law'.[14] As these were rightly presented as heralding the biggest expansion of employment rights for generations, Labour almost immediately came under intense business pressure to moderate them. Any attempt to weaken the package was, in turn, resisted by the unions, overtly with Unite and, more quietly and largely behind the scenes, with the other large unions (UNISON, GMB and USDAW). In the event, when the manifesto was published, while the party decided to ban only 'exploitative' (to be defined) zero-hours contracts and equivocated over the 'single status of worker' question, most other pledges were retained.[15] Almost uniquely, on this issue Starmer more or less held fast to the position he had adumbrated early in his leadership. There were several reasons for this.

Firstly, there was a significant degree of convergence in policies and goals between the leadership and the unions, more so than during the New Labour years. For Blair and Brown, a key to enhancing UK economic competitiveness was labour market flexibility, that is, weaker labour protections than in most of the UK's European competitors. The Starmer leadership has taken a very different approach. Cheap and insecure labour, in their view, discouraged new investment in labour-saving machines, while a demoralised and resentful workforce clinging on to precarious work was an unmotivated one; in both cases, the result was to lower productivity.[16] In addition, for Starmer, creating circumstances and institutions which afforded working people respect, dignity and security seemed to be a matter of deep personal conviction.

Secondly, granting more rights at work meshed with electoral imperatives, with polling indicating that it was one of the party's most popular policies.[17] Further, hard lessons had shown the damaging effects of New Labour's complacency about working-class voters ('they have nowhere else to go'). Starmer's strategists saw workers in 'Red Wall' seats who had defected to the Tories – so-called 'hero voters' – as a key target, and his speeches were peppered with references to defending their interests. More employment rights fitted neatly into this (see Chapter 1).

Thirdly, the leadership understood that managing relations with the unions necessarily took a different form from managing those with the PLP and constituency parties because of the power Labour's federal arrangements gave to its industrial affiliates. With their own leaders, bureaucracies, funds and other resources, the unions could not be railroaded as easily as ordinary members and constituency parties. Further, the leadership recognised that it was virtually impossible to steer measures on key issues (including organisational ones) through Conference without union votes – concessions on workplace rights had often been the quid pro quo. As a result of these three factors, the leadership displayed a sensitivity, a receptivity and a willingness to compromise on matters of high importance to the unions that it did not exhibit on other matters.

Electoral appeal and policy rationality

The Starmer camp framed the options available to Labour in terms of the clash between power and protest, utopian ideals versus tough realism. As Josh Simons, then Director of Labour Together and now a (parachuted) MP, explained: 'So often, the Labour party has lost elections because it clung to unachievable, pious, ideological purity. Labour wins when its agenda is radical but deliverable in the world as it is.'[18] That there is often a tension between office and principles is undeniable, but what the leadership's framing tended to overlook was another clash, just as fundamental, between electoral advantage and policy rationality or, to put it differently, between what woos and what works. We can afford two major examples of this.

The first was Labour's so-called fiscal credibility rule, which required that debt be a falling proportion of GDP by the end of a parliamentary term. This somewhat arbitrary rule was devised to reassure both the voters and the markets that Labour in government would be fiscally 'prudent'. In truth, it should more accurately have been called 'the fiscal incredulity rule'. It was described by the leading macro-economist Simon Wren-Lewis as 'economic illiteracy', by Paul Johnson of the IFS as 'basically silly', by Will Hutton as 'intellectually absurd' and by the National Institute for Economic and Social Research as 'not fit for purpose'.[19] It was also, according to the former chief economist to the Bank of England, Andy Haldane, utterly self-defeating, since its effect was to constrain public investment, lower growth potential and in general weaken the economy.[20] In short, there was 'no economic basis for the falling-debt-to-GDP rule. That rule is there for political reasons, and perhaps in Labour's case because they believe the media and the public want it there.'[21]

The second was over tax. Labour's manifesto stated bluntly that it would not 'increase taxes on working people, which is why we will not increase national insurance, the basic, higher, or additional rates of income tax, or VAT'.[22] Starmer and Reeves had also promised that a Labour government would not introduce new taxes on wealth, raise corporation tax, abolish the upper earnings limit for National Insurance contributions or bring capital gains tax (CGT) into line with income tax (used as a tax-ducking ploy). Virtually all of these taxes (aside from VAT) were progressive, bearing most heavily on the more affluent. Perhaps for this reason they were deemed too dangerous. Instead, the party confined itself to only very minor steps to gain revenue and make the tax system more progressive: scrapping non-domiciled (non-dom) tax status, closing a tax loophole used by some private equity fund managers (referred to as 'carried interest', see below) and adding VAT to private school fees. All this meant that there was little money to go around.

The result was a contradiction between Labour's diagnoses – the woeful state of the public services, record NHS waiting lists, a disintegrating public infrastructure, the desperate shortage of houses, rampant child poverty, a crisis in adult social care and so forth – and its prescriptions: the very modest sums committed. Under the Tories, 'nothing worked'; under Labour, it would, and furthermore, the bill for repairs would be modest: nobody would have to dig deep into their pockets. As the IFS and other think-tanks perpetually pointed out, none of this made sense. Insofar as Labour sought to square the circle, it was by invoking 'reform' and 'modernisation'. These were very vague words that, in effect, performed the function of magical incantations which, through endless repetition, could deliver the promised land. The inevitable consequence for Labour would be a crisis of trust and credibility, which we discuss below.

Many in the party were, in truth, uneasy and even disturbed by the drift of policy, but, during this period, doubts were largely muffled and subdued. Except for the row over Gaza (discussed above), the leadership was little troubled by rebellion in the heavily disciplined PLP. There were a variety of reasons for this. Firstly, and not least in importance, was self-discipline: virtually everyone wanted to place the tumult and turbulence of the Corbyn years behind them. Secondly, the powers of patronage of an incoming Prime Minister are very considerable and, with many jobs needing to be filled in a Labour government, few MPs, whatever their reservations, were prepared to risk personal advancement by irritating the leader. Thirdly, the fear of instant retribution: confronted by a ruthless and single-minded leader quick to resort to disciplinary sanctions, most potential rebels were cowed into silence. At the same time, collective responsibility was strictly enforced for all holders of front-bench positions, with members warned that open dissent would not be tolerated.[23] Finally, most members, both inside and outside the House of Commons, accepted Starmer's right to rule, rooted in the mandate conferred upon him by his sweeping victory in the leadership contest, then bolstered by Labour's swelling poll lead from 2002 onwards – and therefore their obligation to accept whatever decisions he made. The era of weak and contested leadership legitimacy, evident since 2010, had come to an end. The only opposition came from the demoralised, divided and discredited hard left – and even this was episodic.

The 2024 election

The scale of Labour's victory and the collapse of the Tory vote exceeded expectations. Labour doubled its representation in Parliament, winning 412 seats, with an overall majority of 174, the Conservatives sinking to their lowest ever score with 121 seats, the Lib Dems at 72, the SNP at 9 and the Greens at 4. There was, not surprisingly, much exultation in Labour's ranks: Starmer had engineered a resounding triumph in less than five years on from a desperate defeat.

All was not quite as it seemed. If the results in Scotland (where Labour did well) are discounted, Labour's vote compared to 2019 was static (Table 11.1). The turnout, at 60 per cent, was one of the lowest since universal suffrage was introduced. In fact, the real level of public participation was even lower. According to the Institute for Public Policy Research (IPPR), just 52 per cent of those eligible to cast their vote – that is, including the eight million-odd voters who were not registered – did so, the lowest turnout ever since the advent of universal franchise (1928).[24] Party strategists

Table 11.1 *General election votes won by Labour leaders in numbers and percentages*

Leader	Date	Votes won	% of vote
Ed Miliband	2015	9.6m	30.4
Jeremy Corbyn	2017	12.8m	40.0
Jeremy Corbyn	2019	10.3m	32.2
Keir Starmer	2024	9.8m	34.0

Source: House of Commons Library

heartily congratulated themselves on the remarkable 'vote efficiency' of their campaign – winning votes where they were most needed rather than piling them up where they were not. The problem with this analysis was that though it would explain why the party did best in potentially winnable seats (though this was also due to large-scale tactical voting), it cannot explain the failure to win more votes elsewhere. Why, for example, was the total Labour vote in 2024 three million less than it had been under Corbyn in 2017 – a fact that party strategists preferred to forget and banish from the historical record? The election had delivered Labour a thumping majority in the House of Commons, but on a very insecure democratic mandate.

Indeed, even before the election campaign began, reports indicated that alienation from the Tories was not being matched by any enthusiasm for Labour, with evidence of widespread voter apathy. While the leadership had been successful in expunging the party's negatives which discouraged people from voting for it, its ultra-cautious stance was failing to inspire voters. Indeed, in April 2024 one piece of research reported that on key indicators such as fitness to govern and quality of leaders, Labour under Starmer scored lower than under Miliband: the big difference was that the polling figures for the Tories were very much worse.[25] As one Shadow minister observed in July 2023, 'People are crying out for inspiration and hope and something to believe in again, and we haven't given anybody a reason to vote Labour yet.'[26] Labour's triumph was a formidable edifice indeed – but one built on sand.

Early murmuring and rebellions

The economic inheritance of the new government, as widely anticipated, was dismal in the extreme. Growth was very sluggish, productivity sagging, wages and living standards stagnant, and both public and private investment stood well below that of most other Organisation for Economic Co-operation and Development (OECD) countries. Compounding all this was the dire plight of cash-strapped public services, crumbling public infrastructure, a struggling educational sector and crisis-stricken health care, social care and criminal justice systems. The result was that there were a host of demands from multiple quarters, all clamouring for more resources.

It now became even more plainly obvious than before that the leadership had forced the party into a fiscal straitjacket and would struggle to meet these demands. Conveniently, the new government discovered an alarming £22 billion hidden 'black hole' in the public finances left by the Tories, and this was pressed into service to justify the unavoidability of unpleasant decisions (see below). This 'black hole' referred to the gap between a forecast for the government's deficit and what the government's chosen fiscal rule prescribed: a statistical artifice of little real financial import.[27] But the 'black hole' was wheeled out by the new government to justify two decisions which caused much heart-searching in the party: not to reverse the two-child cap on welfare benefits and to means-test the Winter Fuel Payment, hitherto available to all of state pension age.

The decision in opposition not to pledge to remove the two-child cap, as we have noted, caused deep upset in the party, and many expected it to be reversed once Labour was in power. The government refused, on the grounds that it had to fill the 'black hole'. When it came to a vote, virtually all Labour MPs trooped loyally, if reluctantly, into the House of Commons 'yes' lobby, though seven (all members of the SCG) defied a three-line whip and were immediately suspended from the PLP for six months. This was meant as a marker: 'Punishing the rebels sends a loud signal not just to the left but to his many new MPs and the public that Starmer's "changed" party and ruthless streak weren't just for show in opposition.'[28]

The row over the benefit cap was soon overshadowed by another, more unexpected announcement – the means-testing of the Winter Fuel Payment, which had been introduced by Gordon Brown in 1997 as a universal benefit. In future, only those pensioners in receipt of pension credit, about 1.5 million, would be eligible, which meant that about 10 million would lose out. According to *Guardian* columnist Jonathan Freedland, these two decisions were designed to reassure the financial market, who would otherwise have reacted badly.[29] Wren-Lewis riposted that such claims were met, in informed quarters, by 'general and justified derision'.[30] Critics pointed out that the money saved would be very small, and the cut-off point was arbitrary and would plunge many pensioners into fuel poverty. The move was also extremely unpopular and support for Labour nose-dived in the polls, giving it perhaps the shortest honeymoon in British history.

Setting the framework for governing: the November 2024 budget

Rachel Reeves's first budget was unveiled on 30 October. Sympathetic commentators hailed it as 'very much a Labour budget', with its focus on 'taking money from what may be called the upper middle class and the very well-off, and spending it on the public sector, the lower paid and the worse off in society'.[31] By the same token, it precipitated an avalanche of condemnation from the right-wing press.

Spending, Reeves announced, would be raised by £70 billion a year over the next five years, half of the increase to be paid for by tax increases and half to come from additional borrowing. The major beneficiary was inevitably the NHS, released from the life-support machine with an immediate 4.3 per cent rise in its budget, though thereafter growth would trail off: here Labour delivered more than it had promised. Education, justice and local government, all wrestling with immense financial pressures, also did relatively well. Three million low-paid workers benefited from a significant rise in the minimum wage by 6.7 per cent to £12.21, equivalent to

£1,400 a year for an eligible full-time worker. But government projections in the budget suggested that most departments would see very little in the way of additional growth in real income over the next few years, and spending rounds would be extremely tight. The uplift in welfare benefits (1.7 per cent) was lower than the expected rate of inflation for 2025.[32]

Increased borrowing was made possible by a partial loosening of the inane 'fiscal credibility rule'. The new rule took account of public financial assets that result from investment, thereby allowing considerably more room for an expansion of public capital spending. But it stopped short of the logical next step of including not only financial but also public physical assets, leaving the government still inhabiting a very restrictive fiscal framework which would continue to seriously inhibit public investment and spending.[33]

The major problem was over taxation. The government had to scout around for sources of income which did not contravene its electorally driven pledges, alighting on raising employer National Insurance contributions. These were increased by 1.2 per cent, which, it was estimated, would yield £25 billion a year by the end of the forecast period. Whether the measure was consistent with the pledge not to 'increase taxes on working people' was debatable, since the Office for Budget Responsibility predicted that about 75 per cent of the cost would be borne by future depressed wage settlements.[34] There were some tax hikes on the wealthy – CGT was increased, inheritance tax (IHT) reliefs and exemptions were curtailed and a higher stamp duty for additional homes was introduced – but their overall effects were modest.[35]

It was, in fact, a very cautious and unambitious budget. A government serious about reducing social inequality, Sam Freedman has argued, requires 'greatly increased expenditure', and that ultimately could be funded only by taxing wealth.[36] The Labour MP Liam Byrne charted the prodigious rise in wealth disparities since Labour was last in power in his study, *The Inequality of Wealth*. It documented how the average wealth of those in the top 1 per cent of Britain's richest increased thirty-one times more than that of those in the bottom 99 per cent between 2010 and 2021.[37] Since

1990, the overall wealth of billionaires had risen by over 1,000 per cent.[38] Notwithstanding, taxes on wealth have not risen either as a proportion of total taxation or of national income, not least because of multiple exemptions, reliefs and ubiquitous tax-avoidance schemes.[39] As the leading *Financial Times* columnist Martin Wolf concluded, 'much of the current tax system is unjust, notably, but not solely, in failures to tax capital and tackle tax evasion and avoidance adequately'.[40]

The trade unions and the left of the party had for years clamoured for higher taxes on wealth to generate fresh revenue for public services. For example, a Unite-sponsored resolution adopted by the TUC conference in September 2024 called for a wealth tax on the top 1 per cent of wealthiest households: it was calculated that this could raise £69 billion. The tax expert Richard Murphy, who had worked as an advisor to Corbyn, produced a report listing a range of measures that could be implemented to tax wealth more effectively.[41] And a report for the left-leaning IPPR, published just before the budget and written by a group of business millionaires, had called for the equalising of CGT rates with income tax rates, thereby closing a tax loophole.[42] Even impeccably orthodox economic institutions such as the OECD and the International Monetary Fund had called for higher taxes on property and wealth to fund public investment and help reduce inequality.[43]

The budget did raise the lower rate of CGT from 10 per cent to 18 per cent, and the higher rate from 20 per cent to 24 per cent, but fell far short of equalising it with income tax rates, so a lucrative loophole survived. Some exemptions from IHT were lifted (e.g., on agricultural land), and some other regulations were tightened up, but not appreciably so.[44] None of the more radical and redistributive policies advocated by the unions and the left were implemented. 'A tax system,' Stefan Collini wrote, 'is a political philosophy expressed in numbers.'[45] It articulates a judgement about how rewards should be distributed and how far governments should intervene in altering distributions set by the market. The budget in no significant way challenged the existing market-driven and extremely unequal distributional order, nor did government pronouncements suggest that it might be desirable to do so.

One insight into government priorities and perhaps philosophy was furnished by the shift of Labour policy on 'carried interest'. This refers to a complicated tax arrangement under which the income of private equity executives was taxed at 28 per cent rather than at the 45 per cent rate if it had simply been denominated as income.[46] The proviso, as one private equity boss put it in 2007, enabled people like himself to 'pay less tax than a cleaning lady'; the small number of private equity managers benefited, as a result, by £18 million each.[47] Rachel Reeves had previously branded private equity dealmakers as asset strippers and pledged to 'crack down' on 'carried interest', labelling it as an 'indefensible' loophole. Closing it would raise £565 million a year, money which was earmarked to support 8,500 new mental health staff and legal aid for disaster victims.[48] It was one of the few tax pledges included in the manifesto. The industry lobby the British Private Equity and Venture Capital Association (BVCA) responded by launching an energetic and expensive campaign to persuade Labour to change its mind, warning that, otherwise, private equity professionals would quit the country, taking their money with them. Labour succumbed to the pressure.[49] The budget announced a more modest rise to 32 per cent, leaving much of the income from 'carried interest' intact. The 8,500 new mental health staff would have to wait their turn. Champagne, it was reported, flowed in the City.[50]

The amount of money involved was small, but the political message was clear. The BVCA campaign exposed the multiple close connections the financial sector had forged with Labour, as well as reflecting the lengths the leadership was prepared to go to placate the City. This was a conscious policy. In early 2024, Rachel Reeves had lamented that too often, in the last decade, Labour politicians 'have sounded embarrassed about the sectors we excel in. The next Labour government will unashamedly champion the UK's financial services sector.' The decision on 'carried interest' was a sign that the party was true to its word.[51] Rachel Reeves rammed the message home in November 2024 when she told dignitaries from the financial world assembled at Mansion House that tighter rules on banks and investment institutions, introduced after the great financial crash, had gone 'too far'; regulations which discouraged risk taking would be relaxed to enhance the City's global competitiveness. 'The financial services sector,' she added, was 'the "crown jewel" of the UK economy.'[52] Memories of the 2018 crash were fading.

The object of this 'mildly inconveniencing the rich' budget was to avert an immediate breakdown in the public services bled by the years of austerity and economic stagnation. As Aditya Chakrabortty put it, the budget rescued hospitals and schools from collapse, but with little spare cash left to rebuild.[53] The modesty of Labour's redistributory ambitions as manifested in its first budget should have come as no surprise: significantly, the word 'inequality' did not merit one mention in Reeves's speech.[54] Starmer and Reeves had ruled out raising the most progressive taxes, income tax and corporation tax, and 'barely exploited the redistributive opportunities offered by increasing capital gains and inheritance taxes.'[55] Substantially higher taxation on private wealth and on corporations, they argued, would alienate powerful interests whose cooperation was essential, and would provoke capital flight and deter corporate investment. Policy over both tax and regulation must be geared to enhancing the UK's attractiveness to international investors, since it was upon this, the government averred, that a higher rate of economic growth and therefore money for refurbishing the public services depended. But much research indicates that boosting the growth rate is a complex task, and it takes time for its benefits to flow through the economy and yield additional tax revenue.[56]

The question of trust

Questions of trust, credibility and honesty figured prominently in the leadership's strategic thinking. Starmer reiterated the theme during the election campaign: 'I think the public in the last 14 years had far too much of people who say before an election they'll deliver everything, and afterwards they don't. We have to break that pattern.'[57] He and others constantly pointed to the mood of profound political disenchantment within the electorate, what one sympathetic journalist called 'the vast scepticism [of] so many voters' when presented with grandiose promises.[58] Mountains of evidence indeed showed that many voters had lost faith in politicians, in the political process and in the very capacity of governments to improve their lives. Voters did not believe politicians, and the more ambitious their promises, the less their belief – so the reasoning ran. Labour could rebuild trust and rehabilitate politics only by confining their policy 'offer' to carefully costed and modest pledges; anything grander would be treated with cynicism, 'I'm not going to make a promise before an election,' Starmer insisted, 'which I don't think I can deliver after the election.'[59]

Such considerations, as we have seen, helped shape Labour's policy, especially on taxation. A party source summarised and underlined the message during the campaign. 'Keir and Rachel have made clear that our priority is growing the economy, not increasing taxes. We have set out fully costed, fully funded plans, with very specific tax loopholes we would close. Nothing in our plans requires any additional tax to be increased.'[60] In an interview in November 2024, Rachel Reeves admitted that she had been wrong to promise that, aside from VAT on private schools, tightening up non-dom rules and one or two other similarly minor matters, there would be no need for major tax rises. But this was because she, along with everyone else, had been deliberately misinformed by the Conservatives about the 'huge black hole in public finances'.[61]

Only promising what you can deliver is certainly one aspect of trustworthiness, and, of course, the less you promise, the easier it is to deliver. However, the problem of trust in politics can be construed in a rather different way. Bernard Williams identifies two different aspects of truthfulness, which he labels 'sincerity' and 'accuracy'. The former entails that politicians should say what they believe to be true; in other words, their public assertions should correspond with their private convictions; the latter that they should seek to ensure that what they claim to be true is, in fact, so.[62]

Did public statements by Starmer, Reeves and others reflect their private thoughts? And if that was so, did they make sufficient effort to ensure that these private thoughts were consistent with information available at the time? Well before the discovery of the Tory fiscal 'black hole', Labour was regularly being told, not least by influential think-tanks, that its plans simply did not stack up: they could not possibly achieve their goals without more substantial tax rises. For example, in 2023 the IFS had warned that 'unless levels of tax increase substantially, a reduction in the scope of the public services that the British state provides is likely inevitable.'[63] The same point was made by think-tanks closer to the party, the IPPR and the Resolution Foundation, and was insistently repeated. Weren't Starmer and Reeves making promises on taxes which they knew they would have to break? And did they have to make them?

This last question is the crucial one and it takes us back to the 'Ming vase' strategy and the strategic calculations that underpinned it: that nothing be done that might agitate the voters, provide ammunition to the right-wing press or upset the financial markets or corporate sector. This was despite considerable evidence that voters were far more worried about public services, the NHS and the economy than about tax and, indeed, had already factored in what would be inevitable tax rises after the election.[64] 'Treating the voters as mere children,' the *Financial Times* columnist Martin Wolf warned, 'can only guarantee ever-rising cynicism about our politics.'[65] But the logic of the ethic of power, as embodied in Labour's chosen strategy, led ineluctably to subordinating both policy rationality and party principles to narrowly conceived electoral benefit. Heavier taxation on the rich, especially on wealth (such as on property, stocks and shares and other assets) would have affronted the powerful, in business and the media, contradicting the precept of power accommodation, as well as frightening the voters, and challenging that of opinion alignment. This, Labour's leadership judged, was far too risky.

When the inevitable happened, a substantial tax-raising budget, Labour's standing in the polls plummeted, reinforcing voter cynicism about politicians' dishonesty. The party's leaders, and especially its strategists, its professional political apparatus, had too easily convinced themselves that they understood far better than their critics the inner feelings and instincts of the electorate, and they opted to frame the debate in the party simplistically as between power and principle. They responded that their strategy had in fact delivered the goods – a huge majority in the House of Commons

– but this was largely by courtesy of the electoral system: not that many voters had been impressed.

Furthermore, immediately after the budget, the Chancellor declared that 'We've now set the spending envelope for the remainder of this parliament; we don't need to increase taxes further.'[66] How, then, would the government cope with the crisis in the social sector, a major cause, in turn, of the overstretching of NHS capacities? How would it respond to desperate pleas for more money for local councils, many at the edge of bankruptcy? What of the next pay rounds for public sector workers, especially in sectors (health, social care, education) with acute problems of recruitment and retention?[67] All these would provide grounds for unrest in the party.

Labour's crippling cautiousness, its 'Ming vase' strategy, had boomeranged and will continue to do so. The government in the years ahead will have to choose between heavier taxation, especially of the more opulent, on the one hand, or failing public services and continuing high levels of poverty, on the other, whatever the rate of economic growth. The leadership's response to restiveness in the parliamentary ranks has so far been to persist with, even tighten, its stringent and exacting disciplinary regime.[68] The centralisation of candidate selection has delivered to Starmer a sanitised PLP with relatively few left-wingers, which might ease, temporarily, the task of party management. But the underlying problems, not least the flight of voters from Labour and the looming threat of Reform, will not disappear.

Notes

1 Owen Jones, 'There's no point to Labour as a party if it won't pay to pull children out of poverty', *Guardian*, 17 July 2023.
2 Paul Johnson, *Follow the Money* (London: Abacus, 2023), p. 86.
3 Tom Baldwin, *Keir Starmer: The Biography* (London: William Collins, 2024), p. 355.
4 Polly Toynbee, 'Listen up, critics: First let Labour win power. Then scrutinise its real record', *Guardian*, 17 July 2023.
5 *Ibid.*
6 Jim Pickard, 'Starmer under fire over vow to stick with Tory child welfare cap', *Financial Times*, 16 July 2023.

7 Keir Starmer, 'No more missing records or letters lost in the post – I will bring in a totally digital NHS', *Guardian*, 22 May 2023.
8 David Oliver, 'Did the Labour conference offer hope for the future of health and social care?' *British Medical Journal*, 383 (2023), 2377, DOI: 10.1136/bmj.p2377
9 John Curtice and Alex Scholes, 'The role and responsibilities of government', *British Social Attitudes*, 40 (London: National Centre for Social Research, 2023), pp. 20, 22.
10 Andrew Rawnsley, 'Keir Starmer's recipe for power is missing some ingredients – confidence and hope', *Observer*, 20 August 2023.
11 Polly Toynbee, 'Don't listen to the Tories – Labour is right to raise taxes', *Guardian*, 18 October 2024.
12 Jim Pickard and George Parker, 'The Starmer project: Labour's surprisingly bold economic agenda', *The Financial Times*, 6 June 2023.
13 Andrew Rawnsley, 'Scuttling his flagship green policy, Sir Keir Starmer has imperilled his credibility', *Observer*, 11 February 2024.
14 Pickard and Parker, 'The Starmer project'. Under existing employment law, there was a three-fold distinction between employees who enjoyed full employment rights, workers who possessed some of these rights and the pseudo-self-employed who had no employment rights.
15 Labour Party, *Change: Labour Party Manifesto 2024* (London: Labour Party, 2024), p. 45, labour.org.uk
16 Rachel Reeves, *A New Business Model for Britain* (Labour Together, May 2023), p. 28.
17 TUC, '"Overwhelming support" for Labour's New Deal for Workers, including among Tory voters – new TUC poll', *TUC News listing*, 12 September 2023, https://www.tuc.org.uk/news/overwhelming-support-labours-new-deal-workers-including-among-tory-voters-new-tuc-poll [consulted 21 March 2025].
18 Toby Helm and Michael Savage, '"The mother of all U-turns": After Labour's £28bn green policy climbdown, what's left?', *Guardian*, 11 February 2024.
19 Simon Wren-Lewis, 'What does being an Iron Chancellor mean?', *Mainly Macro*, 17 October 2023, mainlymacro.blogspot.com; Editorial, 'The Observer view: Labour's green U-turn has threatened its plan for growth', *Observer*, 11 February 2024; Will Hutton, *This Time No Mistakes* (London: Head of Zeus, 2024), p. 250; Larry Elliott, 'Tax rises will follow UK election unless fiscal rules are ripped up, says thinktank', *Guardian*, 9 May 2024.
20 Andy Haldane, 'The case for rethinking fiscal rules is overwhelming. Rather than exerting useful discipline, they are constraining government investment', *Financial Times*, 16 May 2023.
21 Simon Wren-Lewis, 'Detoxifying government debt, part 1. Debt is also an asset', *Mainly Macro*, 13 February 2024, mainlymacro.blogspot.com
22 Labour Party, *Change*, p. 21.
23 Interview, Chris McLaughlin.

24 Institute for Public Policy Research, *Half of Us: Turnout Patterns at the 2024 General Election* (London: IPPR, 2024).
25 Ipsos, 'The Conservative party brand image hits new low', April 2024, ipsos.com.
26 Zoe Crowther, 'Do Labour's U-turns matter?', *PoliticsHome*, 29 July 2023, politicshome.com
27 Simon Wren-Lewis, 'In presenting a macroeconomic fiscal stance, Rachel Reeves and Labour need to talk about improving public services rather than book balancing', *Mainly Macro*, 10 September 2024, mainlymacro.blogspot.com.
28 Tom Belger, 'Two-child cap: Why Starmer punished MPs who voted to tackle child poverty', *LabourList*, 24 July 2024, labourlist.org
29 Jonathan Freedland, 'After Labour's dour start, there's still hope for sunshine from Starmer and Reeves', *Guardian*, 14 September 2024.
30 Wren-Lewis, 'Rachel Reeves and Labour need to talk'.
31 Martin Smith, Dave Richards and Sam Warner, 'Labour's first budget: Redistribution away from the rich after over a decade of Conservative rule', *The Conversation*, 31 October 2024, theconversation.com
32 Larry Elliott and Pippa Crerar, 'Rachel Reeves bets on public spending increases in budget winning over voters', *Guardian*, 31 October 2024.
33 Simon Wren-Lewis, 'A budget that points the way but doesn't get us very far', *Mainly Macro*, 31 October 2024, mainlymacro.blogspot.com
34 The government decided not to abolish the upper earnings limit on employee contributions, which would have been more progressive and produced a significant boost to revenues, on the grounds that it contradicted pre-election pledges.
35 Dan Needle, 'The budget – a missed opportunity', Tax Policy Associates, 21 November 2024.
36 Sam Freedman, 'Am I being unfair on boomers?', *Comment is Freed*, 22 February 2023, substack.com
37 Liam Byrne, *The Inequality of Wealth: Why It Matters and How to Fix It* (Maumee, OH: Apollo, 2024); Anoosh Chakelian, 'Britain's richest 10% don't think they're wealthy – and that's disastrous in the fight against inequality', *Guardian*, 24 January 2024.
38 Equality Trust, 'Billionaire Britain 2022' (Croydon: Equality Trust, 2023), p. 2, https://equalitytrust.org.uk/; Johnson, *Follow the Money*, p. 57.
39 Johnson, *Follow the Money*, p. 57; Phillip Inman, 'How to reverse austerity? Scrap some of the tax-relief schemes worth £204bn', *Observer*, 16 June 2024; Toby Helm, 'Wealth taxes could raise £10bn to help plug Tory budget hole, say economists', *Observer*, 28 July 2024.
40 Martin Wolf, *The Crisis of Democratic Capitalism* (London: Penguin, 2023). Kindle edition.
41 Richard Murphy, *The Taxing Wealth Report 2024* (Cambridge: Finance for the Future, 2024), taxingwealth.uk

42 By incurring a charge of 20 per cent, the upper CGT rate, rather than 45 per cent, the highest income tax band. Richard Partington, 'Millionaire business owners urge Rachel Reeves to raise £14bn from rise in capital gains tax', *Guardian*, 17 October 2024.
43 Josh Ryan-Collins, 'In ditching a wealth tax, Labour is rejecting growth and embracing bad economics', *Guardian*, 30 August 2023.
44 The UK has one of the highest rates of inheritance tax in the world, but some of the lowest yields because of the many exemptions. Needle, 'The budget – a missed opportunity'.
45 Stephan Collini, 'Where to draw the line' *London Review of Books*, 19 October 2023.
46 Nils Pratley, 'Rachel Reeves's most irritating manifesto fudge', *Guardian*, 1 November 2024.
47 Michael O'Dwyer, Harriet Agnew and Alexandra Heal, 'Private equity eyes a deal with Rachel Reeves on UK carried interest', *Financial Times*, 29 October 2024.
48 Pratley, 'Rachel Reeves's most irritating manifesto fudge'.
49 O'Dwyer, Agnew and Heal, 'Private equity eyes a deal with Rachel Reeves'.
50 Pratley, 'Rachel Reeves's most irritating manifesto fudge'.
51 George Parker, 'Rachel Reeves says Labour would not restore cap on bankers' bonuses', *Financial Times*, 31 January 2024.
52 Heather Stewart, 'Rules imposed after financial crisis have "gone too far" Reeves tells City bankers', *Guardian*, 14 November 2024.
53 Aditya Chakrabortty, 'At last, a government willing to spend – but this budget will expose it to two great dangers', *Guardian*, 31 October 2024.
54 *Ibid.*
55 David Edgerton, 'Britain cries out for new economics. Labour has given it repackaged Tory ideas', *Guardian*, 6 November 2024.
56 Simon Wren-Lewis, 'Why raising taxes substantially is critical for the next Labour government to be sure of achieving its missions', *Mainly Macro*, 26 March 2024, mainlymacro.blogspot.com
57 Alexandra Rodgers, 'Sir Keir Starmer has insisted he can be trusted to deliver his six pledges to voters', *Sky News*, 16 May 2024.
58 Rafael Behr, 'Keir Starmer's caution may be frustrating, but it's right. Voters no longer trust big promises', *Guardian*, 14 September 2023.
59 Rodgers, 'Sir Keir Starmer has insisted he can be trusted'.
60 Emma Dunkley, 'Wealthy sell UK assets amid fears Labour would raise capital gains tax', *Financial Times*, 2 July 2024.
61 Rowena Mason, 'Rachel Reeves: I was wrong on no big tax rises being needed', *Guardian*, 4 November 2024.
62 Bernard Williams, *Truth and Truthfulness: An Essay in Genealogy* (Princeton, NJ: Princeton University, 2002), pp. 129, 131.

63 Isaac Delestre and Helen Miller, *Tax and Public Finances: The Fundamentals*, IFS Report R270 (London: Institute for Fiscal Studies, August 2023).

64 For evidence see, for example, Hazel Sheffield, 'Twice as many Britons want tax rises as want cuts, survey finds', *Guardian*, 1 July 2024.

65 Martin Wolf, 'Democracy should deliver more than cynical public relations exercises', *Financial Times*, 24 June 2024.

66 Mason, 'Rachel Reeves: I was wrong.'

67 Sam Freedman, 'Buying time', *Comment is Freed*, 31 October 2024, substack.com.

68 *Ibid.*

Conclusions and reflections

> What do you mean 'what are we for'? We're here to win.
>
> Jon Cruddas MP[1]

> Surely, politics is made with the head, but it is certainly not made with the head alone.
>
> Max Weber[2]

> If the Labour Party isn't about values, what's the point?
>
> Tim Livesey, formerly Ed Miliband's chief of staff[3]

Since 2010, as before, approaches to party management have fluctuated between two managerial doctrines: centralism and pluralism. The centralist approach was most clearly enunciated by Hugh Dalton, a senior Labour politician in the 1930s and 1940s: 'Let us have free and frank discussions, followed by majority decisions loyally accepted by all. Without some measure of healthy discipline and the submission of the individual to the collective will, there can be no democracy, but only egotism'[4] Centralism's most forceful critic was Richard Crossman, who, as early as 1955, warned that it could be too easily exploited 'to concentrate power in a few hands and change party democracy into party oligarchy'.[5] He advocated a pluralist approach which emphasised the rights of minorities, and he sought, as a party manager in the late 1960s, to maintain both cohesion and effective governance through consensus building, conciliation and mutual adjustment.[6] Managerial centralism was the dominant approach from the early 1930s to the early 1960s, until replaced by a more pluralist approach, which lasted until Blair's accession to the party leadership in 1994. This, in turn, was supplanted with a return to pluralism under Miliband until it regained favour, though in very different forms, under Corbyn and Starmer.

Miliband and pluralism

Miliband was a pluralist by both temperament and choice, but also by circumstance. His victory over his brother David in 2010 was by the barest margin and heavily reliant on union votes, so that he always felt insecure while the party right remained solidly entrenched in the PLP and the Shadow Cabinet, many of whose members queried the legitimacy of his rule. As a result, his grip over the party never matched that of both his predecessors. But he was also committed in principle to a pluralist approach to party management, and his instinct was always to build a broad coalition of support through reaching out to his critics.

Miliband was a staunch egalitarian, convinced, as his political ally Peter Hain wrote, that after 1980 capitalism has reverted to type, with an inbuilt tendency to generate 'shocking degrees of wealth and income inequality'.[7] New Labour, he maintained, had too readily imbibed neo-liberal assumptions about the economy – and had too lightly abandoned what he regarded as Labour's defining principle, the pursuit of equality. This was not, however, the view of most Shadow Cabinet members, nor, probably, of the PLP at large. Pluralism is a technique of party management which relies upon persuasion and maximising consensus, and therefore was not well suited to pushing through the sharp change of ideological direction that Miliband initially favoured. Many on both the front and back benches responded to Miliband's more radical ideas, such as 'responsible capitalism' and 'predistribution', with mounting bafflement, irritation and exasperation. How did they contribute to winning elections? If they did not, what was their point? Indeed, by alienating the rich and powerful, they were positively counter-productive, striking at one of New Labour's principal accomplishments: the rapprochement with big business. It did not help that Miliband and his most senior colleague, the Shadow Chancellor Ed Balls, did not see eye to eye, with the latter increasingly convinced that, to regain economic credibility, Labour must accept a large dose of 'fiscal discipline' and worry less about the coalition's drastic austerity programme and its victims.

Miliband lacked the power, authority and confidence to overcome resistance, and all his grand schemes of ideological rejuvenation faded away. Under pressure from both his senior front-bench colleagues and the party's professional political apparatus, after 2012 he moved towards a more transactional approach to politics and his earlier innovations were replaced by 'a programme of orthodox fiscal transfers to offset the cost-of-living concerns'.[8] As a result, Miliband ended up disappointing the left, but also the right, for temporising and equivocating too much about fiscal discipline. As one of his senior advisors put it, 'we tried to appease everyone and ended up not having a distinctive character'.[9]

As it happened, the most important change that occurred under Miliband concerned organisation, and not policy, and was a wholly unplanned response to the crisis that erupted over the alleged fixing by Unite of a selection contest in Falkirk. As much to deflect attention from Unite and Falkirk as anything else, Miliband came up with a plan to replace the electoral college with an OMOV system for electing the leader – with consequences which absolutely no one anticipated: Corbyn's election as his successor.

Corbyn and managerial centralism

Of the three leaders, the least coherent approach to party management was Corbyn's. His team never evolved a clear strategy and often seemed at the mercy of events, responding in ad hoc ways to multiple crises. With all its rhetoric of democratisation, empowerment and inclusivity, the managerial instincts of the Corbyn leadership were highly centralistic, and power soon coagulated around the Leader's Office (LOTO). In some ways, its approach to party management resembled the social democratic centralism of the decades before and after the Second World War, with its insistence on the binding force of the majority will, as embodied, in this context, in Corbyn's election mandate as well as in Conference sovereignty. It differed, though, in that it relied less upon disciplinary codes than upon rank-and-file mobilisation orchestrated mainly by Momentum to pressure recalcitrant MPs.

The scale of the managerial challenges Corbyn faced was daunting, even unnerving. The Corbyn leadership's ultimate weakness was the narrowness of its power base in the CLPs, in the party's largest affiliate, Unite, and in other, smaller left-wing unions. Its Achilles heel was its minimal support in the PLP. Corbyn's ability to gain a grip on the party was, in addition, hobbled for much of his leadership by a lack of control over the NEC, until too late. The lack of commitment and, at times, active resistance of, senior party officials was an added and at times serious complication. To compound all this, the Corbyn leadership operated in a wider setting in which powerful forces, notably but not solely the media, were unremittingly and irredeemably hostile.

In striking contrast with Starmer's managerial regime, Corbyn's efforts at control were to a large degree ineffectual. Under Corbyn, LOTO lacked the experience, the knowledge and the skills to manage the party effectively. All this was made worse by egregious errors of judgement, best seen in the handling of the antisemitism crisis. That Corbyn's many opponents exploited and exaggerated the scale of antisemitism to disable his leadership seems incontrovertible.[10] But so too was the fact that too many Corbynites, including some at the most senior level, were in denial about the existence of the problem at all. Both sides, as we have seen, weaponised the issue. It was, in truth, an extraordinarily difficult issue to handle. But throughout, the managerial imperative was unambiguous: to contain, defuse and deactivate the issue by emollient gestures and by carefully calibrated concessions. Some of Corbyn's closest lieutenants, such as McDonnell and Lansman, came to understand this, but others, such as Milne and Murphy, did not, and neither did Corbyn.

The antisemitism crisis accelerated the polarisation and factionalisation of the party, to which both blocs, Corbynites and anti-Corbynites, contributed. A very large and influential slice of the right was never prepared to accept Corbyn's legitimacy and felt little if any obligation to show the leader any loyalty, or indeed minimal respect. As John McDonnell observed, 'they viewed the new left-wing leadership as a challenge to their politics, their careers, their whole existence: and they were right'.[11] The two blocs operated in different doctrinal universes with few points of convergence. This was seen most starkly in cases of foreign policy, notably the Israel–Palestine conflict, NATO and the American connection.

The only way in which the leadership could have survived was by broadening its base. This the leadership ultimately was unwilling to do, partly because they did not believe enough would reciprocate, partly because of the absence of trust and partly because the Corbynite left and the right saw the conflict in zero-sum terms. But perhaps most fundamental of all were their radically opposed conceptions of what the Labour Party was *for*.

Here there was a collision between the ethics of power and of conviction, and the gap between the two was unbridgeable. For adherents of the former, politics was, above all, about winning, and everything should be subordinated to that end. For followers of the latter, this was mere opportunism and obsession with personal advancement.

But the ethic of conviction also diverged abruptly from the ethic of responsibility. This recognised that politics was 'a messy, mundane, inconclusive, tangled business, far removed from the passion for certainty'. It held, as Tim Livesey, Miliband's chief of staff, put it, that it was 'not enough to be pure in politics, you do have to get your hands dirty – as long as you get your hands dirty on behalf of people that need your help'.[12] For many on the Corbynite left, this smacked of the evasions and expediencies they saw as typical of Miliband-style soft leftists. They conceived of themselves as politicians of integrity, inspired by the highest ideals and never deflected, unlike their critics, by low motives of personal gain and political manoeuvring. Compromises were acceptable, for example over Brexit, as long as they did not imperil 'the intoxicating consciousness of serving a larger cause'.[13] Hence the obduracy of Corbyn and many of his supporters – though, as we have seen, by no means all – over the full IHRA formulation, on the grounds that two of the examples adduced could be (and in fact were) used to tar principled opponents of Zionism with antisemitism and hence undermine the Palestinian cause.

The corollary of the ethic of conviction for many of those inspired by it was that, since they were the upright and the principled and sole proprietors of the truth, those who disagreed with them must necessarily be motivated by careerism, self-seeking and other malign motives. The ethic was especially pronounced among those who had been inculcated into the often sectarian and intolerant culture of the radical left; inevitably, then, their entry into CLPs during the Corbyn years had disruptive effects, sometimes seriously. As a sympathetic commentator complained, the Corbyn camp exhibited 'rigid group identities that make serious dialogue impossible – not only between left and right, but also with the various shades of soft-left in between.'[14] The impact of such media platforms as *THE SKWAWKBOX* and *The Canary*, with their highly polemical and vituperative style, was especially toxic.

As a result, normative order and the mutual trust upon which it relied disintegrated. Trust can be defined as 'an expectation or belief that one can rely upon another person's actions and words, and/or that the person has good intentions toward oneself'; it plays a key part in lubricating habits of bargaining and cooperation.[15] In high-trust organisations, participants 'share certain ends or values; bear towards each other a diffuse sense of long-term obligations [...] communicate freely and honestly [and] are ready [...] to give each other the benefit of any doubt that may arise with respect to goodwill or motivation.'[16] Establishing the precise degree of trust in a political party such as Labour is very difficult, as there is limited data and no really reliable indicators, but the absence of these trust characteristics during the Corbyn years was obvious, blatant and unmistakable. Lord Kerslake, a former head of the civil service, wrote in a report commissioned by the Corbyn leadership that 'it is in the nature of a broad political party to have competing views and perspectives, and this has always been the case for the Party. What is different here is the way in which factionalism has become embedded in the way the Party itself operates, creating distrust and division.'[17]

As a classic study of trade union democracy observed, 'antagonism between political opponents must be constrained by common goals, agreement over norms and the absence of unremitting personal hostility to prevent conflict from damaging the cohesion and effectiveness of the organisation.'[18] Under Corbyn, no such agreement existed. Labour morphed into a fractured 'low-trust' institution in which divisions were so entrenched that 'attempts at collaborative working were pointless', where 'the opposing camps had little faith in each other's goodwill, integrity and decency' and where a 'debilitating inertia, factionalism and infighting [...] distracted from what all profess to be a common cause – electoral success.'[19] The party had become unmanageable.

Starmer and managerial centralism

This was the party bequeathed to Starmer. His priority was to rebuild a system of robust managerial control, a precondition, in his mind, for eliminating the Corbynite left and rendering the party electable by wrenching it to the right. In pursuit of these goals, Starmer displayed a ruthless determination which his predecessor had never mustered, and he was aided by managerial officials of impressive calibre. His efforts were helped by the restoration of leadership legitimacy. The size of Starmer's victory in the 2020 leadership contest afforded him a powerful democratic mandate, though his authority was solidified only after Labour took a firm lead in the polls in 2022. Other factors that benefited him included the end of bitter disagreements over the proper location of power in the party, with the rebuilding of a large measure of procedural consensus; after the stormy 2021 Conference, there was virtually no appetite to reignite old battles even over the thorny issue of candidate selection. The departure from the party (a few enforced) of many of the more sectarian, dogmatic and intolerant elements (as well as many more who were simply idealists) who had joined under Corbyn greatly facilitated the Starmer project. At the same time, many of those who remained developed, in the wake of the disastrous 2019 defeat, more pragmatic attitudes towards the electorate, along with a greater sensitivity towards the damaging effects of internal party strife. The traditional norms of civility and loyalty to the leadership revived, the latter manifested in the success of the pro-Starmer pressure group Labour to Win in winning elections to key party committees, in electing delegates to the Annual Conference and in selecting parliamentary candidates. As the 2024 election drew near, Starmer had achieved a mastery over the party unequalled since the high point of 'the Blair Supremacy'.

The Starmer government inherited a stagnating economy, failing public services and a mass of intensifying social problems. Difficult decisions were unavoidable. To the extent that the Starmer government is able to accomplish significant improvements in the public services and ease the plight of the disadvantaged in some measurable ways, fissures within the party will be manageable. But if, for example, the government were to administer another dose of austerity by slicing back welfare and if its efforts to rejuvenate the public services were to stall through inadequate funding, disillusionment would be such as to render serious dissension within the party inevitable.

The Starmer government has sought to pre-empt possible revolts in Parliament by, as we have seen, domesticating the PLP through a selection process which has filtered out potential dissidents, enforcing an astringent managerial regime and intensifying central controls. Persistent parliamentary rebels will be suspended from the PLP and perhaps prevented from standing as Labour MPs. But such a regime will be dysfunctional even if effective: dull and unimaginative conformity and discouragement of critical debate will foster a torpid and inert political culture, hardly conducive to the innovative thinking vital if a party is to retain a capacity for revitalisation. But it is unlikely to be effective, even on its own terms, especially if the party's popularity is in free fall.

Whither the Labour Party?

In 2004, Colin Crouch identified social democracy's central problem as being how to strike the balance between retaining 'the dynamism and enterprise of capitalism while preventing firms and their executives from exercising power to a degree incompatible with democracy'.[20] Under Blair and Brown, he suggested, Labour had moved 'beyond the rapprochement and cooperation with business interests which is essential to all social democratic parties to becoming more or less a business party'.[21] This process was reversed under Miliband, cautiously, and then much more sharply under Corbyn, but it has now resumed, despite or perhaps because of the further swelling of business power.

The *Financial Times* columnist Martin Wolf warned in 2023 that 'as wealth and economic power become increasingly concentrated, liberal democracy inevitably comes under threat'.[22] For the former soft left Labour politician Bryan Gould, this 'intensifying concentration of power' was now 'the central and defining issue of politics'; and traditionally, the left's response has been 'to resist and counteract it'.[23] This is no longer the case: as we have seen, accommodation with power or adaptation to *force majeure* is, for the Starmer Labour Party, its key strategic maxim. Why jeopardise the pursuit of public office and endanger one's capacity to effect improvements in the lives of millions of people by challenging the powerful? Furthermore, Starmer's central mission of higher economic growth depends heavily on convincing international investors – corporations, hedge funds, wealth funds, private equity groups and so forth – to invest in the UK economy. From this perspective, accommodation with business is not only desirable but essential.

But such realpolitik will inevitably change the nature of the party. In 2009, Bryan Gould asked two basic questions: 'what the purpose of politics is' and 'what does it mean to be on the left in politics'.[24] As we have seen, the three ethics of power, responsibility and conviction proffered three distinct responses. The third of these has lost all political purchase, the second has been marginalised and the first is now ascendant, exemplified not only by the government's propitiation of business but also by its appeasement of public opinion through the adoption of a tough stance on asylum-seekers and the provision of welfare benefits; for Starmer's chief of staff, Morgan McSweeney, the end of winning over voters 'justified almost any means, no matter how alienating it was to the Labour Party'.[25]

In his classic essay 'Politics as a Vocation', Weber wrote that 'just because power is the unavoidable means, and striving for power is one of the driving forces of all politics, there is no more harmful distortion than [the] worship of power per se'. He concluded: 'power merely for power's sake without a substantive purpose' trivialises politics, transforming it from a vocation into a game.[26] Labour would claim that it does have a purpose, to improve the lives of ordinary people, temper the effects of a market economy, help those without privilege and provide a decent level of social security for all. But its realpolitik approach involves limiting its ambitions to what can be achieved within the constraints of the established framework of power, wealth and privilege. As a result, as Crouch predicted some while ago, Britain appears to be drifting towards a system where 'politics is really shaped in interaction between elected governments and elites that overwhelmingly represent business interests'. Under such a system, the parameters of policy debate would narrow to effectively exclude the 'agenda of strong egalitarian policies for the redistribution of power and wealth, or for the restraint of powerful interests'.[27]

If the net result is that the Starmer government, which has inhibited itself by choosing to wear a fiscal straitjacket, responds to financial pressures by retreating from the core Labour values of a more equal and fairer society which protects the most vulnerable, then the party's future will be endangered. Labour can survive and retain vibrancy only if it can elicit the commitment and loyalty of its members, and without some sense of common purpose to inspire them, both will inevitably languish. If tight discipline inhibits voice, the option of exit will always remain.

Notes

1 Interview, Jon Cruddas speaking rhetorically of the mindset of most of the PLP.
2 Max Weber, 'Politics as a vocation', Reprinted from Hand Gerth and C. Wright Mills (eds), *Max Weber: Essays in Sociology* (New York: Oxford University Press, 1946), p. 46.
3 Interview, Tim Livesey.
4 Quoted in Eric Shaw, *Discipline and Discord: The Politics of Managerial Control in the Labour Party, 1951–87* (Manchester: Manchester University Press, 1988), pp. 37–8.
5 *Ibid.*, p. 159.

6 *Ibid.*, pp. 158–62.
7 Peter Hain, *Back to the Future of Socialism* (Bristol: Policy Press, 2015), p. 106.
8 Jon Cruddas, *A Century of Labour* (Cambridge: Polity, 2024), p. 210.
9 Interview, Stewart Wood.
10 Patrick Maguire and Gabriel Pogrund, *Get In: The Inside Story of Labour under Starmer* (London: Vintage, 2025), pp. 39–40 and passim.
11 Interview, John McDonnell.
12 Interview, Tim Livesey.
13 Joshua Cherniss, *Liberalism in Dark Times* (Princeton, NJ: Princeton University Press, 2021), p. 16.
14 Christine Berry, 'Political economy and Labour's factionalism', *Renewal*, 29:2 (2021), 26.
15 Kurt T. Dirks and Donald L. Ferrin, 'The role of trust in organizational settings', *Organization Science*, 12 (2001), 6.
16 Alan Fox, *Beyond Contract: Work, Power and Trust Relations* (London: Faber and Faber, 1974), p. 362.
17 Quoted in Martin Forde (chair), *The Forde Report* (London: Labour Party, 2022), p. 34.
18 Seymour M. Lipset, Martin A. Trow and James S. Coleman, *Union Democracy* (Glencoe, IL: Free Press, 1956), p. 252.
19 Martin Forde (chair), *The Forde Report* (London: Labour Party, 2022), pp. 6, 79.
20 Colin Crouch, *Post-Democracy* (Cambridge: Polity, 2004), p. 105.
21 *Ibid.*, p. 65.
22 Martin Wolf, *The Crisis of Democratic Capitalism* (London: Penguin, 2023).
23 Bryan Gould, 'Markets in a democracy', *Political Studies Review*, 8:1 (2010), 6.
24 Bryan Gould, 'Constructing a left politics', *Soundings*, 42 (2009), 129.
25 Maguire and Pogrund, *Get In*, p. 370.
26 Weber, 'Politics as a vocation', p. 37.
27 Crouch, *Post-Democracy*, pp. 4, 6.

Index

Titles of books can be found after authors' names.
'n.' after a page number indicates the number of a note on that page.
'*t*' after a page number indicates a table on that page.

Index

Index

Index

Index

Index

Index

Index

Index

Index

EU authorised representative for GPSR:
Easy Access System Europe, Mustamäe tee 50,
10621 Tallinn, Estonia
gpsr.requests@easproject.com

www.ingramcontent.com/pod-product-compliance
Lightning Source LLC
LaVergne TN
LVHW010559100826
845148LV00014B/2768

* 9 7 8 1 5 2 6 1 9 2 2 8 8 *